"In the multitalented and prickly Raphael—novelist, classicist and Oscar-winning screenwriter for *Darling* (1965)—[Josephus] the ancient survivor has found his ideal judge, a man as certain of being a Jew as he is uncertain of the meaning of that fact, much as Josephus himself was. . . . The result is a mesmerizing study that evaluates Josephus's choices within the context of internecine Jewish strife (both real and polemical) and overwhelming Gentile power."   —*Maclean's*

"Novelist, screenwriter and biographer Raphael (*Ifs and Buts*, 2011, etc.) succeeds admirably in recovering the reputation of much-maligned historian Titus Flavius Josephus (37–c. 100). . . . Informed by scrupulous, sometimes exhaustive footnotes and addenda, the book is not simply an arresting biography, but a persuasive history of an era. Like his subject, Raphael's breadth of intelligence works against single-mindedness. Throughout, he quotes the conclusions, often opposed to his reading, of other historians. Raphael is imposingly erudite and at pains to demonstrate it, yet there is a remarkable clarity to the writing, many elegant turns of phrase and a measure of sly humor."
—*Kirkus Reviews*

"Yigadel Yadin, the Israeli general and renowned archaeologist, referred to Josephus as a 'great historian and a bad Jew.' Undoubtedly, many of the Jewish contemporaries of Josephus would have agreed with the latter assertion. Fortunately, Raphael, a novelist and classicist, provides a more nuanced portrayal of the first-century-C.E. soldier, politician, and historian. . . . This is a well-done account of his life and works."
—*Booklist*

"In his marvelous hands, Frederic Raphael transforms Flavius Josephus from the self-hating Jew he is often portrayed as being to the first great critic of religious fundamentalism. *A Jew Among Romans* is especially relevant to a time when Jews argue so furiously with each other."
—Alan Wolfe, author of *Political Evil*

"It is astonishing how many modern themes are thrown up by the vicissitudes of Josephus's life of two millennia ago. With his Cambridge Classics scholar's eye and his customary sophisticated wit—he simply cannot write a dull sentence—Frederic Raphael uses the life of the general-turned-historian to explore the issues of Jewish alienation and assimilation; collaboration versus realism; virility and vanity; identity, love, and the meaning of historical truth."

—Andrew Roberts, author of *The Storm of War:*
A New History of the Second World War

"Only someone with the gifts of Frederic Raphael could have written a book as original and wide-ranging as this one. His purpose is to explore the moral ambiguity of identity and loyalty that Jews from Josephus to Hannah Arendt have tried to deal with ever since the Roman conquest of Judaea. It is exhilarating to read history that properly illuminates the present." —David Pryce-Jones, author of
Betrayal: France, the Arabs, and the Jews

"With subtlety, irony, and acute insight into Diaspora politics, Raphael brilliantly disentangles, from ancient sources and modern scholarship, a psychologically convincing account of this ancient looking-glass war and the elusive individual who was both its chief protagonist and its much-reviled historian. It is a story with endless echoes of—and lessons for—eerily similar conflicts today, and Raphael tells it superbly."

—Peter Green, author of *The Hellenistic Age*

"Frederic Raphael's probing, reflexive essay on the life and legacy of Joseph ben Mattathias, a.k.a. Flavius Josephus, brilliantly straddles several mental and political worlds at once, situating—not always comfortably or comfortingly—its subject between Judaea and Rome, and us between a deeply troubled Roman middle east of the first century C.E. and several scarcely more serene hotspots of the modern western world." —Paul Cartledge, A. G. Leventis
Professor of Greek Culture, University of Cambridge

FREDERIC RAPHAEL

A Jew Among Romans

Frederic Raphael, born in Chicago in 1931, was educated at Charterhouse and St. John's College, Cambridge, where he was a major scholar in Classics. He has translated Petronius's *Satyrica* and is the author, most recently, of *Some Talk of Alexander: A Journey Through Space and Time in the Greek World.* He is a regular contributor to *The Times Literary Supplement* (London). Among his more than twenty novels are *The Limits of Love, The Glittering Prizes, A Double Life,* and *Coast to Coast.* Six volumes of his notebooks, under the generic title *Personal Terms,* have been published by the Carcanet Press. He won an Oscar for his screenplay of *Darling* and wrote the screenplays for *Two for the Road, Far from the Madding Crowd,* and Stanley Kubrick's *Eyes Wide Shut,* among others. He has been a Fellow of the Royal Society of Literature since 1964.

A Jew Among Romans

A Jew Among Romans

THE LIFE AND LEGACY OF FLAVIUS JOSEPHUS

Frederic Raphael

Anchor Books

A DIVISION OF RANDOM HOUSE, INC.

NEW YORK

FIRST ANCHOR BOOKS EDITION, OCTOBER 2013

Copyright © 2013 by Volatic Limited

All rights reserved. Published in the United States by Anchor Books,
a division of Random House, Inc., New York, and in Canada by Random House of
Canada Limited, Toronto. Originally published in hardcover in the United States
by Pantheon Books, a division of Random House, Inc., New York, in 2013.

Anchor Books and colophon are registered
trademarks of Random House, Inc.

The Library of Congress has cataloged the Pantheon edition as follows:
Raphael, Frederic.
A Jew among Romans : the life and legacy of Flavius Josephus / Frederic Raphael.
p. cm.
Includes bibliographical references and index.
1. Josephus, Flavius. 2. Jewish historians—Biography. I. Title.
DS115.9.J6R37 2012 933.0072'02—DC 23 [B] 2012009744

Anchor ISBN: 978-0-307-45635-9

Author photograph © Stephen Raphael
Book design by Robert C. Olsson

www.anchorbooks.com

Printed in the United States of America
10 9 8 7 6 5 4 3 2 1

For Peter Green
Cui dono lepidum novum libellum

CONTENTS

PROLOGUE

In the late 1970s, more than thirty years after I had read classics at Cambridge, I happened, after a chance cull in a bookshop in Périgueux, to get to know the work of the Parisian Hellenists Jean-Pierre Vernant, Marcel Detienne and, in particular, Pierre Vidal-Naquet. I was drawn to him not only because of his exhilarating scholarship; I had already read his early, brave pamphlet *L'affaire Audin,* about the disappearance and torture by French paratroopers of a young mathematics professor in Algiers in 1957. His reward for telling the truth was to be sacked from his academic post.

In a later volume, *La torture dans la république,* Vidal-Naquet analyzed the pernicious use of torture by the French army during its war with the Algerian FLN. A subsequent edition—published in English as *Torture: Cancer of Democracy*—expanded the indictment to include the conduct of the British in Kenya during the Mau Mau uprising and, later, in Cyprus when Colonel Grivas was conducting his guerrilla campaign for Enosis (union with Greece). In his obituary of the scholar, who died in 2006, Oswyn Murray recalled how P.V.-N. had written to a retired French general requesting a copy of his book about the "truth" of the Algerian war.[1] The general had replied that it was "free to the general public, eighty francs for traitors and forty francs to you." P.V.-N. had sent a check for eighty francs.

Even in his treatment of the ancient world, Vidal-Naquet combined academic punctilio with a sense of mission. The past was a key to the present. Interpreting it correctly was a matter not of pedantry, but of honor; scholarship was a department of truth, not of dandyism. If partisan, P.V.-N. was never dogmatic; if polemic, always humane. He was, he said, "vaccinated against orthodoxy."

I discovered that we were both Jews, born within a year or so of each other, of fathers born in the same year. It hardly made us brothers, but it did produce an illusion of affinity. Later, I learned that Vidal-Naquet père had been a constitutional lawyer who was active in the French Resistance. Arrested and tortured, he was, like his wife, murdered by the Germans at Auschwitz. Their son had spent the war in the rural department of the Drôme, protected by the Protestant community around him, but always under the shadow of murderous anti-Semitism. Pierre's awareness both of his Jewishness and of the menace of totalitarian regimes was never merely theoretical.

One detail of his childhood memories I found especially poignant: he never forgave the Germans for making his father "dance." I was not sure what precisely that sinister phrase meant, but it stuck in my mind. Recently, while reading Christopher R. Browning's *Remembering Survival,* I noticed that, in Poland, a camp commandant called Schroth, when urged to shoot a young girl, replied "the beast must dance first."* No further details are given. In his youth, my own father was the amateur tango champion of the world. He danced only when he chose.

On one occasion when I was in Paris in the early 1980s, I found Vidal-Naquet's number in the telephone book. Against my usual habit when it comes to approaching strangers, I called him. If he had not been a Jew, would I have been as bold? P.V.-N. and I spent a rather formal hour together. His flat was large, not copiously furnished or carpeted; but there were many books. We exchanged flattering pleas-

---

* In *Le crime et le silence,* Anna Bikont reports on the massacre, in July 1941, of some six hundred Jews by their Polish neighbors. An eyewitness reported, *"On tuait les nourrissons qui tétaient le sein de leur mère, on frappait à la mort et on obligeait à chanter et à danser"* (They killed babies who sucked at their mothers' breast, they beat people to death and made people sing and dance).

antries, but I cannot claim that, as the French say, "the current passed" between us.

At the end of our conversation, I gave him a copy of one of my books and he took from his wide, sagging shelves a fat volume *La guerre des Juifs,* by Flavius Josèphe. He inscribed it, with practiced briskness, *"Pour F. Raphael avec la sympathie de P.V.-N."* It was, I confess, the first I had ever heard of Titus Flavius Josephus: he had never figured in the classical curriculum. The translation (by another hand) was preceded by P.V.-N.'s long prefatory essay "Du bon usage de la Trahison." When I got home, I read his contribution, which had the pace and punch I had come to expect, but I cannot swear that I finished Josephus's text.

I returned to read Titus Flavius Josephus only in the last six or seven years. When I mentioned him to that great contemporary classicist, my old friend Peter Green, he said, "He's your ideal subject." I remembered Vidal-Naquet's pugnacious essay and was not so sure; but Peter's encouragement sent me back to the archetypal turncoat's lively narrative. I began the long process of reading which had to accompany any attempt to revisit his life and times.

My encounter with Vidal-Naquet was *sans lendemain:* we never met again. But, in the 1990s, I did by chance review the first volume of his autobiography. He wrote to tell me that mine was the only review he had read with pleasure; I had understood him. He had seemed gruff in person; on paper, he became a friend. Later, in another note, he wrote to say that he had been reading the translation Kenneth McLeish and I had done of the works of Aeschylus and that he thought it the best he had ever read in English (he was a keen Anglophile and, Oswyn Murray noted, had an exceptional knowledge of Shakespeare). His kind words about our Aeschylus may have been a courtesy. I prefer to assume that he was exercising the rigor that was his trademark.

I have never subscribed, except for politeness's sake, to any God, including that of the Jews. In my youth, I blamed Him for failing to prove that He existed by doing the right thing rather more often than history showed. And yet, by no brave decision, I am a Jew. What it means to me is the deposit of many of the things it has meant to others.

There is comedy of a kind in the fact that the only people who might now insist that I am not really a Jew—since I neither pray nor abstain from forbidden foods—are other Jews.

I do not go to synagogue; nor do I adhere to any kind of codified morality. I do not believe that the Jews (or anyone else) have some privileged connection with any kind of supernatural power. I neither seek nor shun Jewish company. And yet this concatenation of negatives links me, somehow, with what has happened, and is happening, to Jews in the world into which we have all been pitched. I would not have written about Titus Flavius Josephus (and alluded to other Jews who, in one way or another, followed his errant footsteps) if being a Jew did not mean something to me, at once indelible and imprecise, but I have not done so with any preconceived scheme or demonstrative intent.

With me, as with Vidal-Naquet, orthodoxy makes unquestionable demands, which I can never honor. P.V.-N. was a frequent pamphleteer on Jewish matters. He engaged deeply, sometimes furiously, always sharply with the complexities of French attitudes to Jews and to the rampant particularism Israel came to stand for. Combative against anti-Semitism, he also deplored Zionist chauvinism. Entertaining his contradictions without embarrassment or reticence, he could, it seemed, be both a French socialist intellectual and a Jew *sans complexes*. Irony and indignation slung a bridge between scholarship and *gauchisme*.

I have been an observer, rarely a participant, when it came to the events that, in my own lifetime, have made being a Jew, of whatever brand and by whatever definition, a perilous condition. As a child, I learned, from a safe distance, of the mass murder of millions of men and women and more than a million children with whom I had at least something in common. What kind of a Jew I have been, or have failed to be, is not my subject here. Yet this book reflects on me and I on it, to a degree that others will judge.

As will be seen from the bibliography, I have relied on a large number of books on the subject of Josephus and his times. Specialists will notice that my references are nearly all literary and biographical. Since my principal interest is in Josephus's character and works, and then in a selection of Jews who, in one way or another, resemble him in having been alienated, in a variety of ways, I have concentrated on personalities rather than, for instance, on archaeological evidence. Isaac Newton said that he owed the scope of his vision to "standing upon the shoulders of giants." I confess only to having sometimes profited from standing on scholars' toes.

INTRODUCTION

In a volume published in 1989, Lee Friedlander broke precedent by allowing his shadow to fall into the frame of his photographs. Normally, photographers stalk, and shoot, an image without blotting it with their own phantom intrusion. Historians are schooled to similar unobtrusiveness. A man's style may grace his material, but it should not distort it. The first-person pronoun is discouraged; reliable accounts should appear to have been assembled by a dispassionate recorder. According to "Freedom for History," proclaimed by Pierre Nora and others in 2005, "History is not morality . . . the role of the historian is not to excite or to condemn but to explain. . . . The historian does not introduce current sensibilities into the events of the past. . . . History has no judicial purpose." In practice, the most enduring historical narratives are salted with personality. Gibbon's *Decline and Fall of the Roman Empire,* for instance, is a prolonged pageant conducted by an eighteenth-century impresario whose point of view shades every page. Hardly a phrase fails to convey gentlemanly disdain for cant, cruelty and credulity.

Of all historians, ancient or modern, Titus Flavius Josephus is the one whose own shadow falls most obviously across his work. Yet if the Judaean Jews had not embarked on the rebellion against Rome that broke out in 66 C.E., and reached its climax with the capture and destruction of Jerusalem in 70, no librarian would ever have cataloged an author of that name. Joseph ben Mattathias was the younger of two sons of a substantial landowner.* He was away from Jerusalem on a diplomatic mission to Rome during the turbulent months preceding the outbreak of hostilities, but he must have assumed that he would spend most of his life in and around his native city. He gives no indication that he was any kind of a writer during the years preceding his appointment, at the age of thirty, as governor-general of Galilee. Born in 37 C.E., the historian certainly lived well into the reign of Domitian (81–96) and is generally thought to have survived till at least 100 C.E. Joseph ben Mattathias's life was broken in half by the war of which he supplied the sole extant account. Only some time after his surrender to the Romans did he elect, or consent, to become the historian of the catastrophe that, unlike so many other Judaeans, he outlived.

First, he had had to make his peace with the Roman commanders, Vespasian and his son Titus. After almost three years of collaboration,† he said good-bye, forever, to the "unhappy city" of Jerusalem and took ship, with the conquerors, to Rome. He never set foot again in his devastated and depopulated homeland. Having witnessed Titus's triumphal procession, he was pensioned and repackaged as the Roman citizen Titus Flavius Josephus. Thenceforth he was nothing but a writing man. Like Edward Gibbon, "scribble, scribble, scribble" was his consuming activity; the past was his present. His "damned, thick, square" books (actually manuscript scrolls) were advertisements, and laments, for the Jews and apologies for himself. He remained an unflagging defender of the people among whom he would never again find it safe to live. Only nominally a Roman and no longer at one with the Jews,‡ he was doubly

---

* According to Jewish law, members of the ruling class of priestly origin were not supposed to own land at all, but Martin Goodman (in *The Ruling Class of Judaea*) says that they clearly did. Roman senators were, similarly, not supposed to engage in business or trade. They often presided over consortia of surrogates who acted for them in such profitable activities.

† While Joseph ben Mattathias gave diplomatic help to the Romans, not least by encouraging the Jews inside Jerusalem to come to terms when there was still time, there is little evidence (though no shortage of allegations) that he served as a military adviser. Certainly he was never an active combatant on the Roman side.

‡ To rewrite the scriptures in the form of secular history, as he did in his work *The Jewish Antiquities*, was itself tantamount to apostasy.

alienated. Recalling the past was a way of keeping himself company: "I am never less alone," he wrote, "than when by myself."

No previous losing general in an ancient war had ever crossed the lines to describe the defeat of his own side. The only near precedent was Polybius, a Greek who composed his Roman history in the mid-second century B.C.E. He had been commissioned as a cavalry commander in the Achaean League, when it sided with Macedonia in its war with Rome, but he never went into battle. After the decisive defeat of King Perseus of Macedon at Pydna in 168 B.C.E., Polybius (whose name means "well-to-do") was among a thousand notables taken as hostages to Italy, where they were held, without charge or trial, for seventeen years.

Polybius was soon befriended by Publius Cornelius Scipio Aemilianus, a grandee who took him on campaign, as a privileged observer, in the Third Punic War, which started in 149 B.C.E. Three years later, despite their brave resistance, he saw the Carthaginians slaughtered and their city set on fire. After it had burned for seventeen days, the site was leveled and, it is said, sown with salt, with the ritual purpose of rendering it unable ever to grow again. In fact, a century later, Julius Caesar sponsored the resurrection of what then became a prosperous, docile city in the Roman province of Africa.*

Victory entitled the Romans to call the Mediterranean "mare nostrum": our sea, though the Phoenicians and the Greeks† had been the first to sail it. In now voluntary and pampered exile, Polybius chose as his theme the irresistible rise of the Roman republic. Its social anatomy was designed, as if by fate, to foster military discipline; its mixed constitution—a hybrid of oligarchic and democratic elements—kept

---

* In 494 B.C.E., Darius, the Persian king of kings, meted out similar treatment to the rebellious Ionian Greek city of Miletus, on the shore of Asia Minor. In time, it too recovered its prosperity.

† By "the Greeks," here and elsewhere, I mean only the men, of different cities and allegiances, who spoke Greek and "worshipped the same gods" (though not all worshipped all of them). It has been argued—for instance, by Roderick Beaton in *An Introduction to Modern Greek Literature* (Oxford: Clarendon Press, 1994)—that there was no Greek "nation" until the declaration of independence from the Turks in 1821.

its citizens in step. Patricians and plebeians, officers and men had one common and binding purpose: conquest. Under the leadership of two quasi-regal, annually elected consuls, the Romans held virtue and success to be all but synonyms.

Foreign triumphs brought luxury, and conceit, to Rome. As a resident foreigner, Polybius had to be cautious about criticizing the extortionate greed of the conquerors of Africa, Spain and Asia Minor.* Only by praising his patron, Aemilius Paullus, and his family for their "abstinence" did the Greek historian imply revulsion from the depredations of less fastidious Roman commanders. He seems to have had no qualms about living in the household of a general who—according to ancient statistics—had sold 150,000 Greeks into slavery after his victory in the Macedonian war. Slave labor supplied energy in the ancient world as oil does in the modern.

Unlike Josephus when he sought to account for the fall of Jerusalem, Polybius never hints that Carthage's fate was due to the moral iniquity of its citizens. Child sacrifice was integral to the worship of Moloch, the "Baal" of the Phoenicians, of whom Carthage was originally a colony, but what commentator ever suggested that the Carthaginians were punished because their barbarities excited divine abhorrence?† Their city's obliteration proved only that the Romans were winners; triumph was the proof that they deserved it. As Montesquieu would say, "The ancients conquered without reason, without utility. They ravaged the earth in order to exercise their virtue (that is, their manliness) and to demonstrate their excellence." Homer's Achilles had set the style in the race for primacy.

Who has ever called Polybius a "bad Greek" because he stood for, and exemplified, reconciliation between Rome and Hellas? Mythologi-

---

* The elder Pliny, a well-connected Roman, would be much more outspoken on that subject, but much later and never at his peril.

† Although they did so very rarely, the Romans themselves are said to have resorted to human sacrifice when the gods appeared to have deserted them—for instance, after their humiliating defeat by Hannibal at Cannae in 216 B.C.E. The Athenian leader Themistokles sacrificed three noble Persian youths before the battle of Salamis in 480 B.C.E.

cal affinities bridged contemporary antagonisms. Although Hellenes might be despised for being too clever by half, they were the perennial teachers and counselors of Roman dignitaries. Despite their military superiority, the Romans remained in awe of Greek culture, as Americans used to be of European. Greek art became fashionable in Rome as early as the mid-third century B.C.E., after Sicily had been overrun and pillaged in the First Punic War. By the end of the second century B.C.E., that ardent Hellenist Marcus Tullius Cicero could say, "Italy was full of the arts and literature of Greece." Hellas produced an inexhaustible supply of antique treasures and the texts to enliven them. The official Roman gods were curiously congruent with Zeus and Hera, Poseidon and Aphrodite, Athene and Artemis. Treading in Homer's hexametrical footsteps, Virgil's *Aeneid* attached the Romans to Greek epic myth by depicting them as the descendants of the defeated Trojans. The Mediterranean world was a Greco-Roman seesaw.

After Judaea was finally reduced, in 73, there was no cultural merger. The Jews shared their God, Yahweh, with no one; He lacked any Latin equivalent. The Jews sported no comely statues, no emblematic heroes, no versatile or amorous deities and demigods. Their sacred language, Hebrew, was an inaccessible code;* their Scriptures unamusing and parochial; their diet odd. Judaism had just one crucial, if belated, influence on Roman history: it was a principal source of the Christian churches that would become the ideological enemies of the Jews.

Josephus purported to follow Polybius in making his history "pragmatic." His avowed emphasis was on *pragmata*: acts, deeds, things. As far as the gods were concerned, Polybius ascribed Rome's success entirely to Tyche (Greek for "chance"), a post-Olympian Hellenistic deity, worshipped by Romans under the rubric of Fortuna. Tyche brought good and bad luck,† but she had no moral agenda for man-

---

* In *Is That a Fish in Your Ear?* (London: Faber & Faber, 2011), David Bellos says that the Hebrew citations read aloud from the Torah by the Temple priests were incomprehensible to almost all of the Jews in the congregation and had to be translated simultaneously into whispered Aramaic, the current vernacular.

† In modern Greek slang, *phortouna* can mean a violent storm.

kind and made no compacts. Under her widespread aegis (Tyche is mentioned seventy-eight times in *The Jewish War*), life was a twenty-four/seven casino. Unlike Homer's Zeus in archaic Hellas, Polybius's prevailing deity was never an active moral force supervising the world's game. Here Judaism differed: in the eyes of the priest that Joseph ben Mattathias was proud to proclaim himself, Yahweh had persistent and jealous expectations of His chosen. The Torah promised that the Holy One played a controlling and judicial part in human affairs. Provided His people honored His commandments,* offered due sacrifices, made pilgrimage to Jerusalem for the great festivals, especially Passover, and paid their tithes to the priesthood, there was no limit to His favor; nor to His displeasure if they did not.

Yahweh was nothing if not a hands-on God. The Book of Daniel, one of the last in the official Old Testament, repeated that the Holy One conferred earthly powers on those who deserved them and confiscated them from transgressors. Justice, not luck, would have the last word, which—so the same text promised—would soon be said. The Ethiopian Enoch, probably around the mid-second century B.C.E., announced the imminent end of the world: of the ten "weeks" of human history, eight had already passed. The next two would see the conversion of the world to Judaism and the Final Judgment. Daniel too threatened apocalypse, and soon.

Yahweh's fattened rule book demanded that Jews respect Him at all times, especially by abstaining from any activity other than prayer on the Sabbath. On the seventh day, purists insisted, men were forbidden even to defend themselves. When, in 63 B.C.E., the legions of Pompey the Great attacked Jerusalem on the Sabbath, the faithful were at prayer in the Temple. The barefoot priests continued with their office as they and their congregation were cut to pieces.

In Josephus's eyes, God was a moral enforcer, not a celestial croupier. It followed that Jerusalem would never have fallen, on any occa-

---

* The original ten ordinances handed to Moses on Mount Sinai had been amplified into 613 bylaws. It is said that Yahweh could be offended if a man broke wind without uncovering his head.

Introduction

sion, if He had not had reason to withdraw His sympathy. Why would
the God of the Hebrews turn His face from His chosen people? The
answer had to be that they had sinned. However scrupulous Josephus
might be with regard to sources and evidence, for him there was more
to human history than Polybius's concatenation of *pragmata*.* For the
first modern Jewish historian, facts and moral reckonings were seldom
separate. Yet his situation, when living on pensioned probation in Flavian Rome, required him to tread delicately, especially when telling
the truth. His most genuine sentiments had to be understated. As the
founder of the BBC, Lord Reith, once said, "When people feel deeply,
impartiality is bias."

In *The Jewish War*, Josephus resembles his fifth-century B.C.E.
model, the revered Thucydides, by figuring in his own history as a
less than successful—though more flamboyant—general, and only in
the third person. While both writers assess their own military performances with affectations of objectivity, Josephus sees himself in a more
indulgent, sometimes heroic light. Only in the autobiographical *Vita*,
while revisiting events already described, more soberly, in book III of
The Jewish War, does he abandon his dispassionate posture. In self-
defense, he composed the first example of prose written in the first
person to reach posterity.†

Josephus's Greek revision of the now lost original Aramaic version

---

* The only other ancient historian who could claim to be a practicing priest was
Plutarch. A decade younger than Josephus, Plutarch gained kudos from officiating
at Delphi, but his many historical studies, including even his so-called *Moralia*, were
not influenced by a faith that carried anything approaching the theocratic overtones
of Judaism. Plutarch was the first historian to portray Alexander the Great as the
cosmopolitan missionary of the rule of Reason, which meant, in practice, the universalization of Greek hegemony. See Maurice Sartre, *D'Alexandre à Zénobie*, p. 113.

† Zuleika Rodgers points out, in "Justice for Justus," that one of Josephus's main
sources, Nicolaus of Damascus, appended a (now lost) autobiography to his universal
history. Hence it is not innovative that Josephus should do the same to his *Jewish
Antiquities*. Priority is often a matter of luck. Herodotus is generally regarded as "the
father of history," but he was preceded by Hecataeus of Miletus, whose many works
survive only in fragments. The Parian soldier of fortune Archilochos wrote poems in
the first person in the seventh century B.C.E.

of *The Jewish War* was intended (by him, if not by the Flavians who commissioned it) to set the record straight: he is at pains to make it clear that the Jewish rebellion also involved a civil war between Jews. It is likely, however, that the text was published by the Romans to serve as a warning to Gentile readers in the eastern Mediterranean who might be of a mind to challenge their presence. Its critics accused the author of inaccuracy and distortion. The only one named by Josephus was a certain Justus, whom he had encountered years before, when campaigning in Galilee.* Justus and his father had been notables in Tiberias, a modernized city—named for Tiberius, the Roman emperor from 14 to 37 C.E.—on the Sea of Galilee. Joseph ben Mattathias tried repeatedly to attach its mixed population to the Jewish cause in the nervous weeks before Vespasian marched into Judaea.

Justus survived the war to become secretary to King Agrippa II, the ethnarch of Judaea. It was as an indignant reply to his critic† that the elderly Josephus was prompted to write his autobiographical apology. His *Vita* is limited to its author's early, active years. Only toward the end of his prolific literary career did he come round to writing about his youth, in the tones of a man speaking for himself, if never quite freely. Looking back in anger and anguish, some twenty years after his

---

* The standoff between Josephus and Justus about the origins of the Jewish war prefigures, for recent instance, that between the Oxford historians Hugh Trevor-Roper and Alan Taylor concerning the causes of the Second World War. Trevor-Roper also mounted a polemic against Hannah Arendt's *Eichmann in Jerusalem* (Gloucester, MA: Peter Smith, 1994) and another against Arnold Toynbee, the author of *A Study of History* and an overt anti-Semite. Elie Kedourie's *The Chatham House Version* (New York: Praeger, 1970) is a no less abrasive treatment of *bien-pensant* ideas about Middle Eastern history. An Iraqi Jew by origin, Kedourie regretted that Britain and France had conspired, in 1919, to dismantle the Ottoman Empire. Idleness and indulgent corruption had served the region's populations better than gimcrack nationalism and aggressive sectarianism.

† The stylish precision of Justus's history, now lost, won praise from the ninth-century Byzantine scholar and patriarch Photius. In his original text, Josephus had taken pains to emphasize how much the Jews had in common with other Mediterranean civilizations, but Justus's criticism stung him into adopting the haughtiness of a sophisticated Roman writer to whom Levantines stood for slyness and verbosity.

arrival in Rome, he has the snap of a survivor with a long memory for the dirty tricks of his enemies, not least those on his own side. Old wounds continued to arm his bow.

Josephus's long retrospective survey, *Jewish Antiquities,* appears more impersonal than his other works. Yet it too was part of an extensive effort to sustain the reputation of the Jews. They might have turned their backs on him; he never turned his on them. Like the solitary Sisyphus, he rolled on, in twenty volumes. Composed, as were the Gospels, in the post-classical Greek (derived from the classical Athenian) known as Koine, the common language of the Gentile eastern Mediterranean, *Jewish Antiquities* demystifies, but never debunks, the biblical and subsequent history of the Jews. Advertising their ancient origins and their intimate association with the Creator of the world, Josephus portrays them as a people who, like the ancient Athenians and Spartans, had lost a war but whose qualities merited lasting admiration.

The early sections of *Jewish Antiquities* are a paraphrase of the Hebrew Scriptures. Josephus then continues the story, through the rebellion of the Maccabees against the Seleucid Greeks, to the death of Herod the Great, in 4 B.C.E., when *The Jewish War* (which was, in fact, written first) latches on to it. Josephus's other substantial work, and the last he was able to complete, is his sustained and outspoken counterattack against Apion, an Alexandrian Greek academic and polemicist. A generation earlier, Apion had mounted a campaign against the Jews who had a large and long-established community in his city. He mocked their absurd beliefs and subversive habits. The Jews, he declared, worshipped a God whose commandments required them to behave in irrational ways.

In *Against Apion,* Josephus responded that if the Jewish laws had been proposed by some mythical sage or lawgiver, such as the Spartans' founding father Lycurgus, they would be regarded as eminently wise. In taking this line, he was the prototype of liberal Jewish apologists who give Yahweh credit for putting health warnings on shellfish and pork and attribute to Him the salutary rule that men should rest from their labors, as He did, on the seventh day. It is nice to think that everybody's weekend owes something to the Torah.* Josephus was the first Jewish writer to advertise his people's merits and religion to an alien audience and to retort robustly when they were disparaged. That he was writing, in Rome, at much the same time as the authors of the four Gospels and in the same public language made him the first Jew not only to challenge Apion but also to anticipate the dogmatic anti-Semitism which the Christian Fathers would sanctify in later centuries.

It is commonly assumed that Josephus's Greek translation of *The Jewish War* trots along with his original (now lost) Aramaic version; but even if his command of Koine was not yet fluent, the use of a foreign language involved a certain liberation. Because he was employing an alien terminology, the revision of his text has to have doubled as a commentary on it. To write in Greek enrolled him, to some degree, in a Gentile logic. Like fancy dress, pastiche dispels inhibitions. Men can both lose and discover themselves in another tongue: Baruch/Benedict Spinoza in Latin,† Joseph Conrad in English, Samuel Beckett in French. Even Edward Gibbon's English derives its Latinate cadences from the French that he learned during his boyhood in Geneva.

Josephus was a Judaean Jew of a kind that never existed before the sack of Jerusalem and the destruction of the Second Temple. The war he regarded as a reckless folly had ended with the mass suicide of the zealot garrison of Masada and the eviction of the Judaeans from their social and spiritual capital. Hundreds of thousands died in the war. Joseph ben Mattathias decidedly did not. Apology, of one kind and another, is at the heart of his history. His involvement in the ruin of

---

* In truth, however, the ratio of working to nonworking days in pagan ancient Rome was roughly the same as in Jerusalem; there were fifty days of public holidays in the year, though they were not spaced out on a weekly basis.

† Michel de Montaigne's first language, on the other hand, was Latin; his thoughts were liberated when he wrote his essays—spiced with many Latin references—in his second language, French. Like Josephus, he took a dispassionate and dismayed attitude to the sectarian violence of his times. As a result, he has been regarded, by severe critics, as a trimmer and even as a coward, since he declined to go into plague-ridden Bordeaux, even though he was the city's ex-mayor. Montaigne was descended, on his mother's side, from Sephardic Jews.

his people, first as their general, then as a captive spectator, both certifies its vividness and compromises its neutrality. A hyperactive social animal became a caged and passive solitary; yet exile also brought him to life as a writer.

The attachment, in midlife, of "Titus Flavius" to the Latinized equivalent of the author's original name symbolized the indenture of a Judaean notable to the service of the upstart Flavian dynasty. He would be marked forever as having accepted the favors, and taken the brand, of those who had destroyed his native city and massacred or enslaved its citizens. Not the least of Josephus's sins is that he survived to report news no one wanted to hear. The verbose individual who, from the time he left his native Judaea, never stopped writing about the past of his people, and about himself, has been stigmatized as the incarnation of an uneasy consciousness. Accused of treachery to the cause he once served, he has something in common both with the Wandering Jew and with Judas Iscariot, archetypal embodiments of the Jew as guilt-laden pariah.

The notion, propagated by the Gospels, that "the Jews" had the power to coerce the conscience-stricken Roman prefect Pontius Pilate into executing the innocent Jesus was a key element both in the anathematization of the Jews by Christianity and in the exemption of imperial Rome from the charge of deicide. Orthodox and Roman Catholicism attached that crime only to the Jews, in perpetuity.* No one has ever accused Italians, ancient or modern, of being Christ-killers. As Susan Gubar has said, "Judas is the principal figure through whom Christians have understood Jews and Jewry."†

---

* For a specific modern instance, see Anna Bikont's *Le crime et le silence,* in which the town of Jedwabne's Catholic priest is shown to have incited his Polish congregation to do God's work by massacring their Jewish fellow citizens in July 1941, which they did.

† In *Judas: A Biography,* Gubar quotes Karl Barth, a much-venerated modern (anti-Nazi) theologian, when he sustains the myth of Jewish guilt: "Like Esau the rejected of God, the Jews sold their birthright for a mess of pottage. They did so not with closed eyes but with open eyes. Yet these were obviously the eyes of the blind. . . . Israel always tried to buy off Yahweh with thirty pieces of silver."

Judas was turned into the hate figure in a myth that required God to be an innocent victim whose blood would redeem those who put their faith in Him. The Jew as treachery incarnate is struck from his mold. Titus Flavius Josephus is rarely so cruelly stigmatized, but his survival, capped by his accepting a stipend from the Romans, has made him, in some eyes, a cousin of Judas Iscariot. Yigael Yadin, the Israeli general and archaeologist who excavated the mountain redoubt of Masada, where the Judaean rebels made their last stand, in 73 C.E., said of Josephus, "He was a great historian and a bad Jew."* Is that a verdict which deserves to stand? How are good or bad Jews to be defined or recognized? Yadin's assertion tells us more about the do-or-die ethos with which the Israeli general hoped to inculcate his paratroopers than about Joseph ben Mattathias / Titus Flavius Josephus. Yet the latter's life and work raise questions of morality and of the value of personal identity and testimony. No one—especially, no Jew—can read Josephus without a certain apprehension that Josephus is also reading him. Our shadows too fall across his pages.

* Yadin's determination to make Masada a place in which Israeli soldiers should pledge themselves to stand or die perpetuates a myth of Jewish solidarity that is also self-destructive. In something of the same spirit of antiquarian sentiment, Greek air force cadets are known generically as "Ikaroi," even though the original Ikaros was the first flier to plunge to his death, because he flew too near the sun.

A Jew Among Romans

I

OBSERVED ACROSS THE ABYSS OF YEARS, the rebellion in which Joseph ben Mattathias was to play a leading part appears like a remake of the story of David and Goliath. Despite the fact that, this time, Goliath won, the Jews' defiant last stand, in 73 C.E., while defending the gaunt mountaintop fortress of Masada, in the southern desert, has been used, especially in modern Israel, to illustrate how the flower of the Jewish nation, having risen *en bloc* against imperial oppression, resisted to the last man. For some Zionists at least, the lesson of "the Jewish War" is that the only people Jews can trust are other Jews. The long story that Flavius Josephus lived to tell is less romantic and more complicated.

Ever since Alexander the Great conquered and appropriated the Persian Empire, only to have it break up into fractious kingdoms after his early death in 323 B.C.E., the Fertile Crescent had been a patchwork of fiefdoms, religions and antagonisms. Lacking gorgeous and impassable rivers* or a bulwark of mountains, Judaea was regularly at the mercy of armies, which marched through it or chose to garrison its cities. Two of Alexander's Macedonian marshals, Seleucus and Ptolemy, founded Middle Eastern empires. Their royal successors—Seleucids in Syria, Ptolemies in Egypt—played tug-of-war with Palestine for almost two centuries.

The Romans were only the last, the best disciplined and the most

---

* In 2 Kings 5:12, the Syrian general Naaman says, "Are not Abana and Pharpar, rivers of Damascus, better than all the waters of Israel?"

tenacious of the foreign invaders. As Josephus recalls in *Jewish Antiquities,* Rome's intrusion into Judaea was the result of an unwise invitation from contending Jewish factions: in 63 B.C.E., Pompey the Great, who was playing for bigger stakes in nearby Syria, was called in as arbiter during a fraternal feud between Aristobulus (the last king of the Maccabean dynasty) and his ineffectual brother Hyrcanus, the High Priest. The latter served as a front for a rich, nominally Hellenized Idumaean* called Antipater, who coveted the throne for himself.

Pompey had also been petitioned by a third group of Jews: the pious Zealots,† who craved a return to a hermetic life that acknowledged no secular authority. Ultra-Orthodox, often lower-class, they advocated a purified theocracy, free of alien corruption and, of course, under their own leadership. It was their regular charge against the High Priest and his council, the Sanhedrin, that they habitually faced both (or several)

---

* Idumaea, in the south of Judaea, had been conquered by the Maccabees less than a century earlier. The heroic brothers began as strict Jewish nationalists, but they needed manpower for their war of liberation from the Seleucids. The forced conversion of the Idumaeans legitimized their recruitment in what began as a purely Jewish religious uprising. The hierarchy in Jerusalem never embraced the Idumaeans, even when circumcised, as their equals and brothers. In this the Idumaeans resembled Sephardic immigrants today, mostly from North Africa, who claim to have been discriminated against in modern Israel by the mostly Ashkenazi Israeli establishment.

† Here and elsewhere, I use the term "Zealots," rather loosely, to cover those Jews, distinct from (and opposed to) the Temple hierarchy, who militantly promoted the strict and hermetic practice of Judaism. They had something in common with modern Middle Eastern fundamentalists in regarding the presence of all outsiders, especially the Romans, as an abomination. It should not be supposed that they had any central organization or program. The term "Zealot" is a convenience, but not one which any ancient Jews would have applied to themselves. The sect of eastern European Hasidim, founded in the eighteenth century by Israel Baal Shem Tov, was a wishful throwback to the Judaean Zealots (who are referred to as Hasidim in sources that scholars now regard as obsolete). The modern Hasids suppose themselves to share many of their spiritual notions and social customs with those of ancient Judaea, but they are reproduction antiques, styled, as Zuleika Rodgers has expressed it, by "German medieval pietism and Polish mysticism." Those who live in the Stamford Hill section of London and in Brooklyn, New York, imitate (in costume, posture and social organization) the inhabitants of the Ukrainian shtetls, which were finally swept away by the Nazis.

ways. Zealots were vehement in accusing the hierarchy of being willing to trade Jewish independence in order to maintain their own standing. This did not inhibit fundamentalists from seeking to recruit Pompey to their cause.

The three Jewish parties had in common only the naïve presumption that the Romans would come in, cancel their enemies and then leave. In the event, Pompey did not give priority to a profitless squabble between native pretenders. First he completed the annexation of the Seleucid Empire* to the greater glory of the Senate and the Roman people, and to his own and his soldiers' financial advantage. Only after Aristobulus dared to anticipate his judgment, by raising an army of his own, did the Roman grandee march on Jerusalem.

The supporters of Hyrcanus opened the gates. Aristobulus and his men barricaded themselves in the Temple precinct. Neither then nor in Josephus's day did the city's Jews react with solidarity to external force. After a three-month siege, there was a massacre in which, Josephus says, twelve thousand Jews died, including those unresisting priests engaged in the exercise of their office.[1] Josephus adds a bitter detail: "Most who fell were killed by their own countrymen of the rival faction; others beyond number threw themselves over the precipices."[†]

Pompey became the first Roman to stride into the curtained inner sanctum of the Temple. Perhaps in superstitious awe of its numinous vacancy, he touched nothing. Just over a century later, the curtain

---

* Despite ad hoc concessions to the Maccabees, the Seleucids had never formally renounced their lease on Palestine. Pompey had reason, of a kind, to consider that Jerusalem formed part of the spoils of his war.

† One of those in Jerusalem at the time was the miracle worker known to folklore as Choni the Circle Drawer. Choni's name and fame derived from an occasion when he was said to have drawn a circle in the dust and stood in it, calling on Yahweh to make it rain. It began to drizzle, but he said that was not enough; it then began to pelt with rain, which was too much; when he asked for a "calm rain," steady rain then began to fall, and Choni's reputation was made. Captured by followers of Hyrcanus, he was solicited to pray for their leader's success. He responded by saying, "Lord of the Universe, since the besieged and the besiegers both belong to your people, I beg you not to listen to the evil prayers of either side." He was then stoned to death by the High Priest's followers.

would be only a small part of the booty Titus took to Rome to swag his father's triumph. The survivors among the priesthood, either because of their dignity or by virtue of the revenue at their disposal, had a chastening effect on Pompey. Inclined to fastidious gestures (malicious contemporaries accused him of being effeminate because he would scratch his head with one finger, in order not to distress his coiffure, which was set to resemble that of Alexander the Great), Pompey consented to the Temple being cleansed of blood and then licensed the resumption of the rites. He was remembered by the Jews more for his sacrilege than for his belated courtesy. Two centuries later, a gang of Jews desecrated the Egyptian tomb containing his headless corpse.

In 61 B.C.E., the evicted Aristobulus and his family, having been shipped to Rome, were obliged to walk in front of Pompey's triumphal chariot; but they were spared the customary chains. A large contingent of Jews was also paraded in the ritual of the triumph. Such occasions had the allure of a mobile circus, complete with "floats" representing scenes from the victorious campaign.[2] The festivities usually ended with the execution of defeated leaders, but the Judaeans appear to have been released when the metropolitan circuit was complete.* A number remained to swell the Jewish community in Rome. It grew to forty thousand in imperial times.†

---

* In 56 B.C.E., Aristobulus and one of his sons escaped from Rome to Syria and raised a rebellion. Again defeated and again a prisoner, he must have had considerable resources of charm, ability and gold. He survived in renewed captivity until 49 B.C.E., when, at the height of the civil war between Caesar and Pompey, he was sprung from his dungeon by Caesar's supporters and sent to command the legions fighting against Pompey in what they took to be Aristobulus's home patch, Syria. There his lucky run reached term: he was poisoned by a bounty hunter. Preserved in honey, his body was returned for burial to Judaea, where his old enemy, Hyrcanus II was in office as High Priest.

† In *The Ruling Class of Judaea,* Martin Goodman says that the Jewish inhabitants of Rome were demonstrably in favor of direct imperial rule, so great was their hatred of the Herodians. A good number of them, it is said, were descended from those captured and sold into slavery by Herod and Mark Antony's consular friend Sosius. The Roman Jews and their descendants were concentrated in the Trastevere quarter of Rome, not far from where the popes would restrict their descendants to the gated ghetto which enclosed many of them until after the Second World War.

Two years after Pompey's parade, there were enough Jews resident in the capital for Cicero to complain—while defending Lucius Valerius Flaccus, an ex-governor of Asia—that Roman justice was under threat from a loud swarm of Jews. Since Roman trials were often conducted in the open air, star advocates attracted large, sometimes rowdy, crowds of spectators. Cicero was used to generating sympathy by affecting to fight against intimidating odds. Flaccus had been accused of siphoning off tribute, sent by Jews from all over the Mediterranean, while it was on its way to the Temple in Jerusalem. Adept at playing to the gallery, Cicero had recourse to whatever means would lead to his client's acquittal. He did nothing to challenge the truth of the charges against Flaccus, but claimed that Pompey's recent "victory" in Jerusalem proved that the gods had deserted the Jews, since they would otherwise have defeated him.*

To infer that Rome's "Jewish lobby" acted in an unusual or improper fashion is to take Ciceronian bluster for reliable evidence.† Roman advocacy was a public performance that has been likened to bel canto: it sanctioned whatever bravura flights might impress a jury or amuse the gallery. Rome's Jews are unlikely to have made Cicero as nervous as it served his case to pretend. Cicero's older colleague and fellow littérateur, Marcus Terentius Varro, with no case to argue, acclaimed Judaism as a true *religio*. He rated it above the superstitious cults, with their fetishistic statuary, that flourished in the Rome of his day.

In 48 B.C.E., the civil war between Caesar and Pompey ended with Pompey's decisive defeat at Pharsalus, in northern Greece. He fled to Egypt. When Caesar followed, one of the Ptolemies presented him, on landing, with the embalmed head of his late enemy and onetime son-in-law. Caesar had the grace to seem rueful, but the Egyptian queen

---

* Pedestrian fact makes nonsense of his rhetoric, but Cicero still won his case, the advocate's sole concern. *"Vae victis"* (Woe to the defeated) was a jeering slogan to which, in one form or another, the Jews were to be subjected many times.

† John Rogister, a present-day British historian of Vichy France, has suggested that the Pétain regime's outlawing of Jews in the summer of 1940, soon after France's defeat, was a reaction to their aggressive "lobbying," which amounted, in fact, to seeking exemption from being deported and murdered.

Cleopatra's alluring proximity made him casual about security. Boxed in at Alexandria by a large force of hostile "Egyptians,"* Caesar was rescued, in extremis, by the cavalry of Antipater, the Idumaean chieftain, and his ally Hyrcanus II, whose military skills, on this occasion, matched his priestly eminence. Hyrcanus was rewarded with the ethnarchy of the Jews. Antipater's sons, Phasael and Herod, then twenty-five years old, were named governors of Jerusalem and Galilee, respectively. Neither was fully a Jew; their mother, Kypros, was a "distinguished lady from Arabia."

If his generosity was its measure, Caesar had had a serious fright. It led him to sanction Jews all around the Mediterranean to resume the dispatch of tribute to Jerusalem, thus strengthening the city's economy, since the Temple treasury functioned as a central bank.† Caesar also excused Jews from conscription. In Josephus's view, the settlement gave the Judaeans every privilege short of independence. It was the high point of their relations with the Romans. Only the fundamentalist Zealots, vigilant for righteous grievances (and for excuses to impose their version of rectitude on others), could object to so amiable an arrangement. Caesar's indulgence was typical of Roman methods when recruiting provincials as allies. His exemption of Jews from military service was both a grace and an acknowledgment that, as recruits, they

---

* The term "Egyptians" probably embraces a spectrum of disaffected Levantines. The Romans, like the British in their imperial vanity, made small distinction when it came to labeling indigenous peoples. The aggressive advent of the Romans during the previous century had generated violent resentment in local populations in the Fertile Crescent. In 88 B.C.E., Mithridates VI of Pontus, the ruler of a kingdom on the south shore of the Black Sea, plotted and primed the simultaneous massacre of some eighty thousand Roman and Italian colonists and officials in the region. His rebellion was put down, with difficulty and condign pitilessness, by Sulla and by later Roman commanders, Pompey the last. A revolt that was intended to drive the Romans out of "Asia" made sure that they would stay there. Mithridates maintained fugitive resistance to the Italian presence until 63 B.C.E. When cornered, he required a slave to stab him (he was impervious to poison, of which he had taken regular small doses as a prophylactic). The attack on Caesar is likely to have been mounted by the rump of those who remembered, and resented, the Mithridatic wars in which so many "natives" had died.

† The going annual subscription was half a shekel per adult male.

could be more trouble than they were worth: they would not eat the same food as the other soldiers; however brave they might be on weekdays, many refused to fight on the Sabbath.*

As long as Caesar was busy imposing his autocracy on the rump of Pompey's supporters, Judaea made no urgent call on Roman attention. Seen from the Seven Hills, it was the pacified adjunct of a province under the mandate of the governor of Syria. For those who lived there, however, there was no shortage of bloody incident. Palestine was home to endless feuds, tribal antagonism and coups d'état. Local events frequently reflected what was happening at the center. In 44 B.C.E., the deified Julius Caesar was stabbed to death in Rome, under Pompey's statue. In 43 B.C.E., his protégé Antipater was poisoned in Judea. The killer is likely to have been one of the bounty hunters who could expect rewards for murdering the enemy of any dominant faction. Since Antipater had been Caesar's man, his assassin could hope for profitable congratulations from the great man's murderers.

Rome had divided into two parties. "The Liberators," led by Brutus and Cassius, were confronted by Mark Antony and, very soon, by Caesar's heir and adopted son, the nineteen-year-old Octavian. "That young man," as Cicero termed him, had no right to power (according to the traditional rules, he was not even old enough to run for petty office), but he could call on the fidelity of Caesar's veterans, who had good reason to hope for handouts in land and bonuses. The less constitutional the cause, the fatter the potential dividends: why else were Rubicons crossed?

In Book I of *The Jewish War,* Josephus concentrates on the consequences in Judaea of Caesar's assassination: Phasael and Herod—as conspicuous for his passions as for his panache—made a bid for

---

* In an extension of the sabbatical principle, as decreed in Leviticus, Judaean farmers left their land fallow for one year in seven. The Roman authorities waived land taxes accordingly, but the peasants' (as it happened) fruitful practice kindled jeers from Roman legionnaires that Jews were lazy. It proved a long-running canard: Julio Grondona, an Argentinian football tycoon, said recently that no Jew should be allowed to referee a football game, because it involved physical effort "and no Jew likes hard work."

control of Judaea. In 40 B.C.E., Rome's most reliable general, Mark Antony assumed command of forces in the region; but then, falling under the same spell as his dead patron, he deferred military duties in order to follow the now thirty-year-old Cleopatra to Alexandria. Alert to the divisions and distractions of the Romans, the Parthians— on the eastern flank of the imperial frontier—marched into Syria and on to Jerusalem. Their occupation of the Temple gave Herod and his brother an opportunity to promote themselves as patriotic heroes; but when they attempted to depose the Parthians' puppet, King Antigonus (the last of the Maccabean line), they had no success. Tricked into a parley, Phasael and his father's ally, Hyrcanus, were made prisoners.

Herod managed to slip away to Masada, not far from where he would later build himself a grandiose compound. Complete with a closet theater, decorated with Greco-Roman images, its ruins stand proof of his pagan tastes. The mountaintop fortress was reinforced by Herod, once he attained power, principally as a means of asserting himself over the Jews who, he feared, rightly, never regarded him as their legitimate king. Herod's plethora of castles, armories and fortified palaces is evidence both of the ruler's distrust of his subjects and of his fear of possible rivals.

While in Parthian custody, Herod's brother, Phasael, committed suicide by smashing his head against a rock. Hyrcanus's ears were cut off, so that he could no longer be eligible to hold the office of High Priest (its tenant had to be without physical blemish, of which stammering was not an instance).* Herod rallied to Mark Antony. Amorous and amoral adventurers, the two men had compatible tastes and ambitions. Having left Cleopatra, temporarily, in order to return to Rome, Antony put himself forward as Caesar's successor as top man. Herod wanted to be boss only of the Fertile Crescent. Licensed to return to Judaea, he evicted Antigonus, with the aid of Roman troops, and installed himself as Antony's client king.

---

* Josephus was proud to number the High Priest Simon Psellus ("the stutterer") among his forebears.

Since he had to pay his mercenary army fat bonuses, Herod imitated the practice of murderous proscriptions initiated in Rome by Lucius Cornelius Sulla in 82 B.C.E. when, in revenge for its failure to support his right-wing coup d'état, he decimated the senatorial class and distributed their estates to his confederates. Antigonus's friends and family were killed and their property confiscated. At home and abroad, theft was as good a motive for murder as enmity. No one has ever needed to dislike a man in order to covet his wealth or his office.* To reconcile the urban masses to his rule, Herod eased their chronic unemployment by initiating large public works; as well as renovating the Temple, he had the streets of Jerusalem paved with flagstones. The people were glad to take his wages, but he failed to win their hearts.

Herod knew how to make himself feared, but he never allayed his own dread of treachery. Apprehensive of its independence and authority, he further degraded the venerated office of High Priest by installing an unknown Babylonian returnee, Ananelus, in the post. Said to be descended from the original Zadok, Ananelus's best qualification, in Herod's eyes, was that he had no nexus of support in Jerusalem; he was, in effect, the king's Jew. Not long afterward, however, in order to please his future wife Mariamne, Herod replaced Ananelus with her sixteen-year-old brother, another Aristobulus. When the young man officiated at the Feast of Tabernacles, his handsome appearance and Maccabean lineage made such a popular impression that Herod feared an uprising in his favor. One very hot day, the guileless Aristobulus was taken, by a party of Herod's acolytes, to have a swim in a pool near Jericho. They held him under the water until he drowned.†

Herod was happier in the cosmopolitan society of the Hellenistic Levant than among Jews. He could not resist the high-stakes game of Roman power politics. As Mark Antony and Octavian turned on

---

* Jewish moralists, including Jesus of Nazareth, were alone in the ancient world in regarding wealth as an impediment to virtue. Their attitude was alien to Romans and Greeks (except for a few Cynics, such as the ostentatiously minimalist Diogenes).

† Constantine Cavafy's 1918 poem "Aristovoulos" mentions only the young man's beauty. The poet has it (perhaps ironically) that Herod was distressed by the death, which is attributed to the machinations of Salome and Kypros.

each other, Herod decided to go and see Antony in order to confirm their *amicitia* (the Latin term for "friendship" implied political alliance rather more than personal affection). Josephus records how Herod left Mariamne, the love of his life, in the custody of Joseph, the husband of his sister, Salome, with instructions that, should Herod himself be arrested and executed by Antony, his brother-in-law was to kill Mariamne rather than let her marry anyone else.[3]

Having renewed his deal with Antony, Herod returned to Judaea to find that his instructions to Joseph had been leaked to Mariamne by Herod's mother and his sister, Salome; both hoped to make trouble between the couple. Mariamne's origins were suspect: she was descended, on both sides, from the Hasmonaeans, the royal house that had sprung from the now severely pruned family tree of the Maccabees. Herod had eliminated the Maccabean males, but his love for Mariamne excused her from his habitual ruthlessness. As soon as he was making love to her again, the king swore that she was the only woman he had ever loved. "And a nice way you show it," she said, "giving Joseph orders to kill me!" Persuaded that she had always hated him and that she had committed adultery with his brother-in-law, Herod flew into a frenzy and had her strangled.

Once Mariamne was dead, the king was consumed by regret. He spent hours in anguished conversation with her spirit. Later, he married another Mariamne, said by Josephus to have been the most beautiful woman of the age. Remorse engendered the king's lethal suspicion of the first Mariamne's devious and resentful mother, Alexandra. He was more and more possessed by the paranoia that would transform him into the killer of all but a few of his own sons by his nine wives.

When Antony and Cleopatra were defeated at Actium in 31 B.C.E., Herod collected a large amount of gold and sailed to Rhodes, where the future emperor Augustus was considering how best to divide, and rule, the world.* Although frequently appalled by Herod's conduct,

---

* It is a measure of Herod's parlous situation after the battle of Actium in 31 B.C.E. that, according to Josephus (*Jewish War* I: 519 etc.), the Romanized Spartan adventurer Gaius Julius Eurycles extracted the huge sum of fifty talents from him

Josephus cannot conceal his relish for the skill with which the king played the hand. A few years earlier, after the great Cicero had been proscribed, Rome's finest orator and onetime national hero had been too terrified to go in person to throw himself on Octavian's mercy, lest his murder be preceded by torture. Void of trumps, Herod approached Octavian without uncomely groveling. Making a brazen virtue of his loyalty to the now anathematized Antony,* he advanced it as proof that, once he had pledged his *amicitia,* he never abandoned it. Now that Antony was dead, the lifelong pledge was ruptured; Herod was free to swear that he would be as loyal to the new master of the Roman world as he had been to his enemy.

A cool assessor of other men's usefulness, Octavian agreed to be amused by Herod's chutzpah. He confirmed the suppliant on his throne, extended his realm to include an enlarged Judaea and gave Herod titular authority, as *rex socius* (king and ally), over the many Jews in the empire at large. A million, it is said, were living in Egypt alone. Herod would later claim that he was second in the emperor's esteem only to Augustus's legate and troubleshooter, Marcus Vipsanius Agrippa. Both kings of Judaea on the throne in Josephus's lifetime, Herod's grandson and great-grandson, were named in Agrippa's honor.

Although he refrained from affectations of divinity, Herod was in most regards a typical Hellenistic king, polygamous and uxorious, exacting and lavish. Like the Seleucids and Ptolemies, he was a foreign monarch who tried to please at least some of the people most of the time. He sponsored gladiatorial shows and pagan sanctuaries (including those dedicated to the now deified Augustus, at Caesarea and in

---

by promising to intercede on Herod's behalf with Octavian, whom the Spartan had been shrewd enough to back with a contingent of latter-day Spartiates. Eurycles was the last Spartan to strut the public stage. His avarice was notorious, but the Spartans were renowned, even in their most glorious (and supposedly ascetic) days, for their appetite for money.

* According to Dio Cassius (51.19.3), Antony's birthday, January 14, was "decreed accursed" by the Senate, under Octavian's encouragement. This did nothing to prevent Antony's legitimate offspring and their descendants from occupying high places in the imperial order of things.

Samaria).* He distributed bread to the Gentile populace and made sure that his twin palaces at Masada had stores full of great Italian wines (from Tarentum, in Magna Graecia, and from Massica, in Campania) and a gourmet's larder with, among other delicacies, apples from Cumae and *garum*, a fish sauce, somewhat like a tapenade, from Spain. The fortress, four hundred yards above the southern desert floor, was designed principally as a bolt-hole for Herod in case of a popular uprising. The disunity of the Palestinian population—Greeks, Jews, Syrians, Samaritans, Arabs—was both his strength and his weakness: he could stay ahead of his subjects by playing them off against one another, but he could never weld them into a cohesive nation with common purposes or interests. His army, composed wholly of mercenaries, was in effect an imported police force.

Herod's restoration of the Jerusalem Temple made it the ornament of his capital. Toward the end of his reign, having out-Solomoned Solomon in the magnificence of the reconstruction (in the Hellenistic style), he ordered a golden eagle to be erected over the Great Gate. Did he not know or not care that it was unlawful for strict Jews to allow the image of any living thing to intrude on holy ground? When the king was rumored to have fallen seriously ill, two ultranationalist rabbis, famed for their aggressive piety, proclaimed that his enfeeblement offered a divine chance to strike a blow for God by pulling down the sacrilegious eagle. The Zealots' version of the good Jew made it more virtuous for a man to die for God than for his country. Allegiance to a mundane state, with its practical duties and compromises, was never their prime concern.[†]

Promised that Herod was dying, a posse of young men lowered

---

* In *The Israelites,* Antony Kamm notes that social conflicts over cult became seriously vexed, especially in the case of the Judaean Jews, only after the Romans made gods of their emperors, a view diplomatically confirmed by Philo in his *De legatione ad Gaium.*

† The coinage struck in Jerusalem during the 67–73 war was in honor of "Zion," not of Judaea. Today's Haredim, similarly inward-looking, refuse to serve in the Israel Defense Forces.

themselves on ropes from the Temple roof, in the midday sun. The precinct was thronged with people who gaped or cheered as they hacked down the eagle with axes. Troops were sent in. Forty demonstrators were arrested and taken before the sick king. The culprits confessed, gladly, to chopping down the blasphemous monstrosity. Herod asked who had told them to do so. They replied that it was the law of their fathers. And how could they be so cheerful when they were about to die? Because of the blessings they would enjoy after death.*

Herod convened a public meeting, in which he accused the young men of being temple robbers who had made the law an excuse for sacrilege. Josephus reports that "the people," afraid of some communal punishment, now begged the king to deal as he wished with those who had instigated the crime and with those caught in the act, but to take no action against the mass of the population. Herod confined himself to ordering that the two rabbis and the young men who had lowered themselves from the roof should be burned alive. It was a form of execution alien to Jews, although convicted criminals in ancient Athens, half a millennium before, had sometimes been done to death by being rolled in red-hot ash. The remainder of Herod's troublemakers were put to death more discreetly.

The eagerness with which the citizens called for the execution of those with whom many had sympathized is as craven as it is understandable. The Jerusalem crowd is said some thirty years later to have switched from welcoming the Galilean preacher Jesus of Nazareth to calling for his execution. Pitched among a demanding God, quasi-Jewish kings, a predatory priesthood and an alien imperial power, the Judaean Jews swung from messianic hope to practical apprehension. By playing politics with the High Priesthood, Herod had inclined the

---

* The notion of paradisal resurrection for the faithful long preceded Christianity and Islam, although the Sadducees had no belief in it. The Pharisees had a Hellenized notion of the immortality of the soul. Josephus (*Antiquities* 18: 13–14) says that they taught that there were punishments and rewards "under the earth for the those who led lives of virtue or vice."

masses to vest their credulity in unofficial preachers and outlandish gurus. When such men disappointed expectation, they were abandoned to their fate.

In Jerusalem, the lower classes had no vote and no social status. Unlike the citizens of Greek city-states or the Roman aristocracy and *equites,* they were never required or trained to take up arms in defense of the state. Herod was a typical Hellenistic potentate: his tenure of power depended less on the loyalty than on the defenselessness of his subjects. The lower orders had either to reconcile themselves to meekness or to resort to terrorism. *The Jewish War* goes to great lengths to show that the rising against Rome in 66 C.E. was, in good part, the consequence of divisions among the Judaean Jews. Their internecine friction had sources in events that had taken place long before its author was born.

Herod's anger over the incident of his golden eagle was visited on the latest of his High Priests, who was deposed. Despite devaluation by their frequent, cynical replacement, these dignitaries remained the only traditional interpreters of the law. Yet since their lease was subject to the pleasure of the occupying power, no appointee could hope for unalloyed public esteem. Their contamination was regularly denounced by the Zealots.

Soon after the incident of the golden eagle, Herod's fever worsened. According to Josephus, diviners told him that his debility was punishment for the burning of the rabbis.[4] His derangement accelerated; he hurried to the therapeutic hot baths at Kallirhoe; he distributed bonuses to his entourage; then he repaired to Jericho, where he challenged death itself by devising a "criminal operation." He called all the Judaean notables together, village by village, and shut them all into the hippodrome. He then told his sister, Salome, and her husband, Alexas, that he knew that the Jews would celebrate his death as a holiday. In that case, as soon as he breathed his last, the notables were to be massacred. The whole of Judaea would then have cause to weep on his account.

While the king was still on his deathbed, a party of officials returned from Rome with word that the emperor Augustus had endorsed the execution of Herod's allegedly treasonous son Antipater* (who was being held in prison in Judaea) but that Herod was free to banish him instead. As soon as Antipater heard the news, he offered a fat bribe to his jailers to spring him at once. When this was reported to Herod, it served as a terminal stimulant; Josephus says that he "uttered a cry louder than seemed possible in so sick a man" and sent orders for his son to be executed immediately. Five days later, in 4 B.C.E., he himself died, after reigning for thirty-three years.

Herod's grandiose funeral procession was also a show of force on the part of his son and nominated heir, Archelaus. The latter's succession depended on the approval of the future emperor, Tiberius, to whom he hurried to present himself.† Meanwhile, Herod was buried in the Herodium, which had been readied for him, twenty-four miles outside Jerusalem, where his death was a cause for rejoicing. The citizens, who were still mourning the priests executed by the dead king, demanded that his nominee as High Priest be ejected from office. A Roman detachment, under a tribune, was roughed up by the Passover crowd. A larger force, backed by cavalry, was then sent in. Josephus says that three thousand Jews were cut down and the feast abandoned.⁵

A few weeks later, Sabinus, the procurator of Syria, who backed the

---

* Antipater was the son of Doris, the first of the nine wives by whom Herod had seven children. In 7 B.C.E., with Augustus's reluctant approval, the increasingly paranoid king had had Alexander and Aristobulus—his sons by his beloved Mariamne—strangled for supposedly plotting against him. Backed by his scheming mother, Antipater was restored to favor, but he was soon accused of plotting to make sure of surviving his father by disposing of him. Observing imperial protocol, Herod sought Augustus's warrant to execute yet another of his own sons. Stanley Kubrick's definition of paranoia, "understanding what's going on," is relevant both to Herod and to his Roman masters. Augustus, whom Dryden called a man who "kills and keeps his temper," sent his only daughter, Julia, into ignominious and unreprieved exile for being implicated in a conspiracy, of which the details were successfully suppressed.

† So did a pretender who—sponsored by a devious Levantine operator—claimed to be Herod's dead son Alexander. Like a false Messiah, he gained the support of the Jews in Rome (and of the inhabitants of the Cycladic island of Melos). He was quickly exposed by Tiberius, who, with a rare show of geniality, sent the silly fellow to the galleys. His sponsor was executed.

candidature of Herod's son Antipas for his father's throne, sent in a full legion, with a posse of slaves, to look for the dead king's treasure. Sabinus's courage did not match his greed. Cornered in the royal palace by a massive Jerusalem crowd, he promised to withdraw, hoping that his colleague Varus would arrive in time for him to break his word. There were riots all over Judaea as rival claimants bid for power. When Varus (whose name means, literally, "the crooked one") reached Jerusalem, with a large force, the insurgent Jews dispersed. According to Josephus, the best people welcomed the return of law and order which was enforced by the crucifixion of some two thousand "ringleaders."[6]

The riots and feuds which followed Herod's death confirmed that he had fabricated a grandiose façade for a kingdom with no affection or trust between the ruler and his culturally diverse subjects. His style of tyranny embargoed even the remote possibility of differing strands of opinion and ambition being reconciled by common civility or municipal power-sharing. As a young man, Herod had derived his military prowess from a combination of aggressive flair and personal heroism; but his soldiers had always been mercenaries. Some had happened to be Jews; none belonged to a national army with allegiance to anyone but their paymaster.

Because of its connection with Christian mythology, the history of Herod's rule is better known than that of most minor kings, but his methods and conduct hardly differed from those common to a host of Hellenistic and Macedonian kingdoms. Herod's machinations provided Josephus with some of his liveliest pages, but his résumé of them was there to prove that the Jews were neither worse nor very different from the Romans or anyone else in the Mediterranean world when it came to treachery, egotism and ostentation.

Alternating appeasement with repression, Herod had inflated Judaea into a heterogeneous, quasi-autonomous province, never a cohesive state. Jerusalem had been turned into a gilded reproduction of Solomon's capital in which the king, although a native of the region, was never at home. Herod had secured independence of a kind from Rome, but his Jewish subjects distrusted him too much to identify themselves with the Greater Judaea which his personal demons drove him to expand and embellish. The vast new Second Temple (and the adjacent palace that insisted on its tenant's temporal authority) both dominated and closed off the horizons of the citizens.

The Temple's magnificence was intended to establish its creator as the equal of "Solomon in all his glory." Among all the cities under imperial jurisdiction, Herod's Jerusalem was unique. It bore some resemblance to a mediaeval monastery. Dedicated to a devout calendar, it was at the center of a community that both serviced and profited from its religious status. Tourists filled the caravanserais, changed money, bought suitable sacrificial livestock and marveled at the Temple and at Herod's palace. Eighteen thousand people found employment in maintaining the precinct and its services to pilgrims. The stone carvers and glassmakers were said to be almost as good as those in Sidon. Upkeep of the Temple demanded regular supplies of wood for repairs, animals for sacrifice, oil and incense for lighting and atmosphere. In general, however, since the city's revenues went mainly into the Temple treasury, they did little to fund practical enterprise or to enrich the surrounding countryside. The rigidity of their society froze the Jerusalem Jews in traditional roles and attitudes. Never organized in any military formation, they had no impulse to secular political activity. Herod's golden Temple and its cyclopean fortifications combined to persuade them that, with God's favor, they would be invincible.

II

In the wake of the squabbles and feuds that followed Herod's death, Judaea lost its nominal independence. For want of an indigenous strongman, Augustus subjected the territory to supervision by a sequence of less than distinguished Roman officials subordinate, in theory, to the governor of Syria. Judaea was not a popular posting. Although fertile, and with a number of prosperous cities, many with a majority of Greek-speaking inhabitants, it lacked natural riches. Unlike the empire's wheat-producing provinces—Egypt, Sicily and North Africa—the region's exports were not crucial to Rome's well-being. Its main crop was a stock of gold, which was located, and annually replenished, in the Jerusalem Temple, the repository of tithes and offerings from Jews all around the Mediterranean.

By the time Joseph ben Mattathias was growing up, Palestine was no more than one of the buffers between the Roman imperium and the unconquered Parthians. The latter were formidable horsemen, said by the credulous second-century C.E. historian Justinus to live in the saddle, whether trading or arguing. Their archers were adept at firing parting shots from their bows as they wheeled to gallop in retreat. Legend insisted that their flight was more formidable than their attack. The ancient taste for congruity presumed that their morals, like their tactics, were perverse:* the Parthians were said to be addicted to undi-

---

* It is typical of ancient typologies that those outside the civilized pale were depicted as physically and morally incongruous. Herodotus recorded, even if he did

luted alcohol (civilized men took water with their wine) and to father children even on their sisters and mothers.*

In 53 B.C.E., the Parthians had destroyed the army of Marcus Licinius Crassus. On the way to his death at the calamitous battle of Carrhae, he had stopped off at Jerusalem in order to cull all the gold in the Temple sanctuary. In subsequent years, the Romans made it a matter of honor to recover the "eagles"—the regimental standards—of Crassus's slaughtered legions. They did so, finally, by a negotiation from which both sides emerged with unbruised pride. With rare willingness to settle for a draw, Rome conceded Parthia's independence, in return for a show of diplomatic deference.

The eastern margin of the empire continued to be patrolled with possessive vigilance. Whoever ruled Judaea could never be allowed to face both ways. Soon after Joseph ben Mattathias was born, in 37 C.E., Herod's grandson Agrippa I—who owed his throne to his loudly trumpeted loyalty to Rome—began to reconstruct the north wall of Jerusalem. If completed, it is said, the battlements would have made the city impregnable.[1] Agrippa might then have had decisive leverage on the balance of power in the eastern marches. As it was, after the Roman procurator, Vibius Marsus, reported his uneasiness to the emperor, Claudius ordered that the project be aborted. Forty years later, the unimproved section of the walls was the back door through which the Romans, under Titus Flavius, mounted their final assault.

Agrippa's plan to strengthen the defenses of Jerusalem (where he never lived for any great length of time) had no connection with the

---

not believe, that there existed a race of men called "Hyperboreans" (extreme northerners), who wore their heads below their shoulders. Tacitus said that "Jews regard as profane all that we hold sacred and permit all that we abhor"; but he also said of the Finns—none of whom he can ever have observed—that "among them the woman rules: thus they have fallen lower not merely than freemen, but even than slaves." As for the Germans, they were his idea of noble savages. It is hardly plausible that Tacitus did any fieldwork or "meticulous research" before having fun at the expense of the kind of people with whom he was unlikely ever to have dinner.

* The same was regularly said of the Thracians, whose territory (including modern Bulgaria) bordered northern Greece.

national or separatist aspirations of the Jews. He presumed that, as a securely based local potentate, he would be more impressive, and serviceable, to the Romans, and therefore more likely to be maintained by them in his Levantine hegemony. On the same principle, he later invited five regional princes to a summit meeting at the provincial capital, Tiberias. The king probably meant only to impress his peers into a common front under his presidency. He would look less dispensable if he could preside over the incorporation of Rome's local clients in an anti-Parthian pact. From the point of view of the imperial power, however, his proposed confederacy once again appeared more impudent than helpful. The stronger a provincial alliance, the more tempted its leader might be to play the opportunist. Claudius's response was to subject Judaea to direct rule from Rome. The Jews had little active part in events that, in one way and another, served to pitch them into a disastrous war.

During the years between Claudius's administrative decision to garrison Judaea and the outbreak of Josephus's "Jewish War," the Roman presence was an irritant, as it had been in other parts of the empire, but seldom led to major incidents. As prefect from 26 to 36 C.E., Pontius Pilate caused more outrage among the Jews when he tried to divert some seventeen talents of Yahweh's treasure to fund the building of an aqueduct than he did by crucifying Jesus of Nazareth. If he assumed that public amenities would enhance his popularity, as they might in any other city, he reckoned without the impractical orthodoxy of the Jerusalem community (their principal use for water was for ritual ablutions—for instance after touching corpses—never for hedonistic indulgence). While the Zealots were infuriated by the well-intentioned idea of the proposed aqueduct, none protested against the Sanhedrin's use of its revenues for an ingenious and expensive drainage system to evacuate sacrificial blood from the Temple area.

Pilate could be forgiven for wondering what he had done to deserve such a posting.* By comparison with some of his successors,

---

* Anatole France's story "The Procurator of Judaea" depicts Pilate, in old age, with only a vague memory of a certain Jesus of Nazareth. The Gospels' image of Pilate as

he was, at the worst, inept. One of his first moves, on arriving as governor, had been to establish his authority by smuggling gilded imperial shields into Jerusalem during the night.* When the Jews woke to
the sacrilegious sight of graven images in the Temple precinct, a mob
gathered. It then marched on Pilate's headquarters in the seaport of
Caesarea, a full fifty miles away. The protesters surrounded his house
and lay prostrate for five days. Pilate ordered them to disperse. The
crowd remained immobile. When the procurator called in the troops,
the recumbent Jews bared their throats for the legionaries' swords.
Pilate thought again. The sacrilegious standards were removed from
the Temple. Some thirty years later, while waiting in Galilee for the
Roman onslaught to gather force, Joseph ben Mattathias had reason
to be sorry that the Jews of his own day had not adopted the unglam-

---

a man with a tender conscience ignores the abrupt way in which he had dealt with a
Samaritan "Messiah" who led his followers to occupy Mount Gerizim. The Samaritans' temple was a symbol of secession, but they continued to regard the Torah as
their fundamental law. They claimed to observe the sacred ordinances with greater
punctiliousness than the Jerusalem priesthood (in the thirteenth century, the Provençal Cathars rebelled against papal authority in a similarly fervent, eventually suicidal,
spirit). Pilate's troops were ordered to massacre most of the Samaritan dissidents. The
ascription of patience and fairness to the Romans in the face of Jewish extremism
was a tactic devised, after Josephus's war, to put the followers of Jesus of Nazareth on
the side of the imperial power. The notion, recently revived by Richard Bauckham,
in *Jesus and the Eyewitnesses,* that the Gospels are authentic, because derived from
eyewitness accounts, ignores how often the *terms* in which evidence is given can color
what witnesses claim to have seen. Without any ideological recipe, Josephus himself
offers copious examples in describing his own and other people's acts and motives.
Confidence that the Gospels were beyond question encouraged clerics and theologians to wrap themselves in the mantle of Elijah and speak and write with increasing
assertiveness about the Almighty's wishes and purposes.

* Roman coins, stamped with the emperor's image, were in themselves an affront
to Judaism. Jesus's eviction of the money changers from the Temple may have had
more to do with disgust at the invasion of impious coinage than with disapproval of
currency dealers as such. Jesus, like the Sicarii, but less violent, could more safely vent
his disapproval of the Roman presence by the indirect method of attacking Jews who
traded in the alien currency. Such assaults won popular applause and did not attract
punitive action from the imperial power.

orous tactics of the passive resisters who persuaded Pilate to back down.*

The rank-and-file Roman and mercenary soldiers on garrison duty in Judaea were probably more often bored than malevolent. In the early 50s C.E., when Ventidius Cumanus was governor, a Roman sentry posted in the Temple colonnade was so exasperated by festive Jews jeering at his presence that he turned his back and mooned the lot of them. (How many stolid sentries on public parade have longed to do as much, or more?) The flash of a bare and alien backside, in a holy place, fomented a riot in the tight Jerusalem streets. Josephus claims that thirty thousand people were crushed to death.[2] That figure must be inflated, but evidently there were many casualties. Cumanus calmed things, temporarily, by agreeing to execute the wretched squaddy who had cheeked the pilgrims.

The governor may have harbored some resentment against the Jews for making such a fuss. Soon afterward, a party of Galilean Jews on their way to a festival in Jerusalem, were attacked by Samaritan villagers. Cumanus and his tribune, Celer, were probably bribed to take no action. The Galilean Jews then sought partisan aid from Eleazar,[†] a Zealot chieftain with a mountain stronghold in the region. Samaritan villagers were attacked and killed. When Cumanus intervened in force, Eleazar retreated, but Judaea was already, Josephus tells us, "full of brigands."

The Samaritans appealed to Quadratus, the legate of Syria. He crucified the Jews Cumanus had taken prisoner and had several "troublemakers" decapitated. He then sent the High Priests Jonathan, Ananias and Ananus, the commander of the Temple, to Rome in fetters. A number of other Jews, as well as some of the Samaritan leaders, were ordered to appear before the emperor Claudius, who relished the part

---

* Mahatma Gandhi counseled the German Jews to adopt similar tactics with the Nazis, as he had, with some success, against the British. It is inconceivable that Hitler would have been shamed into a reversal of policy like that of the pragmatic British. Fanatics have no shame.

† His name means, in Hebrew, "God has helped."

of chief justice. Once in court in Rome, the Jews must have both defended themselves and attacked Cumanus with vigor and with some justice. They enjoyed the invaluable support of Claudius's close friend, King Agrippa II, who happened to be in Rome. The Jews obtained a favorable verdict. Cumanus was exiled, but Celer—who had presumably conducted the "police operation"—took the fall: the tribune was returned to Jerusalem for public torture, after which he was dragged round the city and then beheaded. Presumably, Quadratus claimed to have been misinformed and put all the blame on his subordinates. Tacitus indicates that it was now that Pallas,* the emperor's powerful freedman, took the opportunity to vest his brother Felix with full powers in Judaea. He was to be no marked improvement over his predecessors.

The provincials were subject both to Roman taxes and, in the case of the Jews, to the tithes, which kept the higher echelons of the priesthood in the elaborate style to which tradition entitled them. Since the lower ranks of priests benefited least from what it was their duty to collect, they often sympathized with the rural population whose penury they shared. The Talmud records that the Romans built bridges for the sake of charging tolls on those who crossed them; when they borrowed a poor man's donkey, he could expect them not to return it. The Talmud does not, however, note that the sharecropping peasantry had less to fear, financially, from the Romans than from the exactions of the priesthood.

An undercurrent of glamorous (and glamorized) rebellion runs throughout Judaean history. The descendants of Judas of Galilee, a Zapata-like hero of the rural resistance from the first days of the Roman hegemony,† were among those who practiced terrorism in the name

---

* Described by Tacitus as "a man practicing every kind of cruelty and lust [who] wielded royal power with the instincts of a slave."

† Judas led the resistance to the census of 6 C.E., initiated (no doubt to assist Roman and priestly tax collection) by the High Priest Joazar ben Boethus, who was later deposed, only to be replaced by another Roman puppet, Ananus ben Sethi, said by Martin Goodman, in *The Ruling Class of Judaea,* to be a nouveau riche of obscure provenance. He and his five sons dominated the High Priesthood for more than sixty years. None was acclaimed, as tradition required, by a mass meeting of the

of God and liberty. Memories of the heroic Maccabees (the Hammer Men) inspired Judaean Jews to double piety with sectarian violence. In the Jerusalem of Joseph ben Mattathias's youth, the so-called Sicarii, knife men, waged guerrilla warfare in the streets and markets. Heirs of Judas the Galilean, they would mingle with the crowds in the streets and markets, then suddenly draw knives from under their cloaks. They could stab a target* and vanish quickly, sometimes screaming "Murder" along with the panicking crowd.

Militants in colonial territories often flex their muscles, and blood the young, by a campaign of violence against "traitors" or "collaborators" in their own community. This advertises their cause (and leads people to exaggerate their number) without directly challenging the imperial power. Like today's suicide bombers, the Sicarii linked brutality and surprise. Their knives brought them kudos on the street and, no doubt, allowed unscrupulous *capi* to exact "protection" from prosperous targets. Their revolutionary glamour attracted the young and the unemployed, as well as religious fanatics; it also lent cover to sneak thieves and racketeers. Their gangs were united only in the wish to dispossess the ruling junta and usurp its powers.

Turf wars between rival fundamentalist factions inside Jerusalem were a savage feature of Joseph ben Mattathias's early life.[†] The High Priest Jonathan—a compromising diplomat appointed by King Agrippa II to please the Romans—was only the most distinguished

---

people (this by no means implies that the High Priest was ever endorsed by any kind of "democratic" process). Compare the ritual preceding the crowd's cry of *"habbiamo un papa"* when the white smoke proves that the Vatican conclave has made its choice of a new pope.

* Usually Jewish "moderates" (who could be accused of collaborating with the Romans), though M. Sartre claims (*D'Alexandre à Zénobie*, p. 573) that some Romans too were killed. The intended effect of terror was, then as now, to "radicalize the struggle," in this case by eliminating "Hellenizers." Greek ideas were as threatening to the Zealots as Roman government.

† Malachi (the Messenger), the last of the biblical prophets, records the standoff, in the fifth century B.C.E., between "those who fear God and served Him" and "those who do not fear God nor serve Him." See Shemaryahu Talmon's "The Internal Diversification of Judaism in the Early Second Temple Period."

cadaver done to death by the Sicarii. Attacking other Jews demanded less military cohesion than confronting the troops commanded by the provincial governor, Cestius Gallus. The citizens of Jerusalem were divided, irreconcilably, among themselves. Religion and politics were indistinguishable: reference to revealed Truth allowed any compromise to be labeled heresy. Personal ambitions could be dressed, seductively, as missionary piety.

Agrippa II had been appointed to his father's throne in 49. He owed his small majesty to imperial favor, not to inheritance. His continued tenure depended on performance. The king's principal duty was to control his Jewish subjects. Their affection for him was hardly greater than it had been for his great-grandfather; their fear, much smaller. His public image was enhanced by his sister and close companion, Berenice. In order to allay rumors of incest with her brother, she had been married to her uncle, another Herod, the ethnarch of Chalcis, in northern Syria, but on her husband's death she returned to Agrippa II. While her brother had to keep a diplomatic balance between local loyalties—which divided "Greeks" (that is, Greek speakers) from Jews and the overriding requirements of the Romans—Berenice could afford to be undisguised, if only because she was a woman, in favoring the Jews.

Joseph ben Mattathias grew up under the shadow of Herod's vast Second Temple complex. No other god but Yahweh could be worshipped within the city. Gentile tourists were excluded from the inner precinct. A theater and an amphitheater had been built, outside the walls, for alien amusement, but Jews who contributed to such pagan constructions, or enjoyed their entertainments, always risked denunciation as heretics. Jerusalem's primacy was guaranteed by the presence of the High Priests. Their authority dated back to Moses and Aaron. Viewed from outside, the singularity of the Jewish religion, and its ostentatious enactment in the Temple, made it appear that the inhabitants of Jerusalem were united in its esoteric practice and in deference to the hierarchy.

When the Maccabees had gone to war against the Seleucids in 168 B.C.E., they had been fired with tribal zeal, which unified and inspired their Judaean fighters under the banner of Mosaic conformity.

After they had secured the de facto independence of Judaea, however, the surviving Maccabeans usurped the kudos of the High Priesthood and, by filling any vacancy with their own placemen, diminished its sacred aura. Subsequently, the standing of the Temple hierarchy was further eroded by its enforced subservience, first to Herod the Great, and then to Roman officials, to whom the Temple treasury was obliged to supply regular golden eggs. The High Priests and their council, the Sanhedrin, were wedged between a rock and a hard place: while seeking to honor the law of the Jews, they had to placate, if not buy off, a series of Roman governors who had small sympathy for Jewish sensibilities. As a result of their fractious history, the solidarity of the Judaeans was more apparent than real.

Deprived of political freedom, the Jews of Joseph ben Mattathias's youth had recourse to philosophical and religious intensity and division; there were always contending strands of thought and purpose within Judaism. Of the groups centered in Jerusalem, the Sadducees and the Pharisees were the most influential. The New Testament's evangelists had doctrinal and political reasons for making them appear to have been yoked in common hostility to Jesus of Nazareth. In fact, their principal doctrinal disagreement was with each other. Jesus had often expressed himself in more or less Pharisaic terms.*

Since childhood was never a topic in ancient literature, Josephus's *Vita* does not describe his early years. He merely lays claim, through a remote ancestor of his mother's, to "royal" blood (that of the "Hasmonaeans," as the Maccabees were formally known). He also maintains that his father Mattathias's family belonged to the highest of the

---

* In *Jesus the Jew* and elsewhere, Géza Vermès has shown how closely, in truth, His teachings resembled theirs. Jesus is said, in the Gospels, to have reproached the Pharisees for inflexible literal-mindedness; they were even accused of forbidding acts of charity on the Sabbath. This smacks of retroactive denigration. Jesus's near contemporary Hillel, a famous Pharisaic rabbi, told his disciples, "That which is hateful, do not do to your fellow. That is the whole of the Torah. The rest is explanation; go and learn." Such a view hardly amounted to inflexibility. The Christian evangelists sought to disembarrass their Savior of any debt to the Jewish sect with which His teachings had most in common.

twenty-four echelons of the "priesthood." Their status was an inherited social distinction that entitled its holders to benefit from the tithes the lower orders were required to pay. Although Josephus does not give any details of his father's wealth or property, he took pride in belonging to a leading, certainly conservative, family.

Tessa Rajak maintains that, by the time Josephus sat down to write *The Jewish War*, "it would have suited [him] to *present himself* as a Pharisee."[3] It seems overly elaborate to accuse Josephus, isolated in Rome, of sudden Pharisaic affectations. As he indicates, when looking back in his *Vita* to the days when he had choices about his future, the disputatious refinement of the Pharisees was congenial to him from an early age. Their practice of exegesis when interpreting the law turned brilliant teachers such as Hillel into the *maîtres-à-penser* whom any intellectually ambitious young man would wish to impress. Even if F. W. Walbank is right when he claims that Joseph's family favored the Sadducees,[4] Joseph's quick mind is likely to have veered into the fast lane leading to the Pharisaic seminars at which he might flaunt his ingenuity. The Sadducees advocated the dry study of the Torah without any ingenious interpetations. Honoring the law, but not lawyers, they were unlikely to provide the kind of company a clever boy would be keen to keep. If Joseph's family did incline to the Sadducees, it was probably out of vestigial pride in the Hasmonaean connection.*

The Sadducees later had ideas in common with the followers of Epicurus. Neither believed in human resurrection or immortality; both would be condemned by Christianity, which drew much of its imagery from the Pharisaic belief that God "revives the dead with great mercy . . . and keeps the faith with those who sleep in the dust."† In

---

* The Sadducees are sometimes said to derive their name from Zadok the Priest, an affectation of antique lineage that may have appealed to the ruling circle in Jerusalem.

† The idea of the immortality of the "soul," rather than physical rebirth, is closer to Platonism. Pythagoreans, on the other hand, believed in a form of transubstantiation, which accounts for their vegetarianism. In their view "a duck might be somebody's mother." They refrained even from kidney beans, on account of their supposed similarity to human embryos. The Pharisees believed that the souls of the good "passed into another body" (*Jewish War*, II: 162–63).

the *Vita,* Josephus explains, for the benefit of Gentile readers, that the Pharisees were analogous to the Stoics. The latter philosophy affected Jewish thinking as early as the second century B.C.E.; Ben Sira, in *Ecclesiasticus,* recommended its unaggressive, rational virtues, "modest piety, self-knowledge and wisdom." His good Jew was quiet, if not skeptical.

The Pharisees formed a distinct sect only in the first century B.C.E. Early in *The Jewish War,* Josephus recalls how, when Alexander Jannaeus, one of the later Hasmonaeans, assumed the role of High Priest as well as king, the Pharisees were sufficiently incensed to appeal to the hated Seleucids to help overthrow him.[5] Alexander's response was to have eight hundred of them crucified in the center of Jerusalem. He then "butchered their wives and children before their eyes" while reclining, cup in hand, among his concubines. Eight thousand citizens, led by the Pharisees, fled the city. They remained in exile till Alexander died. After his death, when his widow, Alexandra, became queen, she sanctioned the return of the exiles. It was soon said that "she ruled others, the Pharisees ruled her."[6] When she died, her sons became involved in the vicious civil war that led to that fatal invitation, by each of the parties, to Pompey the Great to come to Jerusalem.

The young Joseph was able to savor the teachings of the Pharisee and Sadducee instructors within the gates of Jerusalem itself. To visit the third group in which, as the *Vita* recalls, he took a cruising interest required him to leave the city. The Essenes had turned their backs on the metropolis and set out to return to an uncompromising, primitive form of Judaism. Seceding from allegiance to the Temple hierarchy, some four thousand men had established a number of pious communities, notably in the desert region of Qumran, where the dry climate preserved the Dead Sea Scrolls until their publication in the 1950s.*

---

* During the forty years following the discovery of the first Dead Sea Scrolls, in 1947, it was assumed by scholars that the inhabitants of the Qumran caves, where they were found, were either Essenes or proto-Christians. The messianic tone of the scrolls and their references to the "Son of God" seemed to typify their communities. More recently, as Edward Rothstein summarized in a review of the Discovery Times Square exhibition of October 2011, it has been suggested that the Qumran population was less exclusively sectarian; that the scrolls derive from a variety of sources; and

The Essene "fathers"—the elders of each community—imposed rigorous asceticism on their followers. Initiates had to commit to a three-year period of study before being received as members. Joseph can have visited them only as a dilettante. He considered their Spartan regime, which included cold baths, truly virtuous, but he was not disposed to take the plunge and join them.

Essene communities were organized along communal lines not unlike those set out in Plato's *Republic*.* Initiates had to be meticulous in speech and deed. According to a document found in Damascus Cave 4, Essene justice demanded capital punishment for "apostasy in a state of demonic possession, adultery of a betrothed girl, slandering the people of Israel and treason." Since it is unlikely that any community had the right to carry out such sentences, their rigid penal code seems to belong to a project for the ideal society of the future.

Among the Essenes, transgression of a single item of the Law of Moses entailed expulsion. If anyone so much as uttered the Most Venerable Name, "he shall be dismissed and return no more."[7] The same applied to initiates who murmured against the authority of the commune; the Essene insistence on homogeneity was a form of reactionary radicalism. It aimed to re-establish the hermetic absolutism which had supposedly existed in Jerusalem before the Babylonian exile. The Marxist claim that men once lived in a state of primitive communism, without social distinction, is a similar nostalgia: redemptive hope looks back and forward to symmetrical Edens.†

No mention is made of Essenes either in the New Testament or in

---

that they, and other discovered treasures and artifacts, were accumulated by a mixture of "locals, nomads and invaders." The scrolls composed what amounted to a somewhat eclectic local library. Their authors take different points of view on a number of matters and cannot all have been Essenes of the kind Joseph encountered.

* Plato's ejection of "poets" from his ideal city, because they tended to create deviant or derisive versions of the gods, matched the ordinance of the Torah that proscribed any representation or direct mention of the deity.

† According to Philip Davies and his colleagues, "It is unlikely that [after the return from Babylon] there was a single pure, agreed 'Judaism.'" The beliefs, often found in the Dead Sea Scrolls, in a basic dualism between "two equal and contending spirits" and also in a "fiery end to the cycle of world history" are essentially Zoroas-

later rabbinic literature. They set an example no one cared to follow or even to commemorate.* All Essene property was held in common; only men could be full members. The community was quasi-monastic, wary of division or dissent: a priest had to supervise any meeting of ten or more inmates. A few Essenes had wives, but females were in no way equal to males. Men could be expelled for "fornicating" with their own wives during menstruation or pregnancy or at any time after meno-pause. Sex was licit only if it could result in conception. One of the Qumran caves yielded a document that decreed expulsion for any male who murmured against "the Fathers." It required only ten days' pen-ance for females who did so. Their prattle was clearly of petty account.

Josephus reports that sworn members were expected to be "truth-ful, humble, just, upright, charitable, modest and proficient in distin-guishing 'the two spirits,' truth and falsehood." The Essenes took a Manichaean view of life as a close-run contest between good and evil. Initiates had to be able to recognize a "son of Darkness." Their great demon was the Wicked Priest, almost certainly Jonathan, the young-est of the Maccabee brothers. He succeeded the heroic Judas, who was killed in battle in 161 B.C.E. As valiant as his brothers in fighting for independence from the Seleucids, Jonathan became "Wicked" only when he accepted the High Priesthood under license from Alexander Balas, who had usurped the Seleucid throne. His exemplary opposite was the Teacher of Righteousness, about whose identity Josephus says nothing, probably because he relied for his information more on the apocryphal books of the Maccabees than on the Essenes themselves.†

---

trian ideas. Modern belief in "the Revolution" can be seen as a "philosophical" muta-tion of the same antique notion.

* In the Diaspora, the story of the belligerent Maccabees was equally shunned by the rabbinate but remained vivid in folklore. The Cathars, who resembled the Essenes, have been similarly deleted from Christian history except as a parenthetic warning of what happens to heretics.

† Shemaryahu Talmon (see p. 26) says that the Teacher of Righteousness, whose name remains unknown, was "born out of the existential stress generated by the non-realisation of . . . millenarian expectations." Hartmut Stegeman (in the same volume) claims that Jesus had little in common with the Teacher of Righteousness. Jesus "never initiated a close circle of followers nor anything resembling a 'commu-

The "pragmatism" which the Essenes deplored had something in common with the Lutheran Protestantism which, in Roman Catholic eyes, was a menace to faith. Any departure from esoteric orthodoxy was likely to lead Jews into temptation.* Although the Teacher of Righteousness seems to have died toward the end of the second century B.C.E., wishful Christians have identified him with Jesus or with John the Baptist.† The desire to discover a founding father with rare qualities is common among monotheistic cults and their scholiasts. Freud's *Moses and Monotheism* may have been inspired by the words of Strabo, a first-century historian originally from Amaseia, in Pontus, but long resident in Rome. Strabo says that the Jews left Egypt not because they fled or were expelled but because of their dissatisfaction with Egyptian religion. "Moses . . . one of the Egyptian priests . . . was accompanied by many people who worshipped the Divine Being. He said, and taught, that the Egyptians were mistaken in representing the Divine Being by the images of beasts and cattle . . . and the Greeks were wrong in modelling the gods in human form . . . for God is one thing alone that encompasses us all." Moses impressed "not a few thoughtful men" and led them to "the place where Jerusalem now is."‡

---

nity' or 'church.' . . . [Christianity's] organizational framework [arose] only after his death." Martin Goodman points out that charismatic figures such as Jesus (including Choni the Circle Drawer and Theudas) were admired "precisely because of their lack of institutional authority or social status." And, it might be said, because they were untainted by official compromises.

* Orthodoxy has generated scholars and sages, but Jews have usually had to become in some sense protestant before making names for themselves, whether in science, art and literature or in commerce. Modern Jewish artists, such as Mark Gertler, could be regarded (sometimes even by themselves) as transgressors, because they depicted the human face and figure.

† Since he was known as "the unique teacher," the Teacher of Righteousness may also have served as the prototype of Muhammad, the (last) Prophet.

‡ Strabo adds that the surrounding people were won over by the excellence of Moses's government and beliefs. Strabo, who died a few years before Joseph ben Mattathias was born, was a welcome source for Josephus when he came to the Hasmonaean and Herodian periods. Like Herod's propagandist and another of Josephus's now lost sources, Nicolaus of Damascus, Strabo belonged to one of the Levantine elites which were content to prosper under the Roman aegis.

Jesus of Nazareth, like the Essenes, was drawn to "the wilderness." His precocious reputation too was bolstered by therapeutic skill. Although Essene society was sternly hierarchical, one Dead Sea Scroll declares that if a "bastard" was a man of learning and the High Priest a boor, then the bastard should take precedence. Genius is the trump that wins the trick. Judaism always reserved a fast track for the clever boy. Jacob was Esau's junior, and his son Joseph was not his firstborn; Josephus makes it clear that his own brother, Mattathias,* was senior to him only in years.

Josephus dwells on the Essenes' reputation for accurate prophecy. More than a century earlier, a certain Judas is reported to have given instructions on the signs to watch for and never to have made a mistake in his own predictions. Prophets were to the ancient Jews what economists are to the modern world: they dealt in futures. Géza Vermès claims that the most rewarding augury was by another Essene, Menahem, who foretold Herod the Great's rule over the Jews. When it came true, Herod had the rare grace to dispense the Essenes, who refused to take all oaths apart from the covenant, from swearing loyalty to him. Another Essene interpreted a dream that came to Archelaus, ethnarch of Judaea at the beginning of the first century, to mean that he would rule for ten years, which also proved correct.[8] Josephus makes no mention of these neat accuracies, and their happy dividends, perhaps because he did not wish to detract from what seems to be the uniqueness of his own impending performance in front of Vespasian. The historian knew, of course, that when the time came, Vespasian's reaction to Joseph's own predictions was to prove as gracious as any precedent could have disposed his prisoner to hope.

---

* The narrow range of names in ancient Judaean society can make it difficult to distinguish individuals. Was it hoped that the young would reproduce the characteristics of their namesakes in earlier generations? Despite their innovations, the church fathers shared the ancient desire for impressive antecedents. Jesus's alleged descent from King David aligned him with the Messiah of whom the prophet Isaiah was presumed to have spoken. Although the Jews were diabolized, their fundamental standing could not quite be denied without damaging Christianity's biblical credentials. In the evolution of human religions and social institutions, there are few clean sheets.

The exact meaning of "Essenes" is uncertain. Philo of Alexandria refers to an Egyptian sect who followed a similar way of life as "Thera-peutai," healers, but elsewhere he mentions the Essenes as if they were distinct from them. Some modern sources, spearheaded by Martin Bernal, have incorporated Egypt in the black Africa from which, so they claim, on more or (often) less sound grounds, other societies, especially the Greeks, "stole" their culture. Freud in his mythologizing *Moses and Monotheism* postulated an Egyptian Moses.*

The Essenes' withdrawal from city life and their determination to absent themselves from secular history make them the antecedents of the Hasids of Mea Shearim, in modern Jerusalem. They too abstain from mundane politics, avert their eyes from secular culture and refuse even to acknowledge the existence of the State of Israel.† Since, for them, the coming of the Messiah must precede the creation of a Jewish state, nothing in current secular history has relevance to Hasidic pieties. The Essene writers of the Dead Sea Scrolls left no record of daily life. Natural events were of interest solely as omens of what was to come. Everything was interpreted in accordance with its moral deposit; good or bad harvests were worthy of note only as evidence of the virtue or sinfulness of the nation.

The sense of living in "Last Days" fevered the dreams of many Judaean Jews of the first century. It conformed with the Zealots' tradition of reading the world only in the light of biblical predictions. After Cyrus the Great allowed the Jews to return from Babylon, a sequence of

---

* Antony Kamm, in *The Israelites,* points out that "Moses" occurs in the names of pharaohs such as Thutmosis and Rameses, and alone "as a shortened form of the name of a ruler." This does little to prove the Egyptian origin of the Moses of Exodus, who is said to have become aware of his heritage when he killed an Egyptian overseer who was maltreating a Hebrew slave. To trump Freud's theory, other writers have postulated an anonymous Hebrew elder who taught monotheism to Akhenaten.

† In *Carl Schmitt and Leo Strauss: The Hidden Dialogue,* Heinrich Meier says that as early as 1923, Leo Strauss observed, "When cultural Zionism understands itself, it turns into religious Zionism. But when religious Zionism understands itself, it is in the first place Jewish faith and only secondarily Zionism. It must [then] regard as blasphemous the notion of a human solution to the Jewish problem." Cf. Joseph Roth in *The Wandering Jews.* The music goes round and round.

pretenders and preachers, of whom John the Baptist was only the most charismatic, told audiences that the ultimate vindication of the covenant was all but upon them. In fact, back in the sixth century B.C.E., many Jews chose not to leave Babylon,* where their families had been for two or three generations, in order to go to a "homeland" they had never seen. Jeremiah himself had advised the original deportees not to waste their time in lamentation for what they had lost; they could and should live as Jews wherever they happened to be. As the Romans put it, *ubi bene, ibi patria:* where the living is good, that's home.

The Essenes' "Pauline" attitude to chastity presumed that mundane family life (if not happiness itself) was inimical to holy living. Josephus gives no indication that the sect as a whole took any militant part in the rebellion against the Romans,† but their communities were nevertheless put to the sword when Vespasian swept through Galilee. Nor does *The Jewish War* hint why they were treated with such ruthlessness. It was entirely in character that they should refuse all compromise with the Gentile forces, but their social organization, however "Spartan," was not military. Yet the Romans are said to have "racked and twisted, burnt and broken them . . . in order to make them blaspheme the Lawgiver or eat forbidden food. Smiling in their agony and gently mocking their torturers, they resigned their souls, confident that they would be returned to them."⁹ Were Vespasian's soldiers infuriated by the Essenes' serene self-righteousness or because their settlements yielded so little booty?

The young Joseph stayed long enough with the Essenes to be daunted

---

* Baghdad remained a venerable Jewish center for centuries after Cyrus gave leave to its Jews to return to Palestine. Baghdad rabbis were consulted from all over Europe. It was the main source of more outspoken defenses of Judaism than that of Josephus. Living outside Roman or, later, Christian jurisdiction, Jewish apologists in Parthia dared to classify Jesus as a false Messiah and the Christian Trinity as self-contradictory. In due time, Sigmund Freud declared the doctrine of the Trinity to be a "lightly veiled" regression to polytheism.

† Josephus does, however, mention a certain John, an individual Essene general who was in charge of the toparchy of Thomna, Lydda, Joppa and Emmaus, early in the war. He was killed at the disastrous siege of Ascalon (*Jewish War* III: 9).

by their dignity. As he put it in his *Vita:* "These are men's men, legionaries of the soul, engaged in the serious pursuit of the virtuous life; disciplined, courageous, perfectly just, and contemptuous of the pleasures as much as of the fears that drive ordinary people."* Joseph was also impressed by the charitable funds to which all able-bodied men contributed two days' wages a month. The money was then distributed by "the Guardians" to the sick and to Jews in foreign hands. The model for Christian charity originates with the Jews. While appreciative of the Essenes' qualities, their visitor appears to have had something in common with Ovid when he said *"Video meliora proboque, deteriora sequor"* (I see the better way and approve it, I follow the worse). Before leaving the Essenes, Joseph may have learned to mimic the vatic tones of their elders.† His apprentice years taught him to adapt his manner to whatever audience he hoped to win. Speed in the imitation of attitudes and arguments gave him secret room to be himself through a show of conformity. It was a facility that would serve him well when he came to live in Rome.

Joseph entertained many ideas, and they entertained him, but the breadth of his intelligence worked against single-mindedness. After sampling the three outstanding strains of Judaism, he ventured further into the wilderness to spend time with the man he calls Bannus. No other source mentions him. Was his unlikely name the cover for a Zealot who, as Tessa Rajak suggests, ran some kind of boot camp for young men who wanted to toughen up for the imminent struggle with the Romans?[10] Joseph's voluntary experience of camp life resembles the way in which modern narcissists improve their musculature, and their self-esteem, by going to the gym or running marathons. His decision to take a survival course is more consistent with his dilettantism than with any militant purpose. It gave him a taste of the Hellenic way of

---

* Unless attributed elsewhere, the translations from Josephus's Greek are my own.

† Elias Canetti accused Karl Kraus of "dithyrambic bearing" when he preached self-righteously against European injustices (and Jewish journalism). W. B. Yeats was said to blow himself up like a Celtic bullfrog when delivering public recitations of his poetry.

life.* There is no evidence that Bannus inculcated Joseph with rebellious resolve or military know-how. Roughing it may have given him physical confidence; but his time encamped on the margin of society scarcely amounted to effective (or premeditated) preparation for revolutionary generalship.

* Pierre Vidal-Naquet's *Le chasseur noir* (Paris: Maspero, 1980) tells how young Athenians took time out to live rough in the hinterland in order to learn survival skills before being admitted to full citizenship.

III

Of HIS LIFE between the age of nineteen or twenty and his departure for Italy some six or seven years later, Josephus's *Vita* says nothing. He resumes his self-portrait only after he has been called upon to take part in a delegation about to sail to Rome to argue for the release of a party of priests. They were friends of his who had been arrested on "trivial charges" by Antonius Felix, the Roman procurator from 52 to 60 C.E.* Felix had ordered them to be sent in chains to Nero for judgment. Since he was consistently rough with "the Jews," Felix (who was of Greek origin) gets a good press from the Gentile Saint Luke, both in his Gospel and in the Acts of the Apostles, where the sympathetic Felix is said to have visited Saint Paul in prison. According to Scripture, they discussed "justice, self-control and judgment."[1]

Although Josephus did not write the *Vita* until Domitian was emperor, he was wise, when looking back, to deal delicately with what-

---

* Shaye Cohen (*Josephus in Galilee and Rome*) believes that the priests were, in fact, "significant rebels." This would make the eventual success of Joseph's mission all the more creditable when he returned home. By the time he came to write the *Vita,* it was politic to underplay the priests' rebelliousness in order not to be tarred with the same brush. There is, however, little in his record to suggest that Felix needed serious evidence before bringing serious charges. The wish that Jews should somehow deserve whatever happened to them runs through Western thought; even Jews can be infected by it. George Steiner has devised the noblest *réquisitoire,* which includes the invention of conscience, for which Steiner's *maître-à-penser,* Martin Heidegger, following Nietzsche, put the blame on Socrates.

ever happened during Nero's reign. The latter had been formally blackened by the Flavians, but Domitian is known to have condemned
to death the author of a laudatory biography of Nero's prime critic,
Thrasea Paetus, and of his son-in-law Helvidius Priscus. The last of
the Flavian emperors suspected that the eulogy of a long-dead opponent of autocracy veiled its composer's distaste for his own sadistic
tyranny. It may, therefore, be out of continuing caution that Josephus gives no details about why his friends the priests were arrested
prior to the outbreak of war. If they had been accused of instigating
the riots in Caesarea, it would be tactless, even two decades later, to
remind Domitian that his house historian had been the advocate
of suspected revolutionaries. In fact, Felix is likely to have arrested
appropriate suspects to avoid being accused of fomenting the riots
himself.

Josephus may have insisted that his friends' offense was trivial in
order to excuse his own class from any responsibility for the outbreak
of war. It could hardly offend Domitian's paranoid sensibilities to say
that the historian was impressed by the priests' unwillingness to breach
the dietary laws. They survived on figs and nuts, a diet later recommended, for no pious reasons, by the Greek medical pundit Galen.
The Book of Daniel says that Jews exiled in Babylon lived on dates and
vegetables, a solemn precedent that the orthodox might well imitate.
Josephus's applause for their abstinence suggests that, in his friends'
place, he might have been less fastidious.

He must have had the means and rank, as well as the ambition,
to volunteer for the mission to Rome. All sea journeys in the ancient
world were perilous. Even the best captains preferred to sail within
sight and, if possible, easy reach of land. However, the ship in which
Joseph traveled from Alexandria was unusually large, probably a grain
freighter, which needed deep water. With six hundred people on board,
it foundered in the middle of the Adriatic. In order to survive, the
passengers and crew had to swim all night. At dawn, the eighty stron-
gest swimmers, who included Joseph, were picked up (thanks to God's
grace, he says) by a ship from Cyrene. Had his workouts with Ban-

nus been based on a Greco-Roman curriculum, including marathon swimming?*

Joseph's Cyrenean rescuers put him and the other survivors ashore at Puteoli, the modern Pozzuoli, on the west coast of Italy, a few miles north of the radiant Greek city of Neapolis, today's Naples. It was one of Rome's busiest harbors. The fashionable seaside resort of Baiae was a few miles away across the bay to the north. Joseph never says how, once landed in Puteoli, he happened to make friends with the mime actor he calls Aliturus, "a particular favorite of Nero's and of Judaean origin."† Whatever names and addresses he had been given before he set sail, he had landed in sodden clothes and with none of his luggage. He says nothing about how he acquired a wardrobe or access to the contacts he needed for his mission. If Aliturus helped him from his own hamper of costumes, it gave Joseph an involuntary taste of crossing the line into an alternative world.

In cosmopolitan Italy, Judaism had a modest but modish Gentile following. Jews had established communities in Rome and in many cities around the Mediterranean, all the way to Spain. Upper-class females—Nero's second wife, the delicious Poppaea Sabina, among them—were among the cultural visitors who frequented the synagogues (Gentile "tourists" were welcome, as they were not in the Temple in Jerusalem). Poppaea and her friends could sample an exotic morality. There was even a taste of "democracy" in the proceedings: any male Jew might volunteer, or be called upon, to read from the Torah by whoever had been elected to lead the devotions. The lack of an officious hierarchy made synagogues attractive, as churches would be, to marginal congregants.

---

* Roman notables from Cato the Censor to the deified Julius, were practiced swimmers. Caesar needed to be when, cornered by a band of assassins, he dodged them by diving into the waters off Alexandria. The young Octavian had a similar escape (Suetonius, *Augustus* 8.1.). Herod the Great, another great escaper, built swimming pools in Jerusalem and Herodium; Tiberius had his on Capri, across the water from Naples.

† As Nero's *"epithymios"* (heartthrob), Aliturus, though of Judaic origins, need not have observed Jewish dietary or other restrictive laws.

No character called Aliturus is mentioned anywhere except in the *Vita*. The name sounds like a nickname ("Salty Cheese") earned by a capacity for crisp repartee.* It could be a pseudonym for Paris, Nero's favorite mime actor until he had him executed, perhaps for no greater crime than threatening to upstage him; then again, for the emperor perhaps there *was* no greater crime. Domitian was the fan of another actor called Paris (the name was used generically for pretty fellows, in honor of Helen of Troy's lover). He too was later put to death. Josephus may have slapped camouflage on Nero's darling to avoid seeming to allude to Domitian's disgraced thespian. To be insensitive to the emperor's feelings was a form of treason. Survival under the principate resembled a game of hopscotch; one had to be nimble when crossing a line.

In the golden years of the republic, witty actor-playwrights, such as Plautus, who had once been a baker, and Terence (whose nickname Afer hints that, coming from North Africa, he was dark-skinned) were prize exhibits for smart hostesses. As Aliturus could have told Joseph, neither of these great comic playwrights of the second century B.C.E. had Latin as his mother tongue. Satire and flattery played heads and tails in their repertoire; effrontery was sweetened by clowning. When Plautus's smart slaves outwitted their betters on the stage, their bravado appealed to the plebs; it was a cheerful way of, as it were, singing the blues. The Roman theater, like the Greek, instructed spectators of all classes how to amuse friends and ridicule enemies. Theater people held up entertainingly warped mirrors to propriety.

As Steve Mason emphasizes in his meticulous commentary on the *Vita,* successful performers were often very popular with their mass audience, who appreciated the liberties that talent allowed them to

---

* The Oxford Latin Dictionary lists *alitura* as meaning "feeding, nurture"; at a camp stretch, this might be said to imply personal dishiness. The modern Greek *alitirios* is used as an adjectival noun by Cavafy in No. 13 of his unfinished poems, "The Salvation of Julian," where it means a rascal, which also has a tasty element. To Joseph's alien ear, the pronunciation (if at all like that of modern Greek) of both Aliturus and *alitirios* would have sounded much the same.

take.* Theatrical clowning often verged on insolence; laughter and applause allowed malcontents in the audience to vent their repressed hostility to the ruling elites. Since showpeople were most commonly of alien and low-class origin, the Roman upper class affected scorn for their crowd-pleasing performances. Equated with prostitutes and other louche company, actors were at once despised by the best people and also somewhat feared, since their words and gestures could so promptly excite the insolence of the groundlings. The bohemian way of life also had a certain appeal for sensation-seeking members of the aristocracy, of whom Nero himself was the grandstanding instance.

All the Greco-Roman world was a stage: imposture, bluff and a gift for repartee were part of the armory of success. Joseph had already proved himself a quick study. The time he spent with Aliturus offered him a sight, and the sounds, of a world unavailable in Judaea. He spent longer in Italy during that first visit than he later would as governor-general of Galilee. What did he do and whom did he meet? He says only that Aliturus introduced him to Poppaea Sabina. "Jewish" only by association,† she helped him secure the release of the priests, whose crimes, we may guess, were too boring to merit Nero's attention. She then gave Joseph "large presents" and sent him on his way. Generosity was a routine I-can-afford-it gesture of nobility rather than a sign of particular favor.‡ If Poppaea resembled other historical princesses, she may well have been seduced as much by her own seductiveness as by the young stranger's importunity. Joseph's record promises that he

---

* As early as fifth-century B.C.E. Athens, Nikias, as *choregus* (producer), gave his freedom to a slave, who had played the part of Dionysus to popular acclaim and thus advanced his master's social and political prospects. (See Plutarch 3.3.)

† Josephus terms her *"theosebes,"* god-fearing/worshipping; when it came to Judaism, she was what another era might call a fellow-traveler.

‡ In *Reciprocity and Ritual,* Richard Seaford remarks that in the archaic Mediterranean "giving and counter-giving . . . may be a highly competitive means of acquiring prestige and power." Under the Roman Empire, it might be very dangerous to seem to be in a position to reciprocate the favors of the master of the world. When he sought to retire from public life, Seneca tried to give his huge fortune to Nero, which did nothing to allay the emperor's resentment of his ex-tutor's presuming, as it seemed, to patronize him.

knew how to make a good impression on females. Jewish lineage would do nothing, at that stage, to make him unpresentable in royal circles, where anything rare can alleviate the banalities of protocol.

However much Joseph may have prided himself on finding favor in Nero's Rome, he had no occasion to write publicly about it until after the Flavian dynasty was in power. What might once have added luster to his CV was by then a black mark. The pregnant Poppaea had only a few months to live before Nero, in a fit of rage, kicked her so fiercely, perhaps because she refused him his pleasure, that she miscarried and later died. Like Herod the Great after the execution of Mariamne, her husband was then overwhelmed by remorse, if not for very long.

Steve Mason suggests that, by the time the *Vita* was written, many of its readers would have been hostile to the memory of Nero and of Poppaea. Hence Joseph could hope to entertain them with the story of how a Judaean arriviste made fools of them. Mason even wonders whether the resourceful Aliturus was an invention. This seems a speculation too far: in no other passage does Joseph concede that, in Roman eyes, he could have looked like some kind of uncouth hick. The success of his diplomacy figures among his claims to fame and served to qualify him as governor-general of Galilee. Since Mason never questions that Joseph did indeed secure the release of his friends, he must have needed an inside track of the kind Aliturus was well placed to provide. Why would a historian fabricate an episode featuring leading figures in a discredited regime in order to dress a narrative devised to prove his veracity?

The brevity of the Roman interlude in Josephus's *Vita* leaves the impression that he fulfilled his mission and returned promptly to his native Judaea. He seems, in fact, to have dawdled for some time in Italy. Who would not? Rome was at the zenith of its power and elegance. Augustus had boasted that he found the city brick and left it marble. Despite the effects of the fire, the imperial capital was calculated to dazzle provincial aliens such as Joseph ben Mattathias as he wandered in the polyglot crowds, asking directions in that Jewish accent he never lost. Yet in the last days during which Jerusalem stood as one of the poles of the Mediterranean world, Joseph need not have had any sense of inferiority while he was in loud, often loutish Rome. There is a wide ditch between the bright young tourist, who returned to Jerusalem in order, for a brief spell, to play a commanding part in the Jewish War, and the obsessive and solitary scribbler in Flavian Rome; but the appetite for a Latin life may have lodged in the young Judaean's mind as he tasted the delights of a world elsewhere.

There is no certainty about what (or who) kept Joseph ben Mattathias in Italy so long. What he learned of its history and saw of its conquests is spelled out only in the speech he put into Agrippa II's mouth when the king addressed his appeal to the Jerusalem Jews not to risk everything by all-out war on the superpower. Joseph may have been no less of a Jew by the time he sailed back to Palestine; he can hardly have failed to be more of a Roman.

If only the dates could be made to stretch so far, it would nice to suppose that a ranking actor such as Aliturus, pseudonymous or no, might have introduced Joseph to the most eminent writer, and the richest man, of the time. Since Seneca was a playwright, he must have had friends and clients in the theatrical profession. He had certainly already retired from public life before Nero forced him to bring an abrupt curtain down on his own life in the wake of Calpurnius Piso's conspiracy of 65 C.E., with which the old writer is unlikely to have had any active connection. In the meantime, Seneca had found Stoic philosophy much more preferable than proximity to the increasingly paranoid emperor. It is tempting to imagine a conversation, even a friendship, between the clever young Judaean visitor and the morose elder statesman who had enjoyed the perilous privilege of eminence under a paranoid tyrant. The Pharisee and the Stoic may have had affinities, but any Jew, however self-centered, observed a God-given scheme that implicated him in a community, which Stoicism did not. Although he need have had no premonition of it, Joseph would soon have solitude thrust upon him; Seneca had already chosen it. His long letters to his friend Lucilius were heavy with introspection. Stoicism was not a religion, nor even a morality; it was, he hoped, a recipe for serene resignation. It also disposed him to flirt, at length, with the blandishments of easeful death.

If Joseph ben Mattathias could ever have met Seneca, and if the old philosopher delivered a measure of his habitual sententiousness, the young Jew might well have congratulated himself on being ineligible to climb what Benjamin Disraeli, in Victorian England, would call the "slippery pole" of political ambition. But was Joseph, at the same time, drawn to metropolitan life? And if he did not yet have an inclination to be a writer, might contact with Seneca have sparked it? Did the famous author happen to have a copy of some of his work in an attendant's keeping? He can be imagined dedicating it to a smart provincial, not unlike his young self, with plenty of time, it seemed, to profit from his example. The morbid millionaire philosopher was nothing if not didactic. One piece of quasi-paternal advice would have been typical of him: don't do what I did.

Seneca was a man haunted by dark possibilities. There was a tunnel, some seven hundred yards long, between Pozzuoli—where Joseph happened to have made landfall—and Naples. That dark passageway reminded Seneca of mortality whenever he made himself go through it.[2] His greatest apprehension was of looking foolish or cowardly. Never at home in Rome or in his own skin, he was forever trying to get out of things at the same time as getting into them. Although long resident in Córdoba, in southern Spain, Seneca's family was of old Roman stock. In one of his many letters to Lucilius, he alluded to the siege by Scipio Africanus, during the First Punic War, of Numantia, near Soria in old Castille. When the defenders saw that their situation was hopeless, as Joseph's companions would at Jotapata, they all killed themselves rather than be captured. Seneca praises both sides, but especially the Spaniards who chose to "die in liberty." At the same time, he did not doubt (or did not confess that he doubted) that the conquest of Numantia was legitimate. Since human knowledge did not equal that of the gods, the Spaniards had fought a futile battle both gallantly and, in their own eyes, rightly. Josephus would say the same of the defenders of Jotapata.

By writing plays with elaborate rhetoric and sanguinary plots,* Sen-

---

* Shakespeare's *Titus Andronicus* is as good as a parody of Senecan Grand Guignol.

eca sublimated fears and vanities in an entertaining advertisement for his divided self. Creative schizophrenia is a useful affliction for playwrights. The theater would prove attractive to Jewish writers in the twentieth-century Diaspora: it offered an arena where a man might make an art of splitting himself into a spectrum of characters. His personality could be reflected in their fractured mirror.*

In Seneca's view of Stoicism, a man could trump Tyche—the "contingency" of modern existentialism—by resigning from the world. He made a spiritual exercise of rehearsing death without dying. In this, he prefigures Julien Benda's *Exercice d'un enterré vif* (*Juin 1940–Août 1944*). There was no single Latin word for suicide; *suicida* is medieval Latin, not attested until 1179. To kill oneself was no crime in ancient Rome. It was more the conclusive proof of a free man's self-determination, uncomely only if he flinched when the moment came. Arria, the loyal wife of Caecina Paetus, a Roman senator unjustly ordered by the emperor Claudius to kill himself, took the dagger from her husband's hesitant hand and plunged it into her own breast. Her last breath promised him, "It doesn't hurt."†

Seneca was fascinated by earthquakes and volcanic eruptions. When, during a violent storm in the Bay of Naples, the captain of the ferry told him that it would be unwise to sail, the great man insisted on putting to sea, to test his composure.‡ While still the richest man

---

* From Arthur Schnitzler to Clifford Odets to Harold Pinter, Jews could be both themselves and other people in the play of dialogue and on the expressive rack of silence. The exile of language lies in what was not said; Pinter's pauses were famously eloquent. Isaac Babel said that, under Stalin, he had made silence his art form. It is no surprise that Stanislavsky called the theater "a second home." Like games, it socializes alienation by melding individuals into a factitious team (Bertolt Brecht made alienation itself into a device that allowed his company to tease the audience with purposeful playfulness).

† A seventeenth-century sculpture by Jean-Baptiste Théodon, commemorating Arria's courage, finished by Pierre Lepautre, stands in the Louvre museum.

‡ In a similar spirit, the nonswimmer Shelley would sit, arms crossed, in a storm-tossed boat on Lake Geneva, contemplating *"le grand peut-être."* Byron, who prided himself on his swimming, promised to save him. Shelley, who echoed Keats (and Seneca) in being "half in love with easeful death," told Byron he would do better

in Rome, Seneca took covert pleasure in being transported in a peasant's cart. Like Nero when he went out in disguise for a night on the town, Seneca relished roughing it incognito. However, when a grander conveyance overtook the cart he was riding in, he blushed to think that he might have been recognized and looked foolish in passing patrician eyes. Death offered an emergency exit from a world of pain and from the ordeal of human society, which he described as "a reunion of wild beasts." He had volunteered to renounce his fortune more as a premium to abate Nero's resentment than because he had no appetite for money and its comforts.*

Seneca told Lucilius that if reduced to beggary, he would kill himself. He advised a friend dying of a wasting disease to commit suicide by starvation. It offered the parting gift of a kind of exhilaration, Seneca told him, like fainting. In his seventieth letter to Lucilius, he says "I intend to choose for myself which vessel I travel on and which house I live in, and I shall do the same with death when the time comes to be gone from this life." He must have known the cruelly apposite line of the playwright Publilius Syrus, *"Bis emori est alterius arbitrio mori"* (He dies twice who does so at another's command). Writing itself was, and remains, a way of abstracting oneself from society. Yet living on the edge leads to chronic vertigo; fear and vanity can engender impatience for dignified quietus.†

---

to concentrate on saving himself. On that occasion, their boat came safely to shore. Shelley's survival, tinged maybe with disappointment, may have encouraged him to put to sea, a few years later, in his top-heavy yacht *Ariel,* in which he was drowned on July 8, 1822.

* By contrast, in the 1920s, Ludwig Wittgenstein gave away something close to £1 million, because money was an encumbrance to thought. The most luxurious item of furniture in his professorial rooms in Whewell's Court, Trinity College, Cambridge, was a deck chair.

† Henry James, the loftiest of displaced persons, called death "the distinguished thing." In 1944, Albert Camus published *The Myth of Sisyphus,* which began by stating that there was only one truly serious philosophical problem: suicide. The key question was whether life, with its contingent absurdities, was worth living. Also a displaced person, Camus would later face a dilemma somewhat like the one that con-

In the Roman world, killing oneself was never an expression of existential despair. It was either a response, given in one's own time, to an irresistible command or, as Tacitus recommended, a relatively painless escape from shame or torture. In 65 C.E., Petronius Arbiter, who had been Nero's intimate friend and *arbiter elegantiae,* a dandy and fashion consultant, elected to die, when ordered to do so by the petulant emperor, in a parody of Stoicism. He opened his veins, bled into a warm bath for a while, then bound his wounds and had a drink and a joke with his friends before resuming the process. In deliberate slow motion, he theatricalized (and ridiculed) what men such as Brutus and Cassius had done in noble earnest, when they fell on their swords. Disdaining to take his own death tragically, Petronius lampooned the unsmiling Seneca, whose death concided with his own.

Cicero had said, in his *De Finibus,* that when being alive ceases to please us, *"tanquam e theatro exeamus":* we can always leave it as we might a theater. Both Petronius and Seneca contrived to make such an exit, one in a tragic, the other in a satirical mode. By way of an envoi, Petronius made public a list of all the refinements and perversions in which Nero's sexual partners, of both sexes, had been involved. Did Joseph ben Mattathias's benefactor Aliturus figure in this pornographic dramatis personae? Did Josephus not say that the young actor was *katathymios,* close to the heart of the emperor? Since Nero's affections were rarely entirely sublime, Aliturus could have been among those who sated his appetites and then paid the price for the intimacy he had enjoyed. The virtues of suicide, if it was ever mentioned in Joseph ben Mattathias's presence, must have seemed entirely irrelevant to a young Jew whose ability to swim all night, before capping his first visit to Italy

---

fronted Joseph ben Mattathias: born in Algeria, educated in France, Camus was torn between backing the Algerian revolt, as his socialist friends did (Jean-Paul Sartre *en tête*), and sympathy with those who wanted to keep Algeria French. By conviction a socialist, viscerally a *pied-noir* (a French Algerian), the author of *L'étranger* (*The Outsider*) dealt with his contradictions by taking refuge in reticence. Many "liberal" Jews have found themselves in Camus's quandary: reluctant to denounce Israel, yet unable to endorse its policies. Silence, however, is not their common resort.

with a diplomatic and social triumph, indicated a powerful determination to stay alive. Only a mordant wit, such as Constantine Cavafy, might imagine Joseph ben Mattathias debating, at some sophisticated Roman dinner party, whether it was better to live in compromise or die as a hero, quite as if it were a purely philosophical question.

IV

WHILE JOSEPH BEN MATTATHIAS was probably still on his travels, in early 66, the arbitrary exactions of the local procurator, Gessius Florus, provoked rowdy demonstrations in Jerusalem. He had regularly demanded money from local Jewish communities and, more scandalously, from the Temple treasury. When the governor of Syria, Florus's superior, Cestius Gallus, came from Antioch just before Passover, in the spring of 66, a huge crowd—said by Josephus to have been "three million"—shrieked at him to remove the embezzler. Florus shrugged away the natives' indignation as laughable; he told his superior that his unpopularity proved only how well he must be doing his job. After the governor had returned to Antioch without taking action, Florus seized his chance to incite further trouble. The more unruly the natives, the more plausibly his depredations could be reported as disciplinary measures.

When the Judaeans continued to accuse him of bribery and looting, he declared that he was, in truth, a poor man. Their response was to take up an ostentatious public collection to save him from penury.* It was one of the few Jewish jokes recorded in old Jerusalem; but Florus was not amused. The Pax Romana was generally maintained with a big

---

* Martin Goodman speculates that the collection was made by the sons of rich men, led perhaps by the aggressively anti-Roman Eleazar, the son of the High Priest Ananias, whose status (and utility to the occupying power) protected them against any reprisal from Gessius.

stick. Seven years before, at the other end of the empire, Britain had erupted in a bloody revolt, led by Boudicca, queen of the Iceni. In 61, it cost the local governor much time and many casualties to bring her and her people to heel. Eighty thousand Iceni are said to have been slaughtered. Their queen committed suicide. By mounting a prompt repressive operation in Judaea, Gallus proposed to avoid anything similar happening on his watch.

Studious in her Judaism, Agrippa II's de facto queen Berenice went, in the autumn of 66 C.E., on a pilgrimage from her palace in Antioch to Jerusalem. Attended by an escort suited to her rank and equal to the dangers of the bandit-ridden road from Antioch, she traveled through Galilee and Samaria, down to the holy city. Her visit coincided with a typical display of high-handedness on the part of Gessius Florus. Claiming that "Caesar needed it," he had sent a detachment of soldiers to requisition seventeen talents of gold from the Temple treasury. Whether or not Nero did, in fact, commission the heist, it was a credible excuse: the spendthrift emperor needed all the cash he could command in order to rebuild Rome after the great fire of 64.

Berenice sent officers from her official escort to beg Gessius Florus to restrain his men. Neither charm* nor her putative royal standing made any impression. The soldiers remained obediently out of control. Some of them were incited to teach Berenice a bloody lesson by torturing and killing prisoners in front of her eyes. She fled, with her bodyguards, into Herod's enormous palace, adjacent to the Temple. Later, she had the courage to present herself to Florus again, as a barefoot penitent. He gestured for his soldiers to bundle her away. She was fortunate not to be killed.

Angry young men, led by Eleazar, the son of the High Priest Ananias, demanded that the now customary sacrifices in honor of the Roman emperor be suspended at once. Such action would amount to

---

* Her considerable beauty was said to be outshone by that of her sister Drusilla, whom she hated. The teenage Drusilla was forcibly taken from her first husband by the same Felix who arrested the priests for whose freedom Joseph went to plead. Drusilla's son and and his wife died in an earthquake in Pompeii in 63 C.E.

a declaration of independence. The Temple hierarchy and the prosperous citizens, conscious of the Romans' superior force, preached caution. They feared for their property and their privileges if "the street" took charge of the city. The mob shouted back that they should rely on Yahweh to intervene on behalf of the righteous. The Jewish War was yet another war between Jews, and between generations. The division between ultras and compromisers modernized the ancient breach between the prophets and the kings.

As Florus's reinforcements approached the city, the chief priests tore their clothes in ritual self-abasement. Josephus's account insists that they pleaded with the citizens to keep their tempers. The worst might yet be avoided if they would greet the approaching Romans in a friendly manner. Some did; but their smiles were not returned. The legionaries had instructions to be implacable. In the consequent riots, citizens were suffocated or trampled to death as they panicked through the tight streets. Young rebels climbed onto the rooftops and pelted the Romans with stones and tiles. While dodging the brickbats, units became separated from each other. Gangs of angry militants managed to smash a gap in the colonnade that connected the Temple precinct to the Antonia Tower, the roomy bastion (named after the mother of the emperor Claudius) where a Gentile garrison of up to a thousand men was usually quartered.

The breach in the causeway prevented Florus from getting his loot into a safe place. On the verge of losing control of the city, the procurator summoned the chief priests and their council, the Sanhedrin, to a parley. In an abrupt change of tactics, he told them that he was pulling out of Jerusalem. He would leave behind whatever force they reckoned necessary to restore order. It was at once a climbdown and a threat: the Sanhedrin was going to be held responsible for restraining the mob. The elders would have liked nothing better than to do so; but the same mob looked to them to stand up to the Romans and would hold them to account if they made servile concessions.*

---

* Somewhat similar situations recurred, in more vexed forms, during the Diaspora. In *Remembering Survival*, Christopher R. Browning reports that, in Nazi-occupied

In most of the ancient world, success in war was the likeliest agent of social change. In fifth-century Athens, for instance, the Athenian hoplites, and later the sailors, demanded and received the vote in return for risking their lives against the invading Persians. In Joseph ben Mattathias's Jerusalem, by contrast, social life had an exclusively civilian and religious basis. There was no forum for legitimate politics outside the Temple. Competitive zealotry was the sole means for those outside the ruling circle to exert influence.

The Jerusalem elders assured Gessius Florus that one cohort (five platoons of a hundred men) would be sufficient backup. It was as numerous an alien presence as they could dare to impose on the city without infuriating the mob. The High Priest had the sense, and the nerve, to insist that the Roman contingent not include any of the troops who had just run riot in the city. The procurator must have been badly shaken: he agreed. When Florus led the main body of his men back toward Caesarea, it seemed that the crisis had been defused. However, in his report to the governor in Antioch, he blamed the Jews for the violence he had visited on them. He had to get his word in before the seductive Berenice offered Cestius Gallus a different view.

Since the royal palace and the governor's mansion were not far from each other in Antioch, she and top Roman officials were on the same diplomatic circuit. Berenice had already interceded with the governor, earlier in 66, on behalf of the Jews of Jamnia, a town on the Mediterranean coast, who had been accused of causing riots of which they had been the victims. She had guessed then that Florus had primed the disorder. He could cream off a percentage from those whom he incited to despoil the Jews, less because they were Jews than because they were a plump and vulnerable minority.

Once Gessius Florus's main force had withdrawn from Jerusalem,

---

Poland, "The councils relieved the Germans of much of the burden of managing the Jewish communities. . . . And they served as lightning rods, attracting much of the hostility and resentment of the downtrodden Jews." The difference was, of course, that it was possible for the subject peoples, if they paid their taxes, to negotiate with the Romans in the interest of a quiet life. The Germans always meant to eliminate the Jews and duped some Jewish leaders into involuntary complicity with their plans.

the Sanhedrin was able to claim that the modesty of the Roman contingent left in the Antonia Tower proved that their leadership had saved the day. Nevertheless, Eleazar's Zealots continued to accuse the elders of betraying the covenant by sanctioning the intrusion of aliens on sacred ground. The charge was both true and unfair: compromise was the only way to persuade the Romans to leave the city undefiled by a more numerous garrison. The Zealots elected to raise the stakes. They blocked the payment of taxes and again destroyed the colonnade that the Romans had repaired to give access to the Antonia Tower.

In alarm, the Temple hierarchy sent a deputation to Antioch. King Agrippa met with it in private and expressed sympathy, quietly. More Jew than Roman, but more royal than pious, Agrippa too was between a rock and a hard place. To keep his throne, and to remain able to exercise discreet leverage on the imperial power, he had to reproach the Jews publicly for their reaction to what he acknowledged, in secret, had been designed to provoke them. Perhaps at Agrippa's suggestion, Cestius sent an amiable junior officer, Neapolitanus, to Jerusalem to assess the situation.

Neapolitanus's report was honest enough—or generously enough subsidized—to conclude that the Jews were not hostile to the Romans in general, but solely to Gessius Florus. It would have been nice if only it were true. The unrest grew so menacing that Agrippa II decided to make a royal progress from Antioch to Jerusalem in the hope of dissuading the citizens from the folly of open rebellion. With Berenice at his side, he began by saying that he would not have come if he thought that everyone in the city favored war. Joseph ben Mattathias and his father must have been among those on whose moderation the king hoped to rely when he said that he was aware of the seduction of "liberty" but insisted that the "trifling mistakes" of the occupying power did not warrant a rebellion that was almost certain to be fatal.

Too elegantly composed for a transcript, the king's speech clearly spells out what Josephus thinks he could, or should, have said.* He

---

* Thucydides established the fashion for including "set piece" speeches by leading historical figures, for instance Perikles's "funeral oration" of 430 B.C.E. These com-

has Agrippa begin by declaring that he would never have come to Jerusalem if he hadn't known that "the most honest and sincere of our people" wanted to live in peace. According to *The Jewish War*, the king then delivered a long history lesson to the listening masses. He enumerated the many instances of Roman invincibility and the spread of their empire. Even the Athenians, he told them, who had defeated the Persians at Salamis, were now subject to Rome. It was the same story all over the known world: The Gauls, with their huge population, had had to agree to become the "milch cow" of their conquerors. The Germans too, he insisted, had been tamed.* How could there be any shame in a much less numerous people accepting Rome's universal authority? Some officials might be insolent or rapacious, but Rome itself was benign and irresistible, just as Alexander the Great had been in earlier times. Submission was no shame when resistance was folly. Josephus's model, Thucydides, has the domineering Athenians say the same thing to the islanders of Melos in 416 B.C.E.†

Agrippa's harangue ended with a warning of what would happen if the Jews went too far. The Romans did not make a practice of forgiveness once they had drawn their swords: "To make sure that you serve as an example to other peoples," he cautioned,

---

positions were, so Thucydides claimed, as close as possible to what was actually said, but there was an unmistakable measure of confection. If Josephus made Agrippa's sentiments track his own, it does not follow that the words he put in Agrippa's mouth were false to the king's actual opinions. We depend almost exclusively on Josephus for what we know of the events he describes. As is proved by his account of his own sometimes admittedly deceitful words and actions, it does not follow that his purpose was entirely self-serving.

* Tacitus's *Germania* makes it clear that this was true only in the sense that they had been penned, undefeated, behind the fairly stable borders of the Rhine and the Danube. See Christopher Krebs's *A Most Dangerous Book* (New York: Norton, 2011) for the glossy afterlife of Tacitus's text.

† The Athenians' pitiless treatment of Melos has been taken as the definitive instance of hubris. It followed, in accordance with tragic morality, that Athens deserved to lose the Peloponnesian War. In fact, the vaunted Spartan general Brasidas offered the same ultimatum to the city of Acanthus, near Mount Athos. The Acanthians were pliable enough to yield. (See also my *Some Talk of Alexander*, p. 131.)

they will reduce your holy city to ashes and they will exterminate your race. Even the survivors will find nowhere to hide. Everyone bows down to the Romans, or fears that he will have to. The danger isn't only to the Jews here, but also for those who live elsewhere. There isn't a city in the world that doesn't have a Jewish minority. If you go to war, their enemies will cut all of their throats. The fatal decision of a few will mean that not a single city will not run with Jewish blood. . . . Have pity, if not on your wives and children, on your mother country and its sacred shrine. Spare the Temple and save the Sanctuary and the Tabernacle for your own sakes. . . . As far as I am concerned, as the Tabernacle bears witness, and the holy angels of God and the country to which we all belong, I've done everything I can to procure your well-being. I ask you now to take the decisions which have to be taken and let us together enjoy the pleasures of peace. If you abandon yourselves to your passions, you will have to face the dangers to come without me.

At this point, Agrippa burst into tears, as did Berenice, who stood in conspicuous public view, a surrogate queen, on the adjacent roof of a palace first constructed by the Maccabees. Her earlier courage had made her a popular figure, her good looks an attractive one. The people yelled that they didn't want to fight the Romans, only Gessius Florus. Agrippa told them that by withholding tribute, as the Zealots had demanded, and by continuing to cut off access to the cohort in the Antonia Tower, which overlooked the Temple (its shadow alone seemed to the Zealots to pollute the sacred enclosure), the Jews were already in a state of war with Rome.

Josephus heightens the dramatic irony by stating that many applauded Agrippa's view that they ought to make amends. Since Josephus was "reporting" long after the war, and since there is no other contemporary record, it is impossible to gauge how far he embellished the king's speech with flourishes that both proved his own rhetorical elegance and, as if incidentally, excused Roman ruthlessness by coining a lengthy warning of what would, and did, follow. The crowd is unlikely to have been unanimous in its repentance. According to Josephus, however, Agrippa's officials were able to collect the arrears in taxes with remarkable promptness.

With access to the Antonia Tower restored, everything seemed on course for peace. Like a bad advocate, however, Agrippa failed to keep quiet after he looked to have won his case. He returned to the rostrum to say that, pending the replacement of Florus, the people should do whatever the procurator asked of them. The Zealots had a second chance. They threw stones at the king and yelled at him to get out of the city. It may be that the less militant citizens had already dispersed. Agrippa and Berenice were shouted down and withdrew, in a hurry, to Antioch.

After the royal couple had gone, Eleazar and his Zealots surrounded the Antonia Tower. The diminished Roman garrison was penned inside. The demonstration was probably intended primarily as a show of defiance to the Sanhedrin. Its size and menace broke the nerve of the beleaguered Roman commander, Metilius. He asked for terms under which he and his men could leave the city unharmed. Eleazar promised them safe passage, if they laid down their arms. A bloodless victory would undermine the authority of his father, Ananias, but might not excite the merciless reprisals of which Agrippa had warned. However, no sooner had the Romans given up their weapons than they were set on and cut to pieces.

If Metilius was still in Eleazar's company when things got out of control, it would explain how, when he saw his disarmed soldiers being slaughtered, he had time to beg for mercy for himself. The crowd must have yelled that only Jews should be allowed to stay alive in Jerusalem. Metilius immediately offered to become one. He was circumcised—carnal proof that there was no going back on his conversion—and dubbed with a Jewish name. Josephus says no more about him. The forcibly Judaized Metilius nevertheless has a signal role in the narrative: he was not to be the only man in the war to save his life at the price of becoming what he had never been before.

Did Eleazar deliberately trick the Romans, and then have them killed, or did his men refuse to honor the deal he had struck? Josephus declares that the incident seemed a "great portent" for the Jews, although no more than a bloody misfortune for the imperial power. That it took place on the Sabbath was especially scandalous: decent citizens were horrified that blood had been shed on a day when even righteous actions were forbidden. On the same day, Josephus adds, and at the same time, "as if as a result of divine providence," some twenty thousand Jews in Caesarea were massacred by the Gentile majority.[1]

The two incidents were not causally related, but Gessius Florus was implicated in both. The procurator's name sounds like that of a genuine Roman. In fact, although his patron was Poppaea Sabina, he was a Levantine careerist from the Greek city of Clazomenae, on the eastern coast of Asia Minor, near Smyrna. Until 44, the procurators of Judaea had been sent out from Italy and so had no affinities with the Greek population. After 50, however, these officials tended to be of local Greco-Roman extraction.

Whether or not Florus had promised the Greeks in Caesarea carte blanche before their onslaught against the Jews, it was instinctive, as well as profitable, that he should favor them. He had already done so in an earlier dispute when some Greeks baited the local Jews by siting a new factory directly next to their synagogue. In a parody of proper sacrifice, they fouled the tight access with the blood of a chicken slaughtered on a chamber pot. The blasphemy was calculated to outrage and provoke the outnumbered Jews.

News of the pogrom in Caesarea inflamed the whole region. Jews in mixed communities all the way to Syria reacted by attacking their Gentile neighbors and setting fire to their property. Not all Jews responded with ethnic solidarity. In prosperous Scythopolis (the modern Beth Shean), south of the Sea of Galilee, close to the west bank of the Jordan, Jewish residents announced that they were making common cause with their Gentile neighbors.

When an army of Jewish insurgents advanced on the city, the Scythopolitan Jews made a valiant contribution to the ensuing repulse of the outsiders. Their unexpected courage more alarmed than reassured their fellow citizens. Fearing that the Jews, having proved their mettle, would turn against them under cover of night, the Gentiles asked them to prove their good faith by taking themselves and their families into the local Sacred Wood. Suspecting nothing, they did so. For two days, they were left there in peace. On the third night, when all were asleep, the Gentiles crept in and cut their throats. *The Jewish War* holds that thirteen thousand died.[2] Their property and belongings were appropriated by their murderers.

Josephus makes use of details, such as the surrender of Metilius, to vivify his narrative, much as close-ups add intensity to a movie. At Scythopolis, he zooms in on a certain Simon ben Saul, who was among those who went out to fight beside his Gentile neighbors against the Jews advancing on the city. He killed a good number and, it is said, put others to flight, single-handedly. When the Scythopolitan Jews were attacked as they slept in the Sacred Wood, Simon woke and grabbed his sword, but saw that he was powerless against so many. Josephus says that Simon cried out that he was being justly punished, by God, for having killed so many of his own people in battle. He should have known better than to show loyalty to men who were now proving their perfidy. "But no one," he said, "is going to be able to boast that he killed me." Glaring with pity and rage at his family, he grabbed his father by his white hair and ran him through. Then came his mother, who offered no resistance; after her, his wife and their children. He climbed onto their corpses and lifted his sword high in the air and plunged it into his own neck. This, we are told, was the consequence of a Jew putting his trust in strangers.

Like the surrender and "conversion" of Metilius, Simon's suicide became pertinent to the historian's own story. It also recalls an incident in *Jewish Antiquities* when the Galilean cave dwellers, near a place called Arbel, were resisting Herod the Great's attempts to coerce them into accepting his sovereignty. One old man was cornered by Herod's special forces who had been lowered in baskets to the mouth of his cave. His wife and seven children begged to be allowed to surrender. As Herod watched, and called on him to yield and be safe, the old man stood in the mouth of his cave and killed every member of his family, one after the other, and threw their bodies down the precipice. He raged at the greed and aggression of the king, scorned renewed offers of clemency, and threw himself down the cliff. Demonstrative self-destruction was a feature of Jewish pride.

In Damascus too, Josephus reminds his readers, the citizens turned on the large, unaggressive Jewish minority, even though "almost all of the women of the town were Jews," killed them, and appropriated their belongings. The Romans were rarely alarmed by the mutual slaughter of subject peoples. "Divide and rule" was an old axiom of imperial management. The opportunism that led the Damascenes and others to attack Jewish minorities, under the pretense of eradicating disloyalty to Rome, strengthened the Zealots' argument for outright secession.

V

AFTER GESSIUS FLORUS'S MALICE had detonated even more violent anti-Roman demonstrations in Jerusalem, Cestius Gallus decided to lead the Twelfth Legion, with a full complement of Levantine auxiliaries, into Judaea from Antioch. Agrippa II, like his late father, had to strike a balance between conserving local credibility and not exciting the current emperor's displeasure. To be useful to Nero was Agrippa's best hope of keeping his throne. He had no choice but to supply auxiliary contingents of archers and cavalry to bring his own supposed subjects to order. Agrippa was the head of a formally Jewish royal family that suited the Romans since it was, as Arnaldo Momigliano put it, "alien in its attitude and institutions."[1] The king was authorized to mint only bronze coins; he was part of the small change of empire.

On the way from Syria, Gallus gave notice of his punitive purposes by burning the town of Lydda and killing the few inhabitants who had not left to go to Jerusalem for the Feast of Tabernacles. He and his men met serious resistance only when they reached Beth-Horon, in the Judaean hills. The site had historical echoes. More than two hundred years earlier, in 166 B.C.E., Judas Maccabaeus and a thousand of his freedom fighters had ambushed and defeated a phalanx of four times as many Seleucid Greek soldiers and killed its commander, Seron. He too had been on the way from Antioch to put down a Jewish rebellion. In mythology, Moses's successor, the militant Joshua, was said to have defeated the Canaanites on the same site.* The Judaeans chose to stage their show of defiance in a place of good omen.

The surprising fury and weight of the Zealots' attack punched through the center of Gallus's force. The Jews killed a good number and might have annihilated the infantry, if the Roman cavalry had not charged and scattered them. The Jewish fighters retreated behind the fortifications of the nearby town. As the Romans moved after them, they were attacked from the rear. While they were taking more casualties, many of their pack animals were rustled by an opportunist called Simon ben Gioras, who made for Jerusalem with his winnings.†

The Roman commander elected to dig in behind a defensive perimeter. He was enclosed for three days in a natural pen, which he dared not leave. The surrounding hills were dangerous, with bands of Jews ready to pounce on the Romans if they scattered or straggled. Agrippa II sent envoys, Borcius and Phoebus, to tell the Jewish militants that he might be able to negotiate a truce, and an amnesty, if they would lay down their arms. Many of the local people called out in favor of accepting the offer. This incensed the Zealots. Phoebus was killed before he could say a word; Borcius fled for his life.

Insurgents and residents then began to squabble furiously and at such length that, Josephus reports, Cestius Gallus had time to get his men together and launch a full-scale counterattack.[2] The deflated and disorganized resistance fighters broke and ran. The legion was clear to advance to the closed gates of Jerusalem. Herod's thickened walls looked to be a formidable obstacle, but the Romans must have had

---

* Joshua's insistence, in Joshua 24, on making a "fixed rule" after the people had voted for "undivided loyalty" to the covenant suggests that divisions threatened the cohesion of the Israelites soon after their conquest of Canaan.

† This exploit gave Simon ben Gioras enough kudos to become "toparch" (local commander) of Acrabata. When the High Priest Ananias deposed him from that role, he threw his hand in with the "bandits" who had occupied the Roman base at Masada. Josephus's account of his exploits (*Jewish War* 4: 493 and following) shows how quickly success could double and redouble a man's claim to a leading role. By 69 C.E., Simon would be in effective command of Jerusalem.

word about that unstrengthened section on the north side. An immediate assault would almost certainly have succeeded. Perhaps because his men were exhausted, Gallus stood off for three days. He may have hoped for, or received, placatory overtures from the Sanhedrin.

On the fourth day, he did move on the city. Perhaps some proposed deal had not been realized. To prove that they meant business, the Romans set fire to the timberyard and market, outside the massive battlements of the Temple. Meanwhile, Gallus established his command post facing Herod's palace. Josephus insists that if he had pressed forward, the governor could have taken the town and prevented a full-scale war. What stopped him? Josephus claims that Gessius Florus bribed the Roman cavalry commanders to advise him to back away. If so, Florus's likeliest motive was fear that his superior officer would take evidence from the Sanhedrin of how he had primed the crisis and, more important, embezzled Temple treasure in Caesar's name. It may be that, after the close shave at Beth-Horon, Gallus's cavalry officers warned him that they could not be expected to come to the infantry's aid in the narrow streets.

If, as Josephus also says, the Jerusalem elders had promised the Roman commander that they would open the gates, provided that the attackers advanced in force, they must have been hoping that shock and awe would bring the mob to its senses. For whatever motive, practical or characteristic, Gallus showed himself to be in two minds, as he had been on his previous visit to the city. His hesitation gave Eleazar and the Zealots time to throw Ananias and his "traitor" friends out of the Temple precinct. The city mob pelted them with stones as they fled into their houses.

For the next five days, Gallus made repeated, if lame, attempts to pierce the citadel. On the sixth, he lined up a substantial force, with covering fire from Agrippa's archers, on the north side of the precinct. For protection against missiles hurled from the ramparts, the Romans locked their shields together over their heads, in the well-rehearsed maneuver known as the *testudo* (tortoise). Despite everything thrown at them, they were able to work at undermining the walls. Under their makeshift roof, they were soon ready to set fire to the Temple gates.

The Jews were again in two minds. There was a standoff between those who wanted to resist to the death and those who regarded Gallus's arrival as a divine deliverance. Echoing Homer's *Iliad,* in which the gods abort a truce between the Trojans and the Achaeans, Josephus attributes to Yahweh Himself the decision that the moderates should be frustrated. Where Homer is whimsical, Josephus moralizes: the Zealots had polluted the sacred stones with the blood of Metilius's soldiers, and on the Sabbath day; that transgression alone justified Yahweh's withdrawal of His protection even from his own Tabernacle.

With the city at his mercy, Cestius Gallus backed away. As soon as the legions retreated from the gates, the Zealots counterattacked. In the scramble of the Roman retreat, they picked off a number of soldiers and horsemen. Gallus regrouped on the adjacent Mount Scopus, and camped there. The Zealots must have been audible, all night, yelling defiance and promising holy war. On the following day, the Roman commander chose to march away. He may have calculated—or been assured—that Ananias and his circle, in which Joseph ben Mattathias's father was an influential member, would gain popular credit for persuading him to spare the city. Traditional order restored, and by an economy of means, the governor could then resume the standard practice of saddling the Sanhedrin with the double task of controlling their compatriots and paying reparations. Throughout the empire, by bestowing rank and privileges on native notables, the Romans fashioned groups of collaborators whose interests could be elided with their own.*

Mimetic opportunism may help to explain why, coincident with Cestius Gallus's punitive expedition to Jerusalem, there were murderous riots in the Levant's greatest city, Alexandria. Jews were assaulted (three were said to have been burned alive) by the Greek mob. Rumor

---

* The British followed their example, particularly in India, where princes and maharajahs were incited to send their sons to school with those of their imperial overlords. The Ottoman Turks did something similar by promoting the so-called Phanariots, a Greek Orthodox elite, to supervise their compatriots and to take responsibility for any dissidence on their part.

served in the office of the media in the ancient world. The news that the Romans were out to punish the Jerusalem Jews may have been enough, in a volatile city such as Alexandria, to prime the Greek "Egyptians" to despoil their fellow citizens. Why would the Romans not applaud them for doing in one place what Cestius Gallus was bent on doing in another? The Gentile violence provoked a vigorous response from the long-established Alexandrian Jewish community. The city's Jews had no habit of humility. The experienced local Roman governor, Tiberius Julius Alexander, an apostate Jew, tried to calm things, but when the street battles continued, he brought in two legions and some off-duty soldiers who happened to be in from the desert and were hot for loot. The Jewish quarter was sacked and many Jews killed, despite strong resistance.

Hindsight makes Gallus's withdrawal the action of either a fool or a villain, but he had reason to settle for a draw. His lines of communication were stretched, his numbers insufficient to deal with a mass uprising. In the event, the Zealots were less relieved than frustrated by the Romans' failure to mount an assault on the city. Exalted by sacred texts and messianic convictions, they could believe that the Roman general had pulled back because he was unnerved by the righteousness of their cause. Since the Jews were, at this stage, only lightly armed, Gallus's sudden retreat was similarly read as the Lord's work. For the Zealots, it proved that this was no time to stay passive. They had the will, the means and the Lord's manifest license to go after the Romans.

The Jews were held together not by military discipline, or political will, but by faith in the covenant; it made them fighters for the Lord. Those uncontaminated by Roman connections believed that they would enjoy Yahweh's favor, as long as they did everything He required. Scriptural precedents proved how often the prophets had been right when the kings were wrong. The disappearance of the Romans could only be God's work. Everyone remembered that something similar, and even more dramatic, had happened when Sennacherib and his Assyrians descended, as Byron was to put it, "like the wolf on the fold," only to melt away in the night and never threaten Israel again.

Since the Assyrian invasion had taken place more than seven hundred years earlier, what the Jews remembered was the account of it in the Second Book of Kings. Zedekiah, an early separatist monarch, fortified old Jerusalem against a siege by the vengeful Sennacherib. Zedekiah took the practical precaution of drilling a duct more than five hundred yards long through solid rock, so that the water from the spring Gihon could flow into the city in case of a siege. When the Assyrians actually marched in, Zedekiah was pinned in Jerusalem "like a bird in a cage." He sent his representative to negotiate with Sennacherib's legates. During the parley, the Assyrians were requested to speak Aramaic, rather than Hebrew.* Zedekiah feared that excitable Jews on the walls of the city would overhear, and denounce, whatever deal might be in the making. Even in the eighth century B.C.E., the Jews were divided between extremists and compromisers. Sennacherib's legates declined to be diplomatically secretive. By proclaiming their harsh terms in loud, clear Hebrew, they hoped to terrify the listening citizens into surrender. In fact, they determined them to resist. Even the prophet Isaiah, rarely belligerent, advised Zedekiah to defy the enemy. He seemed inspired by knowledge that salvation was at hand; and so it was: "That night an angel of the Lord went out and struck down one hundred and eighty thousand dead in the Assyrian camp . . . the following morning, they were all corpses."

Cestius Gallus's troops had come a long way for nothing. Footsore retreat turned into dejected scramble. Harassed all the way back to the defile of Beth-Horon, the trudging legionaries were sniped at by archers who scampered along the hillsides. The Roman commander abandoned his heavy baggage, killed all mules not carrying essential kit, and made camp. That night, he devised his only successful ruse: having ordered a battalion-strength rear guard to exchange passwords all night, as if the whole brigade were still inside the palisade, he slipped out with the main force.

At first light, the Jews saw that they had been tricked, raced after the

---

* By Joseph ben Mattathias's time, the vast majority of Jews spoke and understood only Aramaic. Hebrew was no longer their vernacular.

enemy, outflanked them and started to pick them off. In their panic, the legionaries dumped the rest of their siege equipment and other heavy matériel; but nothing could save them. Six thousand are said to have been killed. The Zealots helped themselves to all the munitions dumped on the ground and whatever they found on the soldiers' bodies. The previously illustrious Twelfth Legion never recovered from the shame; it was disbanded.

The Jewish fighters had negligible losses. Their triumph was taken by the Zealots to be proof that the End of Days was indeed at hand. Victory over Gallus was evidence of Yahweh's renewed willingness to intervene on His people's behalf, as long as they went the whole way with His wishes. If the High Priest did not endorse what he could hardly fail to hear, he dared not say so. Meanwhile, back in his palace in Antioch, immune to the threats of the Jerusalem mob, Agrippa must have seen the survivors from Gallus's legions straggling into the city. He knew that if he wished to keep his throne, and his head, he had to be seen to be engaged on the Roman side. Yet if he was going to retain influence over his Judaean subjects, he had to work for a negotiated settlement. However much he wished for peace, he had to prepare ostentatiously for war against the rebellious Jews.

When the Zealots came back to Jerusalem in triumph, with few losses and flourishing Roman weapons, Eleazar and his friends were well-placed to convince the urban masses that they were the new Maccabees. The happy blood on their hands had to be a portent from heaven that the messianic age was dawning. While the Zealots exulted, the Sanhedrin was forked. It could not afford to show dismay at a Jewish victory; yet the elders knew that the Romans were more powerful than the celebrants in the streets cared to acknowledge. Only by seeming to move with the people could the High Priest have any prospect of putting the brakes on them. His situation resembled that of the nineteenth-century French politician Alexandre Ledru-Rollin, when he said of a militant mob on the march, "I am their leader, I must follow them."

Not a few of the Zealots were prone to apocalyptic rhetoric of the kind to be found in the Books of Enoch and Daniel (which was among the last to be added to the Authorized Version of the Bible). Daniel hears the angel Michael tell him, "I have come to explain to you what will happen to your people in days to come." The End of Time would be marked by the tearing up of the temporal calendar. There would be "a period of distress such as has never been," but after it, "Your people will be delivered." Isaiah himself had spoken of a miraculous transformation of the natural order: "Wolves and lambs together shall crop grass upon the mountains and leopards shall feed with kids . . . for He shall make the beasts upon the earth incapable of harm." That would be The Day. Jews who embraced these predictions had so enthusiastic a vision of the moment when Yahweh would spring his people from subjection that political compromise and rational diplomacy were taken to be the disgraceful mark of those with little faith.

Talk of an apocalyptic shift in the world's prospects was not limited to Jews. Despite fundamentalist attempts to keep Judaism ideologically pure, Greek philosophy had seeped into it. Platonists held that our present, fugitive world was only one form of the Ideal World which had yet to be realized, but must supersede it. Hellenized Jewish sophisticates, such as Philo of Alexandria (30 B.C.E.–45 C.E.), syncretized the Jewish creation myth into a hybrid parable: each day of divine activity corresponded to an earthly epoch. The Sabbath was seen as a weekly trailer for the culminating One Day, when a perfect and unchanging world would emerge.

In the late fifth century B.C.E., Thucydides had discounted the possibility that anything that happened in the Peloponnesian War could be attributed to heavenly activity or divine partisanship. According to Thucydides, the course of human fortunes was driven by *anagke,* the impersonal force of necessity. Although Josephus cloaked his narrative in the Thucydidean style, the war he describes can never be understood in a wholly Greek light. No historian could render a full account of what happened if he ignored the mystique that led the Judaeans to disdain mundane reasoning. The Athenians and Spartans had fought the Persians (and later each other), under the banner of "Liberty." Josephus never pretends that the war in Judaea had anything to do with democratic institutions or military supremacy. To the Romans, the Jewish uprising was one more provincial problem; for most of the Jews, it had to be the Lord's work.

For any High Priest to question the possibility of divine intervention would be heresy. However they might wish, in secret, that the victory over Cestius Gallus had never happened, in public the hierarchy had somewhat to applaud it. The folk memory of the triumphant revolt of the Maccabees, just over two hundred years earlier, remained unquenched. The courage and endurance of the five Maccabee brothers had led to the ousting of the supposedly invincible (in truth, decadent and militarily overextended) Seleucid Greeks from the soil of Israel. The precedent armed Eleazar's fighters with aggressive conviction, although they were not above tactical accommodation with anti-Roman Levantine "Greeks."

The disaster that had overtaken Cestius Gallus might be momentous news in Jerusalem. It was less significant to Nero, who was on a tour of arts festivals in Greece. If the fracas in Judaea would have to be avenged, with the obligatory heavy hand, it was never going to be Nero's own. The emperor's self-esteem was built on applause and awards, which he affected not to realize had been rigged in his favor. He was the first ruler for whom the X factor of showbiz trumped statesmanship or martial prizes.* Unlike his predecessors, Nero never campaigned with, and rarely even inspected, the legions whose vigilance maintained his empire and whose muscle secured its revenues. He relied on hireling "publicans" to collect the tribute that he rejoiced in spending on showy schemes, such as his impending Golden House in Rome. He was not merely a maverick spendthrift: great projects were the enduring mark of great emperors. Nero's current scheme was to drive a canal through the isthmus of Corinth.† Although the canal would not be completed

---

* He was not the last: in the 1990s, Prince Norodom Sihanouk, at once head of state of Cambodia and, in his own view, a filmmaker, founded an annual film festival at Phnom Penh, at which he received the Grand Prix every year and was hailed by the media as the best writer and journalist. He also wrote songs and had them sung to the peasants.

† In 146 B.C.E., as a result of a rebellion against Roman occupation, Corinth had been looted and, legend has it, leveled to the ground (archaeological evidence

until modern times, work had started on cutting through the neck of land between central Greece and the Peloponnese.

Nero's self-indulgence and paranoia have tagged him with the reputation of a murderous narcissist; but he did try to enlarge the cultural horizons of the empire. His desire to rival Orpheus as a musician and singer is said to have shocked sterner spirits among what was left of the Roman upper classes. In fact, not a few patricians were given to amateur dramatics; some even liked to work out with gladiators (for whom, so gossip alleged, Roman matrons often had an itch).

Since Judaea and its troubles failed to divert him, Nero delegated a reliable, never brilliant general, Titus Flavius Vespasianus, as a proxy to put his imperial foot down. Now in late middle age, Vespasian seemed no more than another of the modest workhorses on whom emperors, good or bad, could depend to pull their weight in Rome's service. He was not among the fans of the Muses. Neither patrician nor playboy, Vespasian was a professional soldier who had first been promoted thanks to his connections with the emperor Claudius's powerful freedman and private secretary, Narcissus. As a result, he was given a com-

---

suggests that nothing so drastic ever took place) at the end of a punitive campaign led by Lucius Mummius. The position of the desolated city, at the gateway to the Peloponnese, soon attracted Roman colonists, as had the site of Carthage. Eventually, both ruined cities became prosperous again. As time went by, their mostly imported citizens took pride in the fame and antiquity of "ancestors" with whom, in truth, they had no blood connection. None of the Roman colonists who, after the war, came to occupy Jerusalem are known to have boasted of similar links with the evicted Jews. The city did not even keep its name: after Hadrian's definitive pacification of the province, in the wake of the rebellion led by Bar-Kochba in 135 C.E., Jerusalem was renamed Aelia Capitolina (when first captured by Israelites under the command of Joab around 1010 B.C.E., it was called "the city of David"). For almost two millennia, no community around the Mediterranean chose deliberately to identify with the Jews. In the 1930s, however, a group of very poor, previously Roman Catholic Italian peasants elected, under the leadership of Donato Manduzio, a visionary veteran of the First World War, to convert to Judaism. The Jews of San Nicandro, from Gargano, one of the poorest areas in the Mezzogiorno, persisted in what seemed to the Vatican, to the Fascist authorities and even to the rabbinate to be a misguided conversion. After 1945, the young people made aliyah to Palestine, where their descendants still live. See *The Jews of San Nicandro,* by John A. Davis.

mand in the invasion of Britain. Success in combined operations (for which Claudius took triumphal credit) procured him consular rank. If Vespasian lacked brilliance, he was shrewd enough, when Nero came to the throne, to keep his head down while others, including his own patron Narcissus, were losing theirs. He resumed public life, as proconsul in the placid province of Africa, only after Nero's domineering mother, Agrippina, was done to death at her son's command.*

Once back on the ladder that led to high places, Vespasian performed wearisome duties competently and never encroached on the emperor's spotlight. Stolid, without charm or eloquence, he looked to be the last man of whom any highflier needed to be wary. The great Seneca—who had been the young Nero's tutor and then became his prime adviser—lacked Vespasian's reticence. As a writer, Seneca alternated between cogitation on the meaning of life and death and the composition of melodramatic stage plays. If they seem immoderately gory, so too was the imperial court of which he was, for a long while, the intellectual ornament. Roman literature and life shared an obsession with blood; gladiatorial shows at once diverted the people and familiarized them with slaughter. The amphitheater offered its public an education in callousness.

While Nero preferred music, in the Greek sense of the performing arts, especially his own, he was not slow to shed blood when it was other people's. His Hellenism was a genuine affectation. He was more certain of applause in Greece than in Rome, especially after the great fire of 64. In case the fastidious sat on their hands, Nero had been quick to recruit his own band of five thousand fans, known as

---

* She was supposed to be drowned, apparently by accident, in a collapsible boat, but managed to swim ashore and had to be stabbed instead. An oracle had warned her that her son would be the death of her. When her killer came for her, she ordered him to strike at her womb, as Aeschylus's Klytemnestra did, after her son, Orestes, returned to Argos to avenge his father. All the Roman world was a stage. The publicity following Agrippina's clumsy murder was cardinal in turning upper-class opinion against Nero. The earlier prompt murder of his half brother, Britannicus, a potential rival for the throne, had been excused, by that elastic moralist Seneca, as necessary to the stability of the succession.

the Augustiani. They followed him from gig to gig and rose to cheer his performances in the contrapuntal Alexandrian style, which somewhat resembled the modern "Mexican wave." In Rome itself, however, not even Nero's claque could be guaranteed to immunize him against outbursts of plebeian resentment over unfair taxation or the high price of corn. His Byronic curtain speech to the Greeks, at the Isthmian Games at Corinth in November 67, told them that they were again to be free, at least of greedy tax collectors.* Not many years after Nero had done his crowd-pleasing number, the Greeks would have their taxes reimposed, by the same Vespasian who, it is said, had once found the emperor's bel canto so soporific that he fell asleep during one of Nero's concerts. For a non-singing non-patrician autocrat, with a reputation for what Tacitus called *domestica parsimonia* (tight housekeeping), balancing the books counted for more than provincial encores.

Had Nero's gigs included venues in Judaea, he might have reprised his magnanimity. There were, however, no festivals with prizes sufficiently glittering to seduce the imperial vanity. It is unlikely that he would have found the Jews a receptive audience: back in the eighth century B.C.E., the prophet Amos had spoken for the faithful when he said, "I hate the sound of your harps, which make you despise justice." Plato's distrust of the alluring "Lydian mode" is of a piece with Amos's revulsion from the socially disruptive effects of popular music. It continues to be anathematized in strict versions of Islam.†

If its echo ever reached Jerusalem, the emperor's declaration of fiscal independence for the Hellenes might have been taken by the young Zealots as a sign that the Romans were losing their appetite for global domination. The Jews were mistaken, however, if they thought that they were going to get away with murder. The military response to

---

* His speech earned something like the relieved, ambiguous applause that greeted Mikhail Gorbachev when he granted autonomy to the Soviet satellites in Eastern Europe in the late 1980s. In both cases, the cheers were meant to hold the speaker to his word; and in both, unsmiling conservatives at home regarded the liberator as little more than a weakling who was giving away what braver men had won.

† As rock music was by Allan Bloom in *The Closing of the American Mind* (New York: Touchstone, 1987).

the bloody humiliation of Cestius Gallus (which he can have been in no hurry to report in any detail) took longer to organize than a more martial Caesar would have required. Once in train, however, it was in substantial strength.

Titus Flavius Vespasianus carried a big stick more easily than a tune. If the commission to pacify Judaea was not intended as a punishment, it was certainly not designed to set him on the path to glory. Of Sabine origin, born in 9 in Falacrinae, in the Apennines high above Rieti, Vespasian was a workhorse, never a thoroughbred. Persons of Sabine descent were regarded by the Romans as Scots have been by the English: frugal to the point of meanness, but usefully competent and courageous. Like Joseph ben Mattathias, the Roman commander was his parents' second son (his brother, Sabinus, was as eloquent as Vespasian was dour). His father had fought for Pompey against Julius Caesar. Vespasian's aristocratic mother, Vespasia, had married beneath her. After the death of her husband, she made a home to which her younger son was always happy to return; as emperor, he preserved it as it had been when he was a child. Sabinus headed promptly for the lower rungs of the *cursus honorum,* but Vespasia had to taunt Vespasian with being no more than "his brother's footman" before she could kindle his ambition. No orator, he favored action over the law or politics and became a professional soldier.

His first posting was in Thrace, but he returned to Rome in the last, sour years of the emperor Tiberius. He there fell in love with a clever freed slave, Caenis, to whom he remained devoted, even after his marriage. As secretary to Antonia (the sister-in-law of Tiberius and daughter of Mark Antony), Caenis had carried a secret message from her mistress to the emperor, a recluse on Capri, to tell him that his trusted deputy in Rome, Sejanus, was plotting treason. She survived to be Vespasian's right hand as he picked his way through the political minefield of Roman politics.

In 38 C.E., soon after Caligula succeeded Claudius as emperor, Vespasian was elected aedile, but only just: he ranked at the bottom of the list of successful candidates. As the man now responsible for keeping the Roman streets clean of refuse and slops, he had the bad luck to meet the new emperor on a particularly filthy stretch of road. Fortunately, on this occasion, Caligula was more playful than—as he soon became—murderous: he had his bodyguard shovel the shit into the folds of the aedile's toga and passed on by. On another occasion, when Vespasian was at dinner, a stray dog appeared and made him a present of something it had found in the street: a human hand.

To live in Rome was to have a public life or no life worth talking about. Married to Flavia Domitilla, a woman without impressive connections, Vespasian was impelled to crave imperial favor. When Caligula made him praetor (he ranked first on the list this time), he was embarrassed to have to make a series of servile, life-preserving speeches. His great desire was to command a legion. It was granted when Antonia's son Claudius was elevated to the purple and—perhaps prompted by Caenis—dispatched Vespasian to Argentoratum, the modern French city of Strasbourg, whence he and his legion (the Second Augustan) and his brother, Sabinus, accompanied Claudius on the expedition to conquer Britain. The brothers fought side by side, gallantly, and went on, under the overall command of Claudius, to defeat the son of Cymbeline and capture Colchester. Vespasian was recommended to the Senate by the emperor himself for triumphal honors.

In 51, he became consul, but three years later Claudius was dead, allegedly poisoned by his wife, Agrippina. Her son, the seventeen-year-old Nero, became emperor. Vespasian's previous connections were abruptly useless, if not dangerous. He went into provincial retreat for a full ten years. His brother, Sabinus, continued in public service; he was prefect of Rome when half the city was burned down, in 64. Meanwhile, Vespasian was in Africa as proconsul. His stewardship of the province was rigorous, honest and unpopular; the locals on one occasion pelted him with turnips. His Roman house went up in flames in the fire. On his return from Africa, he paid the penalty for failing to enrich himself as corrupt governors regularly did: he had to go into business, trading mules, to retrieve his fortunes. The haulage trade was a good market. Peter Wiseman reports that Nero traveled with a mule-drawn cavalcade of "anything up to a thousand carriages, richly caparisoned and shod in silver."[3]

Nero's desire to make the arts the paramount public activity of the Romans showed innovative flair. Since the business of Rome had always been war, its principal communal pleasures—gladiatorial contests—served to accustom audiences to bloodshed. If Nero had to pander to the gross appetites of the public, he also made it his Orphic mission to refine them. Other emperors marched; he preferred to prance.

VI

N<small>ERO'S DILETTANTISM</small> allowed time for the rebellion in Judaea to organize itself into what the Zealots could claim was a divinely warranted national resurgence: anyone who was not on their side was an enemy of the God who had granted them their victory. It was dangerous for anyone in Jerusalem openly to deprecate the enthusiasm of the victorious Jews. The Zealots' challenge to the Temple hierarchy was as outspoken as their calls for full independence from Rome. The elders of the Jerusalem aristocracy, composed of Mattathias, the father of Joseph, and his peers, may have reacted with private dismay at the triumphalism of the insurgents; in public they had to greet it with polite, and politic, applause. Was Joseph a bad Jew if, on his return to Jerusalem, he tried to persuade anyone who would listen that the consequences of all-out war with Rome would be disastrous?

Since he had succeeded in securing the release of the captive priests, his standing, at least among the hierarchy, had been enhanced. Who was more plausible when arguing against a reckless uprising than a young man who had just proved that the Romans were not impervious to diplomacy? Joseph's recipe for caution was not wasted on the Pharisees, nor on those of his father's class and age. The measure of his new prestige is that his views infuriated the popular leader, Menahem, the Zealot son of Judas, the Galilean bandit and hero. Menahem had recently led an expedition to capture Herod's armory at Masada. He and his men had massacred the small Roman garrison and helped themselves to weaponry, which enabled them to return to Jerusalem and back their leader's claim to command.

Menahem's henchmen soon forced Joseph to take refuge in the inner court of the Temple, where he was quarantined among those of his equivocal opinion. The Zealots were parading a bristling version of faith that brooked no argument. How could there be any question about dying in obedience to the laws that, it was said, were inherent in the Torah? No Jew, they insisted, could make compromises without breaching the covenant. Their introversion was aggressive and dogmatic. In the areas of the city under their control, anyone who stole "holy articles," swore improper oaths, married out or "made an Aramaean their concubine" was treated as a criminal.

Menahem's bid for absolute power had led him and his men to murder the High Priest Ananias and his brother Hezekiah. Ananias's son, Eleazar, had been among the prime fomenters of the rebellion, but family loyalty or personal ambition turned him against Menahem. Outraged by the latter's presumption in dressing in royal robes, he chased his father's murderer as far as the town of Ophel, where Menahem was captured, tortured and killed. Josephus reports that it was hoped in Jerusalem that Menahem's death would bring the insurrection to an end. It did not: Eleazar had returned to continue the siege of Metilius and his men in the Antonia Tower to its bloody end.

Joseph insisted that the tenets of Judaism in no way required that he and the best people in Jerusalem should sacrifice their lives rather than endure patiently. Like the Temple hierarchy, he hoped that time and diplomacy could defuse the crisis. Instead, it escalated. Josephus gives no account of precisely how the old guard and the Zealots came together in what affected to be a government of national unity. In fact, it was never united in trust or purpose. The Zealots were not disposed to moderation, even if they were, for the present, compelled to public reconcilation with the traditional priestly leadership. The hierarchy, on the other hand, could not exercise an appeasing influence on the young fundamentalists unless it seemed to agree to endorse their policy of national liberation. None of the elements in Jerusalem had reason, or any long intention, to abide by the solidarity they sought to impose on the whole of Palestine. Neither *The Jewish War* nor the *Vita* offers a reliable account of the process by which Joseph ben Mattathias was appointed governor-general of Galilee, but his selection must have been part of a compromise, of no reliable duration, between the elders and the Zealots.*

Judaeans at large had their grievances, but they were against the Jerusalem hierarchy as well as the Romans. If it was questionable whether the population had any appetite for all-out war, there was no "democratic" arena in which such a question could even be raised. Can Joseph be blamed if he took the same view which Philo of Alexandria had, two decades earlier, when he recommended that the Egyptian Jews put patient trust in the Holy One? It was wise, and pious, the Alexandrian elder had said, to rely on the antique slogan Saint Paul would rehearse, for alien motives, in his epistle to the Romans: "Vengeance is mine, saith the Lord, I will repay." The moral was: leave it to Him.

Josephus's mixture, in *The Jewish War,* of the pragmatic and the supernatural provides a parallax view of what happened in Judaea. His tour of the riches and pleasures of Rome must have altered his younger self's vision of Judaea's future, and perhaps of his own. He had come back with no furious commitment to Jewish exclusivity. Eclectic before, he was now cosmopolitan; the man with an extra eye is a menace to those who cannot see things his way. Josephus depicts himself as dispassionate and humane. As a rich young man, he was not con-

---

* Martin Goodman suggests that Josephus "lets slip" that his appointment (or election by "the assembly") followed that of other "generals." No scholarly source suggests one qualification that may have made Joseph particularly eligible for the governorship of Galilee: he was a stranger to the region, with no specific ties to any of its rivalrous communities. This gave him some prospect of uniting them without being suspected of partisanship. In Greek mythology, it was often *xenoi*—heroes or divinities from outside—who managed by the force of their charismatic arrival to unite the people in a way beyond the power of an indigenous leader. The figure of the "heaven-sent" marginal figure who unites contending in-groups spills from myth into history: Theodoric, Napoleon, Atatürk, Hitler, de Gaulle and Margaret Thatcher (whose advent enforced unity on a party of contentious males). In Galilee, Joseph did not succeed on a grand scale, but his seemingly miraculous ability to master crowds must have owed something to his outlandishness.

cerned with personal aggrandizement; if he enjoyed his priestly and aristocratic status, he advertised no political or religious zeal. Once on the ground as governor of Galilee in the spring of 67 C.E., he devoted himself to keeping the command of local cities in what he, his father, and their friends regarded as responsible hands. Damage limitation was central to his mission.

Josephus does not even summarize the process by which he came to be appointed. It is unlikely that the Zealots voted for him (if they ever did, they were prompt to go back on their word), but in the early stages, before Vespasian had even landed at Caesarea, they lacked the power to put one of their own people in the post. They must have guessed how difficult Joseph's task was. Whatever happened, his mission would remove a charismatic opponent from Jerusalem. If he succeeded in rallying the Galileans, the Zealots could hope to supplant him; if—as was more likely—he failed, it would tarnish his reputation and reflect badly on whoever had sponsored him.

As far as the Sanhedrin was concerned, Joseph's lack of fanaticism must have contributed to his eligibility as commander in Galilee. By securing the appointment of a quick-witted, diplomatically experienced and well-connected governor-general, the Jerusalem elders left the door ajar for negotiation, even if they dared not declare as much to the people at large. It would be no evidence of their treason if the elders briefed Joseph to combine a show of belligerent purpose with a covert policy of wait and see. He soon found that the Zealots were much more eager for war than the Judaeans at large. Outlying towns and cities, along the Mediterranean coast and especially around the Sea of Galilee, had populations including Arabs, Greeks (or Levantine Greek speakers) and Samaritans,* as well as many Jews who were content to be Hellenized. These disparate communities had little sense of "national" unity, still less any loyalty to the Jerusalem junta that had nominated Joseph as commander-in-chief. Any attempt to recruit and

---

* Although repudiated by the Judaean Jews, at the time of Alexander the Great, the Samaritans continued to regard the Torah as their "Bible" and had their own breakaway temple on Mount Gerizim. See Shemaryahu Talmon, "Internal Diversification."

station a large force in their region could only alarm the rural popula-tion. An army's need for forage is bound to trump even the most ami-able intentions.*

It was crucial to Joseph ben Mattathias's strategy to bring the biggest communities on the shore of the Sea of Galilee under his command. Principal among them was Tiberias, the provincial capital, which had a mixed population of Jews and Hellenized Levantines, and the adja-cent, mainly Jewish, town of Tarichaeae. Joseph was faced with the task of trying to reconcile as many of them as possible into a common front. On his own account, it required him to play the trickster and the action hero at the same time. But then, this is what the Greek god Hermes, Homer's Odysseus and, on occasion, King David himself had done.

Before full-scale hostilities began, young hotheads from a town-ship called Dabarittha (the modern Deburieh, at the foot of Mount Tabor) ambushed a convoy of wagons, under armed escort, containing baggage, clothing, jewelry and six hundred gold coins, the property of Agrippa II and Berenice. Surprised by the value of their haul, the thieves realized that they could not keep all of it without attracting punitive attention either from the king's men or from other highway-men stronger than themselves. They decided to hand their booty over to Joseph ben Mattathias, who happened to be in Tarichaeae.

He scolded them for the affront to the royal family and then depos-ited their takings with the leading man in the city, Annaeus. Josephus says that his intention was to return the belongings to their royal owners, as soon as he had a chance, in order to retain their goodwill. His overt displeasure with the brigands was untypical and unsubtle; hence, it was probably sincere. They had expected congratulations and, no doubt, a percentage of the loot. When they heard that Joseph ben Mattathias meant to restore their stolen belongings to the royal couple, whom they regarded as collaborators with the Romans, the

---

* During the German occupation, peasant farmers, especially, in France's south-west, were expected to supply sustenance both to the Germans and to the Resistance, whose exactions could, at times, be more peremptory, because they were patriotic.

young adventurers went "running by night," Josephus says, through the region, denouncing the governor as a traitor.[1]

By dawn, a hundred thousand men in arms were reported to be crowding into Tarichaeae, bent on doing him bodily harm. Assembled in the hippodrome, they were not all of one mind: some wanted Joseph stoned to death, others to burn him alive. John of Gischala* and Jesus, the son of Sapphias, the chief magistrate of Tiberias, latched on to the highwaymen's grievance. They chose to elevate an opportunistic heist into a revolutionary exploit. Joseph's supposedly craven intentions became central to the indictment of his leadership, of which John was eager to relieve him. When the crowd proclaimed Joseph a public enemy, all but four of his bodyguards deserted him. The first he knew of the commotion was after a mob set fire to the house where he was sleeping. His four loyal guards begged him to get out while he could. He refused. Instead of panicking, he chose to tear his clothes (he was dressed in black) and then—another dramatic gesture—leapt out of the house, having covered himself with cinders. His hands were behind his back, he says, and his sword hung around his neck. This penitential apparition aroused the pity of supporters and friends in Tarichaeae. It also infuriated those who had crowded into the city from outside. They yelled for him to produce the treasure, which "belonged to the people," and to admit that he had made a treacherous deal with Agrippa II.

The outsiders took it for granted that he would not dare to deny the charge. They also assumed that he hoped, by his pitiful makeup, to secure a reprieve. In fact, he tells us, he had a cleverer plan.[2] First—in

---

* Described as a "son of Levi," John of Gischala is said to have at first opposed the revolt from Rome; but then neighboring people from Gadara, Gabara and Sogana, with help from some of those from Tyre, attacked the town of Gischala and burned and demolished it. John armed the Gischalans, rebuilt the town and made it into his personal power base. He then became an ardent revolutionary as well as a commercial opportunist. Josephus takes time out to remark that Levites had been authorized by Agrippa II to wear the same linen clothes as priests. As Zuleika Rodgers emphasizes in "Justice for Justus," it is a mark of Josephus's pride in his priestly standing that he claims that the Levites' presumption excited divine punishment. John's personal history is another symptom of the volatility, if not vacillation, of almost all of the players in the politics of the period, grand or petty.

order to divide the mob—he promised a complete explanation. To get a hearing at all, he must have had a remarkably commanding voice. When the crowd conceded him time to make his case, he responded—like a good advocate—by springing surprises. Entertainment, as well as good timing, is an aspect of successful rhetoric. His first trick was to confess that he had never really meant to return the treasure to Agrippa. But then again, no more did he mean to keep it for himself.

It is not difficult to imagine how Joseph both cued and confused his listeners. By giving them the chance to react in different ways, he was able to control the show. As they jeered or groaned, laughed or frowned, he became their master of ceremonies. Joseph told the people that God would not want him to treat their enemy as his friend or to keep for himself anything to which the people had a right. Having set his listeners a pious puzzle, he solved it for them: "Seeing that your city, citizens of Tarichaeae, had above all a need to strengthen its security, and didn't have enough money to build up its ramparts, I was afraid that the people of Tiberias and a number of other places would try to trick their way into getting hold of the booty. And that's why I decided to put it in a safe place."

If he gave the skeptics a half second to groan, it served to isolate them from the residents. "I did so," he resumed, "in order to have the means to build you a rampart. If you think that's a bad idea, I'll dump the whole lot in front of you and you can help yourselves. On the other hand . . . if what I decided seems to you a good idea, why take it out on someone who was trying to do you a favor?"

The effect of his words was to open divisions among those who, not long before, had been united in baying for Joseph's blood. The inhabitants of Tarichaeae were given an incentive to get rid of outsiders—John of Gischala not least—in order to benefit more fully from Joseph's largess. While the two parties turned on each other, Joseph found enough voice to continue his harangue. He promised to secure funds to fortify the other towns in the region, if they would stop making trouble. By dividing, he could continue to rule.

As the crowd lost cohesion, some of the protesters drifted away. Joseph had bluffed the majority, but he says that two thousand armed men pursued him back to his lodgings and blocked the way out. It was time to pull another trick. He climbed onto the roof and, with a pacifying gesture, silenced their commotion. Literally above the crowd, he claimed to have no idea what exactly they wanted him to do, because they were all saying different things.*

Joseph proposed to arrange things by inviting a deputation to come into his lodgings for a quiet discussion. His cool style must have impressed the hard men, despite themselves. The Jews took pride in their equality, but the uneducated were often susceptible to lordly eloquence. A mixed delegation of the leaders of the militants and of those whom Josephus calls "magistrates" (presumably from places outside Tarichaeae) came forward. Joseph had them taken into the back of the house and locked the front door. He then had them so severely whipped that, as he tells it, they were virtually flayed alive. The protestors outside could hear nothing. They assumed that their representatives were still pleading their cause.

When Joseph had the doors flung open, the bloody men were thrown into the street. Their appearance is said to have provoked such a panic that the rioters threw down their arms and ran away. The story is too unlikely not to have some truth in it. If so, Joseph must somehow have rallied more supporters than his four faithful bodyguards. Some locals were probably as keen as he was to be done with the outsiders. Even John of Gischala backed off—if only to give himself time to try something more devious. Affecting an illness, he wrote to Joseph, as the general-in-command, for permission to go for a cure to the thermal baths at Tiberias. Fooling and being fooled were part of the farce that preceded the tragedy. Josephus claims that, at the time, he did not suspect John of evil intentions. He even instructed his friends in Tiberias to give John a cordial welcome.

Within a couple of days, John had bribed and browbeaten the Tibe-

---

* Years earlier, the emperor Claudius had had a similar experience with two sets of Jews who came from Alexandria to petition him. They fell into such violent dissent in his presence that the emperor ordered that no subject people should ever again be allowed to send more than a single group to speak on its behalf.

rians into abandoning their allegiance to Joseph. Tipped off by a loyal supporter, Joseph went by night to Tiberias. As dawn broke, he was met by a crowd of anxious citizens. John sent word that he was too ill to get up; he would make amends later. Joseph called a mass meeting in the waterfront stadium, where he could address the people from a high tier, backing onto the beach. As he did so, John was rehearsing a party of commandos to kill him. When they appeared behind him and drew their swords, the crowd yelled to Joseph to watch out. He turned just in time, jumped down the twelve-foot-high embankment to the shore and—with two of his bodyguards—tumbled into a boat and set off for the middle of the lake. There was, it seems, already a plan B.

Joseph's supporters in the town ran for their arms and were soon all set to attack John and his gang. Fearing a bloody civil war, Joseph sent word that no one should be killed, not even the guilty. The volatile locals became so alarmed by the prospect of street fighting that they chased John out of the city and back to his power base in Gischala. Having been friendless not long before, Joseph returned to land to find "several tens of thousands of soldiers" ready to go in pursuit of John, now public enemy number one, burn him alive and reduce his native city to dust and ashes.

Josephus says that the scoundrel's backers shriveled to his immediate entourage. However, John continued to agitate and soon recruited another swath of support, whose leaders, all said to be remarkable orators, incited several cities, including Tiberias, yet again to renounce their allegiance to Joseph. This time, the governor responded by arranging for the four ringleaders and their best men to be summoned to help in the defense of Jerusalem. It seemed like a promotion. On arrival, they met a hostile reception from Joseph's friends and had to run for their lives. John, however, had been confident (or cautious) enough to stay, for the present, in Gischala. He would make his move later.

Looking back years afterward, Josephus clearly found it difficult to describe the rogue from Gischala without highlighting his impudence. He reports that in the weeks before the war, while John was trying to displace him as the boss of Galilee, the Gischalan also found time to bargain and bully his way ino a virtual monopoly in the region's copious olive oil production. Olive oil supplied a third of the caloric intake of the inhabitants, as well as being used for lighting, hygienic and medical purposes. John profited from the apprehension of the Jews, especially those in Syria, that they might be using an impure "Gentile" brand, even though olive oil never featured among foodstuffs expressly disapproved by the Scriptures.* John of Gischala bought cheap oil, rebottled it, and marketed it as a purified—"organic," as it were—brand suitable for Jewish consumption. He charged ten times the price he had paid and insisted on payment in Tyrian silver coin, which was unadulterated.

Joseph's determination to stay in his post can hardly have been motivated by the pleasures of command; nor was it seconded by the steadfastness of his allies. Once he had returned to Tarichaeae, the Tiberians called on King Agrippa II to send troops to their aid. The rumor was that a squadron of Roman cavalry had been spotted not far away. It was enough to make the Tiberians solicit help from the same king whose treasure they had been eager to filch. The Tiberian leaders now advertised their resumed loyalty to Agrippa by announcing Joseph's formal banishment. They were, in effect, opting out of taking the Jewish side in the imminent war.

Joseph met the challenge with renewed Odyssean panache. Having ordered all the gates of Tarichaeae to be closed, so that no one could escape to carry word to the Tiberians of what he was doing, he requisitioned all the town's boats. Two hundred and thirty small craft were massed on the lake. Joseph divided the available rowers among the boats, four to each, and led the fleet down the coast toward Tiberias. There he anchored his fleet, far enough offshore for those on the ramparts not to be able to discern how many men were on board each boat. He then had himself rowed close under the walls, with only seven bodyguards in attendance. His enemies yelled the usual abuse when

* It was among the commodities in which Baruch Spinoza's Orthodox father traded in seventeenth-century Amsterdam, as part of a business the philosopher inherited but abandoned.

they first saw him. As he got closer, they began to be alarmed. Fearing that the boats out in the lake were crammed with soldiers waiting for Joseph's signal, they threw down their arms, waved suppliant olive branches and begged him to spare the city.

Standing up in his boat, Joseph scolded them on two counts: they had chosen to take up arms against the Romans and then they had dissipated their forces in civil conflict. On top of that, they had fulfilled their enemies' wishes by closing the gates against the one man who had done the most to fortify their city. The town councilmen, he insisted, should come and explain themselves. Ten of the chief men walked forward. Joseph demanded that they get into one of the boats. They were promptly rowed out onto the sea. Fifty more councillors were invited to follow their colleagues. They too were somehow persuaded into the boats. In the end, Josephus reports, all six hundred of the town councilmen (including Justus and Pistis) as well as some two thousand citizens were transported across the water to Tarichaeae.

It sounds to be another unlikely story. Yet Tiberias would suffer less than other cities in the war; enough of its citizens survived to give Josephus the lie, if he was romancing. Since their docility added luster to his leadership, it is understandable that he should give no further explanation of why the Tiberians obeyed him. Their actions become plausible, however, if a good many, once they had been promised security in Tarichaeae, were glad to get out of their own city. The remaining citizens are said to have called out to Joseph that the ringleader of the revolt was a certain Clitus (possibly a nickname, "Mr. Bigshot"). Their denunciation of him suggests that the majority was interested, above all, in a quiet life.

Josephus claims that he was determined to bring down the curtain on the episode without anyone being killed. To this humane end, he ordered one of his guards, called Levi, to land and cut off both of Clitus's hands. Levi refused to go alone among so many changeable people. Joseph made a show of preparing to jump from his boat, splash ashore and do the carving himself. He looked to be in such a passion that Clitus begged him from the beach to be allowed to keep one of his hands. Joseph agreed, on the condition that the villain cut off the other hand himself, which he did. In this way, Josephus promises us, he managed with a fleet of "empty" boats and a handful of bodyguards to regain control of Tiberias.

A few days later, however, both Tiberias and nearby Sepphoris had once again rebelled against his rule. Levi had evidently been no fool when he refused to go ashore. Joseph licensed his soldiers to go in and pillage both towns. The prospect of loot was the happiest way to motivate his levies. When the booty had been accumulated in one place, presumably for distribution to his troops, he ordered that it all be given back to its owners. He hoped that they would learn their lesson and behave. It is unlikely that the morale of his soldiers was enhanced by his magnanimity. It certainly had no grateful effect on the Tiberians.

Although Joseph was supposedly in the region solely to organize resistance to the imperial power, he found a certain Julius Capellus, who led a faction that wanted to stay loyal to Rome (and thus maintain its hegemony in Tiberias), more congenial, because he was more gentlemanly—and hence more like himself—than Pistis (whose Greek name, if not his practice, promised trustworthiness) and his clever son Justus. Since the latter was to be Josephus's rival as a historian, the portrait painted of him in his youth is unsubtly shaded. In truth, he too resembled Joseph: all of the people involved were playing a double game, without any clear idea of what would count as its vindication, apart from the survival of their persons and property.

Justus took advantage of the unrest to strengthen his personal militia. Indifferent to the nebulous concept of Judaean liberty, he was glad to enroll the rural poor and lead them in raids on the villages around Sepphoris. Tiberias's feud with its neighbor* made it easier to gather volunteers for this purpose than for any national cause. Joseph alter-

---

* Agrippa II had recently presented Sepphoris to Nero as a gift. The city was then promoted to be the capital of Galilee. Justus and his father were keen for local hegemony, but had no wider horizons or ambitions. After the event, Justus had good reason, as a historian (and a survivor), to depict himself and his father as always loyal to Agrippa. (See Mason, *Life of Josephus*, p. 39.)

nated between punitive and placatory responses: he first threw Justus and Pistis into jail, to prove that he had the necessary muscle, and then invited them to dinner. In private, he told them that he knew that the Romans were too strong to be resisted but that he dared not say so, because of the "bandits" who were the common enemies of everyone at the table. Having reminded Justus of how Galilean roughs had cut off his brother's hands, he let his prisoners go. His hope had to be that his dinner guests would appreciate that he was engaged on a policy of candid duplicity. To regard the Jewish War only as an instance, or assertion, of national solidarity is anachronistic. The settling of old scores, the hope of petty power and messianic fantasies combined to instigate a confrontation with Rome that—at least to those who had much to lose—was as unnecessary as it was likely to be fatal. Jerusalem was a fine and golden city, with a volatile population, but it excited small allegiance among the mixed, often mutually antagonistic populations of the provinces.* Their monotheism made the Jews appear both introverted and eccentric. Their peculiarities also sealed what appeared, from outside, to be an enviable mutual dependence. Internally, however, their cohesion was never monolithic. In Judaea, Pharisees, Sadducees, Zealots and Essenes fought their corners with uncompromising partisanship. Samaritans and Idumaeans, even decades after their conversion to Judaism, were relegated to a lower division.

In his *Vita,* Josephus deplores Justus's immoderate language and trickiness. By denouncing the elaboration of his rival's "Greek" discourse, Josephus assumes the straightforwardness that Romans liked to suppose was their natural manner. Deploring a critic's florid vocabulary or outlandish gesticulation is a regular way of recruiting the prejudices of an author's audience against loudmouths.† It can be doubted

---

* Even the French Revolution was, at first, an exclusively Parisian affair. Its spread too led to countercurrents within the population. The repression in La Vendée was the bloodiest evidence.

† When reticence was an aspect of the British idea of how gentlemen should conduct themselves, scorn for "talking with your hands" (often alleged to be a Jewish speciality) was an element of the belief that "wogs begin at Calais."

whether, at the time, Joseph conducted himself with as much reticence and decorum as his later account implied.

Since he was particularly nettled by Justus's criticisms of *The Jewish War*,* Josephus supplies a detailed profile of a man who, like many others, was torn by contradictory ambitions and fears. Justus is accused of intimidating his fellow citizens into joining him, but many can be assumed to have volunteered in the hope of gaining booty or power. Long after the event, Justus claimed to have been steadfastly loyal to Agrippa II, his postwar patron, and to Berenice. Fairly or not, Josephus recalls how Justus made a speech, just before Vespasian marched into Judaea, in which he enthused the mob by denouncing Agrippa for favoring Sepphoris over Tiberias. Local grievances had more leverage than any grand considerations.

Joseph was an intruder with wider interests, but he and Justus had made much the same assessment of the situation. Their later literary feud had more to do with vanity than with patriotism. To upstage Justus as a historian, Josephus adopted the stance of a Roman sophisticate. In this, he inaugurated an enduring tradition: Jewish intellectuals not infrequently have a Jewish *frère-ennemi* who can be assailed with a brand of abusive scorn rarely visited on Gentile critics.†

---

* Since they are never itemized, still less refuted, it is reasonable to conjecture that at least some of Justus's objections were unanswerable.

† Hannah Arendt's peeved reaction to *all* Jewish criticism of *Eichmann in Jerusalem,* not least that of her old friend Gershom Scholem, contrasts with the guarded reproaches with which she responded to Martin Heidegger's infatuation with Hitler. Jewish polemicists regularly display outspoken venom toward those with a provenance not unlike their own, but from which they are, for whatever reasons, earnest to distinguish themselves. Even the Oxford historian (and Zionist) Lewis Namier was capable of alienated condescension. Asked why he spent so much time examining the minutiae of English parliamentary sociology rather than dealing with the great theme of Jewish history, he responded that the Jews did not have a history, only a "martyrology." It is also sometimes alleged that, among themselves, even the most sophisticated and assimilated Jews like to revert to the Yiddish patois in which, supposedly, they are more comfortably at home. According to Adam Sisman's 2010 biography of Hugh Trevor-Roper, Bernard Berenson claimed that this was true even when he and Isaiah Berlin got together, which Berlin denied, with polite indignation.

VII

As Vespasian was reported to be disembarking at Caesarea,* Joseph ben Mattathias moved his headquarters to the hilltop town of Jotapata (today's Yodefat), about ten miles north of Nazareth. He had already ordered its fortifications to be thickened as part of his hurried plans to balk Vespasian's advance on Jerusalem. During his governorship, Joseph had raised, and done his best to train and organize, an efficient Jewish army. He claimed that it amounted to a hundred thousand men.

Statistical exaggeration is a habit with ancient historians. Like old Hollywood producers, they fatten their epics with mammoth casts. Whatever the exact numbers, Joseph's levies lacked the discipline, cohesion and equipment to confront regular Roman soldiers. With few illusions about the result if he were to be caught in open country, his best tactic had to be to hole up and hold out for as long as possible. In the event, he would have enough time, in his tight redoubt, to reflect on the amalgam of grievances, vanities and miscalculations that had brought the Judaean Jews, and himself, to the present pass.

In an annex to his adventures in Galilee, Josephus cuts back to Jeru-

---

* The city, previously known as Strato's Tower, was renovated as a major port by Herod the Great, who dedicated it to the Roman emperor. Until the outbreak of hostilities, its population was a mixture of Jews and Syrians. On the outbreak of war, Josephus says (*Jewish War* II: 447 and following), the Syrians massacred Caesarea's twenty thousand Jews, thus rendering it a safe haven for Vespasian's headquarters.

salem, where he says that the High Priest Ananus "and those of the leading men who were not pro-Roman" (implying that a good number were) set about reinforcing the defenses and importing the matériel necessary for war. While the moderate citizens abandoned themselves, as moderates will, to lamentation, Ananus prepared for war, slowly. Can he be blamed if he still hoped that, by being all things to as many men as possible, he could deflect the Zealots from a disastrous war?

Ananus remained in formal control for almost two years, but his authority was eroded by the Zealot factions, which were also jostling each other for mastery of the elements in favor of total war. Josephus's two versions of events supply an incongruous double portrait of Ananus. A noble figure in *The Jewish War*, the same man appears in the *Vita* to connive at the attempt by a three-man delegation that was dispatched from Jerusalem in the spring of 67 with authority, so they said, to displace Joseph. Their appointment suggests that the Zealot parties, perhaps by agreeing on temporary alliance, had outvoted (or merely bullied) the High Priest and his friends.

Josephus's inconsistent treatment of Ananus argues for his candor. In *The Jewish War* he likes to show himself in a gallant light, but self-justification is not, in that book, his prime purpose. In many regards, Ananus was playing much the same two-faced game as Joseph: both were acting tough and, at the same time, hoping for a last-minute settlement. If Ananus preferred to make concessions at the expense of his own side rather than to excite a bloody confrontation with the radicals, it may have made him a poor friend of Joseph ben Mattathias; but Josephus the historian could see that to betray him might further policies both men had favored. The charge of treason was as easy to bring against Joseph as it would be, a year or so later, against Ananus himself. Neither man was in a position to define, or cleave to, an unequivocal purpose. The more flexible their policy, the more its public expression would excite violent reactions from the militants. To play a double game was their common recourse if they wished both to remain in control of affairs and to compromise with the Romans. How could the elders speak out against the Zealots, whose appeal to the masses was based on the Maccabean myth of heroic Jewish independence? To stay in a position to avoid all-out war, the moderates had to show every sign of preparing for it.

Joseph displayed daring and ingenuity in clinging to his thankless office as governor-general. The likeliest and least complicated explanation of his persistence is that he was doing what he considered to be his duty. Unless his adventures in Tarichaeae and Tiberias are a fabrication, which not even detractors such as his rival historian Justus have claimed, he never flinched when faced with hostile mobs and daunting odds. Relying on surprise and showmanship, he matched a cluster of charismatic leaders, before and after his time.

When Vespasian's legions began marching through Judaea on the way to Jerusalem, Joseph chose to sit tight in Jotapata. With no prospect of halting the Romans in the open, he could pose a credible threat to their flank. He may have had a second thought, and perhaps sealed orders from the hierarchy in Jerusalem; in any negotiated settlement with Vespasian, he was the likeliest go-between. The old hierarchy may have had a large enough majority to secure his appointment, but the young Zealots soon proved numerous enough to revoke it.

As a result, as well as trying to align the local bosses in a common front against the Romans, Joseph had to deploy his ingenuity in frustrating the posse from Jerusalem, which had come to relieve him of his command. Jesus ben Gamala, a former High Priest who remained a leading figure in the High Priest's coterie, sent word, through Joseph's father, Mattathias, warning that the Zealots' deputation had been supplied with forty thousand pieces of silver from central funds with which to persuade the Galileans to dump Joseph.* Can vanity alone account for the vigor with which he fought to keep his post?

---

* Martin Goodman (*The Ruling Class of Judaea*) maintains that the revolt "was led from the start by the ruling class"—of which Joseph's father was clearly a member—"to keep their prominence in Judaean society after the Roman backing, on which they had . . . relied, was withdrawn." This implies that they hoped to have things both ways, but hardly makes it plausible that they should have instigated what put their position at risk and, in the event, led to their own destruction. The argument that "previous incidents" had never led to a serious revolt is thin evidence that it

Josephus says that he was fortified in his resolve by a marvelous dream: "A certain one standing over me appeared to say, 'Look, you who are hurting, calm your mind! Let go of all fear! For the matters about which you are now sorrowful will produce greatness and the highest fortune in every respect. You will set right not only these matters, but many others as well. Do not exhaust yourself, but remember you must also make war against the Romans!'" If it can be doubted whether the message came expressly from the Holy One, the dream need not have been wholly fabricated, not least because, in Josephus's usual style, it combines affectations of election with a show of humility. At the same time, the style of his dream, which implies divine empowerment, may owe something to his exposure to Roman culture: in Cicero's *Republic*, Publius Cornelius Scipio is visited in a dream by his distinguished forebear, Scipio Africanus Major. He is promised a great future career as a servant of Rome and protector of its laws, under the governance of the deity who rules the universe.

Since Jotapata's defenses looked sound, Vespasian might yet choose to bypass a strategically negligible township and head straight for Jerusalem. Joseph would then be left with space and time in which to maneuver. Once the now overexcited citizens had seen a major Roman force marching on the city, a change of mood was possible. Should the saner members of the Sanhedrin then be able to reassert comprehensive control, Joseph would be well-placed to act as their plenipotentiary. He

---

was only the sponsorship of the "ruling class" that caused the events of 66 to escalate. Goodman's account requires Josephus consistently to falsify the situation. Yet no one can deny that the Zealots were far more enthusiastic for war than the Sanhedrin. Men such as Simon ben Gioras and John of Gischala were clearly out of sympathy with Joseph ben Mattathias and, we may infer, with his "ruling" social echelon, which the Zealots had always suspected of facing both ways. Goodman remarks that Jesus ben Gamala had assumed strategic command although he had no "military competence." Many figures in ancient warfare had done the same. As Thucydides recounts, one of the greatest victories over the Spartans in the Peloponnesian War was contrived by the demagogic Cleon, a civilian who had previously done nothing, in the military line, except criticize the tactics of Athens' generals.

was hardly a bad Jew if he belonged to those who hoped, quietly, that it was still possible to come to terms with Rome.

Vespasian circled south and advanced on Jotapata from the east. An experienced campaigner knew better than to leave even an amateur general in a position to cut the legions' lines of communication. He had additional reason for hastening slowly: Nero's undignified profligacy was kindling unrest throughout the empire. Provincial governors, notably Vindex, in Gaul, were rumored to be flexing their muscles. Insecurity fed the emperor's paranoia; he was increasingly distrustful of generals with illustrious reputations. It was not a clever time to draw attention to oneself by fighting a lightning campaign, even if the methodical Vespasian was capable of it. He would be wise to husband his resources and boost the cohesion and devotion of his men by small, preferably lucrative, successes.

Jerusalem could wait. Even disciplined troops camped in the open, under the walls of what looked like an impregnable city, were vulnerable to sickness, to shortage of water and forage, and to volleys of spears and arrows from those high on the walls. Sorties were likely to inflict casualties and depress morale. If the legions were stalled, and became dispirited, and if Joseph remained undefeated behind them, he and his men could sally out of Jotapata and begin a Fabian guerrilla war on the Romans' supply lines. He might even rally enough reinforcements to attack the besieging army from behind. Vespasian would then be the one between a rock and a hard place.*

Jotapata was a small nut, but not easy to crack. Its hilltop location made access difficult for heavy siege equipment. The inhabitants—unlike those of bigger cities in Galilee—were all Jews, not short of provisions and solid in determination to defend their faith, their homes

---

* Skeptics who take Josephus's whole narrative to be tendentious camouflage for his preconceived duplicity argue that the Roman commander's excursion to Jotapata has to be explained by his wish to make contact with the traitor. Is it plausible to suppose that Vespasian would have taken time out to stage a bloody charade, which lasted several weeks, in order to validate a cover story that served no diplomatic or military purpose?

and their families. The craggy site could not be undermined. It had no source of fresh water, but there were underground cisterns in which the townspeople stored the winter rainfall, more generous in the first century than in modern times.

It was, however, midsummer. By July, the town's water reserves were drying up. Immediately after Vespasian's siege began, rationing had to be imposed. Within a short while, most of the cisterns were empty. The defenders could draw water only from a single source, within range of enemy spears. Joseph guessed that Vespasian must be hoping that thirst alone would force an early, soft surrender and allow him to move on to Jerusalem. He ordered some of the garrison to soak their outer garments and hang them over the battlements until the walls ran with water. If he could gull the Romans into believing that he had the resources to hold out indefinitely, they might abandon the siege. Alternatively, if frustration hustled Vespasian into an ill-prepared assault, the defenders could hope to inflict heavy enough casualties to make him back away before he lost any more time or men.

Joseph told the garrison that it was quicker and less degrading to die in battle than to perish from thirst; his own hope was to do neither. As a Jerusalem grandee, he had no family links in upper Galilee. His accent and his urbanity were alien. It required distinct nerve and charm for him to assert himself over the rustics and provincials. What he now revealed of his hopes and intentions was no more than what the Jotapatan garrison needed to hear: they should hold firm and wait for Vespasian to lose patience or for the local militias and—it was pious to say—God to come to their help.

Impatience was not Vespasian's vice. His extant portrait bust shows a forehead triply creased with frowning calculation, a wide, thin mouth and the heavily lidded eyes of a man used to looking at things in a disillusioned light. Not to be hurried or provoked, he surrounded Jotapata's jagged site and waited for his siege engines to catch up with the legions.

Joseph found an ingenious way of resupplying the town by night. He sent couriers out via the western side of the valley, down a defile so steep that the Romans felt no need to keep close watch on it. When in sight of the guard posts, the runners were instructed to cover their backs with sheepskins and crawl. In that way they could be mistaken for slinking dogs. This Odyssean ruse enabled Joseph to stay in cursory contact with Jews outside the city and to bring weapons and fresh food, if very little water, back into it.

After a time, the Romans spotted the camouflage and sealed the defile. Until their artillery arrived, Jotapata remained impossible to storm. Meanwhile, its defenders were securely boxed. Almost seven weeks passed in deadlock. As the town was approaching the end of its resources, Joseph proposed to the leading citizens that he, and they, should slip out under cover of night. The notables refused to desert their families. Joseph had got them into their present fix; he was going to stay in it with them. Joseph argued that if he could get away, he would be able to return with sufficient reinforcements to threaten the Romans from the rear and lift the siege. Then again, if Vespasian heard that his most important enemy was no longer in the town, he might well move on and leave them alone. The Jotapatans were unconvinced. Joseph had to yield to their noisy demands that he continue to lead them.

The Romans hauled their siege artillery close enough to be able to catapult large rocks against the walls. The fortifications began to split and crack. Joseph again showed inventive panache: he ordered sacks to be filled with chaff and hung over the most vulnerable sections of the battlements. His outsize pillows baffled the impact of the incoming missiles.* When the Romans moved their artillery to another section of the walls, Joseph anticipated their line of fire and transferred the chaff-filled buffers. Vespasian's men countered him by attaching reaping hooks to long poles and harvesting the sacks. They then brought up a large battering ram and moved in for the clinching assault.

Joseph retrieved his reputation with the notables by leading a sortie of three groups of commandos. Brandishing burning torches, they

---

* Almost two millennia later, in 1776, the soldiers of Charleston, South Carolina, followed his example when they defended their walls against British cannonballs by filling sacks with palmetto branches. Hence the privileged place of the palmetto on the state flag.

scattered the sentries and set fire to the cumbrous Roman siege train. Driven back by flames made fiercer by an amalgam of bitumen, pitch and brimstone, the legionaries are reported to have been "paralyzed by the Jews' astonishing courage."

Josephus makes the scene vivid with another of his close-ups. One of the defenders, Eleazar from Saba in Galilee, is described raising a huge stone and pitching it from the battlements. It traveled with such accurate velocity that it broke off the head of the battering ram. Eleazar then leapt down and seized the broken piece as a trophy. As he toted it back to the walls, his unarmored body was a choice target for Roman spears. Pierced by five of their *pila,* he still managed to climb back onto the wall and stand there for a triumphant moment before falling to the ground in agony, still clutching his prize.

The defenses continued to crumble. Everyone knew what would follow once the Romans broke through. Vespasian had already served the rebellious Judaeans with notice of his ruthlessness: when he took the town of Gabara, which was void of armed defenders, the legionaries slaughtered all the inhabitants except for small children. Local peasants, many noncombatants, were rounded up and sold into slavery. Josephus is frank in saying that, at that early stage of the war, he considered that the one hope of the Jews was "a change of heart. He himself, he was sure, would be pardoned if he went over to the Romans, but he preferred to die rather than betray his motherland." He may have protested too much, but who can challenge his assessment of the military and political situation? He had cruel evidence of Roman intentions: at Japha, near Nazareth, the largest village in Galilee, the local commander, Trajan (the father of the later emperor of the same name), is said to have killed twelve thousand defenders.

When Roman armies did not massacre all the rebellious colonials they met, it was because it was more profitable to take commission on their sale. Along with prostitutes, slave dealers always followed the eagles. Kickbacks fattened the generals and funded bounties for the common soldiers. Their paltry pay encouraged the rank and file to be eager for the bonuses of success. Soldiering offered the lower classes their only form of gambling, apart from knucklebones.

As the legionaries paraded for the clinching assault on Jotapata, they uttered terrifying war cries. Joseph ordered the garrison to cover their ears. Print mutes ancient history's raucous soundtrack (Livy tells of how besieged barbarians were terrified by the crash of missiles, and Tacitus says that the Germans amplified their war cries by using their shields as improvised loudspeakers). The Romans advanced under cover of their regular *testudo:* crouched under their shields, like a rectangular, articulated tortoise. Aware that their composite shell was impervious to spears or rocks, Joseph ordered cauldrons of boiling oil to be tipped from the walls. The seething liquid ran into the cracks between the shields and scalded the assailants. The tortoise disintegrated.

The Romans now mounted gangways to the breach in the walls. Joseph trumped them by having his men spill a soup of boiled fenugreek, a local vegetable of the pea family, onto the narrow, tilted planks. The attackers lost their footing on the slithery mash. Vespasian reverted to standard procedure: slow and steady. Joseph could only watch as the Romans wheeled up their siege towers. Carpenters added platform to platform until they overtopped the walls. As soon as the weakened defenders had no ammunition to impede the assault, the legionaries jumped from the towers onto the battlements and streamed into the town. Panic followed. The enraged Romans took revenge, and loot, wherever they had the chance. A few Jewish sentries slipped away in the darkness. Many Jotapatans still inside the town killed their families and then themselves rather than be enslaved or crucified. In ancient wars there were worse fates than a quick death.

On Vespasian's orders, the Romans conducted an urgent search for the Jewish general. As the legionaries had surged in, Joseph had been able, "by some divine providence," to jump into a deep pit that communicated with a cave invisible at ground level. The local notables must have alerted him to this privileged hiding place. Some fifty of them took refuge in it with him. They remained in undetected seclusion for two days. Then a woman of their company was captured as she tried to slink away from the town. She revealed the inaccessible cavern where Joseph and the others were hiding.

Unable to lay hands on him, Vespasian sent two tribunes, Paulinus and Gallicanus, to Joseph with a promise of safe conduct. The offer did not extend to the Jotapatans in the cave. Joseph replied that he was staying where he was. How could he know what fate was being reserved for him? His decision not to surrender was endorsed, forcibly, by his companions: they promised to kill him if he made any move to get out. The two tribunes went away. Another, called Nicanor, returned to try again. Said to have been "personally known" to Joseph, he was probably a Levantine Greek member of Agrippa's staff. He was authorized to say how much Vespasian admired his opponent's tactics and that the general would like to talk to Joseph. The message was as civil as it appeared sporting: the Roman commander had himself been wounded by an arrow during the assault. Given his routine ruthlessness, Vespasian's insistence must have had a motive more purposeful than chivalry, unless it was uglier.

Joseph was literally in a hole. The Jotapatans were obdurate that he remain in it with them; the legionaries outside were yelling for the whole gang to be "roasted out of the cave." The Roman rank and file had not forgotten, and lacked diplomatic reason to forgive, how Joseph and his crew had basted their comrades with boiling oil. At this point, we are told, Joseph happened to remember some dreams in which "God had warned him of the calamities coming to the Jews and of the fortunes of the Roman emperors." Since he was both a priest and the descendant of priests, he could pass as a plausible recipient of divine messages. He found the nerve to claim that their proper interpretation had only just revealed itself to him. With the Jotapatan elite huddled around him, he spelled it out in a loud prayer to Yahweh; this procured a moment of solemnity that no pious Jew would choose to interrupt.

Joseph's becomingly sanctimonius exegesis was that God was "visiting his wrath on the Jewish people" and that "all prosperity" had passed to the Roman camp. Because Yahweh had selected him personally to "make known the things to come," Joseph had the authority, and the gall, to announce to his companions that he was bound by a transcendental obligation to deliver himself to the Romans, "that I may live, though I solemnly declare that I go, not as a traitor, but as the servant of the Lord."

This portentous reading of his divine duty, in which he mimicked the vatic style of the prophets, was not endorsed by the Jotapatans. They jostled around him, crying that the laws of their fathers, decreed by God Himself, had endowed their race with contempt for death. "Are you so in love with life, Joseph, that you can bear to live as a slave? How quickly you've forgotten yourself! How many did you persuade to lay down their lives for liberty! False, totally false, was the reputation you won for courage and cleverness, if you expect to be let go by those you have hit so hard. Even if their offer is genuine, how can you stoop to accept it? If you have been enchanted by the Roman success, we shall have to be responsible for our people's good name. We'll lend you a sword and a hand to wield it. Die willingly and you die as the commander of the Jews; if not, you die as a traitor."

Their language may be elaborated; its fury rings true. It is also a testimony to Josephus's willingness, as a historian, to spell out the case against his own conduct. Honesty and evasiveness were not incompatible. Somehow he managed to abate the communal anger sufficiently to institute a discussion of whether suicide was incumbent, not only on him, but also on his companions. By a show of erudition, he contrived yet again to pull rank on his provincial audience. However exasperated they were, they listened to him long enough to be bemused, perhaps impressed, by his sophistry. "Why," he asked them, "are we in such a hurry to commit suicide? Why should we make those best of friends, body and soul, part company? I am told that it is a glorious thing to die in battle. Maybe, when it is decreed by the laws of war and we die at the hands of the victors. If I shrink from Roman swords, I deserve to die; but if they are prepared to spare an enemy, how are we not entitled to spare ourselves? It would be absurd to do to ourselves what we have fought to prevent them doing to us. You say that it is glorious to die for freedom. I agree; when it's on the battlefield and at the hands of those who are trying to take freedom from us. But now they are coming neither to do battle nor to kill us."

What fear, Joseph wanted to know, keeps "us" from going up to the Romans? Fear of death? In that case, must Jews, because they fear death at the hands of the enemy, inflict it on themselves? " 'It is a brave act to kill oneself,' another will suggest. No! It's a thoroughly craven act," he said. "I consider that a pilot would be an arrant coward if, through fear of bad weather, he did not wait for the storm to break, but scuttled his own ship instead." After this schoolmasterly, quasi-Platonic analogy, Joseph resumed the sacerdotal mantle. He reminded his rustic congregation of Yahweh's disapproval of suicide: "Of all living things, there is not one that dies on purpose or by its own act; it is an irresistible natural law that all should wish to live. . . . Do you suppose that God is not angry when a man treats His gift with contempt? It is from Him that we have received our existence and it is to Him that we must leave the right to remove it."

By generalizing the question of what "we" should do, if given a chance to stay alive, Joseph diverted attention, and indignation, from the fact that Vespasian's offer of salvation was to him alone. As if everyone in the hiding place had the same choice between life and death, he encouraged the Jotapatan notables to speculate on possibilities not available to them: "If we choose to die, isn't it better that we do so at the hands of our conquerors? I shall not go over to the Romans in order to be a traitor to myself; if I did, I should be even more foolish than those who desert; for such people, desertion means life, but for me it means only death, my own. I pray that the Romans may prove traitors; if after giving me their word, they put me to death, I shall die happy, because I shall find in the broken word of such liars a consolation greater than victory itself."

This pharisaic reversion to self-importance was more than his companions could tolerate. No sooner had Joseph switched back from the plural "we" to his own first-person case than the Jotapatans rushed at him with their swords, crying, "Coward! Coward!" He retained the mental agility and physical poise to box clever. Later, he described the scene using the third person: "He called one by name, glared like a general at another, shook hands with a third, pleaded with a fourth till he was ashamed . . . turning like an animal at bay to face each assailant in turn. At his last gasp, they still respected their commander; their arms lacked energy, their blades glanced off him and many, while thrusting at him with their swords spontaneously lowered their points."

Joseph had obtained another truce, but he was never going to be allowed to get away from them on his own. He claimed later that he put his trust in divine protection. He was too modest to mention any element of cunning in what he now proposed: "Staking his life on one last throw," he informed his companions that, since they were resolved on mass suicide, he agreed to share their fate. He asked only that they accept an orderly and decorous procession to death rather than involve themselves in scenes of clumsy, uncontrolled carnage. It would be more seemly if they all drew lots and then killed each other in numerical order: the first and the second striking each other, and so on down the line as the luck of the draw had determined. "In this way," he said, "no one will have to die by his own hand." Otherwise, he told them, it would be unfair, when the rest were dead, if one man were to change his mind and save his life.

To be accepted, as it was, without suspicion, his proposal must have accorded with tradition. Five years later, the defenders of Masada would adopt a similar rota when they killed each other, to the last man, woman and child. Josephus reports that his companions "swallowed the bait" and allowed him to draw lots with the rest of them. "Life was sweet, but not so sweet as death," they told each other—especially when their commander was going to die with them.

Whatever the precise method by which lots were drawn, Joseph evidently presided over the procedure. Whether by "divine providence," as *The Jewish War* puts it, or by dexterous manipulation, he himself just happened to draw a number that would leave him alive with only one other man, after all the rest of the party had honored the rites of mutual extinction. Joseph ben Mattathias watched as, when their numbers came up, one after another of the pairs of Jotapatan notables, men and women, stabbed each other. The serial killing must have taken some time. The blood and stench and the cries and groans of the dying filled the bunker.

The tight pit was thick with corpses until it was the last pair's turn to follow their companions in mutual slaughter. The Romans were clustered above them. Joseph now suggested to the single other survivor that they should spare each other. He remained a captain who saw little virtue in going down with his ship. He also had the pious nerve to claim that he did not wish to "stain his hand with the blood of a fellow Jew."* Joseph's proposal was accepted gladly by his fellow survivor. A short time later, "having come safely through two wars—one with the Romans and one with his own people"—Joseph ben Mattathias was being escorted through the Roman lines by his friend Nicanor.

---

* It may be that a Pharisaic priest could be trusted to come up with a timely taboo, but it would be undue cynicism to accuse Joseph of insincerity in recoiling from shedding the blood of his kin. His reluctance to kill himself is of a piece with this: self-killing can also be seen as a form of pollution. Jewish and Greek ideas are compatible on this topic. Richard Seaford points out that in Plato's *Laws* (873c), "suicide is discussed immediately after kin-killing, as it kills the nearest and dearest of all." If there is one undeniable consistency in Joseph ben Mattathias's personal history, it is that he never actually killed another Jew, although he certainly manhandled quite a few of them with tactical ferocity. There is no reason to doubt that he was genuinely appalled by the Zealots' eagerness to slaughter other Jews. Few Romans ever showed an equivalent reluctance.

VIII

LEGIONARIES HURRIED TO SEE the barbarian captive. Was his beard fair or dark? Was he tall or short? What was he wearing? The common soldiers were more than curious: they were hot for revenge. Josephus implies that their officers were less vindictive than impressed by the prisoner's bearing; but then they had taken no part in the *testudo*. Was he defiant or was he careful to avoid his enemies' eyes? His walk required a calculated performance, the head held just so. To seem calm and otherworldly was a literally vital cosmetic. Exemplary execution was still his likeliest fate, probably by crucifixion, but only after he had been tortured, at length. The emperor Caligula cannot have been the only Roman to tell the *carnifices* whose profession it was to torture the condemned, "Make him feel he is dying."*

How could Joseph not imagine jeers and cheers as the lead-loaded lash flayed him before the nails were hammered in? There was no natural, no casual way of living his situation. He must have wondered whether the notables of Jotapata had not taken the easier course. The claim that he was doing the Lord's work had been a plausible excuse

---

* The Nazis were to be adept in that department. In 1941, in the old Jewish quarter of Amsterdam, a band of Dutch Jews attacked a German security police detachment. In Hannah Arendt's words, from *Eichmann in Jerusalem,* "Four hundred and thirty Jews were arrested in reprisal and they were literally tortured to death, first in Buchenwald and then in . . . Mauthausen. For months on end they died a thousand deaths. . . . There exist many things considerably worse than death, and the SS saw to it that none of them was ever very far from their victims' minds and imaginations."

for his breach of faith with the Jotapatans; with the Romans, it would be a necessity, if only he could work it. Was he a hypocrite? In Greek, *hypokrites* meant "actor."* In that sense, he had to be one. What role suited the venue better than that of the messenger of Yahweh, the singular god of the Jews? Joseph ben Mattathias was born for the part of the robed and bearded priest with a divine annunciation to deliver. Truth and imposture dwelt on the same page.

Vespasian's son Titus was a young man in his early twenties, an apprentice in the butchery business. He is reported to have admired Joseph's "courageous attitude" and to have been filled with sympathy for his "youth." A good actor can attract admiration by inducing others to imagine themselves in his place. However, the original order to take the enemy commander alive has to have been Vespasian's. "Clemency" had become the characteristic attribute of Roman leaders, if a prisoner was important enough to merit its exercise. Julius Caesar had been the first to vaunt his willingness to show mercy to vanquished opponents. He was less quick to advertise that he did so in a civil war that he himself had started. In 46 B.C.E., Marcus Porcius Cato,† when besieged in the city of Utica, in North Africa, chose to fall on his sword rather than to accept a patronizing offer of mercy from the dictatorial Julius.

A century after Cato's suicide, when Nero came to the throne, Seneca—first his tutor and now his prime counselor—presented him with an essay in which *clementia* was recommended as the most desirable form of princely grace. There was much to be said (a speciality of

---

* One of its primary meanings is "interpreter," which chimes sweetly with Joseph's performance both with his fellow Jews and, in due time, with the Romans.

† Some Romans regarded the younger Cato as a martyr; others, as a prig. Dante made him a sentinel in Purgatory. As Erich Auerbach put it in *Mimesis,* Cato "stands for the guardian of the eternal freedom of the elect in a place where we are astonished to find a pagan." Nero's brightest poetic protégé, the precocious Lucan, portrayed Cato as the hero of his unfinished epic, *Pharsalia.* The tagline *"Victrix causa deis placuit, sed victa Catoni"* (The Gods favored a winning cause, but Cato a lost one) was a taut obituary on the man whose noble suicide Lucan himself was required to emulate, in 65, at the age of twenty-five, at the command of his onetime friend the emperor.

Seneca's) for encouraging the new prince not to wallow in blood. During the course of his reign, however, Nero's pleasures soon included the extinction of those irksome to him. His only vestige of clemency came in the suggestion that his erstwhile friends kill themselves before things got really nasty. Mercy did, however, remain the emperor's unique prerogative. When Josephus attributed his own survival to the *clementia* of Titus and Vespasian, he was implying that each of them was—in the words of the sardonic Tacitus—*"capax imperii,"* capable of being an emperor. The ascription of clemency to the young Titus may have been a retrospective grace. Josephus's descriptions of Titus's behavior during the campaign suggest that moderation came to him late, if at all.

In the Roman camp, in chains among angry enemies, Joseph had something in common with another isolated Jew almost two millennia later. The French Jewish soldier, Alfred Dreyfus, after he had been falsely accused of treason, was described by the gloating Catholic writer Maurice Barrès as "alone in the universe." At the moment of his public disgrace, when his sword was broken and his captain's epaulets ripped off, Dreyfus adopted an air of stoic resignation. In private he raved and banged his head against his cell wall. Yet he was determined to endure. So was Joseph; but he was no falsely accused scapegoat. He might be somewhat admired by his enemies; he was sure to be condemned by his friends.

By his decision not to die in that cavern in Jotapata, Joseph made himself exceptional. He was now alone as no Jew had ever been before, not even the shorn and captive Samson, "eyeless in Gaza, at the mill with slaves." In Roman custody, committed to continual improvisation, Joseph could not afford to seem either afraid or arrogant. He had to maintain the aura of a sacrosanct prize. His account says nothing of his private feelings. He could scarcely afford them. He was now like a poker player; his concentration had to be on the play of the next card. The odds were still stacked against him. He was kept in irons, under tight guard. Did some of the legionaries hold out their arms and loll their heads in mimic crucifixion? There is no proof that they did; small likelihood that they did not. Not smiling, not wincing, not pleading, not provoking, and ignoring provocation, Joseph had to endure. Baiting the Jew general might be one more spectator sport; but the fate of an enemy commander was a matter only for the emperor. In the same monopolizing spirit, no matter which of his generals had actually won the victory, by Nero's time only the emperor himself could enjoy a triumph and ride in glory through the streets of Rome. The sole national hero in imperial Rome had to be Caesar himself. Vespasian was too seasoned a campaigner not to be aware that under a jealous autocrat, nothing failed like conspicuous success.*

The author of *The Jewish War* gives the impression that Joseph ben Mattathias was at first saved from immediate death so that Vespasian might send him as a present to the emperor. Since the Roman commander had gone out of his way to pluck him alive from the ruins of Jotapata, it remains possible that he had been advised both of Joseph's intelligence and of his utility as a go-between. But if Vespasian was keen to meet and talk to him, why was the prisoner kept incommunicado and in chains for several days? Joseph may have been hoping, or even have been promised, that a ransom would be offered for his release. His father was a rich man in Jerusalem. In any case, calm reserve was his best line. Collaboration would seem more valuable if not promptly volunteered.

On the other hand, if the general was keen for Joseph's cooperation, and Joseph reluctant to offer it, Vespasian may have had it relayed to him that rendition to Nero was imminent. Such a threat would explain Joseph's next reported move: a request for a private word with his principal captor. The way in which it was pitched, and received, hints that

---

* In recent years, Gnaeus Domitius Corbulo, a veteran commander of genius, had accumulated more victories than Nero cared to applaud. Corbulo had already faced a similar problem in 47 C.E., when the emperor Claudius felt upstaged by his successes in Germany. Even then Corbulo was rumored to have commented, "Roman generals were lucky in the old days" (when glory had led to fame and fortune). In October 66, the great general was summoned to the emperor's presence at Cenchreae, in Greece. He was greeted by Nero as "benefactor" and "father." Soon afterward, his master invited him to commit suicide. Vespasian's younger son, Domitian, later married Corbulo's daughter Domitia.

Vespasian may have been hoping for some kind of confidential disclosure. As soon as Joseph had been escorted into his quarters, the general ordered everyone except his son Titus and two other officers to leave.

Whatever the Romans expected, it cannot have been what their captive now chose to say: "You imagine that, by capturing me, you have merely secured a prisoner."[1] If he was as calculating as he needed and knew how to be, Joseph spoke softly, but with unhurried clarity. A quiet voice impels even important listeners to lean forward, attentively. Sacerdotal solemnity and theatrical flair* surely modulated Joseph's diction. The only version we have of his words is in the Greek of *The Jewish War*. There is no evidence that he ever spoke or wrote fluent Latin. The Romans are unlikely to have understood Aramaic. So the Jew probably spoke to them in Koine. Both sides were playing away from home.

As he describes things, Joseph was bold enough to contradict his conqueror before, it seems, he had spoken a word. "No, sir," he said. "No, I come as a messenger of the greatness that awaits you." Was he looking directly at Vespasian and Titus or did he stare blankly, a man entranced, with the divine afflatus upon him? Either way, his good news held their attention. He had no need to gabble. The Romans were waiting on his words. He had managed, in a few seconds, to become less a suppliant than a dispenser of supernatural favors. "Had I not been sent by God Himself," he told them, "I should have known the Jewish law and how a general ought to die."

The implication was that angelic duty alone had forced him to transcend a soldier's obligation to suicide. Who in the tent could have guessed how desperately he had argued to the contrary when in that pit in Jotapata? Once out of it, Joseph ben Mattathias had to become an improvised man: someone who expected to be watched and listened to, by himself not least. From the moment when he crossed the lines,

---

* The 1920s Broadway producer-director Jed Harris, whose original name was Jacob Hirsch Horowitz, always gave "notes" to his cast in an oracular whisper, the better to concentrate their attention.

he had committed himself to being a *performer.* No longer a Jew among Jews, he was conditioned by his alien audience: it played with him; he played to it. He was, in a literal and a theatrical sense, cast among strangers.

The egotist has to be his own writer and his own producer. Like Sir Walter Raleigh,* when he was living on his nerves, at daily risk of disgrace and execution, Joseph had to tack according to every circumstance, and yet be lucid enough to steer through the rough water. Closeted with Vespasian, Joseph assumed the lineaments of a sacred herald. As if on the tragic stage, he played the seer, a makeshift Tiresias, whose oracular magic the general would be well advised to reserve for himself. It is too modern a cynicism to assume that Joseph never believed that the divine grace was on him; as with a method actor, reaching into his own experience to flesh his imposture, a tincture of that belief would lend conviction to his performance. Romans, however hardheaded, were rarely immune to dread of the supernatural content of dreams.†

The most pressing thing on Joseph ben Mattathias's mind must have been the fear of rendition. He confronted the threat immediately. Taking the issue out of his captor's hands, he added it to his own armory: "Do you mean to send me to Nero? What for? How long will Nero and those who succeed him remain on the throne before your turn comes?" Josephus's narrative implies a pause. The reader can imagine a close-up of Vespasian's tough face: those heavily lidded eyes and that tight mouth. When he failed to stop Joseph at that point, the general's

---

* Raleigh also became a striker of attitudes, playing the madman and the courtier, the advocate and the gambler, as occasion required; and at the last he too became a historian, surveying mankind from a lonely, doomed eminence. As he put his head on the block, his last words to the executioner with the axe—"Strike, man, what do you fear?"—remain unrivaled among exit lines.

† In the reign of Claudius, the ex-consul Appius Junius Silanus was sentenced to death after the emperor's third (but not last) wife, Messalina, and his powerful freedman Narcissus both reported dreams that he was plotting against the emperor. In 60, Nero had been alarmed by a comet that, it was thought, signified a change of regime. Vespasian is said by Tacitus to be "not untouched by superstition." The stars in their courses were commonly assumed to have breaking news for great men.

silence promised more than curiosity. Did he recall the story of how Seneca—when confident of his position—had had the nerve and wit to tell the young Nero that, however many people a prince might kill, there was always one man he could never kill: his successor? And did Joseph ben Mattathias see himself as his mythical namesake, the son of Jacob whose interpretation of Pharaoh's dream put him on the way to being the Egyptian ruler's privy counselor?

Joseph staked everything on the insolence of his last question. In that silent second, during which Vespasian could, and should, have forbidden his prisoner even to suggest the possibility of anyone succeeding Nero, the general became complicit with what followed: "You, Vespasian, are Caesar and emperor, you and your son here. Load me with your heaviest chains and keep me for yourself. You are master not only of me, Caesar, but of land and sea and the whole human race."

Now what? Joseph's next words conveyed both a captive's deference and the sanctity of a divine herald. "I ask only to be held in closer confinement if I am taking the name of God in vain." The corollary was that if they believed him, he should be well treated. Whether or not Joseph truly thought that he was divinely inspired, he had bet his life on seeming that he did. Whatever its source, his prediction was calculated to spring an ambition which, Joseph ben Mattathias had the wit to guess, was latent in Vespasian's thoughts. Playing the part of the Jewish priest, he was to the victorious proconsul what Macbeth's witches were to the thane of Cawdor. Yet Jerusalem was not yet captured. Although he had taken a brave part in Claudius's conquest of Britain, Vespasian had no great pedigree or military genius. Joseph's oracular prediction was based on a small victory in a petty province. Its precision about the timing of Vespasian's accession may be the historian's later embellishment,* but what other than its appealing plausibil-

---

* As reported by himself, Joseph was so exact in his prophecy that he warned Vespasian that he would not be Nero's immediate successor. In the event, three other brief reigns—those of Galba, Otho and Vitellius—would indeed precede Vespasian's, in what came to be known as the Year of the Four Emperors. If that detail is not an a posteriori addition by Josephus, it must have been happy news for the general to be told that he would be the last of the quartet.

ity can explain how he came to be recruited to the general's personal circle? Joseph had contrived to become an instant lucky charm.

In the good old days of the republic, Vespasian might have been content with the steady rewards of a routine military career, but in Nero's reign, Joseph ben Mattathias and Titus Flavius Vespasianus had one vital thing in common: neither could safely play safe. Rome had been the scene of an extensive conspiracy just over a year before. The aristocratic Calpurnius Piso was a worthy candidate for the purple, but lacked the steel to grasp it. When detected, Piso committed suicide to avoid execution and his family's loss of their property; but the extent of the conspiracy convinced Nero of the innate treachery of the senatorial establishment.*

Vespasian's willingness even to listen to his prisoner's words was tantamount to treason. As soon as Joseph's divination was not greeted with outrage, his all-or-nothing gamble had paid off. He now had something over his conqueror: what Vespasian had not said and not done. Whatever happened, Joseph was never going to be sent alive to Nero. It was vital that the Judaean priest be given no chance to transmit to Nero his divinely sourced prediction that Vespasian was destined for the purple. Nothing would be more certain to render it void. Vespasian had become his captive's captive.

---

* His suspicions were also aroused against the three greatest writers of his court: Lucan, Seneca and Petronius Arbiter. For Petronius, aristocrat, satirist and dilettante, living well was not so much the best revenge as a form of disdain; nothing surprised him. Only Lucan was directly, and proudly, involved with Piso; but all three littérateurs were candidates for Nero's jealousy. A talent to amuse or instruct might be a way into imperial favor, but too quick a wit or too aloof a philosophy could lead to abrupt exits. Seneca may have known of Piso's conspiracy but played no active part. A dramatist no less than a Stoic, he took the opportunity to lower his own curtain with theatrical solemnity. His brother, L. Julnius Gallio Annaeus, was the governor of Greece (Saint Paul had appeared before him) and had warmed up the audience while Nero was doing his gigs there. He too was invited to kill himself, as a precaution against fraternal loyalty. Roman political tactics were close to those of the Mafia. The domestic scene was littered with excellent cadavers. For the ruling prince, the world was *cosa nostra*.

The twentieth-century Alexandrian poet Constantine Cavafy wrote an ironic poem in which Nero is warned by the Delphic oracle, "Beware the age of seventy-three." Since Nero was thirty years old (of an age with Joseph ben Mattathias), he concluded that he still had plenty of time. But, as Cavafy is pleased to recall, Nero's immediate successor, Servius Sulpicius Galba, was an old man of seventy-three. Another of Cavafy's poems tells of how "the gods abandoned Antony" at the time of his great love affair with Cleopatra (it advises Antony not to complain but to accept that his lease is up). This myth has an echo in Josephus: he says that, months before the destruction of the Temple, strange voices were heard saying, "We are departing from here." The tendentious Alexandrian Origen is quick to interpret them to be those of the angels who supervised Temple worship. As a Christian he took their departure to be a symptom of Yahweh's abandonment of the Jews and Judaism.

The Holy One's writing on the wall had been less ambiguous when it presaged the doom of Belshazzar. In the Book of Daniel, as Josephus would remember, Nebuchadnezzar saw a statue with a golden head, a torso of silver and brass, iron legs and feet partly of iron, partly of clay. When the statue was struck by a rock, its anatomy was quartered. The rock itself became a mountain. Daniel had interpreted this as meaning that there would be four successive earthly powers before the coming of the eternal kingdom. During these convulsions, whatever mayhem was in store, the centrality of the Jews in the divine scheme was not in question.

In the dream Josephus reported to Vespasian, Yahweh announced that He intended to bestow dominion on a Gentile conqueror. Vespasian might have shrugged if Joseph had threatened him with Yahweh's anger, but the news of divine backing was easy to take.* Joseph's ver-

---

* According to romantic legend, Alexander the Great had been similarly grati-fied when the priests of Ammon at Siwah, an oasis in the remote Egyptian desert that he visited in disguise, "recognized" him as the son of the god whom Alexander identified with Zeus. Maurice Sartre reports, in *D'Alexandre à Zénobie,* that while

sion of events was, at a stretch, consistent with his ancestral faith: God favored Jews when they honored His Commandments, but chastened them when they did not. Perhaps because he wrote a secular account of the war, and in an alien language, Josephus's work represented Yahweh in world-historical costume, the emperor's emperor. After due adjustment, the cap of a universal and eternal God would fit neatly on the head of the single, august sovereign of the temporal world. The notion of *translatio imperii*—the passage of power by God's will—and hence of the divine right of kings became an axiom of Western thought* until, in the Enlightenment, the people's will displaced that of a personal god or monarch.

Josephus was the first Jew to offer an overview of the world's history and evolution that was not Judeocentric. In his wake, Yahweh would be deconstructed, through the centuries, by a series of Jewish intellectuals, some religious, many not. A suite of competitive analyses generated schemes of redemption,† in this world if not in the next. Visions

---

Alexander was passing through Palestine, he became affronted when the Jewish High Priest Yaddous denied him the tribute that had been paid to Darius III. However, he was placated after Yaddous came out of Jerusalem to meet him. The conquering king prostrated himself (deference and condescension often use the same currency) and was rewarded with the promise that he would remain the lord of Asia. Alexander then sponsored sacrifices in Yaddous's name and enrolled a body of Jewish soldiers. Some were later disciplined for refusing to build a temple to Marduk, in Babylon, but Alexander reprieved them.

* The British assumption of the imperial mantle was signaled not only by the acquisition of colonies but also by Gibbon's translation of Roman history into one of the glories of English literature and by the transfer of the Parthenon marbles to London. The Church of England, its liturgy and hymns, made God very close to the ideal English gentleman. In his role as the ubiquitous referee, Yahweh has never quite been evicted from the world's game: Einstein was more Jewish than Greek when he said that God "does not play dice" with the universe.

† In private correspondence, Zuleika Rodgers has pointed out that, in earlier Hebrew texts, "the presentation of Cyrus as God's anointed or 'mashiach,' [after] he brought about the return of the exile and the destruction of the first temple, revealed a somewhat similar world view." There is, in my opinion, a difference: Cyrus was glorified by the Jews because, thanks to the Holy One, his actions were central to their restitution in Palestine and to their future prosperity. Josephus's salute to Vespasian

of universal truth, culminating in Marxism, divinized History itself, which became a godless theodicy in which logic or "the dialectic" held inexorable, impersonal sway. Aristotle and Hegel supplied accelerant additives to the mixture that fueled History's course. The desire for an overarching logic that applies to everything is often said to be the legacy of Greek "science"; but the appetite for universal rules, and the belief that they can be divined by human intelligence, is an aspect of the Judaism that Joseph never abandoned.

One of the two Roman officers at the meeting did show himself skeptical of Josephus's capacity to read the future. If the prisoner had prophetic powers, why had he not warned the men of Jotapata that the town would be taken or foreseen that he himself would be captured? Might he not have saved them all a lot of trouble? Joseph replied that he had, in fact, predicted the fall of the town after forty-seven days, and also that he himself would be taken alive (which conveyed the sly suggestion that his surrender honored the will of a Higher Being). Vespasian is said to have questioned other prisoners, who confirmed the prediction. If one of them was Joseph's surviving companion, seconding his savior was the least he could do.

Joseph's assertion that he had fought on although he knew that Jotapata was doomed was less out of keeping with ancient logic than the Roman officer had implied. Stoics such as Seneca took the view that individuals supplied their own lives with meaning by their capacity to endure reversals of fortune with equanimity. Knowledge of coming disaster did not absolve an individual from the need to do his duty; even if the future was inevitable, no human being could be sure what it was. Therefore men should act in accordance with reason, not truth, which only the gods know. Heidegger's notion of "living toward death" modernized Seneca's glum resignation. Seneca had argued, at length, that life was a test with no prizes other than a man's capacity to endure

announced the imminent displacement of the Jews as God's favorites, a prediction that, by the time Josephus was writing his history, had been verified by the destruction of Jerusalem and the Second Temple.

it with dignity. In his *Letters to Lucilius,* he repeated that suicide was the one freedom that no tyranny could deny him. The elaboration of Seneca's arguments suggests that he wished that he found them more of a comfort. Suicide was an emergency exit that Joseph, unlike the philosopher, did not elect to take.*

* The French sociologist Émile Durkheim (1858–1917) discovered the suicide rate among Jews to be lower than that among the rest of the population; persistence against the odds appeared to be a function of their sufferance. There has yet to be a convincing account, if there can ever be one, of why concentration camp survivors— Primo Levi, Piotr Rawicz, Paul Celan among the most renowned—seem often to have "waited" for many years before taking their own lives. That they suffered from "survivor's guilt" is too glib (and too general) an explanation. Each case had a specific etiology: Levi seems to have been possessed by a foreboding that Holocaust denial would render his patient witness futile; Celan, to have been pushed to the limit by a painful love affair.

IX

For Joseph, the good news was that Vespasian had taken his bait, with some pleasure; the less good was that the Roman general's prisoner was a witness to the ambition he had kindled. He had become a real and present danger to his captor. To stay alive, he had to combine discretion with proof that he could be of further use. His own narrative says nothing to this effect; but it was manifest in his conduct. If the Flavians were disposed to leniency, one of the reasons had to be superstitious respect for a man apparently privy to the future plans of the strange, solitary God whose mandate he had transmitted to them.

It would be surprising if Joseph was not aware of the similarities of his situation with that of his biblical namesake, and if he did not somewhat glory in them. Even before he went over to the Romans, Joseph ben Mattathias paraded his distinction from Judaeans who lacked his intellectual and diplomatic education. Although he never alludes to it, the future traveler and versatile historian had been given a name illustrious in Jewish history. Did the original Joseph inspire him to keep calm in the face of important aliens? He must have known, from his earliest years as a student of the Torah, how the precocious son of the patriarch Jacob was said, in Exodus, to have exasperated his eleven brothers, not least by boasting of a dream in which they all bowed down to him. On a trip to the desert, they planned to dump him down a well, but then reprieved him only in order to sell him to a caravan of Ishmaelites, for twenty pieces of silver. The Arab traders transported their smart purchase into Egypt and sold him into slavery.

The young Joseph's renowned "coat of many colors" may be a mistranslation of the original Hebrew, but it flags his ability to be all things, or as many as necessary, to all men. Camouflage and ostentation, mimicry and versatility go together. Like Joseph ben Mattathias, the archetypal Joseph had a knack of making a favorable impression on important persons. As a slave in Egypt, the son of Jacob attracted the sexual overtures of his master Potiphar's wife. When he denied her, she accused him of attempted rape. Joseph was thrown into prison, where two Egyptian officials, who had been locked up with him, told him their dreams. He interpreted them with such pre-Freudian acuteness that when Pharaoh himself had a disturbing dream, one which his counselors were unable or afraid to decode, the smart young Hebrew was summoned to supply an explanation. With nothing to lose, Joseph could afford to tell Pharaoh that the royal dream about the seven fat cows and the seven skinny ones implied that seven years of plenty would be followed by seven "lean" years. During the latter period, the Nile would fail to flood broadly enough to irrigate the fields that, for centuries, would make Egypt one of the fattest granaries of the Mediterranean world. The young prisoner's lucidity led Pharaoh to recruit him as his plenipotentiary with the task of averting the recession he had forecast.* He evidently did so with astonishing success.

As a result of Egypt's cleverly contrived surplus, Joseph's brothers trekked there to buy corn. Brought into the grand vizier's intimidat-

---

* Joseph straddled two worlds, as did countless Jews of talent or genius who administered the affairs of non-Jewish overlords. Such Jews included Samuel ibn Nagrela, the eleventh-century vizier of the Muslim king Badis in the triune city of Granada; "court Jews" such as Joseph Süss Oppenheimer in eighteenth-century Württemberg; Bismarck's banker, Gerson Bleichröder; and Walther Rathenau, who, during the Great War of 1914–18, served the kaiser with technocratic and managerial flair (emulated by Albert Speer when he presided over the Nazi war effort from 1942 to 1945). As German foreign minister in 1922, Rathenau was murdered by those who claimed that "the Jews" had stabbed Germany in the back in 1918. In 1897, he had published an anonymous but "notorious" pamphlet, which, according to Susan Tegel (*Jew Süss*), called on German Jews to "cast off all vestiges of oriental customs and appearance."

ing presence, they failed, of course, to recognize him. There followed a twist echoed in countless plots in Attic comedy and Hellenistic novels. Perhaps as a result of a "joke" contrived by Joseph himself, Benjamin—the youngest of the dozen brothers whose names were later attached to the twelve tribes of Israel—was accused of stealing a "magic" cup belonging to the brother he had failed to recognize. In fact, it had been slipped into his luggage on Joseph's instructions. His motive is not specified. It could have had many colors: furtive generosity that was also an accusation; a parting gift that would allow his brothers to be detained; a means of reminding his brothers that they had better bow down to him now. Benjamin's brother Judah defended the accused so forcefully that Joseph was moved to reveal who he was. That may have been his intention all along. He was as merciful to his brothers as they had been heartless to him.

The whole family, including the old patriarch Jacob,* is said to have migrated to Egypt. They were the first of many. The immigrants, traditionally known as "Hebrews," were at first welcome in Egypt because of their affinity with Joseph. However, their security depended on his sustained ascendancy. Lines of stress recur in Jewish history between those who find high, if precarious, favor with Gentile potentates, and other Jews, without rare qualities. When the grandees lost favor, they were powerless to protect whoever had relied on their patronage. Harold Bloom wrote of "the unhappy dialectic of Jewish existence whereby the Jews of exile perpetually sought everywhere an alliance with the ruling powers, thus further provoking the hatred of the masses."[1]

Even before the Hebrews adopted Judaism, a pattern of dependence and vulnerability was stamped on their history by numerical inferiority and, after they reached Canaan, by geographical location. Any search for some innate psychological inability to assimilate or to ape the supposed civility of their hosts is superfluous. Their allegiance to a singular deity, if diagnosed as a pragmatic detail, rather than as the fruit of rev-

---

* When Jacob died, his embalmed body was sent with an escort of Egyptian chariots and cavalry, and an honor party of dignitaries, to be buried in the cave of Machpelah in Canaan, "the land of his fathers."

elation, suggests the wanderers' need for a supreme and unifying "ruling power" whose benevolence might be trusted, provided always that His people deferred to His ordinances (it is tempting, as Nietzsche did, to call their devotion "slavish"). The consequences of fidelity to Yahweh would prove as ironic as any mythographer might wish.

According to Exodus, Joseph's patron was succeeded by a pharaoh who "knew not Joseph." As a result, the status of Joseph's clients—the entire Hebrew population of Egypt—was imperiled. By that time, on the hinge of the fourteenth and thirteenth centuries B.C., the surge of Hebrew immigrants was felt as a threat to the local population. The new pharaoh, Seti I, then distanced himself from the conspicuous alien who had rectified Egypt's finances. To adapt Descartes's phrase, the ivy was threatening to grow taller than the tree. The foreignness of the Hebrews made it plausible to accuse all of them, including Joseph, of commerce with Egypt's dangerous neighbors, the Hyksos.

Oppression and enslavement followed. The worse the indigenous Egyptians treated the Jews, the more they overestimated the immigrants' numbers. A plan was mooted to drown all male Hebrews at birth. According to the Torah, this form of culling was turned on the Egyptians: their own firstborns were struck down by the hand of the deity who, shortly afterward, would declare Himself to Moses on Mount Sinai and recruit the errant Hebrews into His chosen people.

Although he never rivals the place Moses occupies in Jewish mythology, the original Joseph is designated as "the righteous" by the rabbinic tradition (as it was revised after the fall of Jerusalem). He alone, however, of Jacob's known sons, never lent his name to one of the tribes of Israel. Perhaps he was suspected of being too congenial with foreigners. However, the great polymath encyclopedist Louis Jacobs says that in the Kabbalah (the collection of glosses on sacred texts that began to be compiled in the twelfth century), Joseph stands for the *Sefirah* of *Yesod*, "foundation," the source of all cosmic energy, represented by the organ of generation in the human body, the place of circumcision and the covenant. Hence Joseph and every male who is sexually pure is known as a "guardian of the covenant."

The "coat of many colors," which folklore insists that Joseph the son of Jacob chose to sport, advertised his want of modesty. A High Priest's robes had to be whiter than white, just as his person had to be immune from deformity. Joseph's patchwork wardrobe suggests the volatility of his character. That he should become a master of the Egyptian language and double as a senior functionary of an alien, often hostile country is proof both of his diplomatic skills and of the versatility that enemies could read as opportunism.

Did the story of the original Joseph influence Joseph ben Mattathias's conception of himself? In addition to his capacity for playing many roles, in a variety of costumes, Josephus resembled his biblical namesake in priding himself on his sexual restraint. He too had distinguished origins, showed precocious intelligence, was ill-used (so he insists) by his own people, escaped death by a ruse, and was promoted by an alien prince whose future he forecast, from a dream of his own that he claimed contained a message from God Himself. The validity of his interpretation was established, even in foreign eyes, by his credentials as a priest with prophetic provenance.

Joseph the son of Mattathias too came to enjoy a somewhat favored life in consequence of services rendered to a culture that was not his own. Both Josephs had individuality pressed on them by circumstance. Both had, in a way, been flung into a hole in the ground, from which they were lucky to escape; the first because his brothers' greed trumped their malice, the second by his own agility. Sustained by singular intelligence, both were distinguished by their resilient opportunism. But while Joseph the son of Jacob occupies an honored, central place in the catalog of Hebrew lore* (he was never a practicing Jew, since his life was over before Moses enrolled the Hebrews in the covenant that would bind them into one people under one God), Joseph the son of Mattathias has uneasy standing in Jewish esteem.

---

* Saladin, the great Saracen leader who defeated the Crusaders at the Battle of Hattin, in 1187, and went on to capture Jerusalem, was—according to Anne-Marie Eddé's 2011 biography—regularly compared to "Yusuf," who features in the Quran as "the embodiment of wisdom and righteousness, and as a person who found success in Egypt."

Titus and his father presented their prize with clean clothes and other "valuable gifts." Defeated generals can be flattering company. Joseph ben Mattathias may not have eaten with his captors (their diet was not his),* but he interested and perhaps amused or instructed them. If he was now in a lonely limbo, it was a limbo with cushions. Had he died in Jotapata, history would have had small occasion to remember Joseph ben Mattathias. Having contrived his own salvation, he was able to observe and annotate the disasters that, over the next five years, would overwhelm his compatriots. Parole allowed him to gain firsthand material for the single source on which all accounts of the war in Judaea have had to rely.

He gives no indication of when it came into his mind, or was suggested to him, that he should be the chronicler of his people's fate. There is no evidence that he undertook any literary work until after he crossed the lines and joined Vespasian's camp. All clever young men in Jerusalem learned to read. The best and the brightest became conspicuous by their argumentative acumen in Temple seminars; but there is no record of secular literature during the Second Temple period, nor of any poetry that was not liturgical.† After Joseph ben Mattathias was transfigured into T. Flavius Josephus, and enrolled as a trumpeter for the Flavian dynasty, he became the first of a long line of fluent Jewish commentators and journalists for whom social, political and historical punditry offered a way both of rising above their particular condition and of making names for themselves. Revised nomenclature came to be a common career move among Jews who figured in Gentile societies, from Flavius Josephus to Isaac Babel and Leon Trotsky. The latter's *History of the Russian Revolution* offered a supposedly dispassionate version

---

* In the Second World War, after the Battle of El Alamein, the British general Bernard Montgomery invited his defeated adversary, the German Panzer general Wilhelm Ritter von Thoma, to a desert dinner in his caravan. When this antique courtesy provoked indignation back in London, Winston Churchill defused it by remarking, "Poor von Thoma! I too have dined with Montgomery." Churchill's favorite form of sustenance, alcohol, was banned from the general's table.

† The Song of Solomon is the exception that highlights the rule.

of the events in which he played a leading part, before he was arraigned by Stalin as the Judas of the Communist myth.

In time, Joseph both enhanced and compromised his individuality by putting his pen at the service of Roman masters. They encouraged him to garnish what he knew in a form that advanced their standing. In Josephus's Greek account of the Jewish War, young Titus assumes some of the allure of the legendary and divinized Alexander, the first man to take his own embedded historian, Callisthenes, with him on his conquering travels. As Josephus must have known, when Callisthenes presumed to differ with Alexander, the vainglorious master of the world had him killed. Josephus was able to smuggle brutal truths about the conduct of the legions into his history only by appearing to excuse those who commanded them. His art concealed more than art. To call him a traitorous collaborator underrates his subtlety and simplifies his practice.

He was more devious than a turncoat—and more consistent. Without some measure of slyness, how could he have told as much of the truth as he did? Faced with an alien, often contemptuous audience, he was under the patronage of men whose indulgence could never be taken for granted. Nero had killed the best writers of his time out of jealousy. Later, under the Flavians, even well-born, native Roman historians could be put to death merely for adopting an independent tone. Tacitus tells of a certain Maternus who, during the reign of Vespasian, hurriedly rewrote his life of Cato, the champion of the republic, after a public recital of the text had been greeted as implying a slur on the principate; the laughs, it may be, came too easily. The fact that posterity has read with some ease between Josephus's lines is more of a credit to his artfulness than scholarly detectives are in the habit of conceding.

From the moment he devised a way not to share the fate of the other defenders of Jotapata, Joseph was alone. Isolated from other Jews, he was sentenced to life in the solitary confinement of his own memories and reactions. After the war was over, and spoils were being distributed, Vespasian rewarded him with estates in Judaea; but Josephus never visited them. He was safer in the company, and service, of the Romans.

Despite his new citizenship, however, he was never one of them; nor could he ever again be what he was before. To himself, he remained a Jew; to his surviving compatriots, a pariah.

For almost four years while Joseph was in Titus's company in Judaea, he had to witness massacres in which thousands of Jews were slaughtered, thousands more sold into slavery. Like Bertolt Brecht's Mother Courage, forced to look on the corpse of her son and to react as if she had never seen him before, he was obliged, again and again and again, to hide his anguish. Like Dreyfus, if he wept, he wept alone. His captors did supply him with a Jewish woman to replace the wife from whom he was separated, but she has to have been more comfort than confidante. How could he be sure that his pillow talk would not be passed on to the Romans? Every word he wrote or spoke had to be guarded. He was committed to a form of self-consciousness, and repression, that individualized him, as a Jew and an outsider, to an unprecedented degree.

From the time of his surrender until his departure for Italy in 71 C.E., Joseph ben Mattathias was in close attendance on the Roman commanders. While portraying himself as too gentlemanly to applaud such knavish dodges, Josephus cannot resist telling how, soon after the fall of Jotapata, his personal enemy, John of Gischala, blindsided the credulous Titus. Storming the town of Gischala presented nothing like the difficulty to the Romans that Jotapata had, which may explain why Vespasian delegated its capture to his son. In the usual way, before moving in to assault the walls, Titus called on the garrison to surrender. In ancient warfare, prompt capitulation might procure lenient terms. The longer a town held out, the more certain its ruin and the death or enslavement of its population when captured. Surrounded and outnumbered, John agreed to open the gates and give himself up; but he claimed that, for religious reasons, he could do nothing at all, not even surrender, on the Sabbath day, which had begun at sunset.

Gullible or chivalrous, Titus agreed to wait overnight and mounted only a superficial watch. John and his men took the opportunity to slip out and repair to Jerusalem. Josephus says that God allowed John to escape on that occasion so that he could live to play a catastrophic part as a faction chieftain inside the city; but the moralizing tag reads like a straight-faced coda to the Jewish joke John played on Josephus's Roman patron. Despite his leading role in the revolt, John was able, at the very end, to escape the fate of many of the defeated Jews and somehow to make his peace with Vespasian: he was sentenced to life imprisonment, not crucifixion. Martin Goodman attributes his reprieve to his elevated social status,[2] but others of the same class, such as another Zealot leader, Simon ben Gioras, were not so lucky. Simon had been dictatorial enough to make enemies even among the Jews during the last days in Masada. Arrogance helped qualify him for exemplary execution at the climax of Vespasian's postwar triumph in Rome.*

When Vespasian marched on Tiberias, he must have expected that the city would put up a strong resistance. From his own sour experience of their duplicity, Joseph was able to assure the Roman commander that few of the inhabitants of Tiberias had ever been wholeheartedly in favor of the rebellion. He was proved right when, thanks to Agrippa II's mediation, the leading men of the city agreed to open the gates. As a result, Tiberias suffered no more than a wide breach being made in its walls. The Romans wanted to be sure that they would have easy access if the wrong people—such as Joseph ben Mattathias's prewar supporters—regained control of the city.

Tiberias's neighbor and rival, Tarichaeae, was filled with Zealots who had fled to the safety of walls that Josephus had had strengthened before the arrival of the legions. Its defenses were less substantial than those of Tiberias, where greater funds had been available; but since

---

* Personal charm is a quality in survivors that can elude strict analysis. In Piotr Rawicz's 1961 novel, *Blood from the Sky* (written originally in French and substantially based on his own experiences in the Holocaust), his blond alter ego, Boris, has the lineaments of a modern John of Gischala. He escapes death by conning a Gestapo officer into accepting that he really is the Ukrainian Gentile in whose vocabulary and culture he has dressed himself. Rawicz is almost alone in seeing that the Final Solution could carry elements of foul comedy. John Hersey's 1950 novel, *The Wall,* about the Warsaw ghetto, features a clownish Jew who remains alive only by amusing his Gestapo captors with his sterotypical performance as a capering, cringing Yid, but Hersey could not match Rawicz's hellish authenticity.

their city backed directly onto the southernmost shore of the Sea of Galilee, Tarichaean Jews had a line of retreat that the Romans could not easily sever. The militants had lined up a large number of boats to enable them to evacuate the city and then harass the enemy from the sea. Not everyone was eager to resist, but residents who preferred a quiet life were given no choice.

In accordance with the standard practice of blooding ambitious young officers in combat, Vespasian sent his son Titus ahead with six hundred cavalry. Before the battle, Josephus reports Titus to have stiffened the sinews of his ethnically mixed force by addressing them as "Romans."* He told them that they belonged to a "people" whose reach no one in the whole world had been able to escape. His words were more a reminder of shared *Romanitas* than of any specific racial identity. Fighting for Rome defined its soldiers as Romans, whatever they might be by birth.†

"All the same," Titus went on, "the Jews, to do them justice, have not until this moment flinched from the fight. And since they are managing to keep their end up, despite their disasters, it would be ridiculous for us to back away when we're winning. I'm still afraid some of you may be secretly alarmed by the number of our enemies." Since Josephus has informed his readers that Titus had already sent for reinforcements, there is a squeeze of irony here: the general attributes his own anxiety to some of his men. "The Jews are tough," Titus tells them, "and have no dread of death, but they're also undisciplined, without any experience of organized warfare, more a mob than an army. . . . Remember that you are fighting in armor against men whose bodies are totally unprotected. You're on horseback; they're on foot. You have a commander and they do not." Titus is reported to have emphasized how important daily drills and training were to the Romans. He hardly

* Conversely, on an occasion when Julius Caesar was faced with discontented soldiers, he addressed them as *"quirites,"* citizens, which in a single word demobilized them to the status of mere civilians. They promptly returned to military rectitude.

† In a similar fashion, the regiment of Gurkhas, recruited in Nepal, are traditionally regarded, in the Gunga Din spirit, as British soldiers.

needed to tell them what they knew already; but the redundancy gave Josephus a chance to remind his readers with what gallantry unprepared Jewish irregulars had gone into battle against an experienced military machine.

"What wins wars isn't the number of fighting men," Titus continues, "even if they don't lack fighting spirit. What counts most is courage, even with reduced numbers. The Jews are driven by daring, recklessness, desperation—emotions that flare up when things go well, but collapse at the slightest reverse, whereas we . . . we're controlled by courage, discipline and steady morale. They work wonders when things go well and make sure we hold out to the end, if they don't. Remember: our cause is superior to theirs. They run all the risks of going to war for the sake of their liberty and their homeland. But for us nothing is more important than success. We must never allow anyone to get the impression that we, who've taken control of the whole world, are being frustrated by the Jews."

Titus is made to grace the enemy with patriotic amateurism and his own army with no nobler motive than professional vanity. Insisting that the Romans had every advantage, in equipment and training, Josephus lends heroic luster to the Jews who sallied out from Tarichaeae, even as he deplores their recklessness. They had to confront not only Titus and his cavalry but also two thousand archers, supplied by King Agrippa. While the archers gave covering fire, the mounted men charged in and set about slaughtering the Jewish militants. The whole plain was soon littered with corpses. As the Zealots retreated toward the city, Titus and his horsemen outflanked several groups and cut them down. The remainder bullocked their way back to the city gates. They found them barred. Tarichaeae's original inhabitants had watched their worst fears realized. They screamed at the militants that they were bringing ruin on the city and prayed that, by keeping them out, they might still save their lives and property.

Joseph ben Mattathias had discovered when he was in command that few comfortable citizens wanted a war which they were likely to lose. Despite his role as general, he shared their views. Why, then, had he been so keen not to be ousted from his invidious office when the delegation came from Jerusalem to depose him? He could have resigned; but he stayed, at the risk of his life. His likeliest motives were at once honorable and duplicitous; honorable *because* duplicitous: if he were dislodged, little hope of a compromise peace would remain. When Josephus tells how, at the gates of Tarichaeae, the residents came to blows with the extremists, he supplies one more proof of how the misfortunes of moderate and modest Judaean Jews, himself and his family not least, had been brought upon them by extremists.

The imminent fate of Tarichaeae had very nearly been visited on Tiberias. Vespasian had been enraged by a certain Jeshua, who made off with some unguarded Roman horses. The general had shown clemency in the particular case of Joseph ben Mattathias, but it was rarely his first quality. Josephus now has Titus say what he himself feared, although no Roman is likely to have thought: "God has delivered the Jews into our hands! What are you waiting for? Take the victory that's offered to you. Listen to the Jews yelling at each other even when they've just got away from us. The town's ours if we move fast. Let's hit them before they join ranks again and take the place all by ourselves before reinforcements arrive. That way, we—the happy few!—can say we've beaten the lot of them!" Josephus implies what it would be tactless, even years later, to spell out: the main incentive for Titus and his men to capture Tarichaeae before Vespasian arrived was less the glory than the spoils. If they won promptly, the booty would not have to be shared with the latecomers.

In another vivid close-up, Josephus next portrays Titus leading from the front, in the style of Alexander on his stallion Bucephalas. Titus leaps onto his horse and heads his squadrons toward the lake. Plunging into the water, he rides at the town from the lake side. This daring maneuver is said to have paralyzed the defenders. Most abandoned the ramparts and fled toward the beach. They scrambled into the boats or swam out into the warm water. Jeshua the horse thief escaped into the countryside. Those who had nothing to lose in the city ran for their lives. Civilians who had never had anything to do with the decision to resist were cut down together with militiamen who had left it too late to get away. Josephus first describes an indiscriminate massacre and then, in the same paragraph, observes, "Finally, after having killed all the genuinely guilty men, Titus took pity on the inhabitants and stopped the slaughter." In other words, the legionaries were sated with blood and broke off to help themselves to as many valuables as they could carry before the reinforcements arrived and grabbed a share. Meanwhile, Titus was quick to courier the good news back to his father. When Vespasian rode up, he ordered Tarichaeae to be sealed off. Anyone who came out was to be killed.

The next morning, the veteran campaigner went down to the lake and ordered rafts to be prepared so that soldiers could go after the waterborne fugitives. In those days, there was no shortage of wood in the region. Josephus prolongs the suspense by—in cinematic terms—cutting away to the beauty of the surrounding countryside. Galilee was so fertile that its vines and fruit trees produced crops almost without interruption.* Like Homer with his parenthetical similes, Josephus sharpens the contrast between peace and war by harping on the quality of the region's air and the abundance of its irrigation. One of the springs was held to be a branch of the Nile because it produced a species of catfish (*coracinus*) similar to that found in the lake near Alexandria. Jewish fishermen regarded it as forbidden food, because it had no scales, but it could always be sold to the Arabs.

Once enough rafts had been constructed, Vespasian set about encircling and killing the Jews out on the pretty waters. Their narrow boats had been designed, as Josephus puts it, for "piracy," although fishing must have been their more regular use. The craft held only a few men and were too unstable to fight from. The Jews were helpless against legionaries able to throw their javelins and fire their arrows from the steady base of their rafts. By evening, the whole lake was stained with the blood of more than six thousand defenders. By a possibly deliberate symmetry, the casualties are said to be of exactly the same number as those of Cestius's Twelfth Legion at Beth-Horon.

---

* Géza Vermès suggests that Jesus of Nazareth gave evidence of his provincial origins when he cursed a fig tree, in the environs of Jerusalem, because it failed to produce timely refreshment for him, as trees in his native Galilee did at the same season.

In the days that followed, the stench of swollen and ruptured corpses filled the previously delicious air. Josephus says that even many of the victors were appalled by the effects of the carnage. Vespasian was not one of them. He set up a court-martial at Tarichaeae and proclaimed his intention to separate residents from troublemakers who had infiltrated the city. Some of his officers insisted that it was dangerous to leave any suspects alive. Vespasian agreed that all the Jews had to die, but fearing that wholesale slaughter might reignite a general insurrection, he appeared to proclaim a distinction between guerrillas and innocent citizens.*

Josephus attributes what followed at Tarichaeae to the advice of some of Vespasian's anonymous lieutenants, but would the general have listened to them if they had not proposed what he wanted to hear? There was deliberate ambiguity in Vespasian's proclamation of an amnesty for those who had not already been condemned. Unsuspecting citizens were encouraged to leave their wrecked and reeking city, taking whatever they could carry, and proceed, by a single prescribed route, to Tiberias. Promised that they would be safe, they took the Roman at his word. In their innocence and despair, the survivors of Tarichaeae did not find it amiss that the road along which they trudged was lined with legionaries who made sure that no one dodged the column. Once they had reached Tiberias, the Tarichaeans were herded into the stadium. Vespasian is said to have ordered twelve hundred old and unfit refugees to be executed at once. The phrase "at once" disposes of the matter quickly, but such slaughter required hard, hot work; the victims had to be corralled and cut down, among the screams and prayers of those who were spared only that they might later be sold as slaves. Vespasian auctioned thousands of Jews, of whom only a small proportion can have been involved in active hostilities, to the slave-merchants. Out of

---

* His tactics were of the kind that, two millennia later, Jean-Paul Sartre labeled "serialization." By creating several categories of Jews, distinguished by whatever factitious criteria of age or origin, and seeming to grant some of them immunity, the authorities in Nazi-occupied Europe inhibited their victims from reacting in unison to what was, as it turned out, a common danger.

politeness, he presented Agrippa II with a contingent of captives, who were in truth his own subjects. The king sold them on. The possessions the Tarichaeans had toted with them were distributed among the soldiers who had escorted them to their deaths. Booty and sex were the dividends of ancient war.*

Six thousand strong young Jews were sent by Vespasian to Nero for forced labor on his proposed canal across the Isthmus of Corinth. Whatever ambition Joseph may have kindled or confirmed in Vespasian, the general maintained a posture of deference to his songster sovereign until Nero was safely dead. There were logistical reasons why the siege of Jerusalem was not Vespasian's first objective, but the lack of haste suggests that he had not forgotten Corbulo's fate. The siege of Jerusalem did not begin in earnest until shortly before Passover in 70 C.E.[3] Meanwhile, Vespasian's policy was to campaign unobtrusively and fruitfully enough, in terms of booty, to deserve the gratitude, and enhance the expectations, of his troops. The massacre in Tiberias was less "racist" than prudential: it gave the men some additional pocket money. Their general had to be able to rely on their support when it came to a fight for the purple. By this stage in Roman history, loyalty was a commodity to be bought and sold, not a feature of citizenship.

The assault on Tarichaeae was followed by the siege of Gamala, another hilltop bastion, somewhat like Jotapata. Josephus reports that he had himself had the walls strengthened. As a result, they were "virtually impregnable." Vespasian suffered heavy casualties while trying to reduce the place, but men of the Fifteenth Legion at last undermined

---

* Any female, Judaean or otherwise, who had been a captive, for however short a time, was assumed to have been raped and had to be regarded as unsuitable for marriage, especially to a priest. One of the reasons why Eleazar urged the people in Masada to mass suicide in 73 was to safeguard the purity of the women. The same motive may have applied to the elders in Jotapata. True to his name, Josephus makes a point of denying that he ever used his authority to force himself on women. In this, he was at one with the few commanders, from Alexander the Great, to Scipio Africanus in the second century B.C.E., to Julian the Apostate, five hundred years later, who deplored the violation of women. Ammianus's praise of the last for refraining from taking advantage of beautiful Persian females suggests that the emperor's chastity was not infectious.

the walls and broke in and slaughtered the civilian population. The citadel resisted longer, but a "heaven-sent storm" (*thyella daimonios*) blew in the defenders' faces and helped the Roman javelins find their marks, thanks to Rome's "alliance with God." (Another such favorable wind would be said to help the Romans take Masada.) When all hope was gone, the defenders are said to have flung their wives and children, five thousand of them, down the sheer flanks of the hillside, into the abyss below. The remaining four thousand Gamalans, including infants, are reported to have been cut to pieces or thrown down the walls by the enraged Romans. Only two women survived, but Josephus does say that, during the early stages, "the more venturesome slipped away." He had proposed the same course to the Jotapatans, who had scorned it.

X

Was it evidence of Joseph's treason to the Jews that, after the war, he confirmed his transfer from Judaea to Rome? Whom was he betraying? Upper-class men of foreign birth, such as the Seneca family, had no reluctance about reconditioning and relocating themselves as Roman citizens. When Saint Paul declared that he was both a Jew and a native of Tarsus ("no mean city"), he made a point, at the same time, of flaunting his status as a Roman citizen, which exempted him from flogging and, unless he was very unlucky, from summary execution.* For most people in Josephus's time, nothing was more desirable than to be integrated into the imperial system. Spaniards, Gauls and Greeks converged on Rome. Even in later centuries, the tribes—Goths, Alans, Huns—who overran the empire were keener to have access to its benefits (and to the levers of power) than to destroy it: Theodoric the Goth was a more effective Caesar, in Ravenna, than the last official emperor, Romulus Augustulus, ever was in Rome.

---

* Revolutionaries often expect their enemies to abide by civilized rules that they themselves disparage: in flight from Stalin, Trotsky presumed that the English would extend their bourgeois tolerance to giving him asylum. Like Czar Nicholas II, when he appealed to his first cousin George V, he was mistaken. Safely in America after escaping Nazi Germany, Herbert Marcuse stigmatized Western democracy for its "repressive tolerance." In 1960, the terminally ill anti-Western activist Frantz Fanon sought expert treatment in America. Terrorists guarding hostages in the Middle East have asked their help in securing green cards so they could emigrate to the United States.

Jerusalem was the capital of a province that never made convincing patriotic claims on its inhabitants. When the Jews of Scythopolis sided, disastrously, with their Gentile neighbors, they were defending no bigger a territory than their own city and their own property and no grander a principle than their right to hold on to their local independence. They disdained wider allegiance.* Judaism might make absolute demands, but religion had no territorial boundaries. Jewish nationalism was an exaggerated defense of religious exclusivity. Judaea was not a Jewish state; it was a state with many Jews in it.

Throughout his exiled life, Josephus remained a polemic pamphleteer in defense of Judaism. At the same time, he made no secret of abiding hostility to those belligerent Jews whom he rated as no better than usurping gangsters.† Josephus's denunciation of what others call "freedom fighters" was consistent with his view that they had provoked the Romans to commit the atrocities he had observed. The Zealots' endurance may have been heroic; it was certainly folly. As Joseph saw it, fanaticism triumphed in Jerusalem, not only over common sense but also over decency. The extremists exulted in the ruin of all the Jews who failed to be in their camp; they killed any who tried to escape it. Like Saturn, revolutions regularly consume their own children; but the Zealots were as savage in consuming their elders as they were in disputing leadership among themselves. Josephus refused to see the war as inevitable, or holy. In his view, if individual men, Jews and Romans, had behaved differently, Jerusalem need never have been destroyed.

For a full two years after the fall of Jotapata, there was a stand-

---

* The modern Druses have adopted a Scythopolitan ethic: they agree to be subject to whatever power commands the area in which they live. Alone of non-Jews, Druses who live within the borders of Israel serve, with marked diligence, in the Israel Defense Forces. Despite allegations of dual loyalty, Europe's Jews have been equally patriotic within the boundaries of its nation-states. German Jews who had been decorated for gallantry in the Great War were sent, in first-class carriages, to their deaths in concentration camps; French Jews decorated for fighting against them were, in theory, exempt from deportation. In practice, Marshal Pétain refused to acknowledge their claim on his protection.

† As Bertolt Brecht would the Nazis, in *The Resistible Rise of Arturo Ui.*

off inside the walls of Jerusalem between the High Priest Ananus and his supporters and the Zealots who had installed themselves in different fortified sections of the city. The factions barred access even to kindred militants. All of them hated the elders; they also distrusted, and often murdered, each other. Despite his eminence, Ananus was never quite strong enough to arrest John of Gischala and the other radicals; nor could they unite to dispose of him. The internal *stasis* (the Thucydidean term for civil conflict or class war, frequently used by Josephus) continued until John resorted to accusing Ananus of being about to sell the city to the Romans. Two of the Zealots, Eleazar and Zachariah, both from priestly families, then wrote to the Idumaean tribes in the south of Palestine, urging them to save the day by bringing their forces to Jerusalem.

Ananus still had enough support to be able to close the gates of the city against the "twenty thousand" tribesmen who rode up in answer to the Zealots' call. It would be pretty to suppose that they came only because the Temple and the city were in danger of being surrendered to the Gentiles, but would they have traveled north in such numbers without the promise of a share in the spoils of revolution against the old hierarchy? Standing on a high tower, alongside Ananus, a revered elder priest called Jeshua made an appeal to the Idumaeans massed under the walls. His reported words are surely more elegantly phrased than what was actually said, but the gist of his speech rings true. Ananus may have been too old or too shaken to speak out.

Jeshua must have had the aura and the volume to procure a respectful hearing. "Here you are," he told the Idumaeans, "ready to take sides against us with men whose vices have no limit. You've answered their call more promptly than if you had been begged to repel a foreign invasion. If I thought that you were just like the Zealots, I might not find your enthusiasm absurd. But you're not. Look at them up close and each of them deserves a thousand deaths. . . . They're nothing but brigands who have desecrated holy ground. . . . There they are now, shamelessly drunk, pigging themselves on the plunder of people they've murdered. And then look at you, your vast army, the sparkling spectacle of your strength. Anyone would think you'd come to help us as allies against a foreign foe. It's a scandal to see a great people like yourselves up in arms to help a band of outright criminals. . . . I can hear some of you calling, 'What about the Romans?' and 'Treason' and claiming that you're here to liberate our capital city before we sell it. That charge is a lie." Jeshua denied, at length, that the hierarchy had any intention of negotiating with the Romans. He wished, loudly, that the Idumaeans had come to purge Jerusalem of the murderers and wreckers inside the city. He would then have been glad to welcome them. However plausible, his words were also patronizing: the hierarchy clearly wanted the Idumaeans to go back where they came from. The unmistakable, and unforgivable, implication was that the tribesmen might be Jews of a kind, but they had no place in the city except at the service of the Sanhedrin.

One of the Idumaean generals, Simon son of Cathla, replied by accusing Jeshua of hypocrisy. He and his men would stay where they were in order to defend "the house of God" against the enemy outside and the traitors within. The Idumaeans were incensed that the Zealots had failed to find a way of getting them into the city. Once in arms, they expected some action and, no doubt, some reward. They stayed where they were, out in the open. The gates remained barred.

That night a tremendous storm broke over Jerusalem, with raging wind, torrential rain, sheet lightning and thunder. Josephus says that the Idumaeans at first took the tempest as a sign of God's displeasure at their coming in arms against the city. Ananus and his friends were equally sure that He had come out on their side. The tribesmen huddled together under their long shields, in a makeshift *testudo*. As a result, they suffered less from the weather than Ananus supposed. Josephus says that the High Priest had kept the walls fully manned. In the middle of the night, however, some of the key sentries, at the approaches to the Temple, fell asleep. The Zealots were able to get hold of saws from the Temple workshops and sever the beams that secured the gates. No one heard anything because of the noise of the storm. The Idumaeans poured into the city.

Angry with Ananus and Jeshua, they immediately allied themselves with the extremists. Within a short time, they were proving their "bar-

barous and bloodthirsty" credentials by attacking the good citizens, whose young men tried in vain to defend them. Josephus says that eighty-five hundred civilians died in the ensuing massacre. The outer courtyard of the Temple was deluged with blood. Ananus and his colleagues were murdered by men who then stood on their bodies before throwing them to be "devoured by dogs and wild beasts." Josephus concludes that the city was, from that moment, beyond salvation.

The successful revolutionaries conducted a prolonged and brutal purge in which twelve thousand "young nobles" are said to have been killed. They also mounted show trials of alleged traitors. One of their choice victims was a distinguished man also called Zachariah, who not only had what Josephus calls "a burning hatred of wrong and a love of freedom" but was rich and important enough to question their hegemony. Having accused him, without evidence, of being in touch with Vespasian, they convoked seventy men in high public positions to form a jury to judge—or, rather, to condemn—him.

Zachariah defended himself with such spirit, and denounced the Zealots with such accuracy, that his accusers became the accused.* Seeing that they were about to lose the case, the Zealots curtailed his trial and called for the seventy notables to bring in their verdict, "keen to discover whether they were ready to risk their own lives for the sake of justice." When, despite intimidation, the seventy brought in a unanimous verdict of "not guilty," two of the Zealots murdered Zachariah, in the middle of the Temple (yet another pollution of the sacred site)

---

* As did Georgi Dimitrov, in 1935, when the Nazis arraigned him for causing the 1933 Reichstag fire. Dimitrov was a Bulgarian Communist who happened to have been in Germany at the time. As Hannah Arendt describes it, "He was . . . confronted with Goering whom he questioned as if he were in charge of the proceedings . . . thanks to him all the accused, except van der Lubbe, had to be acquitted. His conduct was such that it won him the admiration of the whole world, Germany not excluded. 'There is one man left in Germany,' people used to say, 'and he's a Bulgarian.'" During the Shoah, when the Nazis demanded that their Bulgarian allies hand over all their Jews for extermination, more Bulgarians turned out to be men than anyone had imagined. Its government, alone of all the rulers of Balkan states, refused to deliver their Jews. Bulgaria's northern neighbors, the Romanians, horrified even the SS by the wanton ferocity of their pogroms.

and jeered over his dead body "Now you've got our verdict too, and your trials are over!"

Josephus says that the Zealots drove off the seventy recusant jurors with the flat of their swords, failing to kill them only because they thought it better to humiliate them in front of everyone. The Idumaeans could not hide their revulsion. A renegade Zealot then spelled out to them how they had been duped into conniving at the ruin of Ananus and his people, none of whom had had any treasonous contact with the Romans. The best thing would be for them now to go home. The Idumaeans first broke open the jails and sprang some two thousand prisoners, who immediately fled the city to join Simon ben Gioras's bandit rebels in the Judaean hills, where they commanded the approaches to Jerusalem. In the spring of 69, Simon was strong enough to move back into the city and challenge the hegemony of John of Gischala.

After most of the Idumaeans went home, the mass of the population hoped that the worst of the terror was over, but Josephus says that the Zealots, less ashamed than relieved by the departure of their belatedly squeamish allies, became even more murderous. The Idumaeans who did remain in the city later grew disillusioned with the extremists and, in the spring of 70, were able to surrender, on fairly lenient terms, before the final debacle. Immediately, however, there was another purge, in which the only victims named were a certain Gurion, said to be "democratic" and devoted to liberty "if ever a Jew was," and Niger, from Peraea, who had been outstanding in an early battle at Ascalon, soon after the expulsion of Cestius Gallus.

Niger's earlier heroism did nothing to save him from the remorseless Zealots. As they paraded him through Jerusalem, he protested furiously and drew attention to his battle scars (in this he resembled his namesake, the outspoken "black" Cleitus, who saved Alexander the Great's life at the battle of the Granicus and was later killed by Alexander in a drunken rage). As soon as the Zealots dragged Niger through the gates of Jerusalem, he realized that they meant to kill him and leave his corpse for the dogs to eat. He pleaded with them to allow his body to be buried. When they denied him even that, he cursed them and called the vengeance of Rome down on their heads, as well as famine, pestilence and slaughter. He even had time, Josephus says, to add civil war to the misfortunes he wished on his murderers.

After Niger's death, the terror continued in the city. As in the emblematic case of *stasis*, on the island of Corcyra, in 427 B.C.E., during the prelude to the Peloponnesian War, even those who did not take sides were accused of arrogance, especially if they had enviable property. Jesus of Nazareth was not alone in saying that people were either with him or against him. Death was the sole penalty for giving offense to the Zealots. Only men without pedigree or possessions were immune.*

Josephus's narrative now cuts back to the Roman camp. Informed of the *stasis* in Jerusalem, his generals urged Vespasian to march directly on the city while the population was distracted by civil war. The commander-in-chief argued against undue vigor; it would unite the enemy. It was better to leave them to tear themselves apart and wait for the garrison to be weakened by the growing number of desertions. As long as Nero remained on the throne, Jerusalem could be left to fester. The Zealots and their henchmen killed so many people that bodies accumulated in the streets or were thrown over the walls to rot in the open. Kinsmen who tried to bury their dead were themselves threatened with death. Josephus repeats that there was a time-honored prophecy that the city would be captured and the Holy Temple burned, if the citizens fought each other and if Jews themselves polluted the house of God.

---

* Marxists attach similar immunity to unalloyed proletarians and the "class justice" they dispensed. Michel Foucault defended the French Revolution's Terror (and that of the Iranian ayatollahs) in the same preemptive spirit. Principled killing is at the sharp end of logic; hence Auden's 1938 camp version of Marxism, relishing the "necessary murder." G. B. Shaw was of the same view, saying that "states" had the right to choose whom to kill. He backed totalitarian ruthlessness—puckishly, of course. René Cassin's formal enactment of the notion of "universal human rights," after 1945, has to be seen as an assertion of the individual's claim not to be subsumed under statistics. It so happened that Cassin (1887–1976) was an emancipated French Jew as well as a jurist. An early supporter of General de Gaulle, he returned to active Jewish allegiance as a reaction to the Holocaust but, in the French style, he universalized the lessons to be learned from it.

Whether or not he had taken Joseph ben Mattathias's dream prediction to heart, Vespasian's tactics were sound, and in character. It would be a signal achievement to capture Jerusalem, but it had to be at the right moment. There were political as well as tactical reasons to be in no hurry. Although few of his officers could be allowed to guess it, Vespasian was fighting a campaign on two fronts. He had to keep his men in good humor for an infinitely bigger prize than *Judaea Capta*. His greatest ambition was to capture Rome.

Nero's popularity had survived the great fire of Rome in 64, thanks to the prompt measures he took for urban relief, and it had not been dented, except among the upper class, by the bloodthirsty repression of the aristocratic Pisonian conspiracy of 65 C.E. If the people never ceased to be amused by his panache, Nero's unmanly indifference to threats on the empire's borders lost him the respect of the military commanders on whom his tenure depended. His treacherous treatment of Corbulo clinched the conviction of provincial governors and generals that they had no more to fear from challenging him than from succeeding in his cause. Despite the contempt of the senatorial establishment, Nero might not have been driven to (assisted) suicide if he had shown more spirit. In the event, rumors that Vindex, in Gaul, and Galba, in Spain, were preparing to unseat him were enough to unnerve the last of the Julio-Claudian line of emperors.

In the course of the second year of the Judaean campaign, young Titus was literally blooded. By the beginning of 69 C.E., he could be entrusted with command of the siege of Jerusalem. Meanwhile, his father had gone to rally support in Alexandria for his imperial ambitions. Thanks to Tiberius Julius Alexander, the prefect of Egypt, Vespasian received solid enough military backing to be able to sail for Italy after two of his rivals had been eliminated in, as it were, the semifinals. The noblest, and least remembered, was Otho, the second of the four emperors (and the onetime husband of Nero's beautiful wife and Joseph ben Mattathias's benefactor Poppaea Sabina). When the pretender Vitellius marched against him, Otho chose to kill himself, although his chances of remaining emperor were not negligible. Unlike more successful candidates down the ages, Otho did not care to have it on his conscience that he had led Romans to kill Romans. Vespasian was not so squeamish. By defeating Vitellius in the final, he made Joseph ben Mattathias's predictive dream come true. His lease on the throne would last ten years, and he would die of natural causes.

The fate of the third emperor of the year 69, Vitellius, at the hands of Vespasian's soldiers (some of whom might have been at Jotapata), illustrates what might well have happened to Joseph ben Mattathias: Vitellius was dragged from where he was hiding, paraded naked through the streets of Rome, pelted with abuse and missiles, his head pulled back, a drawn sword under his chin, and was then thrown down the Gemonian steps toward the Tiber, beaten to death and then decapitated.*

Josephus recounts the horrors of the war in Judaea in a cool manner until he comes to the siege of Jerusalem itself. Having described how the whole of Vespasian and Titus's large force was massed around the city, he apostrophizes the "unhappy city" in a style that, even in its Greek recension, echoes Jeremiah. To those like Yigael Yadin, the prophet himself must have seemed another "bad Jew" when he advocated accepting that Jews should make a life elsewhere if the odds were irresistibly stacked against them. Contrary to that view, the modern Israeli Sabra Yehoshafat Harkabi held that the Jewish rebels of 67 should have honored Jeremiah's advice. Thomas Idinopulos counters with the view that the Jews of Jeremiah's day were "not confronted by the actual danger of national extinction through cultural dissolution."[1] Can it really be claimed that first-century Israel had no due way of reacting to a cultural threat except by risking and—as it turned out—procuring the destruction of Jerusalem? If there had been an effective Jeremiah in the city at the time when Vespasian was advancing on it, the consequences would have been infinitely less ruinous. Idinopulos insists that the Great Revolt of 66–73 "preserved a sense of Jewish

---

* His body was thrown into the river and his head carried round the city on a pole. Vespasian himself arrived after the savagery but did not reproach those, including the "rapscallion" general Marcus Antonius Primus, who had tortured his predecessor. Vitellius had begun public life as Tiberius's catamite, gambled with Claudius, became a charioteer under Gaius and, it is said, sung along with Nero, a paradigm of rising and falling in imperial Rome.

national uniqueness . . . a creative and lasting contribution to Jewish history."*

Whatever tears Joseph ben Mattathias shed as he looked back, he could not, during the siege itself, afford to manifest too much sympathy for his fellow countrymen, even though he had many friends and relatives, including his brother and his old mother, inside the walls. It is some testimony to his credibility that he mentions in *The Jewish War* that his mother never forgave him for his defection to the Romans. Does the third-person narrative account for his dispassionate candor? The narrator was not quite identical with the person he describes, even when it was himself.

Joseph's survival has to have depended on the intelligence he provided. Speaking Aramaic, the language of the natives, he was well-placed to convince the Romans that, until the end, he was the likeliest negotiator with those inside the city. He begged the Jewish leaders repeatedly to curtail the sufferings of the innocent.† He seems also to have been authorized to promise leniency to members of his own class who came over to the Romans. Several did in the last days of the

---

* In *The Jews Under Roman and Byzantine Rule* (Jerusalem: Magnes Press, 1984), Michael Avi-Yonah goes further: "If we regard Jewish history as a whole . . . the Zealots were successful in their struggle. . . . The destruction of the Temple and the elimination of Jewish statehood widened an already existing gulf between Judaism and its environment . . . no conciliation in the fields of art and literature could bridge it. . . . If Israel has kept its national identity . . . the only nation of antiquity to do so . . . this is due . . . to the warriors of two lost wars against the Romans. From the point of view of Jewish nationality, their [the Zealots'] desperate undertakings appear in a positive light, however much one can regret the amount of suffering caused to the community and to individuals." The secular version of much the same argument has been advanced by Eric Hobsbawm in defense of the "experiments" of Communist regimes, especially in the Soviet Union but also in China, as a result of which some sixty million people died from ideologically justified famine.

† Thomas Mann did something similar, in the Second World War, in broadcasts to the Germans he had quit in 1934. Mann dared to say, "All the heroism lies in enduring, in willing to live and not die." He was referring to a remark of Frederick the Great's, but the saying applied, to some degree, to himself and his acceptance of abuse and exile. No sane person has accused either of the Mann brothers of being "bad Germans."

siege, among them Ananus ben Bagadatus, who had earlier supervised the execution of would-be deserters. He was regarded with distaste by Titus, but was allowed to retire "honorably" to Gophna (the modern Jifna), at the base of the Samaritan hills.

Martin Goodman argues that the landlord class, which Josephus regularly distinguishes from the Zealots and "brigands," was more deeply implicated in the rebellion than it suited him to concede after the event.[2] In his view, it was "mendacious" to claim that those who fought on were all low-life scoundrels whose wickedness prevented them from admitting the futility of the struggle. Josephus's portrayal of the Zealots, in the winter of 68–69 "running riot in the city, dressed as women while they murdered and looted" is said, by Goodman, to be "ancient invective at its most blatant." Must he be right? It is hard to believe that the class war that undoubtedly took place in Jerusalem, from the earliest months of the war, did not lead to the confusion of theft and murder with the hazards and malice of revolutionary "justice." As for dressing as women, might this not have secured them immunity from search or suspicion as it has terrorists wearing burkas in modern circumstances?

Josephus denies that the Romans were superior in anything but military efficiency and resources. He had seen their machine in action; he witnessed pillage, rape, killing, the auction of captives. His memories were the reward and the cost of being a witness. It would have been suicidal openly to question the right of Vespasian to crush the rebellion, but his portraits of unsavory or cynical Roman officials, especially when "Greek," were as scathing as those of the Zealots who had usurped power inside the city. What witness of the events at Tarichaeae (where the Romans had tortured captives, at length, in front of those on the city walls) can be blamed for begging the Jewish commanders to allow noncombatants to quit Jerusalem? Joseph's tears at the heartlessness of the Zealot leaders were those of a sincere crocodile: he wept for a fate he now stood every chance of escaping. Yet he returned again and again to the walls of Jerusalem and called on the defenders to come to terms while they had the chance. He was literally in no-man's-land; there had, until then, never been a Jew quite like him.

On one occasion, he was knocked unconscious by a stone, to cheers from those on the ramparts. He claims to have been rescued by Titus himself. His depiction of the young Titus is loaded with ambiguity. Celebrated as bold, and often ruthless, the young general is also revealed as naïve. During the siege of Jerusalem, after a heavy ram had been wheeled close to a tower on the notorious northern flank of the walls, a "charlatan" called Castor, with ten comrades, tried to ambush the Roman engineers. They were chased off by a volley of arrows. Later, when the tower seemed about to topple, they stood up as if in despair. Castor raised his hands and begged "Caesar" to have pity on them. Convinced of his sincerity, Titus shouted to Castor that he should encourage the rest of his companions to do the same.[3]

Five of Castor's platoon appeared to agree that they should surrender. The other five called out that they would sooner die than be slaves. They brandished their swords and, as far as could be seen in long shot, thrust them into their breastplates. They fell to the ground, as if mortally stricken. Titus and his staff were amazed at their courage and pitied their fate. During this, an archer let off an arrow, which struck Castor near his nose. He plucked it out and waved it at Titus, claiming that he had been unjustly used. Titus was furious with the archer and asked Joseph to go and give Castor a hand. Joseph suspected a trick and refused. How did Titus look at him at that moment?

Castor called out to his enemies to send a volunteer to receive all the money he had on him. A certain Aeneas, a deserter to the Romans, offered to go. His Hellenized name suggests that, if a Jew, he may never have been a Zealot. As he ran forward, holding his skirts out to catch the cash, Castor hefted a large boulder and flung it at him. The stone missed Aeneas (an apt name for one who survived a siege) but hit another soldier who had run up beside him, hoping to cadge a coin or two.

Titus is said by Josephus to have drawn from this petty incident the grand conclusion that pity was futile in warfare and cruelty the best policy. Since Castor's charade was staged at least a year after the extermination of the helpless citizens of Tarichaeae, and of many others elsewhere, there has to be irony in Josephus's assertion that the Roman commander-in-chief resolved on pitilessness because of a prank in which a common soldier was bruised by a boulder. Might Titus's outburst have been primed by the fact that Joseph had witnessed him looking foolish?

When the bombardment resumed and the tower did collapse, Castor set fire to what was left. He and his comrades then jumped through the flames into a subterranean vault. This show of courage, Josephus says, again impressed the Romans. They thought that the Jews had genuinely flung themselves into the fiery pit. The implication is that the Gentiles had failed to see through a trick that Josephus himself recognized. This vignette is typical of the "clips" with which he intersperses his panorama of the war. It also illustrates his ambivalence. Although Joseph's instinct, at the time, was to distrust Castor, he cannot conceal his amusement at the rogue's Odyssean slyness. Castor and his crew, when they put on their show of committing suicide, re-enacted Joseph's own disappearing trick after he had leapt into that secret chamber in Jotapata, from which he too had emerged, although not to fight another day.

Like the convert centurion Metilius, Castor makes one appearance and then vanishes from Josephus's story. In Greek mythology, the brothers Castor and Pollux are sons of Zeus. They had cult in Sparta and, appropriately enough, lived half their time below the earth. The dichotomy that sets Athens against Jerusalem obscures similarities between Greek *poneria* (impudent rascality) and what came to be known in Yiddish as chutzpah. The Jew Castor outsmarts Titus, as Odysseus did the Cyclops Polyphemus. The story implies both that the man was a clever trickster and—since Joseph guessed that he was up to no good—that it took one to know one. Josephus seems to have cast himself in the role of the divine Castor's twin brother, Pollux, the will-o'-the-wisp who, in mythology, knows how to get out of tight spots. Joseph had done as much when he found a way out of the charnel house in Jotapata.

If Josephus's enormous literary output was a prolonged attempt to put a good face on his translation to a Roman underling, it is only fair to say that during the siege he did everything he could—even though, in the end, it amounted to very little—to avoid the spilling of Jewish blood. Out in no-man's-land, he tried to talk the Jews into surrender, for as long as there was any hope of averting the culminating horror. He submitted to the obscenities and missiles with what a modern mind might interpret as masochistic courage. If he was a coward because he had failed to die, he was also egregiously brave; if a traitor, it was to a reckless nationalism he never favored, not to Judaism.

XI

Tiberius Julius Alexander arrived in Judaea, probably in early 69 C.E., in order to become Titus's effective chief-of-staff during the siege of Jerusalem. He had already played a cardinal part in Vespasian's successful bid for the throne. As prefect of Egypt, he had command of the legions needed to ensure that the outsider won the big race. His duty in Jerusalem was to ensure that Titus had professional backup and the necessary resources for the final assault on the holy city of the Jews. Born in Alexandria, Tiberius Julius appears, on the face of it, to have been one more Roman provincial officer, able, ruthless and with no private sentiments that might infect his public allegiance. In fact, he had been born a Jew, the nephew of the Alexandrian Jewish sage Philo, whose wealth and intelligence confirmed him as the natural leader of the community.

As a young man, Tiberius Julius chose not to "stand by the principles of his people." Severing his connection with the Jewish faith, he exercised the kind of freedom that was easy in Alexandria, but unthinkable in Jerusalem. He features in *The Jewish War* as an important but marginal personage. He is always described formally, and at a distance. Historians continue to seek the roots of "anti-Semitism" in the supposed "Judeophobia" of the pre-Christian world. The brilliant career of T. Julius Alexander offers negligible evidence of it. He was no more distrusted or scorned by those with whom he had enrolled than others of whatever social or geographic provenance who made careers and fortunes by conforming with the ethos of the predominant power.*

By the time he and Titus landed, in 69 C.E., at the head of a fresh Roman force of six thousand men, Tiberius Julius was at the peak of an adroitly managed career.† Years of experience had qualified him as an able and necessary adviser to Vespasian's headstrong son. It was not Alexander's first visit to Palestine. As an already thoroughly assimilated Roman citizen, he had been appointed procurator of Judaea from 46 to 48, during Joseph ben Mattathias's boyhood. He was drafted to replace Cuspius Fadus, who had had to deal with Theudas, a rabble-rousing preacher who persuaded a throng of Jews to follow him out of Jerusalem, into the desert and up to the river Jordan, which he promised to divide by a Mosaic miracle.‡ Fadus had him arrested and beheaded, which reduced his charisma. Using the occasion to chasten the Jews further, Fadus canceled the privilege, granted by the emperor Claudius, that permitted the High Priest to keep his elaborate vestments, symbolic of his election, on Temple premises. The procurator ordered them to be sequestered under Roman control in the Antonia Tower. This petty measure excited an outcry loud enough to induce the emperor Claudius to replace Fadus with the young Tiberius Julius, perhaps on

---

* In his mixture of administrative savvy with mercantile opportunism, Alexander had something in common with Joseph Süss Oppenheimer, but he incurred none of the odium that, in the eighteenth century, in predominantly Lutheran Württemberg, led to the arrest and judicial lynching of "the Jew Süss." Süss's misfortune was to be a scapegoat for the hated Catholic duke he had served so well. Susan Tegel notes that Süss had a copy of Josephus in his library.

† Josephus says (*Jewish War* V: 41), in G. A. Williamson's version, that "he was entrusted with command as a reward for having been the first to welcome the newly emerged imperial dynasty and with splendid faith to throw in his lot with theirs when the future was uncertain."

‡ Martin Goodman remarks that the attraction of messianic figures such as Theudas was precisely because of their "lack of institutional authority or social status" (*The Ruling Class of Judaea,* p. 78). The cult of Dionysos (the divine outsider) was similarly external to the Greek city and defied its rulers. Seaford (*Reciprocity and Ritual*) offers a very full account of Dionysos as the ambivalent force that brought both disruption and regeneration to the city.

the advice of King Agrippa. The latter, with his gift for being in the right place, had been present in Rome when Caligula was stabbed to death by one of his bodyguards, Chaereas, in 41 C.E.

Caligula's uncle Claudius was still alive only because he had been discounted as a drooling dodderer.* Without Agrippa's smart (and self-interested) encouragement, Claudius might never have stepped up to become emperor. Once installed, he proved as generous as he was grateful by honoring Agrippa's request that he go easy on the Alexandrian Jews still under arrest in Rome. Tiberius Julius Alexander's father, Philo's brother, was among those released. Thanks to a reference from Agrippa, Philo's nephew was granted equestrian status without having to do preliminary military service. It was no impediment to his accelerated progress that he had been born a Jew. However, having been in Alexandria during a particularly vicious spasm of sectarian violence, conducted by the Alexandrian Greeks against the Jews, he was probably glad to be appointed *epistrategus* (district officer) in the more peaceful Thebaid, the area around modern Luxor. His abandonment of Judaism was primed by no spiritual epiphany. As a nominal Gentile, he was not converted to any new enthusiasm, except for his own advancement. He and his younger brother Marcus (who died in 44), had common business interests. Alexander's activities as a Roman official aided his acquisition of a steadily enlarged fortune in trade and banking. In combining public duties with an eye for private gain, he was no different from any Roman careerist.

In 46 C.E., he had been in the Roman service for only five years when he was sent to govern Judaea. Josephus reports that, to mark the style of his administration, Alexander ordered the crucifixion of

---

* The Roman autocratic scheme, apparently so solid, was the result of what François Mitterrand (referring to General de Gaulle's engineered ascension to power in 1958) would call a *"coup d'état permanent."* Augustus had endowed himself with the trappings of constitutional propriety, but he was an unelected tyrant who had come to the throne along bloody tracks. Each Julio-Claudian emperor succeeded the previous one with uneasy presumption. Attachment to the imperial family shortened the life expectancy of any attractive alternatives to the incumbent ruler.

Jacob and Simon, sons of the Galilean Zealot called Judas. The last of his dynasty was the Eleazar who died heroically at Masada in 73. They had formed a nexus of outlaws whose power to intimidate tithing tax collectors, Roman or priestly, won them credibility as champions of the common people. Their hostility to authority was expressed in the fundamentalism that lent righteousness to resentment.

Claudius or his advisers may have imagined that Alexander's Jewish origins would enable Fadus's successor to handle Judaea's inhabitants more adroitly than his predecessors had and to be more acceptable as a keeper of the peace.* In the event, the young Tiberius Julius remained in Judaea for only two years. He could not be accused of an excess of moderation toward the Jews during his brief tenure. It may be that, recognizing the province as a place where reputations were more easily lost than enhanced, Tiberius Julius contrived an early transfer. It is unlikely to have been granted because Claudius disapproved of his heavy-handedness. Crucifying Jews never earned anyone bad marks; at least not until the Jews themselves could be accused, by Christian polemicists, of having practiced it in the case of Jesus of Nazareth.

After 48 C.E., Tiberius Julius Alexander spent much of the next fifteen years serving on the eastern borders under the great Domitius Corbulo. In 66, he was personable enough to be given the mission of going to meet the Parthian prince Tiridates in order to escort him on the first stage of his journey to Rome, where Nero confirmed him, with great pomp, as king of Armenia. The king kept his throne for

---

* The British had the same hopes when they made the Jewish liberal politician and philosopher Herbert Samuel their high commissioner in 1930s Palestine. In trying to abate communal conflict between Jews and Arabs, Samuel leaned over backward so far that he approved the selection of the virulently anti-Jewish Amin al-Husseini as grand mufti of Jerusalem. A well-intentioned English Jew awarded supreme authority to a fanatical enemy of the renewed, and increasing, Jewish presence. In imperial administration, it is seldom enough to be decent and fair-minded. David Lloyd George, who was neither, remarked of the philosophical Samuel (whose liberalism was not of the Welshman's brand), "When they circumcised him, they threw away the wrong bit."

only another six years before he was evicted by an invasion of Alan tribesmen. The Roman emperor might be supreme, but he was not omnipotent.*

Tiberius Julius Alexander chose to live by his wits. Joseph ben Mattathias had that choice forced upon him. By 69, when the apostate arrived in the Roman camp outside Jerusalem, as a senior member of Titus's staff, Tiberius Julius had played for high stakes and won. While his mentor, Corbulo, had been forced to suicide, Tiberius Julius was promoted to prefect of Egypt, the grandest post available to anyone of equestrian rank. As things turned out, Nero installed the Alexandrian apostate as governor of his native city in time for him to play a key part in helping Vespasian become the fourth man, in that single year of 69 C.E., to acquire the purple. Tiberius Julius Alexander was the last military emperor-maker until troops intervened to settle the succession after the death of Commodus in 192. As in 69, four emperors once again competed for power.

On his return to Judaea, Alexander showed no reluctance, no split feelings, no remorse. He had already been in charge of the repression of the Alexandrian Jews when fifty thousand of them are said to have been slaughtered, probably by some of the same troops he now brought to Palestine. Josephus's narrative supplies no close-up of the great apostate. He gives the impression that he himself was in friendly contact with Titus, but Alexander was an infinitely more important member of the young commander-in-chief's entourage. Tessa Rajak suspects that Joseph ben Mattathias could have had closer links to Tiberius Julius than he cared to confess, both in his youth and in the period before the war.[1] In that case, Joseph's famous dream of Vespasian's ascendancy could have been prompted, if not scripted, by what he had heard being mooted in the procurator's circle when he was in Alexandria waiting for his boat to Italy. Nevertheless, the implication that Joseph was playing (or taking advantage of) some previously plotted part requires Tiberius

---

* Almost three centuries later, Constantine the Great's enrollment under the banner of the Christian God would, he hoped, ally divine might (and favor) with temporal power.

Julius to have been improbably indiscreet in the hearing of a young Judaean on his way to plead a case at Nero's court.

One of the great imaginary conversations in world history would be between Joseph ben Mattathias, as he still was during the siege of his native city, and Tiberius Julius Alexander. The latter, who was so much at his ease in Roman company (and, no doubt, in the officers' mess), is not unlikely to have asked Joseph why he did not make a clean break with the doomed Jews and become a wholehearted Roman citizen. Joseph was clearly dismayed by the Zealots' takeover of Judaea. He had already gone so far toward divorce from orthodoxy, and been so ill-used by those still wedded to it, that Alexander might well have wondered why the turncoat did not complete his translation to *Romanitas*. The reluctance of Diaspora Jews, even those without any preference for Jewish company, formally to renounce Jewishness, if not Judaism, is a trait as persistent as it often appears inexplicable.*

Josephus's writings offer no analysis of his motives or of his states of mind. The price of his survival, and of his ambiguous loyalties, was that he lived on to stand for Yigael Yadin's idea of a "bad Jew." Tiberius Julius Alexander, on the other hand, succeeded so well in standing away from the shadow of his ancestry that he passed into historical limbo with no more tarnished a reputation than that of one of the countless hard men, not of Roman birth, whose careers involved making war on those who challenged Rome's hegemony.† It is a nice irony that when Tacitus felt disposed to put him down, he described Alexander as "an Egyptian."

In 1945, Jean-Paul Sartre would say of the French that they had lived in shame a period which the British had lived in pride. Josephus

---

* A source that must remain anonymous has told me that he was once reproached by the great ancient historian's wife for speaking to Sir Moses Finley in a "Jewish way." The quondam Moses Finkelstein was, she said, now a Buddhist.

† Heinrich Himmler's deputy Reinhard Heydrich, one of the architects of the Final Solution, would be the darkest instance of the Jew turned Jew-killer, if the rumors of his ancestry are anything more than a spiteful canard put about by those who resented his handsome ascendancy in the Nazi hierarchy, which, according to Dawidowicz (*The War Against the Jews*), they are almost certainly not.

might have said much the same of himself when he compared his life in the Roman camp with that of Tiberius Julius Alexander. Unencumbered by piety, the latter never made the mistake of being on the wrong side. Unlike Alexander, Josephus clung to his ancestral faith and, as he proved by the terms of his annunciation to Vespasian and by his own commentary in *The Jewish War,* never discounted Yahweh's role in human affairs.

In the prelude to Titus's final assault on Jerusalem, Joseph returned and made yet another appeal before the walls. He was greeted, as before, with howls of derision and more stones. Yet he claims that his reappearance brought hope to the "common people."[2] He promised the garrison that surrender, even now, would save the city, but that once Vespasian's men stormed the city, there would be no mercy for anyone. At the end, Josephus bursts into direct speech, as if unable to contain himself in cool *oratio obliqua:*

> You fools, you forget who your real allies are when you fight the Romans with your own arms and muscles! What other enemy have we ever conquered by those means alone? But when, on the other hand, did God, their founder, not avenge Jews who were victims of injustice? Look around and see what kind of place you are setting out to fight from and what a powerful ally you are defiling! Do you not remember the prodigious acts of your fathers and the terrible enemies that this Holy Place has seen off in the past? You are making war not only against the Romans but against God!

As he did when addressing the notables in Jotapata, Joseph slipped into the sacerdotal mode: the Jews' only means of salvation lay in obedience to Yahweh's laws. He would repay the injustices visited on His people. In the spirit of Philo, Joseph recounts Yahweh's most dramatic interventions:

> Our fathers in Egypt, oppressed and humiliated by foreign kings for four hundred years, when they could have defended themselves by force of arms, didn't they choose to trust in God? Who hasn't

heard what He did to Egypt, crawling with pests and consumed by all kinds of diseases . . . after which our fathers were led to safety . . . God himself guiding them to become guardians of His Temple? Take the time when the Holy Ark was stolen by the Syrians. Did not the Philistines and the idol of Dagon live to regret it, they and the whole nation of plunderers? Their private parts dripped pus and their guts dropped out with their food, until the very hands that stole the Sacred Ark brought it back, to the sound of cymbals and tambourines and with all kinds of offerings in expiation. It was God as our general who directed what your ancestors did when they renounced violence and left everything for Him to decide.

In the rhetorical manner of Cicero, he says that he is not going to talk about the bloodshed that has been taking place inside the walls, and then does so. At the end, his anguish bursts out:

A man does well to run from a house of shame and to regard its occupants with disgust. And you believe that God can still be with people who are bursting with wickedness, God who sees all that is hidden and hears what is not said? But then, what is not said or kept secret by you people? What is there that isn't all too obvious, even to your enemies? You parade your crimes and every day you compete to do something worse. You put iniquity on a pedestal as if it were a virtue. But there is still a way out, if you care to take it. The Holy One is quick to forgive those who confess and repent. You hard-hearted fools! Throw down your arms. Shame on you when your homeland is in ruins! Turn around and look at the beauty you are betraying. What a city, what a Temple! How many nations heap tribute here. Who can want all this to go up in flames? Who could want it all to disappear? What could more deserve to be saved forever? You people have hearts harder than stone! . . . Oh I know, I know that in the middle of it all is my mother, my wife, my family, which is not without nobility, my house with its glorious history, and I may seem to be giving you this advice only to save them.

There has to have been a pause, during which the advocate allowed the jury members, as it were, to have a moment of triumph in which they could shout that they were sure that this *was* his only reason. He could then spring his last surprise: "Go ahead then, kill them all! Take my family's blood in exchange for your own salvation! Yes, I'm ready to die too, if only my death can bring you to your senses."

Whether they applauded, fell silent or went on heckling him, the citizens were still trapped. The Zealots treated all talk of surrender as treason and killed anyone who attempted it. With their own casualties mounting, the Romans were daily less disposed to distinguish between civilians and rebels. Despite the double danger, quite a few refugees managed to sneak out of the city, taking whatever of value they could carry or, in the case of precious jewels, swallow. Many fell into the hands of scavenging Arabs and Syrians, who ripped open their bellies to retrieve the valuables. Titus is reported to have been appalled by the barbarity the Roman presence had triggered but noted, "Avarice scorns every penalty."

As things reached the final stages of savagery, in which the Temple itself became a killing ground for competing bands of extremists, Joseph concluded that "God had condemned the whole nation."* Josephus concedes that the Romans had won, but—on closer reading—the ultimate responsibility is attributed to God. Yahweh was chastening the Jews for their iniquities rather than siding with their enemies. Wary of how he expressed it, Josephus never abandoned hope for the resurgence

---

* This verdict would be appropriated by Christian preachers, such as Saint John Chrysostom, the man with the golden mouth: "Although Jews had been called to be adopted as his sons, they fell to kinship with dogs; we who were dogs received the strength through God's grace to put aside irrational nature . . . and rise to the honor of sons." (For Saint John Chrysostom's dicta, see Malcolm Hay, *Europe and the Jews*.) Disinheritance was transformed into a genocidal warrant by other theological enemies of the Jews in later centuries. Cain and Abel became archetypal figures. The Latin historian Ammianus Marcellinus (born in Syria in 330) depicted the brothers as "the first Christians" and the murder of one by the other as conduct "worse than that of wild beasts." Saint Augustine made Cain stand for the Jewish people, his brother for Jesus: "Abel, the younger brother, is killed by the elders of the Jews . . . so the voice of the Holy Scriptures accuses the Jews."

of Jewish fortunes. His wariness is a small Jewish joke at the expense of the guileless censors, and of modern critics who read him as no more than a rented propagandist.

He encapsulates the terminal horrors of the siege in a close-up of a mother called Mary, the daughter of yet another Eleazar.[3] She was a rich woman of good family who had taken refuge in the city as the Romans advanced. Most of the property she had packed and brought into the city from east of Jordan was pillaged by "party chiefs"; the remnants of her treasure was stolen by their henchmen. Filled with uncontrollable rage, she loosed a tirade of curses, which infuriated the looters. Finally, "in defiance of all natural feeling, she laid hands on her own baby. 'Poor little thing,' she said. 'In war and famine and civil war, why keep you alive? When the Romans come there will be only slavery, even if we live that long. Hunger is with us already and the Zealots are worse than both.' She killed her son, then roasted him and ate one half . . . saving the rest." The Zealots sniffed the "unholy smell" and threatened to kill her if she didn't give up what she had been cooking. When she did, "they went away quivering. They had never before shrunk from anything, and did not much like giving up even this food to the mother."

Josephus appears to be telling the story to prove the depravity of the Jews: "Caesar disclaimed all responsibility in the sight of God for this latest tragedy. He had offered the Jews peace and self-government with an amnesty for all offenders." It is not clear when exactly these terms had been proposed. Neither Titus nor Vespasian had, at any earlier stage in the campaign, shown a disposition to amnesty. Whatever Joseph ben Mattathias might have meant by "self-government," it cannot have been anything close to autonomy. Yet Titus is made to seem only now to decide to "bury this abomination of infanticide and cannibalism under the ruins . . . and would not let a city in which mothers fed themselves in that way remain on the face of the earth."

Josephus proceeds to read Titus's mind: "While he made this clear, he was thinking also of the desperation of these men. They would never see reason after going through all the agonies that might so easily have been avoided by a change of heart." The effect of the siege becomes the justification for ending it with the obliteration of those whom it drove to cannibalism. Can anyone but Titus himself have been expected to read this account of his motives with complacency?

Although he must have known of it, Josephus does not allude to the grisly precedent in Jeremiah when Jerusalem was under siege by the Babylonians. The prophet had been put in prison for subversion (even in those days, there was angry dissent among the Jews) and witnessed the last days of the siege. "Death has climbed through our windows," he wrote. "Little children beg for bread. None gives them a morsel. Those who feasted on dainties lie famished in the streets. Those reared in purple have embraced refuse heaps." Finally, in Lamentations, he says, "With their own hands, tender-hearted women have cooked their own children."

Josephus reports that there was some final attempt at a parley, but Titus then makes a long speech in which he rehearses a number of the examples which Agrippa II is also said to have listed when he was trying to dissuade the Jerusalem Jews from rebellion. Carthage, the Britons, the Germans (claimed now to be the slaves of Rome) are all paraded in metaphorical chains. There was, Titus is made to say, only one reason for the revolt: "You were incited against the Romans by Roman kindness . . . like beasts you bit the hand that fed you."

It took a further three weeks to build the siege platforms necessary to allow the Romans to complete the capture of the inner precinct. As the legionaries swarmed through the streets, contending Jewish factions were still trying to loot what was left of the city's treasures. The inner courts of the Temple complex had not yet been stormed. Two Romans, no doubt equally intent on loot, were captured alive. One them of was brutally murdered and "dragged round the city," like a surrogate Hector. The other—said to have been a cavalryman—was handed over to a Jewish officer called Ardalas, who blindfolded him and proposed to cut off his head in the sight of the besieging army. The blindfolded man managed suddenly to duck away and ran back to the Roman lines. Josephus remarks that Titus could have had him executed, but simply stripped him of his arms and dismissed him from the legion, a fate "to anyone with self-respect" worse than death. Does the vignette of that desperate, blindfolded man running from one camp to the other, and then left alive but without honor, carry an element of self-portraiture?

The last hope of the faction leaders and their gangs lay in hiding out in the sewers of the city.* Josephus has no doubt that the Jews in the tunnels would have had recourse to cannibalism if they had not been captured. Meanwhile, the Idumaeans inside the city preserved their tribal solidarity.† They succeeded, even in the last stages, in coming to terms with Titus, whose character, it seems, was to veer between grand gestures and pitiless fury. One of the priests, another Jeshua, was granted a safe conduct if he handed over some of the Temple treasures. He also brought out a quantity of rare incense and the curtains through which Pompey the Great had entered the sanctuary, after the Romans marched into Jerusalem on that first fatal occasion, more than a century earlier.

When the city was finally subdued, Josephus reports, nearly a hundred thousand prisoners were taken and over a million people had died in the siege.[4] (Tacitus put the figure at six hundred thousand.) Many had been trapped in Jerusalem only because they had come to the city for Passover. Even if the figures are again excessive, they suggest that until the last stages of the siege there was no great shortage of food or water within the walls. Perhaps the long tunnel dug by Zedekiah eight hundred years earlier was still bringing water from the spring called Gihon. The besieging Romans, on the other hand, had often been short of water; some of their forces had even deserted to the Jews.

In the aftermath of the killing and looting, Josephus was sent by Titus to a village called Thekoa to check whether the terrain was suitable for a "fenced camp." This has to have been the lowest moment of his collaboration. Many prisoners had been crucified. More would be,

---

* As the Polish partisans did in Andrzej Wajda's film *Kanal.* In both cases, none escaped. A recent Polish film, Agnieska Holland's *In Darkness,* tells the true story of a handful of Jews from Lwów who survived by hiding, for fourteen months, in the rat-infested sewers of the city. They were brought food by a "righteous Gentile." According to the film's postscript, when the latter was killed in a road accident in 1945, it was said, loudly, by other Poles that this was Jesus's judgment on him for helping Jews.

† So did the Sephardic Jews from Thessaloníki in Auschwitz.

when enough timber had been cut or requisitioned to nail them to. Of the war, the siege, the massacres and the reprisals, Joseph could say, as would Abbé Sieyès on being asked what he had done during the French Revolution: "I survived." When Joseph and his imperial master sailed for Italy, they left Jerusalem a smoldering husk. No city since Carthage had been so callously obliterated.*

The war did not end with the capture and sack of Jerusalem in 70. The pacification of Judaea continued for three more years, until the reduction of Masada and the defiant suicide of its entire garrison and their families, 960 in all. Echoing Josephus's pessimism, Eleazar—the last of the family of Judas the Galilean—was to veer between grand gestures and pitiless fury. He told his men that the fall of Jerusalem, which God Himself was said to have founded, meant the end of the Jewish people; there was nothing left to live for. Josephus reports that the Romans were amazed by the determination of the doomed garrison in Masada to dispose of themselves and their families.

The archaeologist Kenneth Atkinson questions the myth of mass suicide at Masada by remarking that there are no mass graves at the site.[5] Nor is there any evidence that the siege was as prolonged as folklore insists.[†] Atkinson also questions the Josephan claim that only Eleazar and his company of ultras and Sicarii were involved in the defense. He insists that priests too were involved. If so, how badly is Josephus's account damaged? As Josephus himself proves, priestly rank was a matter of social caste; it had nothing to do with spiritual vocation. And if the defenders did indeed die to the last man, woman and child, who would have stayed to bury them in a mass sepulchre suitable for mod-

---

* Almost two millennia later, anti-Semites in Arthur Schnitzler's and Theodor Herzl's Vienna would chant "Hep, hep, hep!" (an acronym for *Hierosolyma est perdita*) when they encountered a Jew. For two thousand years, scattered Jews repeated the pious wish "Next year in Jerusalem" as they celebrated Passover.

† The posthumous cult of those who, for the sake of the city, died in battle or in obedience to a loyal oath was not unusual in Greek lore. The much-respected Attic shrine of Aglauros was in honor of the daughter of Cecrops who "voluntarily killed herself in response to an oracle promising to Athens victory in war in return for a suicide" (Richard Seaford, *Reciprocity and Ritual*, pp. 212, 214).

ern excavation?* The Bible shows that the detritus of ancient wars was often left for the dogs to eat.

Another archaeologist, Mordechai Aviam, considers Josephus's description valid.[6] Remains of legionary equipment at Gamala confirm that a number of Romans did die there (more than at Jotapata). Aviam also thinks that, while Josephus may have exaggerated the scope of his command (many commanders do), he was certainly in charge of the defense of Jotapata.

No one has challenged Josephus's story that he witnessed seven thousand defenders being crucified around the walls of Jerusalem. It is the more credible since he says that he managed to retrieve three of his surviving Jerusalem friends from their executioners. Two were taken down after they had been mounted on—but probably not nailed to—their crosses. Whatever the limits of his treason, Joseph must have rendered considerable services to the Romans. He reports, not without vanity, that Titus offered him "whatever he wanted" when the city fell. He limited himself to asking for mercy for his brother and fifty of his friends, as well as for some two hundred Jews who had been imprisoned in the Temple, presumably the few "moderates" who had survived the purges of anyone who did not favor total war. Joseph also asked for custody of "some sacred volumes." Although Joseph had spent almost four years in the Roman camp, Titus was not, it seems, tired of his company. If he had been no more than an interpreter of the Jews' language and a now redundant go-between, Joseph might well have been left to take his chances when the Roman forces departed. His unblinking narrative testifies to his resolve to see things through to the end.

---

* Atkinson also suggests that the fall of Gamala, the hill town that somewhat resembled Jotapata, came about because Joseph revealed a vulnerable section of the walls to the Romans. He reasons that, since Joseph had, before the arrival of Vespasian, spent money on reinforcing the walls, he knew where they could best be undermined and so shortened the siege. Josephus's account may be melodramatized and—like all ancient histories—statistically unreliable, but if it is even roughly true, the Romans had a hard time reducing the place. That Gamala did eventually fall to the Romans scarcely entails that it was betrayed.

Since the *Vita* was written in Greek, it is not surprising that its main character pastiches the allure of Homer's Odysseus. Like Joseph ben Mattathias, the Greek hero had none of Achilles's reckless urge to live and die gloriously, and young. *Metis,* the cunning intelligence that the Greeks admired in Odysseus, was Joseph's prime quality. It had no nobler aim than to surmount whatever challenges and traps life might throw in a man's path. In Homer, in myth and in Sophocles's plays, Odysseus was portrayed as, in many respects, despicable; trickery was his great resource, as it was of his patron goddess, Athene. Reluctant to serve in the war against Troy, he faked evidence to revenge himself on the noble Palamedes, who had conscripted him to quit Ithaca. Odysseus was, in truth, a scoundrelly charmer whose resilience matched his determination to prevail.

The wooden horse was Odysseus's typically sly idea: leaving it as a gift for their gods, he relied on the Trojans' piety to procure their own downfall by wheeling it, and its hidden freight of Greek elite forces, into their city. Odysseus's singular concern was his own survival. Yet he remains the Greek with whom readers most happily identify and whose character inspired a catalog of recensions. In Joseph ben Mattathias's lifetime, Petronius Arbiter refashioned Odysseus into the antihero of his *Satyrica,* called Encolpius.* Like Odysseus and Joseph ben Mattathias, he will resort to whatever it takes to stay alive (all three survive shipwreck). Different as they may be, they each possess the attributes of charm, durability and double-dealing.

* Literally "in the crotch." In my translation of the *Satyrica,* I call him "Mr. Crotchety."

XII

JOSEPH HOPED, in vain, that the Jews in Jerusalem would surrender the city before it was too late; but however the siege ended, he must have been conscious that his utility to the Romans would then cease. What would become of him? If he was a turncoat of a kind, he never sought to exempt himself from the Jewish cause. In this he differed, for example, from a certain Antiochus, an apostate Jew—"son of a respectable father"—whose claim that the city's Jews were planning to burn down Agrippa II's capital prompted the pogroms that literally inflamed the Syrian city.* Despite his services to them, Joseph was too compromised, in the eyes of the Roman military, to hope for access to the *cursus honorum*. His most plausible role was that of oracular savant. His "annunciation" of Vespasian's coming glory, after he emerged from Jotapata, was timely but not unique: according to rabbinic tradition, Johanan ben Zakkai, a leader of the Tannaim, a Pharisaic sect trained in the oral tradition, later came out of besieged Jerusalem, where he had preached "moderation," and he too hailed Vespasian as *"Imperator."*[1]

Vidal-Naquet notes that, after his comely (if somewhat banal) salutation, Johanan received imperial permission to found a rabbinical college in Jamnia (modern Yavneh).[2] The Romans were ruthless, but they had none of the doctrinal animus that later armed European Christendom with vindictive zeal. After Jerusalem fell, the forced abandonment

---

* Damascus, the capital of modern Syria, was the locus of the blood libel that, in 1840, was seconded by the French consul in the city.

by the Jews of the ceremonial rites, and of the sacrificial cults associated with them, altered the practice of Judaism beyond easy recognition. It could no longer be centered in Jerusalem, except in the memories and hopes of its practicants. Biblical scholarship and rabbinic counsel were all that remained of the theatrical flamboyance of the High Priests and their acolytes in the Second Temple period. The sects that had thronged its courts lost the focal point that had held their disputatious dissidence together.

The Sadducees, as well as the Essenes, are said to have "disappeared"; but not for the same reason. The Essenes had been massacred. The eviction of the Jews from Jerusalem had the incidental effect of disbanding the Sadducees, if only because their worship centered on Temple ceremonial and dutiful repetition. The rabbis who met at Yavneh after the war agreed, however dolefully, on an "extraterritorial" version of Judaism, centered on discourse and texts. Johanan ben Zakkai inspired them to neo-Pharisaism. His tailoring of its practices allowed the studious style of Judaism alone to survive as a force strong enough to rival, and question, Christianity. As a result, the evangelists had reason to pillory the Pharisees of Jesus's time and to depict them, retrospectively, as His principal and priggish rivals. Freud's "narcissism of small differences" impelled Christians to widen the distinction between Jesus and teachers such as Hillel into a chasm. The de-Judaizing of Christianity grew more obsessive as time went by. It became psychotic in the mysticism of the "saintly" twentieth-century apostate Simone Weil, who wanted to amputate the Old Testament from the Bible and delete the influence of Roman civilization in order to substitute Hellenism and Platonism as the sole antique sources of Christian doctrine. The long standoff between Christianity and Judaism has always had the lineaments of a civil war. The two sides understood each other all too well.

By the end of 69, Vespasian, already sixty years old and of undistinguished origin, had become the ruler of the known world. His worthiness to be emperor was validated, in the eyes of the citizens of Rome itself, by the lavishness with which he was able to celebrate the subjugation of the Judaeans. Was anyone disenchanted enough to remark that his triumph was the first in which a Roman general had treated the suppression of a revolt in a minor province as if it were a new conquest? The advertisement of the pillage and destruction of Jerusalem added luster to the Flavians. His triumphal parade through Rome was a living newsreel. A family without impressive pedigree became instantly glorious. The nascent Colosseum—funded, so an inscription announced, by "the spoils of Judaea"*—was a monumental lesson, from which others were advised to learn. Under the shattered walls of Jotapata, Vespasian had been happy to take Joseph ben Mattathias's words as a divine omen; on his deathbed he would resume the Sabine realism that had been his mark as soldier and emperor. His last words—*"Vae puto deus fio"* (Alas, I think I am becoming a god)—convey succinct skepticism about the existence of any celestial scheme of the kind that, according to Josephus, had sanctified his autocracy.

Whatever might become of his native Judaea after the war, Joseph would certainly be a marked man if he stayed there. His years with the Roman army had been an education in duplicity. For the rest of his quite long life, he would always be intelligent but never forthright, never wholly himself. Like Racine's Christian, he might have said, "My God, what a cruel war! I find two men in myself." Life in the Roman camp, under often scowling surveillance, had required willful self-control. His writing proved an extension of the same exercise. Skillful verbosity offered a way of at once making a name for himself and secreting unspoken feelings. Josephus was the first of many exiles who, whatever their internal dissidence, impersonated conformity with a dominant culture. Need there be anything "typically Jewish" in such imposture? Roman and Greek education encouraged the emulation of noble models. Schools of rhetoric combined "creative writing" with dramatic impersonations. To be an advocate, in court and politics, was an exercise in style. To make a name for oneself was the common goal. Under tyrants, ancient and modern, outspokenness has been a luxury

---

* Unlike Nero's Golden House, which was intended to occupy the same ground and which was going to be paid for only by exacting taxes.

few could afford. Imposture may have its secret pleasures but, for the survivor, public conformity is the rule.*

Memories were all Joseph could carry with him when he sailed for Italy with Titus in 71, together with the booty from Jerusalem and the "tallest and most handsome" of the prisoners,[3] who were destined to be butchered to make a Roman holiday. Titus reserved one trophy for himself: Agrippa II's sister Berenice. He had fallen in love with "the Jewish Cleopatra" during the campaign.

A dozen years older than the emperor's son, she was, according to ancient standards, a mature matron of forty-five by the war's end. She is not said by Josephus to have tried to influence Titus's conduct toward the Jews as she had that of Gessius Florus. The fact that she is unmentioned in *The Jewish War,* after the outset of hostilities, suggests its author's tacit disapproval of a woman whose passion, or opportunism, was greater than her faith. There is a hint of Essene condescension toward female levity in the indulgence with which Berenice is spared solemn censure.

She continued to live with her brother in Antioch until they both traveled to Rome two years after the fall of Masada. The complaisant Agrippa was appeased with praetorian status and by an extension of his royal lease. Berenice and Titus resumed their passionate relationship for four more years. Since Agrippa stayed in Rome at least some of the time, it is likely that Josephus had occasion to solicit detailed information about the war. Their correspondence seems to have continued for

---

* Osip Mandelstam's 1933 poem deriding Stalin's "cockroach whiskers" was enough to lead to his long persecution. When Stalin telephoned Boris Pasternak and asked his opinion of Mandelstam, Pasternak was famously frightened. After he had finished equivocating, Stalin is said to have remarked, "Is that the best you can do for your friend?" Pasternak survived. Mandelstam did not. Stalin did not execute Mandelstam, but he made it clear that his minions should do nothing officious to keep him alive. It is impossible to present a clear picture of Stalin's vexed relations with writers without acknowledging how many of those he murdered were Jews. One was the short-story writer Isaac Babel, who said, early in Stalin's reign, that he had discovered a new art form: silence. It proved too loud for the tyrant. In 1940, he was accused of being a Trotskyite, tortured and then shot.

a while.* Suetonius says that Titus promised to marry Berenice, but that when he succeeded Vespasian, in 79, *raison d'état* prevailed. Titus was led to believe, perhaps by catcalls when he attended the Games, that the Roman public would not accept an Oriental princess, now over fifty years old, as his Augusta. Racine prefaces his tragedy on the subject by quoting Suetonius's curt text: *"Titus, reginam Berenicen cui etiam nuptias pollicitus ferebatur statim ab urbe dimisit invitus invitam."*† In the play itself, Racine makes the Romans' visceral dislike of all royalty the sole motive for Berenice's eclipse.‡

If Racine has it right, Berenice proved an unselfish, if tearful, Cleopatra: she agreed to renounce the man she loved for the sake of his reputation and future glory. It is tempting to see her rejection by the Romans as foreshadowing the failure of Jews ever quite to be accepted in European society, but Racine depicts her as unacceptable only because she was a "queen"; and the Roman people, he says, abominated royalty: *"Rome haït tous les rois; et Bérénice est reine."* Her Jewishness was irrelevant. In his 1844 essay on the play, Sainte-Beuve depicts Racine's Béré-

---

* As a species, historians play with inquisitive skill on the reminiscential vanity of those with privileged access to great places (and great beds).

† "Queen Berenice, whom it is said he had promised to marry, was immediately sent away from the city by a Titus as reluctant to expel her as she was to go."

‡ Racine's tragic heroine had an afterlife in the French brothels of the belle époque, which often featured a raven-haired beauty known as *la juive* whose exotic favors were particularly desirable. A conspicuous literary example is "Rachel when from the Lord" in Proust's *À la recherche du temps perdu,* another work in the Josephan tradition of redemptive recollection. In the Faubourg St.-Honoré, Jewish women of rich provenance had a greater exchange value than males. Two Rothschild sisters, both friends of Proust's, became the Duchesse de Gramont and the Princesse de Wagram. Proust's fictional Swann—based on a blend of Charles Haas and Charles Ephrussi—epitomizes the exquisite flâneur who, by his idiosyncratic assimilation and wealth, detaches himself from the mass of Jews, but never quite denies his Jewishness. It is suggested only obliquely that Proust's narrator has any "Israelite" connection. The desire to conceal Jewish origins is ridiculed in the character of Bloch, a Jew so reluctant to speak his name that he changes it to Jacques du Rozier. The young Bloch's pseudo-Homeric vocabulary is an early *fuite en avant,* a run for clever camouflage. His later assumption of a *particule,* the signal of aristocracy, conveys the sarcasm the snobbish Proust displayed for snobs less stylish than himself.

nice as "scarcely a Jew, already a Christian, that's to say, resigned" (to her eclipse); "she will return to her Palestine, and perhaps meet some disciple of the apostles who will show her the way of the Cross." There is no evidence that the resilient lady did anything of the kind. She came back, hopefully, to Rome after Titus was emperor, but her lover refused to see her. According to Ronald Syme, there is erudite, if larky, speculation that the fifty-year-old beauty then married the elderly king Sohaemus of Emesa, who, like Agrippa II, had supplied auxiliaries to Vespasian's four legions at the siege of Jerusalem.[4]

After his arrival in Rome, the renamed Titus Flavius Josephus was housed on the fashionable Quirinal, not in the main imperial compound on the Palatine. One of the consequences of his Roman citizenship was that it severed the connection between him and his children. Vespasian allotted him a stipend in order to write the history that would, on the face of it, glorify his patrons. These favors did not imply that Josephus was a member of the emperor's suite. He was never formally dignified as his *amicus*. The new imperial family enfranchised a long quota of arrivistes and hallmarked them with "Titus Flavius" before their Romanized names. Placatory donatives were distributed to clients whose gratitude would solder them to the new regime.

If Josephus was free to walk among the Seven Hills, did he find time to visit the new three-dimensional advertisements of Titus's victory? His illustrated arch was part of the stone furniture that conveyed what Ezra Pound called "news that stays news." The lapidary headlines on the Flavian monument told passersby that Titus "subdued the race of the Judaeans and destroyed the city of Jerusalem, which by all generals and kings of races previous to himself had either been attacked in vain or not even attempted." In the ancient world, when it came to rendering a falsehood true, no one was more convincing than a good stonemason. Hadrian's defeat of the Bar-Kochba revolt proved almost as great a military achievement as the Flavians', but it had no equivalent billboard in Rome.* As an addicted Hellenist, Hadrian cared more

---

* Hadrian was a more vindictive enemy of the Jews than Vespasian or Titus, whose repression lacked the "racial" animus of the later emperor. It prompted Tacitus

about his reputation in the eastern Mediterranean, where his monuments are plentiful.

Vespasian took a certain pride in his lack of august lineage. The great, now deified, Augustus was beyond criticism, but the last of the Julio-Claudians, Nero, was so disgraced that the Flavians made a virtue of their detachment from him. The new emperor took all available measures to make himself and his dynasty legitimate and respected. He built for the public's pleasure rather than for his own gratification. He despised affectation and artiness: when a young man came to thank him for being made prefect, Vespasian was affronted by his use of perfume and retracted the appointment. "You should have smelt of garlic," he told him.[5] The emperor nevertheless commissioned several works of literature, apart from Josephus's, for the glorification of his regime. Silius Italicus, Valerius Flaccus, Papinius Statius and other poets did their rococo best to embellish the Flavians.

The most influential (and durable) writer of the time was Marcus Fabius Quintilianus. The first professional literary critic and an almost exact contemporary of Josephus's, he wrote an oration in defense of Queen Berenice (perhaps as an exercise in winsome contrariness). He did not hail any of the epic poets of the day as a latter-day Virgil. Vespasian might be as ruthless as Augustus had been, but he was never as pretentious: when one of the literati flattered him by tracing the emperor's pedigree to Heracles, who was said to have visited Sabine Italy, he was greeted with "roars of rustic laughter." No such laughter would be tolerated by the church when it came to the improbable travels and miraculous achievements of Christian saints and apostles.

Flavian loot from Jerusalem decorated Rome's Ara Pacis, the Altar of Peace, which became a dynastic museum. It was swagged with the great curtain from the inner sanctum of Herod's Temple. Artifacts from Jerusalem centralized world power in the metropolis where they were on display. Most of the exhibits were looted yet again, in 455, when

---

to say, "In their treatment of Judaea, the Romans made a desert and called it peace." If only for the sake of an epigram, he afforded himself a thin measure of pity for the victims of the war.

the Vandal king Gaiseric conquered and sacked Rome. Almost a century after that, Belisarius, the great Byzantine general—a latter-day Corbulo whose victories served Justinian much better than Justinian treated him—repossessed "the ornaments of the Jews" and dispatched them to Jerusalem, for the enhancement of the Christian community's trophy cabinet.

In the decade during which he acted as Vespasian's deputy, Titus's generalship earned him a reputation for *saevitia* (savagery). Suetonius says that even the Roman people, who had never witnessed its fury, feared his accession (rumor and gossip were the only ancient mass media). Josephus knew much more than he could ever write, if he hoped to survive. Steve Mason points out that Josephus's effort to absolve Titus from direct involvement in Temple destruction "fits ill both with the Flavians' celebration of it (on the arch) and with the account—quoted, probably from Tacitus, by Sulpicius Severus—that Titus himself decided that the Temple *should* be destroyed," for pragmatic not pious reasons.[6]

Mason maintains that Josephus said as much as he dared to depict Titus as a callous conqueror; like a literary *sicarius,* his knife was concealed in the folds of his style.[7] Later Jewish legend has it that Titus died an agonising death, only two years after his accession to the throne, in retribution for the desecration of the Temple. For those who choose to read history as a plot, death is seen as the secret agent of divine justice. In his *Lives of the Caesars,* Suetonius reports only that, on his deathbed, Titus said, "I have made just one mistake." It is less likely to have been the sack of Jerusalem or the abandonment of Berenice than dying so young that his brother was left in sole charge of Rome. The unstable Domitian instituted a fifteen-year reign of terror, which Josephus had the wit and agility to survive.

Josephus's only society comprised people whom he could never wholly trust. If he was not quite like the man Tacitus describes as "running the gauntlet of the staring streets," shunned by everyone, he seems to have led an unobtrusive life. He is said to have lodged in what is now the Via delle Quattro Fontane, far enough away from Trastevere to suggest a fear that he might not be safe in the area where most Roman

Jews chose to live. If he lacked friends, he was not short of enemies. Not long after the war was over, a certain Jonathan, alleged to be a fugitive Sicarius, fomented sedition in Cyrene. When he was captured by Catullus, the local procurator of Libya, he was said to have implicated three thousand of the "wealthier Jews" of the region, whose goods Catullus appropriated "for Caesar." The procurator (possibly a descendant of the poet's family) dispatched his captive in chains to Rome. In the emperor's presence, the prisoner alleged that Josephus had sent him weapons and supplies.[8] It is not improbable that Jonathan wanted to implicate the hated collaborator in a plot with which he had no connection. His evidence, extracted under torture or in fear of it, failed to convince Vespasian. Jonathan was executed and Josephus confirmed as the owner of "considerable land" in Judaea. This was taken by Josephus to prove "the providence of God, who delivers judgment on the wicked"; in pragmatic terms, it indicates that he was still professionally useful to the emperor.

Josephus mentions that he took a new wife (his fourth) but offers small account of the people he knew in Rome or of the attitude to him, or to Jews in general, in the aftermath of the repression in Judaea. Malicious rumors dogged him through the reigns of the three Flavian emperors. The sadistic Domitian was his unlikely champion against his detractors; he is said to have punished Josephus's eunuch slave when he reported his master's supposed machinations. Josephus's ability to charm Roman women may again have served him well: he says that Domitian's wife, Domitia Augusta, "never ceased showering him with favors."[9] Josephus's last wife, "of good lineage," bore him two sons, Justus and Simonides (surnamed Agrippa). Their Greco-Roman names—either oddly or deliberately chosen to flatter a rival historian and a source common to both—suggest that he expected his children to be assimilated into Gentile society. The Hasmonaean connection no longer had any residual luster.

The only patron to whom Josephus offers direct, brief thanks was a certain Epaphroditus, whose identity is uncertain. If he was the freedman Marcus Mettius Epaphroditus, he was a renowned teacher of grammar and a former tutor to the son of the Egyptian prefect Marcus

Mettius Modestus.* A specialist in Homer, Hesiod and Callimachus, he had a big library that would have been useful to Josephus. Another Epaphroditus was Nero's former secretary for petitions (*amanuensis a libellis*) who helped expose Piso's plot against Nero in 66. Just over a year afterward, when everyone else had deserted the court, he was asked by the tremulous emperor to steady his hand while he committed suicide. This second Epaphroditus survived into Domitian's reign but was then executed, less because he had done anything wicked than as a warning to anyone else who might care to help hasten an emperor on his way to oblivion. Tyrannies breed duplicity; the courtier often doubles with the assassin.

Josephus remarks of his benefactor that "he himself has been associated with great events and diverse vicissitudes." This inclines Steve Mason to favor the second Epaphroditus as his patron. Hannah Cotton and Werner Eck take a contrary view.[10] Learned conflict proves only how little can be proved about Josephus's Roman fortunes. First-century Rome has been described by Vasily Rudich as "an uncanny world of illusion and delusion, ambivalences and ambiguities on all levels of social interaction."[11] Even though Nero had been blacklisted, criticism of the dead emperor was taken personally by Domitian, since it was, in the younger Pliny's words *"de similissimo"*: about a bird of very similar feather. Perhaps the paranoid emperor knew that his nickname was "the bald Nero." It remained prudent not to boast of favors received, however indirectly, from Nero's circle. This may explain the brevity of Josephus's account of his connection with Nero's empress, Poppaea Sabina. (Had he been more of a Suetonian gossip, he might have mentioned that she kept a stable of five hundred she-asses to provide milk for her bathtub.)

---

* Lucian's sardonic article "On Salaried Posts in Great Houses" suggests that erudition like that of this Epaphroditus was no passport to an easy life or to social eminence when dining out in Rome. Lucian makes it clear that alien intellectuals who provided great families with their academic house pets were always in danger of humiliation or ejection. That men such as Josephus's patron were themselves liable to be patronized indicates Josephus's own nervous standing on the social ladder.

XIII

THE EMPEROR DOMITIAN'S ATTITUDE to the Jews was never benevolent, but benevolence was not his first quality in any regard. The historian Cassius Dio says that in 95 "Domitian slew, along with many
others, Flavius Clemens the consul, although he was a cousin and had
to wife Flavia Domitilla, a relative of the emperor. Both were accused
of atheism, a charge on which many who drifted into Jewish ways were
condemned. Some of them were put to death, the rest were at least
deprived of their property. Domitilla was merely banished to Panda-
teria. But Glabrio, who had been Trajan's colleague in the consulship,
was put to death."

Martin Goodman claims that this purge proves that the "concern
of the state" was the rise of "atheism."[1] Is it likely that such an abstract
delinquency, for which there is not even a specific Roman word, was
of importance to a paranoid and sadistic emperor? It is more plausible
to suppose that the usual mercenary motives, not "anti-Semitism" or
the imposition of some kind of pagan propriety, were behind the killings. It is an anachronism to presume that the rebellion in Judaea must
have engendered widespread hostility to Jews in Flavian Rome. There
were no religious wars or pogroms in Europe until after the triumph of
Christianity. Nor were any media available to turn news into a form of
incendiarism. The distant losers of the Jewish War were known merely
as Judaeans. Daniel R. Schwartz maintains that, despite Agrippa II's
menacing words during his speech in Jerusalem, Jews elsewhere were
not identified with them and did not suffer their fate.[2]

Josephus's contemporary Epictetus of Hierapolis, in Phrygia—a freedman of the same Epaphroditus, Nero's secretary, who may have been Josephus's benefactor—also compares Jews to Epicureans and Stoics: members of a philosophical rather than a "national" category. The fall of Jerusalem had no theological deposit for the Romans, simply because they had no theology; the crushing of the Judaeans had only administrative consequences. It is, however, true that in Domitian's reign, the *fiscus Judaicus* was extended to tax all those who adopted "the Jewish way of life."[3] This was less a dogmatic sanction against Jews than a way of raising revenue. If Domitian had been an ideological anti-Semite, he would have been capable of decreeing that he had "forbidden them to exist," as—according to Cassius Dio—he did with the tiresome Nasamones (whom Lucan called *"gens dura,"* tough guys) in Libya.

Some historians argue that Judaism has to have been very unpopular after the Jewish War; but if the tax (first imposed by Titus) was worth levying, a large number of people must have been liable to it. Conversion to Judaism is also said to have become a "plague"—in other words, fashionable. It supplied a new band of taxpayers, some of them wealthy Romans who, as had Poppaea Sabina, flirted with the exotic. The supplementary charge of "failure to sacrifice to the common gods" also entailed the confiscation of property by the emperor, which suited his exchequer but had little to do with his morals.

Those deputed to enforce (and take commission from) these exactions are unlikely to have made a scrupulous distinction between Jews and Christians. Both, being monotheists, seemed equally addled. Suetonius does, however, say that the tax on Jews was "levied very keenly." Judaizers were prosecuted for evasion along with those who concealed their origins. "I recall being around," Suetonius says, "as a young man, when a ninety-year-old man was inspected, in front of the magistrate and a very crowded gallery, in case he was circumcised." The degradation of suspected Jews has rarely lacked a cheerful, prurient audience. In Rome, an added humiliation was that the revenue was diverted to the treasury of Jupiter Capitolinus.

The main motive of imperial actions was economic. Vespasian

put a tax on urinals, the contents of which were used by tanners as a source of ammonia. When his son Titus made the prim objection that it was unworthy to get revenue from piss, his father replied *"Pecunia non olet"* (Nothing smelly about money). Peter Wiseman has pointed out that when *pissotiers* were invented, in 1834 by the prefect of Paris, Comte Rambuteau, they became known as *vespasiennes.*[4] Among other, grander places, Vespasian's name has been found stamped on lead ingots from the mines in the Mendip Hills, in southwestern England. "A pig of lead," Wiseman concludes, "is no bad memorial for Titus Flavius Vespasianus."

Tacitus wished that the destruction of Jerusalem had put an end to Jews and Christians alike.* Tacitus's stylish snobbery was not animated by any spiritual investment in Mars or Venus; he deplored the infiltration into Rome of people who had exclusive and alien habits. Jewish unwillingness to eat with Gentiles was not seen as a mere dietetic foible. Ovid's versified almanac, the *Fasti,* makes it clear that Romans at table believed themselves *adesse deos:* in the presence of the gods.† Hence not to sit with them implied shunning their divinities. In the time of the Maccabees, the Greek citizens of Ptolemais, which was outside the Hasmonaean realm, instigated a general ordinance requiring local Jews to take part in a ritual feast to celebrate the Seleucid king's birthday. Those treasonous enough to lack Greek appetites were to be put to death and lose their property.

Soon after Domitian was assassinated (and his name formally blackened), the new emperor, Nerva, rehabilitated Flavius Clemens and announced on his coinage that the abusive tax on Jews had been canceled.[5] The new motif replaced the slogan *Judaea capta,* which had

---

* In a similar spirit, when Henry Kissinger was asked what he thought about the Iran-Iraq War, he replied, "Pity only one side can lose." George Walden heard him say it.

† The Olympian gods actually sat at table with mortals until the Lydian king Tantalus took gastronomic innovation to the point of serving his divine guests with the flesh of his own son, Pelops. This put an end to any such commensality. It was and is, of course, unthinkable that Yahweh should participate in a meal, although he is always properly thanked for providing it.

figured on Domitian's coinage fifteen years after the event. The last of the Flavians had needed all the kudos he could mint. Nerva had played no part in the Jewish War, but in November 97 he was forced by the Praetorian Guard to adopt Trajan (the commander of the legions in Germany) as his successor. Trajan bore the same name as his father, the Marcus Ulpius Trajanus whose fame derived from the ruthlessness he had shown in the Jewish War. Renewed advertisement of the subjection of Judaea would fortify the new emperor's legitimacy.

Josephus's literary life was solitary and retrospective; his topic was the world he had left behind in Judaea. In the *Vita,* the first thing he declared *in propria persona,* when looking back some twenty years after his arrival in Rome, was that his Jerusalem family was "not unremarkable." His priestly forebears are said to have belonged to the grandest of the twenty-four levels into which the traditional priesthood had been divided. Their status entitled them to the highest percentage of the tithes paid by the laity. Late in his life, Josephus rehearses his ancestors' eminence in order to promote his authority with an alien readership. The exile's narrow freedom depended on the skill with which he could present himself as the kind of upper-class man Gentiles would respect if he had been of their number. The impersonation of what the Romans wanted him to be led Joseph ben Mattathias to play first the seer, then the go-between and finally the ex–military man turned aristocratic scribe.

The greatest tribute aliens paid to the Roman way of life was to crave access to it and, once admitted, to assimilate its protocols. In literature, established metrical maquettes, taken from the Greeks, allowed poets such as Horace, Martial and Lucan to emulate their metropolitan peers. As the empire widened, previously alien peoples—first Italians, then Gauls and Iberians, followed by others, such as Britons, from more uncouth parts—were recruited to citizenship with calculated generosity. The emperor Claudius wanted to exclude those ignorant of Latin, but bribery or indifference often breached his pedantic fence. Less than two hundred years later, Caracalla decreed formally that every free-born person living within the boundaries of the empire should be regarded as a citizen. Caracalla is said to have been "mentally unstable," but he cannot have been all bad, unless tolerance is a vice: Saint Jerome records that the emperor had a grudge against his own father because he had witnessed a playmate of his being "seriously punished because of his Jewish religion." There is little record of similar indignation on the part of any Christian, however virtuous.

For centuries, provincial grandees and artists converged on Rome. Seneca listed the worldly reasons that pulled citizens from all over the Mediterranean onto the roads to Rome: ambition, the call of public office, diplomacy, luxury, desire for a liberal education, the theater, networking, manliness, and the prospect of classy ways of getting rich and famous. In Rome, the right style carried no traces of a provincial accent.* Outsiders were, by definition, contemptible or absurd. Aristotle had lent logic to vanity when he said that "barbarians" were natural slaves. His views licensed the self-righteous imperialism of his pupil Alexander the Great. "Prejudice" and civility were indistinguishable. John G. Gager claims that Tacitus pandered to the "anti-Semitism of conservative senatorial groups,"[6] but Tacitus was at least as keen to amuse himself as to crave applause from what had become, by his day, an upper class without the grace and gravitas that nostalgia attributed to the great figures of the republic. How many senators deigned even to know what Jews were exactly?

Josephus's failure to compose in Latin does not prove that he lacked the competence to learn its syntax. Despite having "consolidated" his knowledge of Greek, he admitted to poor pronunciation in alien languages.† With his usual ingenuity, he then made a Jewish virtue of

---

* The Romans themselves, like other muscular imperialists, had small mimetic aptitude when pronouncing foreign languages. When, in 281 B.C.E., they were negotiating with Tarentum (a Spartan colony in Magna Graecia), the bad Greek of the leading Roman ambassador, Postumius, is said to have been "so ungrammatical and strangely accented that the Tarentines could not conceal their amusement." (Cited by Mary Beard, reviewing Stephen Halliwell's *Greek Laughter* in the *Times Literary Supplement,* Feburary 18, 2009.) The Romans did not see the joke and brutally appropriated Tarentum.

† It does not entail that he lacked written fluency any more than Henry Kissinger did in *Diplomacy.* Accentual mastery is not necessary for competence, and need

his limitations: "Among us, they do not favor those who have mastered the accent of many nations and made their speech frilly with elegance of diction . . . they consider such a pursuit common—not only among . . . the free, but even among domestic slaves who desire it. . . . They acknowledge wisdom only among those who master the legal system and can bring out the force of the sacred literature."

The end of the war in Judaea left Josephus isolated between two worlds, a condition in which few Jews had been before and in which many after him would find themselves. Translated to Rome, Josephus walked among bruising reminders and relics of Jewish humiliation.* The Colosseum grew to be the largest. The paradox of life as a writer in exile was that once he had adopted the mask of another culture and residence in its capital, he was liberated to be more intelligent, because more ambiguous, than in his own.† For centuries, the Delphic oracle had specialized in cleverly cryptic utterances. Classical forms, from Homer to the Hellenistic novel, shaped Josephus's voluble discourse. He was not alone in such ambitious travesty: Saint Luke's gospel was emulous of Greek narrative models. Conformity with current styles won readers and lulled censors. Josephus's contemporary Quintilian, the prototypical literary critic, said that, in good writing, he looked for hidden meanings accessible only to the sophisticated: irony implied the opposite of what appeared on the page.‡ Sub/versions are the catacombs in which writers can embalm secret sentiments.

In the analyses of Christian apologists, Josephus was scrutinized, as

---

not inhibit brilliance, on the page. Joseph Conrad's spoken English was sometimes incomprehensible.

* One can imagine him deliberately choosing not to look at them, just as certain Frenchmen, like the family in Vercors's *Le silence de la mer*, refused ever even to acknowledge the presence of the Germans during the Occupation. Vercors was the pseudonym of Jean Marcel Bruller, an Alsatian Jew (as Alfred Dreyfus had been).

† As an exile in post-1945 Paris, E. M. Cioran—a Romanian tainted by his anti-Semitic and Fascist past—assumed a new identity by dressing his morbid *pensées* in the aphoristic *morgue* of an eighteenth-century French aristocrat (he also paraded a belated philo-Semitism).

‡ Archaism has the same utility. Josephus's use of Thucydides's fifth-century term *stasis*, when alluding to the civil war in Jerusalem, served to remind Roman readers

time went by, for secret winks and nods. Dots were not only joined but also, when necessary, inserted: his words were distorted and glossed* to lend him the oracular voice of a near Christian and so to align him with the version of Agrippa II who, in the Acts of the Apostles, said to Saint Paul, when the latter was arraigned in front of the king in 60, "Almost thou persuadest me to be a Christian." Christians assume that Agrippa's "almost" lacked ironic content. When the sentence is translated into Koine and said aloud, a hint of sarcasm breaks cover.

The abasement of the Judaean Jews was an instant and abiding signal to Christians that they had graduated to the position of God's chosen people. For Vespasian and Titus, the boast of *Judaea capta* enhanced their imperial credibility, not their righteousness. Christian fathers were the first to declare that "the Jews" were not only defeated but damned.† Roman legislators considered that the destruction of Jerusalem entailed no more than that the Judaeans no longer had either a communal identity or a geographical heartland over which a king could properly preside. As a result, although Agrippa II had not failed to supply auxiliaries to Vespasian and had hosted Titus's victory games (featuring "the entertaining deaths of great numbers of Jewish prisoners") in the city of Caesarea Philippi, he lost his throne as well as his sister-consort, Berenice. Josephus was then free to depict his now redundant patron, whose policies before the war he had called "peace-

---

how common it was in Italy itself, without Josephus ever alluding directly to the turbulence of recent Roman history.

* Steve Mason points out (*Life of Josephus,* p. 225 and following) that Josephus was alleged to have endorsed the divinity of Jesus of Nazareth by saying, "This man was the Christ." The term meant only "wetted, anointed" and was meaningful to Jews (while never implying divinity), but never to Greeks of the period, for whom Chrestos was a common slave name.

† The organizers of the new faith appropriated, consciously or not, the taxonomy that, in Aristotle's philosophy, warranted the righteousness of Alexander the Great's assault on the Persian Empire by designating "barbarians" —all non-Greeks—as natural slaves. Mutatis mutandis, Christians became the equivalent of Aristotle's Greeks and the Jews their proper inferiors. Further pious work darkened the Jews into the henchmen of the devil and the embodiment of treachery.

loving and courageous" (that is, the same as his own) in scathing terms: Agrippa is condemned in *Jewish Antiquities* for financing idolatry in Berytus (today's Beirut). Later in the same book, he is accused of causing divine wrath to descend on Jerusalem. Josephus also chides two of Agrippa's sisters for marrying unconverted Gentiles. Clearly, far from flirting with Christianity, he remained an unreformed Jew. Its gossipy detail also suggests that *Jewish Antiquities* was intended at least as much for Jewish readers, especially in Alexandria, as for inquisitive Gentiles.

After 73, to be a good Jew became a matter less of hierarchical standing than of observing the commandments and their bylaws. In the conditions of what became permanent dispersal, the priesthood lost its mystique. Sacrifice was never again part of Jewish ritual. In the Diaspora, rabbis were regarded as teachers rather than lawgivers, although—as Isaac Bashevis Singer remembered in *In My Father's Court* (1997)—the laity often solicited the in-house judgment of venerable sages.* Jews clung to their faith by obeying ancestral obligations to the Holy One. The standoff between Jews and Christians moved into the realm of ideas, to which the enlistment of both Plato and Aristotle as proto-Christians added Hellenic flavors. As Christian propaganda flowered, proselytizing pamphleteers, from John Chrysostom to Saint Augustine, depicted the Jews as an undifferentiated crop of deicides.†

Any charge—the blood libel the earliest and most persistent—might become an article of faith or folklore if it denigrated "the Jews." Like ancient slaves, they had no human rights. In the lubricious vocabulary of Christian malevolence, relayed by the Nazis, Jews are often said not

---

* Rabbinic verdicts were not enforced by any civil power, but they were generally honored as immeasurably more just than any judgment a Jew might expect in a Gentile court of law.

† After the Shoah, some citizens of the self-announced most Catholic country in Europe persuaded themselves, and hoped to convince others, that the Jews had killed Poland, "the Christ among nations." The Jewish victims of the Nazis and, in many cases, of Polish malice were transformed into the perpetrators both of their own and of Poland's misfortunes. Survivors were murdered or driven, forcefully, into exile.

really to be men.* In self-conscious refinement of the same sentiment, circumcision has been read, by some Freudians, as symbolic castration. It is more plausible to see it as the mark the community makes on its members: even in the most private acts (excretion and copulation)† Jews are reminded of a corporate, corporal allegiance.

The recurrence of the same first names in Josephus's narratives— Jesus or Jeshua, Eleazar, Matthew (Mattathias), Simon, Joseph, Jacob— suggests that, in Second Temple Judaea, family continuity and status were more important, as they were to upper-class Romans, than individual distinction or career; hence the unsentimental view of childhood and the paucity of autobiography and of any but rudimentary personal details about most ancient people and heroes, unless they had some signal defect or precocious merit (the infant Heracles was said to have strangled two snakes sent to kill him by the jealous goddess Hera). Blemishes might be remarked—for instance to disqualify a priest—but no one tells us whether Herod the Great, for example, was tall or short.

Fifth-century Greeks and Romans, in the great days of the republic, were equally disposed to regard "private life" as a form of dodging the column; militant citizenship was the essence of manhood. Pericles, in his funeral oration of 431 B.C.E., rejected the "idiot," a citizen who thought only of his own private life, as un-Athenian; no Roman patrician could secede honorably from the *res publica,* "the public thing"; hence the shame of exile and its solitude. Idiocy, in the Greek sense, was a form of unsociable selfishness, at least in the fifth-century city-state. In the Hellenistic world, self-preservation became the overriding

---

* Isaac Cardoso (in Yerushalmi's *From Spanish Court to Italian Ghetto*) testifies that it was common in seventeenth-century Spain to believe that male Jews menstruated. To read circumcision as a form of emasculation is a pseudoscientific gloss on the same notion. Arnold Schwarzenegger was never so Austrian as when he spoke of "girlie men," a description that, according to Otto Weininger, applied especially to Jews (of which Weininger was one by birth). Schwarzenegger was being no more anti-Semitic than he was intelligent.

† Cf. W. H. Auden, in pious mode, in 1944: "Everything [man] does, from going to the toilet to mathematical speculation, is an act of religious worship, either of God or of himself." (*The Complete Works of W. H. Auden,* vol. 2, *Prose: 1939–1948,* edited by Edward Mendelson, p. 229.)

concern; Epicurus supplied a philosophical justification for preferring provincial privacy to metropolitan ambition.* In Rome, sexual excess or romantic obsession (like that of Catullus and, later, of Sextus Propertius) was both a poetic trope and a form of dissidence.† Under the laws promulgated by Augustus, in his belated embrace of conjugal propriety, official Roman policy—like that of the Essenes and, later, of Roman Catholicism—made procreation, an essentially *social* activity, the sole righteous form of sexual behavior.‡

Augustus extended the vigilance of the imperial apparat to include the arts, especially literature. The most effective form of control was through generous grants to those, Virgil and Horace in particular, whose genius embellished the new order and found roots for it in mythology. In the republic, historians such as Sallust had expressed

---

* Cultivating one's garden was a less arduous form of the rural life that, in Greco-Roman literature from Hesiod to Varro and Virgil, was regularly celebrated as more honest than politics or commerce. Apprehension about money and its power begins almost as soon as the invention of coinage in the sixth century B.C.E. For a cogent analysis of the influence of coinage on ancient society and philosophy, see Richard Seaford's *Money and the Early Greek Mind*. In his *Politics* (58 a 37), Aristotle considered moneymaking "unnatural" as against the self-sufficiency of the agricultural way of life. When they were confined to the ghetto, money-lending became the Jews' main form of enriching themselves, when they could. The ancient anathema on such activities laid them open to another charge metamorphosed from ancient moralities (Roman senators were forbidden to be involved in trade, although they almost all gambled on the equivalent of the stock exchange).

† Latin lovers found a truer, supposedly more sincere, world elsewhere; passion justified absenteeism. André Malraux said that eroticism is "a way of escaping one's era"; hence both its attraction and the (now derelict) fence of pious prohibitions surrounding it.

‡ Although known to be practiced, homosexuality was officially deplored or ridiculed among the Romans. All penetration was conquest and therefore manly; but to be penetrated was to be demeaned, hence effeminate. Oral sex was explicitly ridiculed by Catullus and by Martial, as was masturbation in the biblical case of Onan (who may have been practicing coitus interruptus as a means of birth control, as men often did when contraceptive devices were unavailable). The ancient world needed all the babies its inhabitants could make, especially if they were males. The turnover of warriors in ancient Greece meant that it was more important for Spartan women to be pregnant than faithful; this led to the emancipation of female citizens, who were even allowed to own and inherit property.

their disapproval (or personal disappointment) in a more or less overt critical style. Writing in the reign of Augustus, Livy chose to go back to the foundation of Rome and to proceed no further than the Battle of Pydna (Polybius's nemesis), in 168 B.C.E. Livy's antiquarianism may have suited his temperament; it also avoided the risk of giving offense to the *princeps* (Augustus wrote his own *Res Gestae,* the official history of his achievements).* Poets such as Sextus Propertius made bold to deviate from the obsequious line followed by those laureates who touted for imperial favors, but he did so only with nervous effrontery. Although born (around 57 C.E.) during the reign of Nero, Publius Cornelius Tacitus, a socially eminent senator, was careful not to publish his caustic histories (which had a limited, sophisticated audience) until he was living under the indulgent aegis of Trajan and his successors. Tacitus's acid account of the succession of imperial tyrants that had ended with the death of Domitian flattered the Antonine emperors in whose genial light they were written. With all his social advantages, Tacitus bided his time before denouncing the aberrant Julio-Claudians. His unguarded eulogy of the old republic was a form of rhetorical conservatism which borrowed antique lustre to flatter the modern facsimile of a vanished aristocracy for whom honor and patriotism had prompted a principled and often brave way of life.

Under the upstart Flavians, of whom the deranged Domitian was the last, even native Roman citizens had been wise to wrap their sentiments in Delphic ambiguity. As a naturalized Jew, Josephus worked under the rubric which the brave and solitary Spinoza would adopt, in the liberal, but changeable, climate of seventeenth-century Holland: *caute* (be careful).† Josephus's verification of his *akribeia* (accuracy) in the light of Vespasian's and Titus's dispatches and of Agrippa II's comments helped turn his sources into his collaborators. The diatribe Josephus launched against Justus of Tiberias, in the *Vita,* suggests that the

---

* Winston Churchill made sure that, as soon as possible after World War II, his own prompt history of it should become the primary source for assessing its major figures.

† Spinoza wore a signet ring with *Caute* incised in it (Nadler, *Spinoza,* p. 244).

latter's criticism may have been sharpened because he was left out of the loop of subsidized authorities.

It has been claimed that the Aramaic version of *The Jewish War* was commissioned to alert the Parthians to the futility of provoking the Romans. If the original text resembled the Greek, it was an improbable book for anyone to read on horseback, whichever way an equestrian might be facing. Of the Greek translation, Josephus says only that it was made "for the benefit of the emperor's subjects." If it found an appreciative audience among the Jews of Alexandria, they took its moral to be that assimilation was the wisest course. By the second century, most of them had adopted Greek names and embraced the cosmopolitan culture against which the Zealots had risen in ruinous revolt.*

---

* Alexandria's population would remain a polyglot amalgam until Gamal Abdel Nasser took the chance, in the late 1950s, to evict both Jews and Greeks, not a few of whose ancestors had been resident in Egypt centuries before the Arab invasion, and to appropriate their houses and goods.

XIV

MARTIN GOODMAN is the most recent of several historians who have set Jerusalem at the opposite pole to Rome. He posits Jerusalem as a sort of spiritual Carthage: its destruction in 70 C.E. left Rome and its emperor to enjoy what the Chinese called "the mandate of heaven" and Christian apologists *"translatio imperii"*—regime change graced by divine fiat. As the symbolic home of revealed religion, Jerusalem has more often been placed at the opposite pole to Athens, which is made to stand for science and the humanities. Alexandria, by contrast, was a quite new foundation, willed into existence in 331 B.C.E., only three and a half centuries before Joseph ben Mattathias's birth. When Alexander the Great added Egypt to his bag of conquests after defeating the Persians, he created a city to stamp his authority, and name, on the most venerable state in the Mediterranean.* It is

---

* Herodotus set the style for regarding Egypt as the most antique of ancient societies and the source of Greek civilization, philosophy and mathematics. The impenetrability of Egyptian hieroglyphics encouraged the belief that they encrypted age-old wisdom. In recent years, tendentious theorists, primed by Martin Bernal's *Black Athena* (London: Free Association Books, 1991), have bundled Egypt and Africa into a single entity whose civilization, along with that of Asia, they claim to have been plagiarized by Europeans, led by the Greeks. What was true (and rarely denied) concerning alien influences on Greek art and literature has been exaggerated, sometimes to the point of absurdity: for instance, Aristotle has been accused of stealing his philosophy from the library of Alexandria, which was not constructed till well after

tempting to think that anyone of Joseph's cosmopolitan tastes would have been much more at home as a citizen of Alexandria. Its large Jewish population was of a markedly different temper from that of Jerusalem.

In a cardinal position, between east and west, Egypt's capital city was literally flashy: its harbor's towering lighthouse, on Pharos Island, advertised the city's wealth, welcome and innovative ingenuity (*pharos* became, and remains, the Greek word for "lighthouse").* It was a place of opportunity, as New York was at the beginning of the twentieth century. Its population was descended almost entirely from immigrants—many Jews and more Greeks, of various Hellenistic stripes. When pleading in favor of Rabirius Postumus, that otherwise ardent Hellenist Marcus Tullius Cicero could call Alexandria "the source of all trickery and deceit."† Cicero's contemporary Diodorus Siculus was less alarmist: in his view, no city could rival it "in elegance, extent, riches and luxury."

Although their biblical connection with Egypt went back to the Hebrews' enslavement under the pharaohs, Alexandria's emancipated Jews lived in a Hellenized city. Egyptians never figured among its elite. As in Los Angeles, everything that made the city great was built on sand. The upstart Ptolemies had soon displayed the cultural ambitions of well-heeled intruders. Their voluminous library and illustrious Mouseion (home of the Muses) were ostentatiously endowed. Salaried professors and librarians staffed an institution where schol-

---

his death. For an account of Afrocentrism as an assertive and distortionate ideology, see *Not Out of Africa* and *History Lesson: A Race Odyssey*, both by Mary Lefkowitz.

* The island of Pharos figured in myth as the home of Proteus, the changeable Old Man of the Sea. The lost satyr play that followed the *Oresteia* of Aeschylus involved a comic encounter between Proteus and Menelaus, who was on his way home from the Trojan War.

† Not without reason: Rabirius had lent money to King Ptolemy Auletes of Egypt, who refused to pay him back and then threw his creditor in prison. Rabirius escaped to Rome, where he was arraigned (perhaps at Ptolemy's instigation) for illegally funding an African potentate. He was acquitted, just.

arship and "music" enjoyed a virtually autonomous domain. Alexandria's Mouseion founded a new school of poetry, precious and arcane. In the third century B.C.E., Callimachus and his imitators (two centuries later, Catullus was among their smart Roman followers) created verbal artifacts in the spirit of Fabergé's exquisite baubles for the last czars. Specializing in recondite allusion, Callimachus played the cultural arbiter: small was beautiful, less was more. Embellishing a mythology concerning gods in whom they had no ardent faith, the scholar-poets of Alexandria were encomiastic parasites on a Hellas that no longer existed. Art was an alternative to life; poetry, a gloss on religion and a faith in itself. Cicero called Catullus and his friends *neoteroi,* a pun combining tribute to their youth with a hint that they were firebrands. In *The Jewish War,* Josephus regularly uses *neoterizein* to denote the instigators of social revolution, ancient Angry Young Men.

Literature had been among Alexandria's earliest exports. The first translation into Greek of what would be known as the first five books of the Old Testament is said to have been commissioned in the third century B.C.E., when seventy-two Jewish translators, all imported Jews, were sequestered on the island of Pharos at the peremptory invitation of King Ptolemy II Philadelphus. The separate sections of the text were alleged to have meshed miraculously into a seamless narrative. It is a pretty story, but scholarship has since proved that the Septuagint (which incorporated other texts as well as the Torah) was written by different hands at different times, as was the Quran.*

Alexandria's Jews might take their God and His ordinances seriously; but they could not deny or ignore that they were citizens of a great trading center and the neighbors of an intellectual forcing house. The lure of assimilation is caught in Constantine Cavafy's 1919 poem "Of the Jews (A.D. 50)," about a young man "from a family affiliated

---

* One of Spinoza's sharpest weapons, after he had crossed the line into apostasy, was the philological expertise that enabled him to state that the Torah could not be the seamless word of God, transmitted through Moses, since it was the work of various hands over a long period of time.

to the synagogue." In it he claims to care less for Hellenism's cult of physical beauty than for what he "wants to remain forever . . . one of the Jews, the holy Jews." Cavafy concludes:

> *But he didn't remain anything of the sort.*
> *Hedonism and the Art of Alexandria*
> *Held him their addicted son.*

Friction between Jews and Greeks was not uncommon and, to the Romans, not unwelcome: it justified their self-righteous presence as keepers of the peace. Egypt's grain crop was more important to the Roman economy than Alexandria's academic verses, although Roman poets liked to feed on them. Unlike Judaea, Egypt was the emperor's personal fiefdom. Its governors were always *equites,* members of the often mercantile and well-heeled middle class. The best of them could be relied on for administrative competence. Alexandrian Jews suffered more regularly than its Greeks from Roman repression, yet part of their unpopularity was due to a Greek tendency to identify the Jewish presence with Roman imperialism. The city's pivotal position required it to be policed with repressive severity. Its streets were said to be safer than those of Rome itself.

Apion, a local grandee related to the last of the Ptolemies, profited from his connections to become head of the Alexandrian library. He and his colleague Chaeremon wrote a history of Egypt barbed with disparagement of the Jews. Apion provided early evidence of the compatibility of erudition and fraudulence when he derived the Jewish word for "Sabbath" from an Egyptian word for a disease of the groin. His mention of Moses having climbed Mount Sinai suggests familiarity with Hebrew Scriptures, but Apion had been equally happy to retail the oddly persistent story that the Jews worshipped an ass's head (*kanthelios*) that was kept in the Jerusalem Temple.

Since the Hellenized Apion had died in 48 C.E., Josephus was free to vent his scorn and amuse his Gentile readers by putting down the old Homeric scholar as an "Egyptian." He must have known that the Romans found Egypt's animal cults outlandish. More important,

Cleopatra's notorious alliance with Mark Antony (who was said to have been subjugated by her Oriental charms)* had left Egypt's old ruling dynasty with a rancid reputation. No Roman emperor could take offense at a writer who belittled anyone connected with the Ptolemies. *Against Apion* was a prolonged apology for Judaism in which Josephus could exercise his polemical resources without risk of any response from their target. No one in Rome would argue with his jibe that, although the Jews might have been defeated from time to time, the Egyptians had never been free men at all, since they always served tyrants. He takes the opportunity to repudiate the charge that the Jews had a lackluster history of political insubordination and military failure. Misfortunes did not prove lack of courage. He cites the Athenians and the Spartans: "The latter universally agreed to be the most courageous of the Greeks, the former the most pious," he writes, noting that neither of them had escaped defeat in battle. Here he succumbs to the antithetical manner of his model, Thucydides. In fact, the Spartans were both courageous and—as Herodotus had pointed out—exceptionally pious. In 490 B.C.E., they had failed to reach Marathon in order to participate in the Athenians' victory over Darius because they had dared not abridge the religious festival of the Hyakinthia. They arrived only in time to congratulate the victors, laconically.

Apion must have suggested that Egypt had been spared calamity because of its true piety and prudence. In repudiation, Josephus lists a great number of temples, of all faiths, that had been destroyed, without including Herod's in Jerusalem. "No one," he concludes, "blames these things on the victims but, rather, on the perpetrators." Nowhere does Josephus accuse the Romans directly of the willful destruction of the Jerusalem Temple. He does, however, have Eleazar, the defender of Masada, complain that the Romans' uprooting of the Temple was

* According to Lemprière's classical dictionary, Antony was often lampooned as the sozzled Heracles being spanked with a slipper by Cleopatra playing the part of Omphale, the queen of Lydia with whom the mythical strong man was hopelessly besotted.

"*houtos anosios,*" an extremely unholy act. By putting the words in a rebel mouth, Josephus was able to appear to disown them, but it was still he who put them there.*

Apion also alleged that when the Seleucid king Antiochus IV Epiphanes entered the same Temple, in 173 B.C.E., he discovered a captive Greek who was being fattened for the annual sacrifice of a Gentile. Antiochus IV was the monarch who, by his furious repression of the Jews, incited the Maccabean uprising that eventually evicted the Seleucids from Judaea. Antiochus IV's "eyewitness" evidence smacks of a bad loser's parting shot.† Apion's recital of the plan to sacrifice the plump Greek was a seminal instance of the blood libel that, with a variety of Christian embellishments, would endure, despite its regular rejection, sometimes by ecclesiastical dignitaries, and metastasize into Islamic anti-Semitism and eventually feature, in our own times, on modern Egyptian (and thus Alexandrian) television.

The great Jewish commentator Philo makes no mention of Apion,

---

* He may also have been making an oblique reference to Seneca. Nero's éminence grise had accepted that political enemies or menaces (such as the emperor's half brother, Britannicus) could be murdered and conquered cities pillaged, but he is said to have drawn the line when Nero started taking treasure from temples, of all denominations, in order to pay for his architectural extravaganzas. Paul Veyne (*Sénèque*) says that, at this point, Seneca's versatile conscience required him to withdraw from public life.

† In the early years of his reign, Antiochus IV Epiphanes had been a genial Epicurean. The notion that the king conceived a vocation to universalize some kind of pagan monotheism does him undue honor. No potentate proposed a single god for all humanity until after the third century. Since Antiochus IV's ban on Judaism made a specific target of the Zealots in Jerusalem, it is possible that it was delivered after a warning wink from the Seleucids to the Jewish Hellenizers to make themselves scarce. Jews in other parts of the kingdom do not appear to have been severely affected, although circumcision was formally banned. The Temple became a condominium for Zeus and for Baal-Shamim, the god of the Philistines (Antiochus's personal deity was the Sun, with which he identified himself, perhaps for its golden gleam). To complete the profanation, the Seleucids slaughtered a pig on the high altar. In *From Alexander to Actium* (p. 515), Peter Green concludes that "all that Antiochus aimed to achieve was the elimination of a rebellious local group by abolishing the code that sustained it." The Seleucids had no time for missionary zeal.

although the two philhellenic scholars were contemporaries and, to some extent, two of a kind.* Philo could only have been an Alexandrian. His ignorance of Hebrew and his fluency in Greek prove that he would have been out of place in Jerusalem. Unlike his Romanized nephew, the apostate Tiberius Julius Alexander, Philo never renounced the Jewish faith. He did, however, read the Torah in a Greek light: his biblical commentaries reconciled Jewish and Platonic ideas. He also attended Greek games, went to the races in the hippodrome and enjoyed the theater.†

For Philo, the narrative in Genesis spells out the logical order of things, but does not entail their serial creation. His version chimes with Saint John's Greco-Christian notion of the Logos as the beginning of everything.[1] Philo's life was decorous and scholarly. At Jerusalem, his ideas might have made him a target for the Sicarii; in the Jewish community of Alexandria, he was revered as a sage. In dignified old age, after violent riots in the city, he was persuaded to lead the Jewish delegation that went to Rome, in 39, to plead with Caligula against the Alexandrian Greeks who had fomented the trouble for which they now blamed the Jews.

Herod the Great's grandson Agrippa had been the emperor's boyhood friend. He and Caligula lived in privileged isolation on the island of Capri, where—according to Suetonius—the elderly emperor Tiberius moped in pedophile misanthropy, an autocrat who splashed out only in his swimming pool, where he liked to be attended by a shoal of succulent minors. Agrippa had been sent from Judaea to Rome

---

* So too, in postwar England, were the philosophers Bertrand Russell and C. E. M. Joad, whose broadcasts popularized the phrase "it depends what you mean by . . ." When Russell was invited to review a book by Joad, he declined by saying, "Modesty forbids . . ." Philo may have taken the same attitude to the writings of the posturing Apion.

† Philo noted how, at a performance of Euripides's lost play *Auge,* the entire audience cheered two lines exalting "Liberty." The charm of the Greek way of life disposed an Alexandrian Jewish poet called Ezekiel to go so far as to write Greek-style tragedies.

in order to be educated and also to live unthreatened by the wrangles between Herod's heirs.* Fruit of a variety of mothers, they resolved the issues of inheritance by alternating fratricide with appeals to Rome.

In 37 C.E., Tiberius died and Caligula became emperor. Agrippa was rewarded by his youthful companion with the throne of Judaea. Almost immediately, there were violent anti-Jewish riots in Alexandria. They may have been encouraged by the prefect of Egypt, Avilius Flaccus, who had been in the post for five years. As long as Tiberius was on the throne, Flaccus had acted with impartiality toward Jews and Greeks. The prefect's principal office was to keep the peace and to make sure that the grain fleet sailed regularly to the new entrepôt at Ostia, built by the emperor Claudius. Alarmed by rumors of Caligula's execution of Macro, the praetorian prefect, and of Tiberius's grandson Tiberius Gemellus, among others left over from the previous reign, Flaccus chose to make trouble between the communities and then to side with the Greeks. What better than a spasm of sectarian strife to render his experienced services indispensable?

Apion's polemic, to which Josephus was to make belated reply, dated from this period. It justified the hostility of the Greeks (and Flaccus's partiality in their favor) by the charge that the Jews were not legitimate citizens; parasites from "Syria," they occupied "undesirable" parts of the city. The Lower East Side of New York and the East End of London were, for many years, similarly said to be infected by those who had no choice but to live in them. Jewish religious practices had little to do with Apion's case; they might be bizarre, but there was no unified Gentile doctrine with which they clashed, as there would be when dogmatic Christianity became mandatory. For native Egyptians and Greeks alike, the local Jews were resented not least because their presence was identified with that of the same

---

* Herod's treatment of his family had been so vicious that—according to Macrobius, a fifth-century pagan anthologist—the emperor Augustus remarked that he would sooner be Herod's pig than his son.

Romans who, under Flaccus's leadership, had turned so violently against them.*

* In the 1930s and 1940s, the Zionist presence in Palestine would excite a similarly dual rage on the part of the Arabs: overt when it concerned the newcomers and by implication against the imperial power that had introduced them. The British government had been obliged, reluctantly, to honor the 1917 Balfour Declaration. Neither the Foreign Office nor the military establishment welcomed it. Many in both departments sided with the Arabs, who were more picturesque and less argumentative. A. J. Balfour's apparent pro-Semitism was based on much the same belief in the arcane powers of "the Jews" to affect the world economy as was held by anti-Semites. In the dark days of the Great War, it had seemed a good investment to promise them something as vague as a "national home"; it would amount to no more than a slice of the as yet undefeated Ottoman Empire. When, after the Allied victory, the carving had been done, rare British soldiers, such as Orde Wingate, supported the Jews and trained the Haganah to resist Arab attacks. Even Wingate's partisanship was primed by the calculation that, in preserving Britain's communications with its Indian empire, the Jews would be more dependable allies, if only because they would have fewer friends, than the Arabs. During the Second World War, Wingate went to command the Chindits in Burma. He died in defense of the jewel in Britannia's crown, which the British soon renounced, as they would responsibility for the antagonisms in Palestine which their policies, and cartographers, had generated. If disdain for wogs and Jews was a commonplace with the British all over the world, it rarely issued in programmatic persecution. The overriding imperial prejudice, ancient and modern, has been in favor of maintaining the empire. Nevertheless, in "Shooting an Elephant," George Orwell recalls how amazed he was to hear an Indian "admit," without shame, "I am a Joo, sir!"

The confection of nation-states in the Middle East was largely the result of rectilinear decisions made in European chancelleries. After the enforced breakup of the Ottoman Empire, boundaries were decreed that took small account of the divisions, cultural and religious, among the communities they enclosed. Iraq, in particular, was a factitious amalgam. Its instability was designed to make its disparate elements rely on the British to hold the ring. The small, obstinate community of Assyrians, who refused to be acquiescent, were bombed to virtual extinction by the RAF during the 1920s. Saddam Hussein would be following an old Whitehall policy when he crushed the Marsh Arabs, of whose independent way of life Wilfred Thesiger wrote an involuntary elegy.

One of the expressions of the English genius, in the period when Britannia ruled the waves, was the invention of games, cricket and soccer in particular, in which conflict was socialized, violence sublimated, fair play respected. Common to them all was the paramount role of the referee or umpire, whose decision had to be accepted

In 39 C.E., Herod's grandson Agrippa landed in Alexandria on his way to assume the throne in Antioch. He was met and jostled by hostile demonstrators. A local clown called Carabas dressed up as "the king of the Jews" and parodied Agrippa's strut. The mob called on Governor Flaccus to put images of the new emperor in the local synagogues, a provocative demand that he himself may well have scripted, knowing that it was bound to meet with doctrinaire Jewish opposition, which the Greeks could interpret, loudly, as disloyalty to Rome. Flaccus took the opportunity to rescind the Jews' citizenship. They could then be pillaged and murdered with impunity. A number were killed and wounded, but the community defended itself and fought the Greeks to a standstill. Flaccus alleged that Jewish Zealots from outside Egypt had imported the violence, but his men failed to discover the expected stocks of arms in the Jewish homes they looted.

With some courage, Agrippa returned to Alexandria after the pogrom. Having investigated its source and conduct, he denounced Flaccus to Caligula. The governor's connivance must have been flagrant: the prefect was sent to the island of Andros and later executed. Philo interpreted this outcome as "indubitable proof that the help which God can give was not withdrawn from the nation of the Jews." The same determination to see God's hand in the affairs of men was to find a sorry parallel in Josephus's history of the disaster that would afflict Judaea after Philo's death.

On reaching Rome, in 39, Philo and his friends had a difficult time with Caligula. The audience turned into a shouting match between Jews and Greeks. The emperor—primed by an Egyptian named Heli-

---

without cavil if the players wished to remain, so to speak, on side. Teaching the world to play up and play the game elevated the imperial power to the role of disinterested arbiter. Only bad losers challenged its decisions or doubted its good faith; cheating was social treason. The regulation of leisure, and an appetite for admission to its rites, became a means of social indoctrination, both at home and abroad. The greatest of compliments was to say of a native that he was, or very nearly was, "a white man." A retired British Palestine policeman once told me that the real pity was that neither the Jews nor the Arabs ever learned to play cricket.

con, whom Philo refers to as "an abominable, execrable slave"—called the Jews "god haters" who did not believe him to be divine. How was it, he was prompted to ask, that he was acknowledged as a god by everyone else? Philo must have supplied a calming answer. Caligula soon proved more interested in teasing the Jews than in theological inquiry. Why should he take seriously the beliefs of people who refused to eat something as delicious as pork? (Romans rarely ate beef or mutton.) In an excess of amiable impatience, the emperor wished a plague on both their houses, Greek and Jewish, and dismissed them from his presence.

Philo probably considered a draw to be an excellent result. Nevertheless, several members of his delegation were kept in custody in Rome. The emperor's belief in his own divinity was no joke. Later in 39, when Gentiles in Jamnia, on the coast of Judaea, erected an altar in Caligula's honor, their Jewish fellow citizens were provoked, as expected, into pulling it down. When the local procurator, Capito, reported the incident to Rome, the emperor was incensed. Rage had become Caligula's characteristic condition. He ordered Capito's superior, Petronius, the legate stationed in Syria, to install a colossal statue of him in the Temple in Jerusalem.[2]

Instructed to use all the force needed to honor the emperor's decision, Petronius was astute enough to hasten slowly. He marched into Palestine with two full legions and the usual auxiliaries, but quartered them in the largely Greek city of Ptolemais (founded by the Egyptian dynasty at a time when it had control of the region). Petronius then commissioned a large statue of the divinity from the best sculptors in Sidon (whose artists were famed for their excellence). Philo reports that he negotiated simultaneously with the Jerusalem authorities, hoping that the Sanhedrin would find a peaceful way to indulge the emperor's desires. He hoped in vain: when the news of Caligula's intentions reached the streets of Jerusalem, a throng of citizens marched on Petronius's headquarters in Ptolemais in order to demonstrate, yet again, the Jews' implacable opposition to the emplacement of a graven image.

Petronius remained cool. Conscious that he could not do as Caligula wished without a wholesale massacre of Jews, he ordered the craftsmen in Sidon to take very, very great care, and all the time they needed, to make their statue a masterpiece worthy of its donor. He then informed Caligula of the scrupulous aesthetics behind the delay. The governor was pleased to add that, in the interim, the mood in the province was peaceful enough for a good harvest to be gathered. The emperor was not amused or appeased. Fortunately, however, Agrippa happened to be in Rome. He used his emollient skill to persuade his boyhood friend to cancel the imposition of the statue in the Temple precinct. In return, Agrippa promised, he would have altars set up in Caligula's honor in other Judaean cities. He knew, as Caligula seemingly did not, that such statuary was already a common embellishment in Hellenized communities. Jewish residents might avert their eyes from pagan images, but they had to tolerate and do business among them.

Knowing nothing of Agrippa's démarche, but aware of growing tension in the province, Petronius wrote to the emperor requesting that the order to impose the statue on the Temple be rescinded. As an administrator, he did the sensible thing; but his letter was delivered to a paranoid psychopath. Going back on his word to Agrippa, Caligula ordered a huge new statue of himself to be made in Italy. He proposed to ship it to Palestine and have it inserted all of a sudden into Jerusalem. Pending its construction, he sent word to Petronius, advising him to commit suicide. As it happened, the emperor was stabbed to death before the governor's deadline. It requires a hectic determinist not to reflect that, if Judaea had been governed by more officials of Petronius's qualities, the disaster Josephus recorded need never have happened.

Philo remains a remote and austere figure, but his patient humanism, spiced with amiable guile, was typically Alexandrian. The Ptolemies' city featured the great Alexander's tomb, but it had no presiding deity and no scriptural embroidery. Its hybrid population, if fractious, was more devious than dogmatic. The aesthetic skirmishing of its academics was testy but recreational, not religious. Its abiding ethos was a conflation of vanity, stylishness and opportunism. Alexandria may have seemed unstable and often, as Cavafy said, "frivolous," but it was also durable.* The stylish self-indulgence and idle tolerance of its miscellaneous elite—Jews, Greeks, Levantines, Copts and Muslims—sustained the ethos of antique Alexandria until, in 1956, it was ethnically cleansed by Gamal Abdel Nasser.

* In his *Ateli Piimata* (Unfinished Poems), edited by Renata Lavagnini (Athens: Ikaros, 1994/2006), Cavafy has one of the later Ptolemies, "The Doer of Good (or Evil)," declare that the Alexandrians are "superficial (*elaphros*) through and through." The irony is that Cavafy's ruler is himself fat and dozy, and nothing like the manly and forceful Macedonians from whom he takes fatuous pride in being descended.

XV

ALTHOUGH ITS FIRST EXTANT USE was by Josephus in the *Vita,* autobiography is scarcely an exclusively Jewish mode. It is, however, a recurrent means of expressing the solitude that haunts or dignifies the exile. For the Jewish intellectual, especially once he repudiates—or no longer has access to—community, the blank page becomes his only inalienable territory. In the first person singular, Josephus reverts to a world that, by the time he was writing about it, no longer existed. He is the first of countless retrospective Jewish solitaries.

Josephus pays tribute to his father both for his sense of justice and for the education he gave his two sons. He says that by the time he himself was fourteen, he was applauded on all sides because of his passion for literature. He can mean only the Scriptures and his glosses on them: "the chief priests and leading citizens" are said to have kept coming to him for elucidations. Cicero remarked, after dilating on his own achievements, that "it would be better if another had said it." Josephus's good report of himself chimes with legends of famous men who declare their genius by their precociousness. Apollonius of Tyana, a Cappadocian mystic and miracle worker of the generation before Josephus, was said to have spoken, as a small child, with astonishing grammatical rectitude.*

---

* With an exemplary use of parenthesis, Edward Gibbon said, in a footnote, "Apollonius of Tyana was born about the same time as Jesus Christ. His life (that of the former) is related in so fabulous a manner by his disciples, that we are at a loss to

The Temple and the synagogues, like the great European universities and the stern examinations for the Chinese mandarinate, offered an arena in which bright students could parade competitive ingenuity. The young Jesus of Nazareth distinguished himself through a similar ability to astonish his elders. Spinoza's genius was first revealed when he amazed the presiding rabbi of the Amsterdam synagogue from which he was later expelled with contumely. Excellence creates distance between the successful candidate and the examiners who, until he trumps them, sit in judgment on him.

Josephus wrote with filial devotion about his mother, who was in Jerusalem throughout the siege,* but childhood was not a topic for the record in ancient societies. During his time in Rome, Josephus must have observed how Roman grandees filled their houses with the statues of famous forebears (graven images, by Judaic standards). In the Roman courts, patrician advocates fortified their speeches, and sometimes secured instant acquittal, by recounting the achievements of the defendant's ancestors. Reference to his mother allows Josephus to validate the quality of his authorship by announcing that he had royal blood: a remote maternal ancestor was related to the Maccabees. Josephus may have hoped that this tenuous "royal" connection would enable him to pull rank on his Greco-Roman readers.

His description, in the *Vita,* of the three years of his adolescence which he spent touring the main schools of Jewish thought and practice is phrased to give the impression that his education, like that of any ranking Roman, involved making a choice from a buffet of philosophies (Cicero took garrulous pride in savoring a variety of Greek

---

discover whether he was a sage, an impostor, or a fanatic." (*The Decline and Fall of the Roman Empire,* vol. 1, p. 328, n. 71.)

* He reports that, presumably because of his own defection, she had been put in prison, where she was told that he was dead. She responded that she had "foreseen that this would happen ever since Jotapata and that even when he was alive, she might as well have had no son" (*Jewish War* V: 544–45). Martin Goodman (*The Ruling Class of Judea,* p. 210) gives Josephus no credit for reporting his mother's bitterness, but that he does so argues at least somewhat against the notion that he concealed whatever failed to suit his book.

ideas). There was, however, a basic asymmetry between Josephus and his Gentile readers: Jewish cultural aspirations were both exalted and limited, by the covenant, from the moment Moses brought the Ten Commandments down from Sinai. The tablets of the law did not tell the Hebrews what they might do to be rated good Jews, but what they had not to do. The "jealousy" of the Holy One preserved community (and continuity) by inhibiting deviation. Obedience to Him alone would allow the Jews to prosper, on the land the Lord their God had given them, "unto the thousandth generation." Innovation was never a good thing.*

The distinction between "Jerusalem" and "Athens" was patent both in the social structure and in the divinities of the two cities. Monotheism concentrated the wandering Hebrews into a common allegiance. The commandments supplied focus, a hearth for those without a home. Their discipline kept Moses's company spiritually in step as they headed for the promised land. It could not avert divisions once they had found it. Monotheisms, like monoliths, may not bend; but they regularly crack. All three enduring versions have suffered from acrimonious and often bloody schisms.

Social stresses in Judaea were expressed in doctrinal antagonisms (as they would be in sixteenth- and seventeenth-century Europe). As Leo Strauss insisted, mundane reason can never reconcile the children of a revelation with those who cannot, or will not, see it.[1] Jerusalem might be a great city but it was never, in the Greek sense, a polis. The irrational, and seemingly irrelevant, reason why Jews of the Middle East

---

* T. S. Eliot's "Tradition and the Individual Talent" was a tract in favor of educated humility and unromantic conformity to classical models. Seeking to be unduly original was a form of heresy. Eliot's aesthetic was more Jewish than he might have liked. He too can be categorized as some kind of a Josephus. As an immigrant from the United States into 1920s London, he adopted the manners and tone of a culture in which he could better express himself than in the land of his birth. His deprecation (in *The Idea of a Christian Society*) of "free-thinking" Jews just might conceal an apprehension both of their mockery and of a vestigial, if camouflaged, similarity to them. Eliot's *miglior fabbro*, Ezra Pound, another immigrant into European culture, with a Judaic-sounding first name, propounded an unbridled version of anti-Semitism. *Pace* Freud, there is also a narcissism of supposedly large differences.

were drawn into conflict with Greek neighbors and with their Roman masters was the Second Commandment. The Mosaic ban on "graven images" led the Jews to defy, and exasperate, a succession of foreign sovereigns. Josephus supplies plentiful instances of how the horror of desecration inspired them, repeatedly, to risk their lives against overwhelming odds.

Greeks fought and died for their freedom or their vanity; but what Greek of any city or allegiance chose to die rather than to allow a statue to be set up in his city or an "impure" animal to be sacrificed on one of its altars? Pythagoras was a vegetarian (he would not eat kidney beans because they resembled human embryos), but he did not expect his followers to die of starvation rather than chew on a chop. A law without practical utility was taken to require Jews to fight to the death for a principle that the worship of an abstract deity alone could impose. Like circumcision, the Second Commandment* denoted them by what they did not have in common with surrounding cultures.

Joseph ben Mattathias knew that the "Jewish War" might never have taken place without the delusive precedent of the Maccabees' triumph over the Seleucid monarchy in 167 B.C.E. Their rebellion was triggered by a demand by King Antiochus IV Epiphanes (his full, typically overblown title declared him "God Manifest, Bearer of Victory") that a pig be sacrificed, on an altar dedicated to Zeus, within the Temple precinct of Jerusalem. The order, from a king whose name alone was blasphemous to Jewish ears, was an expression not of orthodox Hellenic theology (there was none) but of exasperation with Jewish subjects who failed to give him the respect and—if there was any difference—the revenues he required.

---

* The iconoclasts of Byzantium, who reacted violently against the veneration of icons, showed equal zeal in vindicating the Second Commandment. The Puritans under Oliver Cromwell displayed similar destructive ardor; like the passengers on the *Mayflower,* they saw themselves as latter-day children of Israel. The decoration of Christian churches and the advertisement of the faith through images of the crucifixion and illustrations of the Holy Family aligned Christianity with pagan styles as against the austerity of Jewish sacred architecture (even though this too was sometimes richly ornamented).

When the High Priest refused, as Antiochus knew he would, to defile the Temple's altar with porcine blood, the king signed an edict banning the practice of Judaism altogether. He also proposed to defile the name of Jerusalem by attaching "Antioch" to it, in his own honor. His domineering actions had nothing to do with racial hatred. Cities were often renamed or hyphenated to emblazon a ruler's fame. Why else is the world badged with Alexandrias? Jews might be feared or disliked, their solitary god despised or ridiculed; but conceit and covetousness required no ideological license. Juvenal and Tacitus are often cited as evidence of ancient antipathy to Jews because they wrote scornfully about them; but the list of people or peoples whom the sour patrician and the déclassé misogynist depicted with admiration is not a long one.* It is true that, in his *Germania*, Tacitus seemed to find merit in the German tribes who, in 9 C.E., had pushed the Romans back across the Rhine, but his eulogy of the brawling northerners was intended more to highlight the effete decadence of contemporary Rome than to recommend the savage practices of the barbarians.

Judaism never threatened Antiochus IV; bankruptcy did. His decree was designed to hit people who had failed to pay up where it hurt them most.† Antiochus IV's closure of the Temple and the suppression of its cult would show the Jews who was boss.‡ Their unsociable God was

---

* Juvenal accused Jews of "misanthropy" and "arrogant exclusiveness," apt charges from a snobbish and solitary satirist.

† A tactic employed, with explicit relish, in Jerusalem in 1946 by General Evelyn "Bubbles" Barker, when—following the right-wing Irgun Zvei Leumi's bombing of the King David Hotel (of which a warning had been delivered to the hotel switchboard, but not acted upon)—he decided on the communal punishment of "the Jews" by "striking at their pockets and showing our contempt of them." Barker's mistress, Katy Antonius, was the widow of a renowned Lebanese-Palestinian Arab intellectual.

‡ Antiochus IV was on the rebound from a humiliating encounter. In 168 B.C.E., as he led his army into Egypt, he had been halted by a Roman delegation, led by Popillius Laenas. As Livy reports the scene, when the king held out a friendly hand, the senator demanded whether he would promise to evacuate his forces from Egypt. Popillius then drew a circle around Antiochus with his rod and said, "Before you step out of this circle, give me an answer to carry back to the Senate." The king hesitated and then complied, after which Popillius shook his hand and greeted him (we can imagine with what condescension) as "friend and ally."

a matter of indifference; the confiscation of what was left of his treasures was irresistible. The effect of Antiochus's ban was to make strict religious observance the binding form of allegiance for Jews when battling for independence, both then and in Josephus's war. The Zealots stiffened the Hasmonaean fighters into a uniform force. Exclusivity also divorced them abruptly from the civilized Levant, whose inhabitants, ever since the time of Alexander the Great, had acquired Greek accents. For many Jews, as for no one else, cultural assimilation became synonymous with treason.

In truth, as he must often have been reminded as he was writing *Jewish Antiquities,* Joseph ben Mattathias sprang from a mulch of cultural contradictions. The Semitic "bedrock" that F. M. Donner, for instance, claims to have been so solid under the Greek overlay of the Levant was riven with cracks. In the heyday of the Seleucid Empire, smart young Jews, derided by the Orthodox as "Antiochenes," took to going to the new gymnasia, where men exercised naked, in the Greek style. Embarrassed by what Gentiles took to be a deformity, some capped their penises with prosthetic foreskins. A number of Hellenizers ceased circumcising their sons.

There was, however, a limit to assimilation: "liberal" Jews might work out with their Gentile neighbors, but it was a transgression too far to eat with them or to admire their art. There is no evidence that the Hellenizers, who included some of the Temple priests, ever intended to abolish Judaism or to mesh with pagan practices. The allegation fueled the fundamentalist surge among the Jerusalem lower orders.* Unlike the Greek demos of Thucydidean times, the Jerusalem mob had no class consciousness: their labor was not vital to the local economy; nor was their muscle essential to the defense of the city. They found solidarity

---

* Its anti-Europeanism presaged the sentiments in the Tehran bazaars before Iran's Islamic revolution of the 1970s. Resentment and exclusion from power often assume the form of spiritual enthusiasm; consciously or not, the ayatollahs reprised the Persian magi's resistance to Alexander the Great in the name of the One God, Ahura Mazda.

only in accusing the upper class of heresy. The Greek habit of impersonating their gods and of depicting them onstage, quarreling, making
love between themselves and with humans, was intolerable to Judaism.
Man was said to have been made "in God's image," but Yahweh himself was invisible—although Moses had been granted a brief glimpse
of His hind parts during their summit meeting on Mount Sinai—and
unportrayable. The secluded emptiness of the Holy of Holies in the
Temple implied that, even where He was at home, He was not to be
seen or visited, as Zeus might be at Olympia and Athene was, in gilded
Pheidian majesty, in her Athenian Parthenon.

Yahweh's austere Second Commandment ensured that, although
there were some decorated synagogues, Judaism sponsored no sculpture, no secular art, no public spectacles. There could be no Jewish
Pheidias or Polygnotus.* The effect of Jewish obedience to the Second Commandment was immeasurable. The terms of the covenant
embargoed Jews from freedoms of which Greeks, if only by chance,
had early experience. The Attic theatrical festival of the Great Diony-
sia, instituted by Peisistratus in sixth-century B.C.E. Athens, was never

---

* Even in the twentieth century, Mark Gertler, brought up in the Orthodox East
End of London, wrestled with ancestral demons when he became a figurative painter.
In more pretentious mode, the painter Balthus, born Balthasar Klossowski, adopted a
lordly title and fabricated a Gentile lineage. Graced with the airs of an eccentric *châte-
lain,* he disembarrassed himself of ignoble Jewish origins and inhibitions. Prepubertal
nymphets were his favorite subject.

Marc Chagall had the nerve, after the Shoah, to revise the archetypal, implicitly
anti-Jewish image of the Crucifixion and replace the suffering Jesus with a Ukrainian
Jew as the emblem of martyrized humanity. The uses of tact had been exhausted.
Chagall broke a mold that can never quite be repaired: he made art a means of challenging the iconography in which, for centuries, Christianity had had a free hand in
caricaturing Jews and Judaism. The Polish Roman Catholic establishment responded
by raising a crucifix on the site of Auschwitz. It assumed that an institution that
had preached anti-Semitism for centuries, and kept silent during the Shoah, had
proprietary status in a place where hundreds of thousands of Jews and few Roman
Catholics had died. Many Jews were dispatched to the camps by governments, such
as that of Father Tiso in Slovakia, of which priests were in charge. The crucifix was
later removed.

conceived as an intellectual or political forum; it became both.* An aristocratic populist, Peisistratus bluffed his way to tyrannical power by rolling into Athens in a chariot, accompanied by a young woman rigged to look like the goddess Athene. She was an advertisement for which there could be no equivalent in Jerusalem. What would have scandalized any Jew was taken by educated Athenians to be no more than buffoonery and by the common people as proof that Peisistratus enjoyed divine favor, or at least that he had divine nerve.† His theatrical festivals began as a mixture of traditional folk drama and religious masque. The Greek stage drew from a ready-made roster of dramatis personae in the mythical repertoire of heroes, gods and monsters such as the Minotaur.‡ Although Peisistratus had no such intention, tragic and comic dialogue came to school Attic audiences in self-expression. As it evolved, the theater armed Athenians with the power to think, and speak, for themselves and to question the gods while continuing to honor them with festivals and sacrifices.

The Olympian gods were superhuman, but they spelt out no decisive morality, unless placating their ill humor (and satisfying their copious sexual desires) was moral. Zeus was a usurping parricide whose brute force was opposed by the maverick Titan Prometheus, the first proponent of the rights of man. The Titans had been the Olympians' predecessors as rulers of the world, but they were defeated by the superior firepower of Zeus and his allies. There was something slightly Josephan about Prometheus: since his capacity for foresight

---

* Recent scholarship (cf. W. R. Connor, cited by Seaford in *Reciprocity and Ritual*, p. 244n.) claims that the Dionsyia, in its full-blown form, was developed by Kleisthenes to celebrate the overthrow of the Peisistratid tyranny.

† The processional entrance of a god into the city was a feature of the sacred calendar in ancient Greek cities. It is no great stretch to see the emphasis on Jesus of Nazareth's procession into Jerusalem on Palm Sunday as a Hellenizing element in the Gospel narrative.

‡ The Minotaur may have figured, if only in a nonspeaking role, in Aeschylus's lost Cretan trilogy. If the tragedy was followed, as might be expected, by a burlesque "satyr" play, the Minotaur can be imagined as taking some kind of talkative part as a prototypical Caliban.

had warned him that the Titan cause was doomed, he came over to the Olympians. When they were victorious, Prometheus lent his wit to their parties, without ever quite being one of them. To amuse them, he fashioned human beings out of clay, as toys for the gods. After Athene had breathed life into them, just for fun, Zeus feared that they might become Prometheus's private army. He exiled them from Olympus and condemned them to shivering mortality. Prometheus then stole divine fire to keep them warm and cook their food.* Cooking was of itself a declaration of human independence, for which Prometheus taught his creatures to apologize, after a fashion, by making burnt offerings to the gods.

A benevolent Lucifer, he instructed mankind in how to deceive the Olympians: while ascendant smoke from the fat and bones delighted the nostrils of the immortals, the best cuts could be kept back for human festivities (fat priests are an ancient species). Prometheus was humanity's intermediary on high, a proof that intelligence could trump even the gods.† For the Greeks, comedy was an element in the play between gods and men, and between gods and gods. The Holy One of the Jews suffered no ribaldry and entertained no rivals.

Judaism could never tolerate the polymorphous insolence of Greek literature or the salty babble of Athenian democracy. As the psalmist put it, "Happy the man who does not sit on the bench with those who mock." The Greeks liked nothing better.‡ Their drama engendered

---

* There is nice irony in the fact that the classic study of the role of the raw and the cooked in the structure of human societies was written by an unreligious twentieth-century French Jew, Claude Lévi-Strauss, a wandering anthropologist who confessed that he detested going on his travels.

† Carl Jung regretted that no such figure was incorporated, as a kind of joker, in the triune Christian Godhead.

‡ Dialogue loosened Greek tongues; Aeschylus made controversy an art form. In the *Persae,* he imagined (if a little gloatingly) what it felt like to be on the losing side in the war which had made his own city, Athens, the mistress of the Aegean. With Euripides, tragedy veered toward satire: the gods became questionable. Aristophanes openly poked fun at war, slavery and phallocracy (although he made out that gyne-cocracy would be even worse).

new ways of looking at gods and men. Postclassical "journalism" was the other agency of Greek skepticism. The second-century Hellenized Syrian essayist known as Lucian wrote a notorious piece mocking the senility of Pheidias's great statue of Zeus at Olympia. Once regarded as virtually the god himself, it was now a sad old thing, more pitiable than revered. Lucian was, for many centuries, filed by severe classicists as "the Syrian Semite," but his chatty insolence must have given a sophisticated readership what it wanted.*

Plato had used his dialogues to condemn the "poets" who portrayed the gods as frivolous and immoral, but the Greek genius for contradiction and mockery—of which Plato himself was a copious exponent—would never go back into the bottle. A play such as Aristophanes's *Lysistrata,* which mocked the futility of a ruinous war that was actually in progress, by imagining a simultaneous sexual strike by female Athenian and Spartan pacifists, was never conceivable in Jerusalem. Aristophanes's scorn for what amounted to a Greek civil war between Athens and Sparta never earned him the accusation of being a "bad Athenian." If Joseph ben Mattathias had had a theater available and the talent to mock the savagery of the Zealots and the silly war they were bent on, he would almost certainly have earned himself the sharp attention of an unamused Sicarius.

Hebrew literature was never playful with regard to the Holy One. No Jew could question the paramountcy, still less the existence, of Yahweh and still be a Jew. There was no devious Prometheus in the Torah, no rampant Priapus, no tipsy Dionysos, no shameless Silenus.† The

---

* The notion that pagan society was yearning for some unifying, therefore monotheistic, moral principle is part of a Christian exercise in giving the Logos an integral part in European history. G. W. Bowersock, in *Late Antiquity* (Cambridge, MA: Harvard University Press, 1999), doubts whether, in practice, there was ever a "conflict" between paganism and Christianity. They lived side by side, and the former certainly infected the latter; but it makes small sense, if good propaganda, to postulate some Hegelian "progress" from ancient theologies to one of greater spiritual refinement.

† King David was the subject of heroized admiration, but his story never generated a cult that threatened the uniqueness of the Holy One. There could be no frivolous diversity in Judaism. David's deviousness, not least when it came to Bathsheba, the wife of Uriah the Hittite, manifests something akin to Odysseus's *metis:* excusable

Scriptures made the drunken, unbuttoned Noah a shameful laughing-stock to his children. In Joseph ben Mattathias's Jerusalem, the only public rituals were liturgical repetitions.* The mutual denunciations of the Jews were the debates of the deaf. Jerusalem embraced no public arena in which to enact or discuss them, no assembly for public debate, no means of resolving differences or deciding policies by the votes of the people.

In Athens, no preconceived idea was sacred. There were religious festivals, monuments and sacrifices, but no unquestionable, full-time hierarchy. The city's priests could, like Sophocles, also be its generals (not a very good one, in his case) and its poets. Although Socrates was formally arraigned, in 399 B.C.E., for corrupting the youth and for "introducing other, brand-new gods" into the city, the motives of his accusers were political. His allusions to his personal *daimonion*—something between his conscience and his guardian angel—issued from a vanity that irritated some Athenians, but no priestly caucus had decisive influence in classical Athens (although a priest did pro-pose the decree outlawing "irreverence"). Socrates might be associated, in the public mind, with the recently evicted tyrant Critias and with the turncoat chancer Alcibiades, who had played for both sides in the Peloponnesian War, but he was never arraigned as a "bad Athenian."† What condemned the mock-modest philosopher to drink hemlock was less any alleged heresy than his flippant arrogance in proposing, as a just penalty after his conviction for "perverting the young," that he be given a pension for life. A larger majority voted for the death penalty than had found him guilty as charged. The Athenian sense of humor had its limits.

---

perhaps, but scarcely exemplary. Solomon in all his glory had a flamboyance (in song and in grandiose architecture) not unlike that of Nero, but his reign ended in schism and disaster, which ascetic and celibate moralists could read as a divine judgment on the excesses which others might envy.

* The nation of priests developed no legislative forum for revising or laicizing society.

† Unlike Joseph ben Mattathias, however, he refused to save his life by going into exile.

Themistokles was the first politician known to challenge a pronouncement of the Delphic oracle, where Apollo was held to put words in the mouth of his divinely inspired Pythian priestess. Sprung from a serpentine source, she was renowned for her ambiguities. In 480 B.C.E., when the oracle was asked how to deal with the invading Persians, the Pythia's advice was to "trust the wooden wall." Athenian conservatives claimed that the words could refer only to the original flimsy timber palisade around the Acropolis. According to them, the god was proposing that Athenians make sedentary piety their only strategy. In effect, the old guard was resigned to Xerxes's overlordship of Hellas, if not to becoming the ancient equivalent of the Ottomans' Phanariots, a nice class of quisling.

Themistokles did not attack the oracle directly; he accused his opponents of its unsubtle interpretation.* "The wooden wall," he told the Athenian assembly, did not have to refer to obsolete battlements but could be a divine reference to the new triremes whose keels had been laid down—thanks to Themistokles's own foresight and as a result of a democratic vote—during the previous few years. This revision of the oracular message had something in common with the glosses on the Torah by which Jesus of Nazareth and Joseph ben Mattathias announced their precociousness; but when the Athenians voted to take to the ships and sail to the island refuge of Salamis, they put liberty before piety: they left the temples of their gods to be burned by the Persians. Thanks to Themistokles's tactics, they won a great victory.

By a somewhat Josephan irony, Themistokles himself fell out of favor with the Athenians and, within a few years, was ostracized. He fled into exile at the court of the Persian king, who respected his genius and made him the governor of a province in western Asia, where most of the citizens were, in fact, Greeks from Magnesia. Themistokles

---

* The Spartans, by contrast, were inflexible in their deference to the Delphic oracle, from which they derived "their entire code of laws and discipline" (Paul Cartledge, *Ancient Greece*). If Themistokles was some kind of a Pharisee, the Spartans were Sadducees; they admitted no clever glosses on the fundamental and immutable laws.

crossed a line he himself had earlier drawn. Yet after he was dead, his body is said to have been repatriated to Athens. Typical, if not exemplary, Themistokles was never called a bad Greek.

The Hellenes had no covenant. Although the Orphics, like the Pythagoreans, in their search for purity and salvation, refrained from eating meat, no holy scriptures dictated the Greek diet or circumscribed the Hellenes' conduct, sexual or social. The Jews were Jews because they honored the Torah. Originally homeless fugitives, they could never claim, as Athenians did, and the Germans would, to be "autochthonous," sprung from the soil. Jewish identity was a function only of communal allegiance to Yahweh, never of their place of birth (His ubiquity matched their rootlessness). Descendants of runaway slaves who had spent forty years in the wilderness, the Jews defined their unity above all by reference to the covenant that bound them. The Torah was their wooden wall: it clamped them behind an intractable tradition which they could never abandon without losing what determined their identity.

When Josephus applies the word *demokratia* to the decision-making process in Jerusalem, it is to persuade Gentile readers that there was nothing mysterious or esoteric in the social arrangements of the Jews.* The truth was that, in Joseph ben Mattathias's Jerusalem, the common people—its equivalent of the Athenian demos—had a say only when they shouted or agitated in the streets. If the masses sought to dislodge the old hierarchy, it was never to make any abrupt political alteration to the social system. The Zealots proposed only that the High Priest be chosen by lot rather than by the hereditary succession, which, in practice, had been honored more in the breach than in the observance.† In Jerusalem, since they

---

* Josephus also translates the Sanhedrin as the "Gerousia," as if it had authority as unquestionable as that of the Spartan council of elders. The notion that popular demonstrations are evidence of a desire for democracy, or that "protest" is in itself democratic, is a persistent illusion.

† In classical Athens, most municipal offices were filled by drawing lots among the citizens. For the properly superstitious, recourse to chance left room for the gods

played no practical part in the government, the poor and the unemployed were ripe for seduction by extremists. Ultra-orthodoxy, and the xenophobia that braced it, offered the only revolution for which the Jerusalem masses ever agreed to unite, temporarily at least, and fight.

---

to make their choices prevail. Since any Athenian citizen thus had the possibility of taking office, the process also abated envy or the fear of a political fix. Dr. Johnson defended the hereditary peerage in a somewhat similar spirit: since access to a title was due solely to the luck of being born into the aristocracy, no thinking man should resent the ascendancy of fortune's favorites.

XVI

In his preamble to *The Jewish War*, Josephus assumes the high ground by accusing his critics and rivals of having sought only to establish the superiority of Rome by disparaging the Jews. How, he asked, could the Romans be proved great by being said to have overcome puny opponents? The ex-general glorifies the resistance of the Jews by emphasizing the bravery and the resources required of their conquerors in order to overcome it. Tact coincides with sincerity when he chides the Zealots for their recklessness and for the internecine slaughter which followed it. He even suggests that the final disastrous conflagration in Jerusalem was due to the indisciplined fury of the legionaries rather than to a direct order from Titus. The latter certainly did nothing to stop it, though he may have regretted it on the morning after, just as Alexander the Great was said to have been ashamed of the burning of Persepolis.

Josephus treats Christians, en passant, only as a band of essentially Jewish eccentrics. Until the fall of the city in 70, the members of "the Jerusalem church" were conspicuous in honoring Orthodox traditions in the Temple. Led by James, the brother of Jesus (who was co-opted after the martyrdom of the disciple of the same name), they respected the Nazarene's teachings but never ventured to proclaim His divinity. It was unthinkable for James and his friends to offer cult to the Virgin Mary as "the Mother of God." Nor does any extant Hebrew or Aramaic text accuse her of the virginity which became canonical as the result of a wishful translation of the Greek *parthenos*.

Early forms of Mariolatry had more appeal to Gentiles familiar with female deities such as Cybele, "the Great Mother," than to Christians of Jewish origin. The New Testament's Diana of the Ephesians, the Greeks' Artemis, was a famous virgin goddess (and also a goddess of childbirth, although never herself a mother). The so-called House of the Virgin Mary has become a tourist attraction in Ephesus. It is a modest dwelling not far from the single pillar that is all that remains upright of the Temple of Artemis, one of the Seven Wonders of the Ancient World.

The liquidation of the "Jerusalem church" was a significant, if incidental, consequence of the fall of the city, and of the massacre and dispersal of its inhabitants. Since James was the brother of Jesus, he had been able, although a late recruit, to pull rank over Saint Paul and his admirers. Religion, like revolution, was a family business; seniority counted. After James and his friends had disappeared in the cataclysm, Pauline apostles outside Judaea had no rivals for doctrinal hegemony. Pseudo-Hegesippus glossed Josephus, in the fourth century, to make him say "God delayed the imminent end of the war until ruin could involve much—almost all—of the Jewish race. God expected . . . that the enormity of their crimes would increase until, by the heaping up of impropriety, it would equal the measure of His supreme punishment." The presumption that Christians were the spokespersons of the Almighty became habitual; so did the attribution to all Jews of whatever a particular group or individual might do, or might be said to have done. It is now generally conceded that there is no such thing as a Jewish gene; Jews may be all sorts of things, but they are not a scientifically identifiable "race."*

After 73, Christian evangelists made their separate peace with Rome by distinguishing themselves from the defeated Jews. Melito, the Christian "bishop" of Sardis in the second century, is quoted as saying, "You cast the Lord down, you were cast down to earth. And you, you lie dead, when He went up to the heights of heaven."[1] Melito's rhetoric

---

* For this reason, in the United States, individual Jews cannot seek protection from persecution under anti-racist legislation.

was sharpened by the fact that cosmopolitan Sardis had a very large synagogue from which he was hoping to siphon supporters. Shimon Applebaum maintains that there were "intimate and excellent relations" between Jews, Greeks and Christians in the city in the early third century.* Melito was selling Christianity, not remarking on the degradation of local Jews.

Thanks to the destruction of the Temple, the evangelists were free to remodel Christianity into the righteous antagonist of "the perfidious Jews," as the Roman Missal would label them until Vatican II, at Pope John XXIII's urging, excised the phrase, if not the sentiment, from Catholic practice. The long reluctance of the Vatican to recognize the State of Israel illustrates how God has continued to be assumed to be an agent in history, delivering due punishments and rewards, of which statehood was thought to be one. If the Jews could come to rest, especially back in Jerusalem, it did something to blight the notion, sacred to messianic cultists (including the Quakers of Spinoza's time), that their wanderings would end only when Christ returned to sit in judgment on mankind.

Theologians and rabbis have been variously resourceful in justifying the ways of God to men, especially since the Shoah. Their logic has scarcely differed from that of Josephus: however mysterious His ways, God had to honor the free will that, conveniently for His defenders, He had granted, irrevocably, to human beings. Their sins were their own; their punishment or redemption was up to Him. Some ultra-Orthodox rabbis have hinted that the Shoah was the Holy One's response to the scandal of assimilation, the self-willed sin of emancipated European Jews.† Like Josephus, such authorities deny that the Gentiles can be the primary agents of the disaster that overcame their people. Could any-

* See John G. Gager, *The Origins of Anti-Semitism*, pp. 99–100. On p. 31, Gager cites G. F. Moore as saying that "Protestant [especially Lutheran] scholarship . . . engaged in covert polemic against Roman Catholicism by projecting distasteful aspects of Catholic belief and practice onto Judaism and attacking them in that guise." Another instance of metastasized zealotry.

† The tendency to fanaticism and intolerance within Judaism should not be underestimated. In his autobiography, *Vixi*, Richard Pipes records that, in mid-

thing but some kind of Talmudic casuistry attribute the deaths of six million people, a quarter of them children and infants, to the displeasure of a God at the supposed misuse, by some of them, of the free will with which He had endowed them? It remains true that such a notion of effect and cause lies at the root of unreformed Judaism. Self-accusing vanity has kept some Jews at least convinced that the viciousness of their persecutors can be explained only if they are so important to Yahweh that they merit condign chastisement. Punishment and priority become indistinguishable.*

With his Jewish critics, Josephus could afford to be polemical. He honored one tradition—denunciation is among the oldest art forms exercised in the Bible—and initiated another: the invective that Jewish writers and intellectuals so often reserve for one another. In mutual recrimination, they speak and write without the reticence forced upon them by Christian repression. Benedict Spinoza was only the noblest example of Jews who attack Judaism, to the satisfaction of Christians who lack the wit to see that, mutatis mutandis, his disdain for those who believe in miracles and resurrection applies, with even greater force, to their own faith.†

---

nineteenth-century Lwów, a newly arrived "Progressive" rabbi and one of his daughters were murdered by an Orthodox Jew who had poisoned their food.

* The case of Donato Manduzio, mentioned earlier, provides guileless evidence. Ignorant of any of the inflections of Judaism that had accumulated as a result of exile, humiliation and Talmudic or rabbinic gloss, he interpreted what he came to know of the modern world, and of the Shoah in particular, with unsubtle candor. In April 1945, as a now convinced Jew, he told the Roman rabbinate that Europe's Jews had perished for their failure to observe the Jewish law. The Nazis were merely the instruments of Yahweh's wrath. In Flavian Rome, Josephus had to be wary of saying out loud that, if the Jews resumed allegiance to the Mosaic law, they might become rulers of the world. The guileless Manduzio, in post-Fascist Italy, knew no such reticence. (See John A. Davis, *The Jews of San Nicandro,* pp. 144–45.)

† Spinoza's later equation of God with nature, in the formula "*Deus sive Natura,*" had the logical consequence of discountenancing miracles, as if en passant: if God was identical with nature, and miracles were, by definition, unnatural, the deity would contradict His essential nature by performing them. Without saying so (his loud scorn was reserved for Judaism), Spinoza's formula proved Christianity to be by

In 64 C.E., after the great fire that had devastated Rome, Nero had
preferred to arrest and brutalize Christians rather than Jews. Before
the war in Judaea, cranky innovators were a likelier target for public
suspicion than members of a recognized, somewhat fashionable cult.
Nero inaugurated the public games with which he hoped to retrieve
his popularity by turning a number of Christian martyrs into human
torches.* In response, apocryphal Christian texts dressed the emperor
as the Antichrist, whose wanton persecution of their faith would trig-
ger the final destruction of Rome. His death, in 68 C.E., did not deliver
all that the Christians had hoped for, but it must have suggested that
things were going their way.

In an antiphonal variation, the Jewish "Sibylline oracles"†—
composed soon after the incineration of Jerusalem in 70—announced
that the deposed emperor was still alive. Although he had, in fact, been
driven to commit suicide two years earlier, Nero was declared to have
fled from Rome and joined her eastern bugbear the Parthians. With
their help, the bogeyman would return to the charge, put an end to the
Roman empire and accelerate the End of Days. In this way, Nero too
was credited with "messianic" resurrection.

After the Roman reduction of Judaea, Jewish brigand chiefs are said
to have remained in control of swaths of Parthian territory, although

---

definition absurd. It is not surprising that Spinoza admired the Dutch republic and
advocated democratic rule and free speech, although his own was hedged with caution. In *Natural Right and History,* Leo Strauss was more outspoken: "By uprooting
the authority of the ancestral, philosophy recognizes that nature is *the* authority."

* In due time, the Inquisition provided a similar spectacle for the faithful by
burning Jews (old women as well as men) in the long series of autos-da-fé that entertained the virtuous. Michel de Montaigne (1533–1592), whose mother was of Sephardic origin, remarked, "It is putting a very high price on one's conjectures to have
someone roasted alive on their account." His humane irony did nothing to curb the
salutary practices of the church.

† So called in imitation of the Roman "Sibylline books," supposedly inspired by
the Cumaean Sibyl from whom auguries were taken in times of crisis. The works of
Virgil, who lived for a time near Cumae, took on a similar aura. The so-called *sortes
Virgilianae* involved seeking guidance from a random selection of his lines.

the Jewish kings Anilaeus and Asinaeus had been deposed at the time of Joseph's birth.[2] Conversion to Judaism—as in the later case of Queen Helena of Adiabene, an Assyrian kingdom centered in today's Kurdistan—was a way of declaring independence from Roman tutelage. Helena was so ardent a Jew that, the story goes, she moved to Jerusalem for the last fifteen years of her life which ended in 56 C.E. Her elaborately rosetted sarcophagus (which served for a time as a water trough) is in the Israel Museum. A number of the sons of proselytes from Adiabene rallied to the Judaean cause during the siege of Jerusalem.

Jews outside the Roman imperium reacted to the sack of Jerusalem with unintimidated indignation. Josephus, like almost all Jewish writers of the Diaspora, especially after the triumph of Christianity, could never afford to express himself so recklessly. In the Middle Ages, anti-Christian texts written in Babylon, and beyond the reach of inquisitorial vengeance, continued to be unguarded. Shylockian sufferance was not a racial badge but a skulking concession to European domination. Since it also carried an undertone of banked grievance, it did little to allay the malice of Christendom; the worse the Jews were treated, the more keenly their enemies suspected them of plotting unspeakable revenge. The Christian conscience expressed itself in demanding even more repressive measures. As in ancient Egypt, whatever "the Jews" showed no detectable signs of doing—whether it was kidnapping Gentile children* or poisoning the wells—was commonly construed as evidence of their conspiratorial deviousness. The Jews were never in the clear. Among themselves, consolatory myths of election and loyalty favored an endogamous and unchanging solidarity.

No one recorded the year or the manner of the death of Titus Flavius Josephus. It may, however, be unduly romantic to assume that

---

* There is no evidence than any Christian child was ever kidnapped for ritual purposes by any Jew anywhere. In the aftermath of the Shoah, however, Jewish parents and relatives of children who had been secreted by Catholic institutions, and baptized in the process, managed to retrieve their purloined offspring only with the greatest difficulty and often after prolonged wrangling.

he was entirely without honor or entourage in his exile. Eusebius, the Christian bishop of Caesarea in the fourth century, says that a statue honoring Josephus had been erected in Rome, but does not specify by whom. Since personal commemorative statuary was contrary to Jewish tradition, it may be that the Flavians commissioned it for services rendered. It would be a pretty irony if Josephus's sons had become sufficiently Romanized to celebrate their father's fame (or vindicate his name) by an act of aesthetic apostasy. In any case, neither Justus nor Simonides left a noticeable mark on the society into which, if his choice of their names is any indication, he hoped they would be at least somewhat assimilated.

As a historian, Josephus would have a long, unended afterlife. The craving for Christian unity, regularly proclaimed in Rome and elsewhere, implies the hope for the eventual elimination or conversion of those who will not go along with it. Faith and coercion are old allies. As a result of Christian readings, Josephus's work, like his character, has suffered from frequent posthumous resection. Imaginative clerics interpolated whatever might enhance their visions or brace their faith. His Victorian translator, William Whiston, appears the slyest, perhaps because he seems only inadvertently biased. He thought he was rendering a faithful version, and so he was: one that chimed with his own creed.

Josephus can hardly be blamed because Crusaders took his works with them as a guidebook to the city whose inhabitants they put to the sword with affectations of godly purpose. His defense of Judaism was less keenly honored. In the so-called Slavonic fourteenth-century manuscript, a passage was "discovered" in which Josephus was made out to endorse the divinity of Jesus of Nazareth. Étienne Nodet, a French Dominican, would like this "restoration" to reveal Josephus's "interest in a very Jewish Jesus movement in Judaea, different from the Christianity he encountered only in Rome."* The implication is that

---

* See the notes and appendix to Nodet's translation, *Flavius Josèphe: L'homme et l'historien* (*Josephus: The Man and Historian* [New York: Cerf, 2000]), of the translation by Henry St. John Thackeray (1929).

Josephus was some kind of General de Gaulle *avant la lettre,* a leader in exile planning some "reorganized Judaism." This ambition is held to explain why he is uncited in rabbinic sources; neither were the Essenes nor the Maccabees.

In reliable manuscripts, Josephus alludes to Jesus only casually, but he does use the superlative (*deinotatos*) to highlight both his cleverness and his aura. The same term designates others, such as the rabble-rouser Theudas, who are depicted as no more than charismatic miracle workers in the tradition of the first-century C.E. figure Hanina ben Dosa and of Choni the Circle Drawer of the first century B.C.E. Because Josephus's work lies at the intersection of history and myth, creeds and ideologies (from Christianity to Zionism), he provokes responses that carry perennial freight. His text was further improved to make Josephus say that the Temple was destroyed solely as punishment for the Jews' crucifixion of Jesus of Nazareth. Other Christian enthusiasts concocted a correspondence—cited by Saint Jerome and Saint Augustine as if it were genuine—between Josephus's contemporary Seneca and Saint Paul.

Uriel Rappaport has gone as far as to say that "the claims Josephus makes about his achievements during the war, as well as the personal qualities he ascribes to himself, are unsubstantiated and outlandish."[3] Since Josephus supplies the only account available, it is quite proper to question aspects of his story, but he can hardly be blamed for supplying no corroborating (or self-contradictory) texts. As for "outlandish," the term sounds dismissive or disdainful, but antiquity is, as L. P. Hartley put it, "a foreign country"; it required rare qualities to survive in it, especially as any kind of a leader. Alexander the Great set the style for leading from the front by being the first over the tall battlements of Tyre. It is hard to conceive that Joseph ben Mattathias's enrollment by Vespasian did not owe something to the extraordinary and soldierly qualities he showed during the siege of Jotapata.

Rappaport backs his view by recourse to psychiatric jargon: Josephus is said to have dissembled his failings by creating an "Ideal Ego." The charge is at least somewhat plausible because quasi-tautological:

most people, especially authors, tend to do the same. The components of Josephus's public personality are said to have "provided a response to the pressures he faced. . . . Pro-Roman but pretending otherwise, Josephus had recourse to *legerdemain* to avoid confrontation with enemy forces." If Rappaport thinks that Joseph would have been a better general by meeting the Romans in open battle, he understands nothing of the military odds. After the Roman legions had been almost annihilated at the battle of Cannae in 216 B.C.E., Quintus Fabius Maximus was nominated temporary dictator. His tactics were to shadow and harass Hannibal's armies but never to be lured into direct combat. The dictator's methods were, by Roman standards, outlandish if not unmanly, but they were also effective.

Josephus's ambiguities may shock Rappaport; Plutarch would have found them unsurprising. In his "Advice to the Politician," he says, "if war comes, leaders have to be duplicitous: they must be in command of a revolt that cannot succeed, and try to steer toward a just climbdown." In Rappaport's account, the central episode of the siege of Jotapata is a fantasy, in which the historian uses tricks that "must have been copied" from military handbooks. A more genial view would be that Joseph had learned a trick or two from whatever old hands, or old handbooks, were available. He never suggests that no one had ever resorted to the tricks he used; disguising his couriers in sheepskins was a remake of Odysseus's ruse to get his men safely out of Polyphemus's cave. Taking his own presumption as evidence, Rappaport concludes that Joseph ben Mattathias was not involved in the defense of the town. The story of his survival "lacks all historical value, except to reveal . . . Josephus's double life between Rome and the Jewish nation." Little detective work is needed to show that Joseph had had contacts with the imperial power. As for "the Jewish nation," was there any such entity?

Rappaport tells us as much about himself as about Josephus. His psychodramatized reading of the historian's life and character is itself open to metapsychiatry. Not even Justus, Josephus's fierce contemporary critic, suggests that events of the kind Josephus describes did not take place at Jotapata or elsewhere. The animus directed against

Josephus generates a black-and-white moral crux. It ignores the simple truth that Joseph did not need to be pro-Roman in order to be anti-war. He was not necessarily false to his native city if he did all he could to prevent its destruction. It is going a little far then to accuse him of being responsible for it.

XVII

JOSEPHUS STANDS AS THE INITIATOR of the Jewish writer's long trek along an unending "road into the open."* The charge that the culture and art of the Jews is parasitic rather than authentic derives essentially (hence inescapably) from their dispossession of Jerusalem.† Josephus has been accused by literary surveyors of tailoring *Jewish Antiquities* in symmetry with the Greco-Roman history of Dionysios of Halikarnassus. With scarcely surreptitious animus, his critics point out that Josephus's Book X ends with the fall of Solomon's Temple, Book XX with the fall of Herod's.‡ The implication is that Josephus is not to be trusted as a historian because he imposed a certain shapeliness on his work. In truth, it is as likely that he sought to blend with the going literary models as it is certain that Roman writers, in prose and verse, made a similar virtue of the sublime plagiarism of Greek models. Solitude gave Josephus the time for the aesthetic refinement of his mar-

---

* An expression used, with some irony, in the title of a 1908 novel by Arthur Schnitzler.

† After the suppression by Hadrian of the revolt of Bar Kochba in 125 C.E., no circumcised person was admitted into "Aelia Capitolina," as Jerusalem was officially renamed.

‡ Richard Seaford argues, in *Reciprocity and Ritual,* that the shapeliness of the *Iliad* was fashioned only at the end of its protracted evolution to the "authorized" version of the sixth century B.C.E. Prosaic history took on the lineaments of epic and, in its formal structure, mimicked the idea of "justice," which moralized both epic and tragedy (comedy found small place in it). The Holy Grail of historians is to discover the pattern that runs through the past and present, into the future.

ginal existence. His case was exceptional only because he lived an isolated life: in antiquity, Jews did not, as a rule, hide their heads or seek, like Marcel Proust's Bloch (or, indeed, like Proust himself), to pass themselves off as reproduction Gentiles, although the more assimilated of them, when writing in the vernacular, imitated earlier masters.* As Richard Wagner showed, the charge that "the Jews" lacked originality was the expression of programmatic anti-Semitism. It is at least tempting to see Europe's long and varied efforts to disqualify the Jews from civilization as a symptom of the repression of how much Christianity owes to what Pope John-Paul I had the belated grace to call his "older brother Joseph."†

Some estimates of the size of the Jewish population of the Roman world at the time of Josephus's war put the figure as high as 10 percent. This number, or anything close to it, greatly exceeds the tally of Jews resident in Judaea before the alleged dispersal of its population, even when it is combined with that of Alexandria. It follows that adherents of Judaism, whether by birth or by conviction, were widespread. The speed with which Pauline Christianity recruited converts suggests that Jewish messianic imagery had shaped audiences to be receptive to the Gospel of a modified, often quasi-Pharisaic, monotheism. For the Jews themselves, the ruin of Jerusalem and the destruction of Herod's Temple was a disaster with enduringly agonizing consequences, especially as it was depicted in Christian mythology. What happened in Judaea did not, however, lead to any crisis of faith, or campaign of persecution, in other parts of the Mediterranean. The large Jewish community in Alexandria continued to have vexed relations with its Gentile neighbors, but the tendency to assimilate seems to have secured it from any sustained repression. The Romans saw no necessary seditious con-

---

* Who does not? André Malraux put it succinctly: "One does not become an artist by looking at life, but by looking at art."

† With deconstructive effort, a master of the subtle arts might read even T. S. Eliot's somewhat regretted line "The jew is underneath the lot" as an involuntary recognition of the outcast's fundamental role. The Khazar king in Yehuda Halevi's *Kuzari* (see p. 228) is more gracious in recognizing that both Christianity and Islam gained their presumed validity from their dependence on Jewish Scriptures.

nection between the Judaeans and other Jews, though they took the opportunity to raise extra taxes.

Christianity came to replace Judaism not least because it universalized (and cannibalized) themes already present in the Talmud and in what came to be called the Old Testament. Christians of various kinds, down the centuries, would gladly have dispensed with the Jewish sources of their own religion. They were embarrassed by its roots among the people from whom their Savior had sprung and to whom He chose exclusively to preach and whom they now derided as little better than vermin.* The standoff between Christians and Jews has elements of the *stasis* Josephus described within the precincts of the Temple, in which one sect or faction of Jews was literally at daggers drawn with another over matters of doctrinal detail and political ascendancy. Even the quarrels between Arian and Orthodox Christians, between Monophysites and Homoousians can be seen as a revision of the disputes between Sadducees and Pharisees that Joseph ben Mattathias witnessed in his youth.

It took more than three centuries after the fall of Jerusalem for Christianity to achieve the critical mass that, thanks to the declaration of Constantine, promoted it to primacy among the many religions and cults in the empire. Even then, Constantine never sought to impose the Christian faith on his subjects. Pagan practices of one kind and another persisted in Europe deep into the Middle Ages. Judaism was eclipsed, but it never dwindled into the obsolescence that Arnold Toynbee, for malevolent instance, wished upon it. The venom with which the Christian fathers denounced Judaism (Saint Louis† burned its books before more diligent Christians proceeded to burn Jews) is proof of the infuriating persistence of the ancient faith. The vindictiveness of the Holy Inquisition indicates a morbid obsession, on the part of Mother Church, with rescinding the debt Christianity owed to the first "People of the Book." In the so-called Dark Ages and for some

---

* Nazi artists devised images of an "Aryan" Jesus, blond and blue-eyed. The Mexicans pay homage to a black Madonna. Icons are rarely a good likeness.

† King Louis IX of France (1214–1270).

centuries afterward, Spanish Jews found themselves much more happily at home with the followers of Muhammad. The Arab conquest of Egypt, in the seventh century, was no gentle takeover (the burning of the libraries of Alexandria reciprocated the great Alexander's sack of Persepolis), but the Prophet had specifically recommended respect both for Christianity and for the Jews, whom he had hoped to convert to his faith. His version of monotheism chimed more easily with that of the Jews than with the mystery of the Trinity. If Jews were scarcely treated as equals by the conquering Arabs, their habits of worship, their diet and their social life were generally respected.

The spread of Judaism in the late Roman Empire must have been particularly easy along the southern shores of the Mediterranean. Alexandria was a cosmopolitan stew (in several senses) with no long attachment to any of the Greco-Roman gods. Egypt had exported its antique cults, most noticeably that of Isis, to Rome, but Alexandrians were nothing if not eclectic. Alexandria's Jews were vigorous and had no marked sense of inferiority. Why should they have been reluctant to share their religion and spread its influence? Many of them were Hellenized and at least bilingual. The traffic of ideas is likely to have been in all directions. As the Arab conquest extended westward, it must have taken adventurous Jews with it.

By the eighth century, the Arab advance across North Africa had reached almost to the Atlantic and was spilling across the Pillars of Hercules, from Morocco into Spain. Within a century of their ejection of the Visigoths, the invading Arabs, under the leadership of the first of the Umayyad dynasty, had established their caliphate in El-Andalus.* It is not unduly fanciful to see their capital city as Alexandria born again. For several hundred years, Córdoba had a sumptuous culture under a benign and tolerant series of caliphs (successors of Muhammad) who tolerated the arts and fostered the interplay of Jewish, Christian and Muslim thinkers and poets. The work of Ibn Gabirol, one of the great-

---

* In Arabic "the well-watered place." After the *Reconquista,* Andalucia lapsed into aridity due to the Christian neglect of the irrigation system installed by the Semites.

est and earliest of Sephardic poets, embodies a variation of themes from Jewish, Arab and Latin sources. Medicine and philosophy, with their emphasis on accuracy and truth, provided bridges that sprang from particularism toward common ground.

Many of the subjects of Abderrahman I (756–788 C.E.) were of native Spanish, more or less Christian, origin; a high proportion was only superficially Islamicized.* Abderrahman I chose Jews and Christians as his close aides rather than Arabs; since their preferment derived from him alone and would end if his autocracy were deposed, he could rely on their loyalty. The splendor of his city and his court laid a heavy burden of taxation on the population. There were frequent revolts during the eight generations of Umayyad rule, but the Jewish community never featured among the dissidents. Whenever Christian enthusiasts rose against the Umayyads, the Jews sided strongly with the Muslim regime. The caliphate's reputation for tolerance and patronage attracted a flow of Jews from North Africa, Syria and Egypt. By the early tenth century, its golden age was symbolized by the glittering palace of az-Zahra. Under Hakam II (961–976 C.E.), the invention of the cusped arch allowed the great Mezquita, with its seeming infinity of aisles and columns, to become one of the wonders of the world. Córdoba's quarter of a million inhabitants made it the largest city in Europe at the time. In Córdoba, as in Alexandria, bilingualism was a commonplace, at least among males. Scholars from all over Europe came to ferment the intellectual mix. In Muslim Spain, Judaism was as much respected (and perhaps as profitable, for the socially ambitious) as Christianity.†

The Jewish renaissance in Spain produced a series of outstanding individuals. Their literary, medical and philosophical brilliance was

* Raphael Loewe, *Ibn Gabirol* (New York: Grove, 1991), passim.

† In *The Invention of the Jewish People* (London: Verso, 2009), the Israeli historian Shlomo Sand excited an outcry by claiming that Spanish Jews in the happy years of the *convivencia* can by no means all have been descended from those dispersed from Palestine. Against Zionists who insist that all Jews derive from the original Judaeans, Sand maintains that North Africans, of various tribes, were likely to have been converted to Judaism before or soon after immigrating into Iberia.

hybridized by outside (mainly Arab) influences, but they were not lamed by any sense of belonging to an inferior caste. Muslim Spain was a place where any number of Josephs were able to flourish.*

Jews such as Hasdai ibn Shaprut (born in Jaen around 910 C.E.) served the Muslim caliphs and kings in high positions and with much greater security and panache than was ever available to the seventeenth-century "court Jews" in central Europe.† Under the Arabized name of Abu Yusuf, ibn Shaprut was Abderrahman III's supreme authority on Jewish matters. Because he spoke fluent Latin, he was also the caliph's chief emissary when it came to the Christian states. In 948, in order to establish diplomatic ties, the emperor Constantius VII Porphyrogenitus sent a delegation from Byzantium with the priceless gift of a Greek manuscript of Dioscorides's *Materia Medica*. The caliph asked Constantius to send a Greek teacher,‡ who collaborated with ibn Shaprut in making an accurate translation of botanical terms into their local Arabic equivalent.

Spanish Jews lived dangerously, but sometimes gloriously. After the victory over Almeria in 1038, the triumphant vizier of Granada, Samuel ibn Naghrela (the only Jew to hold quasi-sovereign power in

---

* Twelfth-century Toledo even produced a historian somewhat in the Josephan style. The rabbi and physician Abraham ibn Daud is said, in Yosef Yerushalmi's *Zakhor*, to have "understood history by viewing it schematically." Making symmetry a priority, he tampered with chronology in order to procure what he took to be the key to future events. Pattern was prescriptive, as the Marxist dialectic would be. Events in themselves were noteworthy only if they conformed with a destined place in the historical plan. Hegel repeated this facile scheme when he found significance in the repetition of a key event: Napoleon's defeat at Leipzig became ominous as the prelude to Waterloo. Hegel's conclusion that history operated on the rule "two strikes and you're out" was echoed by Marx's famous "history repeats itself first as tragedy, then as farce."

† Joseph Süss Oppenheimer (1698–1738), commonly known as "Jew Süss," was only the most emblematic of the Jews who served as advisers and tax-gatherers to any number of princes in the three hundred or so petty states of central Europe. Süss was in effect a scapegoat whose execution served to appease the mutual detestation of two sets of Christians, Catholic and Lutheran. Susan Tegel's *Jew Süss* provides a useful epitome of the affair and its malicious uses.

‡ The delegated *didaskalos* was a monk called Nicholas.

the Middle Ages)* decreed a "Second Purim" and circulated a Hebrew poem of celebration. Had Granada been defeated, however, Naghrela and all the Jews under his aegis might well have been killed or expelled. Two generations later, in 1066, when the Andalucian *convivencia* was supposedly at its most amiable, some four thousand Jews were slaughtered in riots in Granada, even though (or because) the city was nicknamed "Granada of the Jews," on account of the number of Jews at the highest levels of the sultan's administration. His vizier, Samuel ibn Naghrela's son Yosef, the builder of the Red Fortress, now known as the Alhambra, was crucified by the rioters. Against strict Islamic law, he had commissioned Christian craftsmen to decorate the Alhambra's harem (its windows overlook the Court of the Lions) with representations of the human figure. The syncretism of the senior members of the emir's court contrasts, as it did in Córdoba, with the tight sectarianism of the lower orders. Their exclusion from power, like that of the city mob in first-century Jerusalem, turned religious fervor into the principal expression of the resentments of the plebeian Moors.†

In eleventh-century Andalusia, the Jewish poet and philosopher Yehuda Halevi furnished a prime example of the mélange of influences. At home with Arabic literature and music, he composed poetry that sometimes mimicked the Arabic "girdle song." It was accompanied by music (on lute, drum and guitar) that has left plangent traces, Jewish and Arab, in flamenco. In Andalusia's golden age, starting in the middle of the eighth century, the caliph Abd al-Rahman and his successors in the great city of Córdoba were blessed with longevity. Untroubled by hereditary jostling, their dynasty procured a period of social stability. During Europe's Dark Ages, they had time to open a wide, bright window, looking onto the Mediterranean, which had, for centuries, allowed the easy transit and exchange of men and ideas.

---

* There was, however, a Jewish duke of the island of Naxos in the Cyclades, in the early sixteenth century. Joseph Nasi, a Sephardic refugee, was appointed by the Turkish Sultan Selim II.

† The role and sentiments of the Muslim Brotherhood in modern Egypt are not dissimilar in its rejection of "civilized" syncretism and alien supervisors.

The caliphs' copious libraries matched those of the Ptolemies in Egypt, which ardent Muslim invaders had torched not many years before. Córdoba's great Mezquita announced that the Umayyads were the masters of Iberia; but Hillel Halkin notes, in his study of Halevi, that that great monument was oriented not toward Mecca, but southward, quite as if it were situated in Damascus, from which the Umayyad Arabs claimed to have sprung.[1]

Halevi was born, in the early 1070s, either in Toledo or in Tuleda, farther north in Castile. From early youth, he was fluent in Hebrew, Arabic (the secular mother tongue) and Spanish; verse and versatility went together. Literature is as often a means of social advancement as of self-expression.* Combining innovation with deference to tradition, Halevi was by turns lyric poet and, later, the advocate of an uncompromising version of Judaism.

His long prose dialogue, *The Kuzari,* has led him to be taken for both a prototypical Zionist and a chauvinist mystic. He is seen in a variety of lights, which his critics themselves often supply. The fragility of the *convivencia* helps to explain Halevi's belated, but then increasingly plaintive, yearning for Jerusalem. His appetite for Zion came to match the passion that, in younger days, had been spent on the anonymous love of his life. Evidently a beauty, she was not the woman he married. In the style of the Arabic poets, and of the Provençal troubadours, the unattainable was the thing he most desired. Pain tempts the poet to treat God as both supreme and not wholly beyond reproach. There is a flash of Jewish egalitarianism in such presumption.

In 1099, Pope Urban II, the godfather of the First Crusade, put an end to a period in which—among the educated, at least—interfaith

---

* Many of New York's twentieth-century literary intellectuals were opinionated arrivistes, quick to be fluently in command of their assumed culture. Outsiders, whether Lionel Trilling and Alfred Kazin or George and Ira Gershwin, can commend themselves to the established order by the ostentation of their ingenuity; they excite, they instruct and, if they are part of what was known in the 1920s as "the show business," they had better entertain. Theater and the movies were powerful incentives for assimilation. Golden age Hollywood stars were often allotted Gentile-sounding names: Kirk Douglas, John Garfield and Edward G. Robinson among them.

argument and mutual respect were not uncommon. His successors sought, and fought, to homogenize and centralize Christendom. North of the Pyrenees, Catholic orthodoxy became the price of admission to the blessings of civilization; dissent—as the Cathars would learn during the Albigensian Crusade of the early thirteenth century—meant death. Men such as Petrus Alfonsi, a Spanish Catholic convert from Judaism, and Peter Abelard (whose vision of Christianity was less dogmatic than the pope's) had written dialogues that, while insisting that Christianity was superior to Judaism, showed scholarly respect for Jewish sources. It is hard to believe that the exposure of Abelard's affair with Héloise was motivated only by moral outrage; it also served to smirch the "liberal" theology of which he was the outstanding exponent. Six centuries later, Spinoza's conspicuous chastity deprived both Jews and Christians, of all denominations, of any convenient opportunity to depict him as a libertine atheist.

Halevi's *The Kuzari* was a response both to Christian polemics and to Jewish waverers. Just as Plato had attacked "the Sophists" for rhetoricizing truth, Halevi's dialogue challenged philosophers and their rationalism. Of these, the most significant in Jewish thought had yet to be born: Moses Maimonides was still only a baby when Yehuda Halevi quit Córdoba, in 1140. The great libraries in the city were already replete with translations of classical texts. Aristotle's notion of a universal and impersonal divinity is said, by Maimonides's enemies, to have polluted *The Guide of the Perplexed.* His own perplexity was caused not least by the difficulty of reconciling the interventionist God of the Jews with Aristotle's unmoved mover. The tension between faith and logic has never been resolved: the square may sit tight in the circle, but it can never square it.

Halevi's dialogue is more than a tract; he was an artist as well as a thinker. His certainties arose from his doubts and from his fears. *The Kuzari* questions as much as it answers. Its inspiration springs from fascination with the Khazars, whose kingdom dominated the northern Caucasus in the centuries immediately before Halevi's birth. Having elected—from whatever spiritual or pragmatic motive—to adopt a monotheistic faith, the Khazar king is said first to have consulted

Christian and Muslim divines before deigning to quiz a rabbi, whose maligned faith had had little appeal for him. However, when he learned that both Christianity and Islam based the authenticity of their theology, as each professed, on the books of the Jews, the king decided that their "truth" had, logically, to be parasitic on that of Judaism: where they veered away from the Torah, Christians and Muslims had therefore to be diverging from the truth into the speculative. The king agreed to be circumcised and turned the Khazars (or at least its ruling order) into what Arthur Koestler would call "the thirteenth tribe."*

Halevi ranges beyond interfaith disputation. His fictional rabbi confronts the issue of determinism five centuries before Baruch Spinoza's bleak and bold declaration of human bondage. The rabbi's defense of free will is defiantly mundane and surprisingly modern. He might be an Oxford philosopher of the 1950s when he says to the king, "We are free to choose because we instinctively feel that we are and act in accordance with our feeling. This is not something that can or needs to be proved by philosophy. It is an empirical reality, the denial of which would be as foolish as denying the existence of our bodies or of the world around us."† Determinism may have its logical sense, *sub specie aeternitatis,* as Spinoza came to put it, but what human being lives his daily life solely in the light of eternity?

Halevi's defense of human liberty, and of the empiricism it encourages, is obstinately of this world. At the same time, his eclecticism has abrupt limits. His rabbi holds the smallest demand of ritual obedience to be unquestionable: "There is no room in the worship of God for guesswork, logic or considered judgment. If there were, the philosophers would have achieved by means of their intellect twice as much

* In *The Thirteenth Tribe,* Koestler proposed, however fancifully, that many Ashkenazim must stem from Khazari proselytes, rather than, as Zionist legend insisted, from dispersed Judaeans. Koestler even drew profiles to show that the "Jewish" nose was in fact a legacy from the Eurasian genetic pool.

† The twentieth-century Oxford philosopher J. L. Austin remarked that he had never met any "determinist" who actually lived as though he were not free to do one thing rather than another. Marxism compromised with a notion of necessity in history that could be accelerated by those on the side of the inevitable.

as the Israelites." Halkin reads this to imply that "the commandments, if executed correctly, have an objective impact on things, just as—to resort to a scientific analogy—combining hydrogen and oxygen in certain proportions and no others yields water."[2] "Just as" is a brave attachment to a tendentious analogy. In Halevi, as in Josephus, the very fact that he was writing secular literature in a pious cause admits a tincture of the irony Quintilian hoped to find in books worth reading.

In Halevi's maturity, the effervescence of his love poetry, and his spirited use of Arabic themes, no longer satisfied him. Abandoning worldly ambition, he turned his thoughts, like those of many contemporary Arab poets, to the fate of his soul. The decision to jettison the comforts of the *convivencia* and to set off, alone, for Zion was, no doubt, primed by piety. Despite María Rosa Menocal's seductive depiction of the caliphate as a haven of tolerance,[3] the *convivencia* never welded the three monotheisms, still less their celebrants, into a cohesive "nationality." Nevertheless, its persistent obsession with *pura sangre* hints at Christian Spain's later and unrelieved apprehension that Jewish and Arab blood must flow in many Iberian veins. Halevi's love songs suggest how great was the lure to cross the line.

As instability and the intolerance of the Almohads, a dynasty of Muslim fundamentalists from Morocco, began to pinch out the Jews, Halevi sought a resolution of his polymorphous life. For whatever amalgam of motives, he set out to honor his nostalgic dream of Jewish election by emigrating to Palestine. In 1140, he sailed for Egypt. The Alexandrians' enthusiasm for his by now famous company tempted him to linger where Maimonides himself would come to die.* In his last poem, however, Halevi praises the favorable wind that, he prays, will carry him on to Zion. His final journey was from the crusaders'

---

* In his Levantine exile, Maimonides became one of Saladin's team of doctors. Medicine was a tempting road to privileged status for non-Muslims in the Islamic world but not without dangers. In 1715, a famous Greek physician, Andreas Likinios, who had previously cured Sultan Ahmed of smallpox, went—after the Ottoman capture of Monemvasia—to claim his promised exemption from being enslaved. He was hanged instead. (See *Monemvasia,* by Haris A. Kalligas, p. 87.) The Jewish doctors accused of plotting to kill Stalin narrowly escaped a similar fate.

port of Acre to the gates of Jerusalem, where, as he prayed at the Wailing Wall (all that was left of the Second Temple), tradition says that he was almost immediately trampled to death by an Arab horseman. Saint Teresa of Ávila (the turreted city not far from Halevi's putative birthplace, Tuleda) might have reminded him of the dangers of answered prayers.

Halevi's vision of humanity is scarcely "liberal." He regards other religions as akin to "medical mountebankery," a subject with which he was familiar since, like Moses Maimonides a generation later, he was a practicing physician (as well as a Levite). Halevi "qualified" as a doctor (to do so a man had only to announce that he was one) by reading Greek medical texts, in Arabic translations; he had no clinical training. In the tenth century, Salerno, south of Naples in Italy, had the sole practical medical school in Europe.* Since medieval medicine was largely a matter of prescribing herbal remedies, combined with a soothing or impressive bedside manner, its practice rarely did much harm.

Maimonides's own knowledge of medicine may have encouraged him in his view that "any human being can be a prophet," depending only on God's will. In some Orthodox circles, the accusation still attaches to him that he dismantled the traditional specificity of the Jews by his willingness to admit converts. Here he challenged *The Kuzari,* in which Halevi, for all his literary eclecticism, claimed that only a born Jew is biologically capable of prophecy: "Its influence can be bestowed only on those high enough on the ladder of Being to receive it." Hillel Halkin maintains that this "unprecedented" chauvinism derives less from conceit than from intimations of despair over the morale of the Jews. Having for centuries been useful civil (and military) servants to both Christian and Muslim caliphs and princes, the Jews in Halevi's day were increasingly marginalized as religious absolutism (mostly

---

* According to legend, the Jew Helinus, the Greek Pontus, the Arab Adela and the Latin Salernus were the cofounders of a school unequaled in fame for three centuries. It possessed a unique library of Greek and Arabic texts, taken from the adjacent monastery of Monte Cassino. Medicine promoted a therapeutic universality beyond the scope of any revealed religion.

Christian) carved deeper dividing lines between once more or less compatible communities.

Halevi's urgent defense of Jewish priority in God's scheme was almost certainly excited by the massacre, in 1099, by the first crusaders, of all the Jews (and Muslims) in Jerusalem. He implored God to roast the crusaders "in coals made from their Cross," an imprecation that sorts ill with the notion, common in the later Diaspora, that Jews never entertained active hostility toward those who persecuted them. Maimonides, for all his aloof intelligence, refers to Muhammad as "the Madman" and hopes that the bones of Jesus will be "ground to dust." Echoes of classical Greco-Roman rhetoric and disdain (as practiced by Seneca, the greatest of Cordoban émigrés) lingered in the prose style of the intellectuals of Muslim Spain.

Maimonides tried to steer a middle course between oral and confidential teaching, which was permitted, and teaching in writing, which—in the Pharisaic tradition—was not. Private correspondence with a close friend was taken to resemble confidential conversation; hence Maimonides's *Guide of the Perplexed* appears to be addressed to his friend and favorite pupil, Joseph (yet another of the same name). In *Persecution and the Art of Writing*, Leo Strauss describes how, in the following decades:

> the continuity of oral tradition presupposes a certain normality of political conditions. That is why the secrets of the Torah were perfectly understood only as long as Israel lived in its own country in freedom, not subjugated by the ignorant nations of the world. Particularly . . . when the supreme political authority rested in the hands of King Solomon who—according to Maimonides III, 26—had an almost complete understanding of the secret reasons of the commandments. After Solomon, wisdom and political power were no longer united; decline and, finally, loss of freedom followed.
>
> When the nation was led into captivity [in Babylon], it sustained further loss in the perfect knowledge of the secrets. Whereas Isaiah's contemporaries understood his brief hints, those of Ezekiel required many more details . . . to grasp the sacred doctrine. . . .

Decline of knowledge became even more marked with the discontinuation of prophecy itself. Still more disastrous was the victory of the Romans, since the new Diaspora was to last so much longer than the first. As time went on, the external conditions for oral communication of the secrets of the Torah . . . grew increasingly precarious.*

As the Cordoban *convivencia* was increasingly menaced by the Almohads, the moment was imminent when it would be impossible to speak without fear. For that reason, Maimonides decided he had to write down the secret teaching. He thought it his duty, despite Talmudic prohibition, to give such written explanations of biblical secrets as would meet the conditions required for an oral tradition. As Strauss puts it, Maimonides had to become "a master of the art of revealing by not revealing and of not revealing by revealing."

Maimonides took the Bible to be the work of a single author, not so much Moses as God Himself. It is on this issue that Spinoza would part company both with Maimonides and with Judaism. Orthodoxy offered him no choice: doubt of God's authorship was tantamount to apostasy. The law is, in this respect, less elastic than faith, and less mutable than myth: for Maimonides, the Torah *had* to be perfect, hence homogeneous, in content and form. He could never accept that what seemed to be its formal deficiencies—abrupt changes of subject, repetition with variations—were due to compilation by unknown redactors from divergent sources, as Spinoza's philology claimed to have proved (and few scholars would now deny). The text's disjunctions were taken by Maimonides to be "purposeful irregularities, intended to hide and betray a deeper order, a deep, nay, divine meaning." According to Leo Strauss, the *Guide* mimics the Bible's lack of manifest order and abrupt

---

* Wittgenstein's famous concluding words in the *Tractatus Logico-Philosophicus* (with its parodic allusion to Spinoza), which were translated, gnomically, as "Whereof one cannot speak, thereof one should keep silent," can be read, in a Straussian light, as implying that unspoken things lie behind its apparent terminus. No wonder that, as will be seen, Wittgenstein later described his thought as "100% Hebraic."

changes of topic.[4] In a mutation of Josephan ambiguity, Maimonides offers a cryptic version of the cryptic.

As the *convivencia* broke up, under the pressure of militant Catholicism, Spanish Jews usually sided with the "Moors," with whom, if Shlomo Sand is even slightly right, they had racial, dietetic and communal affinities. Leo Strauss emphasized that revelation has for both (religious) Jews and Muslims "the character of Law (*torah, shari'a*) rather than of Faith . . . [it is] not a creed or a set of dogmas, but a social order, if not an all-comprehensive order, which regulates not merely actions but thoughts or opinions as well." Muslim hostility to Jews—for instance, in eleventh-century Granada—had more to do with resentment of their ascendancy than with ideology.* The increasing militancy of the Christian church expressed itself, in the years before the Reconquista, by seeking to evict Judaism from its theological primacy and the Jews from any influence in the world's game. The force of argument, circumstance and force itself led to the increasingly beleaguered condition of Jewish communities, Sephardic as well as Ashkenazi (Christian soldiers who enrolled for the First Crusade did their basic training, as it were, by massacring the Jewish civilian population in the Rhineland).

In thirteenth-century Spain, the Jewish apostates Pablo Christiani and Petrus Alfonsi were prototypes of those who deserted their ancient faith, albeit for reasons of conviction, and transformed themselves into its evangelizing enemies. Saint Paul is the God-struck prototype of such enthusiasts. His vision of Jesus is proof that the dead can be remodeled into the antithesis of their living selves.[†] In 1263, the great Rabbi Nach-

---

* In Northern Ireland, the "sectarianism" of Catholics and Protestants was superficially "ideological" but was also the expression of Catholic resentment at the empowerment of an alien ascendancy that defined (and justified, not to say sanctified) its rule by flagging its allegiance to the Church of England and its titular head, the queen.

† Holocaust deniers have made the Shoah itself into a Jewish fabrication, designed to extract blood money from those who were accused by the Jews of killing millions more than actually died. Fantastic versions of the same syndrome have proposed that Hitler himself had some Jewish blood. In this way, anti-Semitism itself can be represented as a function of Jewishness.

manides was conscripted to take part in a disputation with a Dominican friar in Barcelona. Before it began, he was warned by his friend (and medical patient) King Jaime I of Aragon that he might defend Judaism but that he must never, on pain of death, dispute the veracity of Christianity. The Jew was confined, metaphysically, to "playing for a draw." A winning argument was likely to cost him his life. In the case of Nachmanides, even a draw put him in danger. Thanks only to Jaime I, he was able to get away before the Dominicans laid hands on him.*

The Jews, with their arcane language, weird paraphernalia and exclusive rites, had a reputation for recherché powers that accompanied them down the ages, arming their medicine with a tincture of diabolical knowledge. Jewish doctors were both privileged and suspect. Stalin arrested, and would have murdered, all the "Jewish doctors" who had been convoked, because of their expertise, to service the Kremlin. When they proved incapable of immortalizing its paranoid occupant, it remained plausible, to the Soviet public, and to Joseph the Terrible, that Jews should be given to devious duplicity.†

In sixteenth-century London, Ruy López, Queen Elizabeth I's Marrano physician, was executed on suspicion of being a spy; treachery was taken to be the mark of the Jew, not least when he swore that he no longer was one. The queen herself could not save López from the scaffold.

---

* The same monastic order would save a good many Jews when they were being rounded up in Nazi-occupied Italy. It also assisted the flight of Nazis such as Adolf Eichmann.

† Formal Judaism had no place for spells and amulets and inscribed skulls and all the paraphernalia of witchcraft and sympathetic magic, but they recur in the folklore. Their common use in ancient Judaea has been established by archaeologists. Jesus of Nazareth and his followers clearly believed in evil spirits—why else did the Gadarene swine run over that steep place into the sea? In *Jewish Antiquities,* Josephus describes, without apparent skepticism, how a plant with a flamelike color, which emitted a brilliant light, was fatal to touch. It could be plucked only by having a dog tied to it and then sacrificed. As with the magic Greek "moly," the root could then be used to expel demons, simply by being "applied to the patient." Medicine still has a hint of magic, if not the diabolical, about it. The willful illegibility and esoteric terminology of medical prescriptions have continued to carry a vestige of medieval abracadabra. More naughty than malicious, Vladimir Nabokov, a philo-Semite with a formidable Jewish wife, referred to Sigmund Freud as "the Viennese witch-doctor."

As he was publicly disemboweled, the London crowd was amused that he repeatedly proclaimed himself as good a Christian as his tormentors. Shylock is said to have been based on López. However "humanely" Shakespeare allowed the baited Shylock to speak for himself, the English of his day treated "the Jews" with much less generosity than did the Venetians, whom Shakespeare was pleased to satirize. While Jews were formally banned from entering England, the Serene Republic had the mercantile sense to make Jews somewhat welcome, although they were sequestered in their ghetto.

Shakespeare may have had firsthand experience of Jews, since a small community of Marranos were his neighbors in Elizabethan London, but they were well-advised to keep their heads down and their identity secret. It remains typical of the fissile habits of Jews of differing provenance or shades of practice that the ghetto in Venice contains synagogues from which Ashkenazi and Sephardic Jews excluded those who did not share their origins or adhere to the distinct minutiae of their rites.

The ghettoization of Jews in Christian Europe was forced upon them, but there was also a certain acquiescence: Judaism was an esoteric faith. The tradition of the minyan, which Josephus saw institutionalized among the Essenes, requires the presence of other Jews for valid worship. In the Christian imagination, the ghetto created a cloche for bogeymen, for necromancy and for conspiracy; for the pinched Jews, it was also a home from home, albeit joyless and menaced by pogroms. The ghetto became a pressure cooker, heated from without by the sleepless imagination of the persecuting church. The blood libel, for which there was never the smallest evidence, was of a piece with the Christian capacity for believing what was incredible.* The burning of witches and Jews was a vindication of faith that was also an acknowledgment of doubt.

Spanish inquisitors and poets such as Lope de Vega "seriously"

---

* With unsurprising symmetry, the charges of infanticide and cannibalism were leveled first against the early Christians; see H. S. Versnel, *Ter Unus: Isis, Dionysos, Hermes—Three Studies in Henotheism*, volume 1 of *Inconsistencies in Greek and Roman Religion* (Leiden: Brill, 1990).

believed that Jewish males could be detected because they menstru-ated and, so the story went, had tails.* Jews are still sometimes said to be "racially" prone to hemorrhoids and, of course, to have telltale noses.† Yosef Yerushalmi describes how, in seventeeth-century Spain, Isaac Cardoso—a Marrano physician who later escaped to the freedom of the Italian ghettos, where he reverted to Judaism—treated an alcalde of the court, Don Juan de Quiñones, for hemorrhoids.‡§ Quiñones had used his learning and library to compile a treatise proving that Jews had tails, were "subject to menstrual periods, and blood, as punishment for the grave sin which they committed." The author's own piles were "so huge and great, and accompanied by blood and pain, that they actually seemed tail-like. . . . I then said to him: 'Your honor must also be liable in the sin of that [Jesus's] death.' . . . He began to laugh and said he did not agree with this, for he has been well proved to be an *hidalgo* of La Mancha." The absurdity of anti-Semitic myths is often conceded in polite circumstances; but they are too serviceable to be forgotten.

In 1492, the conclusion of the Reconquista drove the mass of uncon-verted Jews out of Spain. On the face of things, those who remained had no choice but to embrace Catholicism. Their sincerity was soon questioned. The so-called Marranos, or Judaizers, were easy targets for neighborly malice. A distaste for pork or a reluctance to work (or even to light a fire) on a Saturday was enough to excite suspicion. Many Jews who fled from Spain and, later, from Portugal found refuge in the Netherlands, where the Christian population, which included many Protestants, had fought a brave battle, physical and spiritual, to eman-cipate themselves from Catholic Spain.

---

* According to Jonathan Sumption, in *The Hundred Years War* (vol. 3: *Divided Houses*), the Scots said the same of their allies the French in the 1380s, when the lat-ter landed north of the border and failed to bond with the rugged clansmen. Scots continue to speak, if sometimes, ironically, of the "Auld Alliance."

† In *HHbH*, Laurent Binet reports that when the Germans decided to remove Mendelssohn's statue from the roof of the Prague opera house in 1941, they selected the image with the biggest nose, only to discover that it was Richard Wagner's.

‡ Martin Luther also suffered excruciatingly from piles, which may account for his obsessive use of excremental imagery, often at the expense of the Jews.

With rare if wary grace, the Dutch authorities tolerated the immigrant Jews forming their own communities and building synagogues. In return, Jews were expected to keep to themselves and not attract attention to their idiosyncratic habits. Tolerance had its repressive consequences: the Amsterdam Jewish authorities formed a petty Sanhedrin. Their inquisitorial vigilance over their congregations' orthodoxy reciprocated the Gentiles' watch over them.

Steven Nadler cites Shabbatai Bass, a Polish scholar who visited the Amsterdam community in the 1640s.[6] He reported seeing "giants [in scholarship]; tender children as small as grasshoppers . . . kids who have become he-goats . . . prodigies because of their unusual familiarity with the entire Bible and with the science of grammar. They possessed the ability to compose verses and poems in meter and to speak a pure Hebrew." It was in this forcing house of heads-down intellectual precociousness that Baruch Spinoza began to distinguish himself.

The rabbis were close to being the absolute rulers of the community. The discipline that produced prodigies also demanded obedience, not only from the student. It was vital to avoid exciting the disapproval of the Dutch authorities. The result was a kind of voluntary ghettoization. Dissent from orthodoxy was visited with punishment that echoed the practice of the Inquisition from which so many of the community had fled. The story of Uriel (or Gabriel) da Costa exemplifies the fate of transgressors. His father had been an authentic Christian, his mother a "Judaizer": publicly Christian, but secretly cleaving to the old religion. Da Costa studied canon law and began a career within the church, leading a pious life. He was, however, riven by doubts concerning the afterlife and by the difficulty of reconciling Catholicism with reason. In his early twenties, he resigned his benefice and, with his mother and two brothers, repaired to Amsterdam, where he recrossed the line into Judaism. His three brothers were circumcised and studied Jewish rituals and duties. The Torah had trumped the Gospel.

Quite soon, Uriel grew disillusioned by rabbinic practice. He found that the Law of Moses had been distorted and embellished by the "inventions of the so-called Jewish sages . . . additions totally foreign to the Law." In attacking the Talmudic annexes to the Torah, he was as much an antique Sadducee as a modern rationalist. He argued that the soul was mortal and that there could be no afterlife, no eternal reward or punishment: "Once he is dead, nothing remains of a man, nor does he ever return to life." When he published his heretical opinions, they also offended the Dutch authorities, who arrested and fined him. His book was publicly burned (one copy survives). Da Costa wandered around Protestant Europe but found no welcome. When he returned to Amsterdam, he tried to reconcile himself with the local rabbinate, but soon reverted to his militant heterodoxy. He concluded that the Mosaic law itself was a human fabrication: "it contradicts the law of nature in many respects and God, the author of the law of nature, cannot contradict himself."*

This seemed to portend a final breach with the Jews, but da Costa soon retracted his words and tried, he wrote, to "reunite myself with them and fall into step . . . aping the apes, as they say." He did not prove steadfast in that effort. He was soon denounced for having sought to dissuade two Christians from conversion to Judaism: "they did not know the yoke they were about to put around their necks." In 1633, a year after Baruch Spinoza was born, da Costa was again told that he would be expelled from the community, unless he submitted to a flogging. He refused and was cut off from all Jewish contact.

Seven years later, poor and lonely, he agreed to be humiliated. According to his own account, in the *Exemplar Humanae Vitae,* he was stripped to the waist, in front of the assembled community, tied to a pillar and given thirty-nine lashes, "as required by tradition . . . a psalm was sung during the flagellation." He was then allowed to dress but led to the threshold of the synagogue. "There I laid myself out . . . and all who came down to exit the synagogue passed over me, stepping with one foot over the lower parts of my body. Everyone, young and old, took part in this ceremony. Not even monkeys could exhibit to the eyes of the world such shocking actions or more ridiculous behaviour."

The account is so stark and so vile that it might include interpola-

* The quotations are from Steven Nadler (*Spinoza: A Life*), on whom I rely in this account of da Costa's life and death.

tions by an anti-Semite, as has indeed been suggested, though with small conviction. It is sadly unsurprising that the vindictiveness with which Jews have been treated, from at least the time of Joseph ben Mattathias, should be assumed into their conduct toward each other. It was rarely marked by magnanimity even before the sack of Jerusalem. Da Costa's brave vacillations, into and out of and back into Judaism, recall the words which Blaise Pascal ascribes to men as a whole: "Does he exalt himself? I lay him low; does he humble himself? I exalt him and continue to contradict him until he comprehends that he is an incomprehensible monstrosity." A few days after writing the *Exemplar,* in which he also chided the Amsterdam magistrates for not protecting him from "the Pharisees," Uriel da Costa killed himself.

Baruch Spinoza was eight years old at the time of da Costa's ritual abasement. He may have been among "the young" who witnessed it. There is no doubt that da Costa's life and opinions had a bruising impact on the Amsterdam community. Spinoza's education was strict in its orthodoxy. His teacher Saul Levi Mortera was an authority on halacha, the interpretation of the law. Something of a rationalist, in the Maimonidean tradition, he sanctioned pictorial images when they were not objects of worship, but he considered that "Jews who are not circumcised and who do not observe the law in lands where they are not permitted to do so [for instance, in Iberia] risked eternal punishment." Mortera too was pitched between uncompromising orthodoxy and the wider intellectual and scientific world of northern Europe.

One of the important influences on the young Spinoza was his Latin teacher, Franciscus van den Enden, an unfrocked Jesuit who, when Baruch was his pupil, confessed to being no more than a "vague deist." Amsterdam Jews were, in some regards, bound by the same rules which Nachmanides had had to observe in thirteenth-century Catalonia; they were forbidden, above all, to engage in theological discussion. To question the divine origin of the Torah entailed the severest *cherem*: total severance from the community. The right of the *parnassim,** the

---

* Carl Djerassi's *Four Jews on Parnassus* (New York: Columbia University Press, 2008) makes play with the convergence of Jewish and classical culture in imagin-

elders, to excommunicate "the unruly and the rebellious" was a function both of orthodoxy and of apprehension, lest their Gentile hosts turn against them (Amsterdam Jews, like others in Europe, had no right of tenure or citizenship). The double bind of esoteric presumption and public deference to alien authority prefigures the tragic fix in which so many of Europe's Jews found themselves under the Nazis. The self-policing of the Amsterdam community was at least somewhat echoed, during the Shoah, by Jewish "leaders" as corrupt as Chaim Rumkowski (the self-styled "king" of the Lodz ghetto under the Nazis) and as well-intentioned as Leo Baeck, the Berlin rabbi who concealed the truth about the camps in order to lessen the dread of those he failed to warn of their imminent fate and who was vilified, after the event, for his reticence, by moralists who were never forked by his dilemma.

Spinoza, like so many precocious Jews before and since, was at first a brilliant student and then a flagrant apostate. His heretical ideas had traces of da Costa's: "Nature is a unity, a whole outside of which there is nothing . . . but if Nature is just the substance composed of infinite attributes, the underlying productive unity of all things, then Nature is God." The mental agility learned with Mortera enabled Spinoza to hurdle the limits of orthodoxy. Latin and mathematical models became the alien means by which he revised his reading of the moral world, as the use of Greek had emancipated Josephus, perhaps despite himself, from the blinkered perspective of the Jerusalem Jew he had once been. Once evicted from the Amsterdam community, Baruch Spinoza was free to turn his calm indignation on a target at which he might fire as incautiously as he chose: Judaism itself.

Bertrand Russell called Spinoza the "noblest" of all philosophers; his logical elegance was the ornament of his genius. In solitary and austere dignity, he had recourse to a system that approximated to mathematics in its abstract apparatus. By composing his ideas in Latin, he attached

---

ing a posthumous (often acrimonious) meeting between Walter Benjamin, Theodor Adorno, Gershom Scholem and Arnold Schoenberg on the mountain the Greeks took to be sacred to the Muses.

them to the Erasmic enlightenment, of which, in time, he became the most radical exponent. Encoding his urgent convictions in the seemingly dispassionate guise of syllogistic rationalism, Spinoza contrived to be heterodox without descending to rhetorical bombast. His conversion to the European philosophical manner enabled him to efface the prints that marked him as a Jew. Like Joseph ben Mattathias, he signaled his change of track by adopting a Romanized version of his name: Baruch became Benedict. Writing in Latin, and advocating the contemplation of life "*sub specie aeternitatis*" (in long shot, as it were), he eschewed ephemeral disputes.* He inaugurated what Jonathan Israel designates as "the Radical Enlightenment" by hiding his personal light under a bushel of verbiage.†

Since the public philosophy of the time (and the laws of the Dutch Republic) left him free to attack Judaism without fear of Christian reprisal, it has been supposed that Spinoza's greatest quarrel was with his own "superstition." Certainly he directed his scholarship to the demolition of its pretensions, not least that the ancient Hebrews "surpassed other nations in their wisdom or in their proximity to God." As a precocious philologist, he claimed (as few now doubt) that the books of the prophets were "heaped together" long after the events they affect to describe. Their miracles might impress the simple but are impossible: everything, he came to say, has a natural cause and explanation. It requires no great elasticity to see that everything Spinoza remarks about Judaism and its God can be applied, mutatis mutandis, to Christianity, against which he says nothing. He never refers directly to the resurrection of Jesus Christ, but he could hardly fail to be con-

---

* In a similar spirit, the Annales school of French historians, led by Fernand Braudel, adopted a policy of looking at history in the slanting light of the "*longue durée.*" What mattered was what transpired in the long run. In this way, the blips of actuality (for instance, what happened in France, not least to its Jews, during the Occupation) became negligible. As if by coincidence, the *annalistes* favor the long-term play of patterns over the bumper-to-bumper traffic of cause and effect.

† See Jonathan Israel, *Radical Enlightenment: Philosophy and the Making of Modernity, 1650–1750* (Oxford: Oxford University Press, 2001).

scious that it was (and is) the pivotal miracle on which all Christian hope turned. Its veracity had supposedly been established by the fall of Jerusalem as recorded by Flavius Josephus. The humiliation and eviction of the Jews was the price, decreed by God, that they paid for failing to recognize His son. Belief that Jerusalem might be redeemed by the return of the Jews to their ancestral home bolstered the mania that spread through the Diaspora as a result of the messianic pretenses of Shabbetai Zevi in 1666.*

Believing that the moment of return to Zion was at hand, many Jews, including sane citizens in comfortable circumstances, sold up and prepared to emigrate to Palestine. Spinoza was not among them. He argued only in favor of free choice and the love of justice, of which democracy is the best guarantee. It is, he said, in his *Ethics* "a disaster for a state to grant religious functionaries the right to issue decrees or to concern themselves with state business." He adds that it is "clearer than the noonday sun that the real schismatics are those who condemn the writings of others." Nevertheless, the Huguenot diplomat Jean-Baptiste Stouppe said that Spinoza was "a very bad Jew and no better Christian. . . . His [theologico-political treatise] undermines the foundations of all religion." The charge was not meant kindly, but it shows conspicuous understanding of the thrust of Spinoza's arguments. Baruch/Benedict Spinoza's genius is as marked as his inability, like that of so many Jews, to pull away definitively from his roots. It is said that Spinoza drew excellent portraits, including a number of himself, though none has survived; it was the nearest he came, apart from his letters, to a first-person statement. His only equivalent to Josephus's in the literary self-portrait *Vita* was a wordless profile.

Spinoza led a deliberately reclusive life. He was always courteous to his landlords and neighbors, but never sociable. Although he corre-

---

* In the view of some Christians, "the Jews" had to return to Zion, prior to being converted to Christianity, before the Second Coming could take place. This synthetic idea has led some right-wing Christians (who might, before the Shoah, have had Fascist sympathies) to be enthusiastically, if not belligerently, pro-Israeli.

sponded with the great minds of his time, he lived—somewhat as Josephus did in Rome—in a ghetto of one. Unlike Josephus, he remained celibate.* Advocating radicalism, he felt no call to detach himself from his roots by any ostentatious apostasy. Spinoza was always identified disparagingly as a Jew even by those, such as Leibniz, who did not deny his innovating genius.† Without public ambitions, Spinoza was not tempted to the kind of pragmatic "belief" that disposed later men of genius, such as Heinrich Heine, to embrace baptism as the price of emancipation from the hobble of Jewish origins.

In the nineteenth century, Benjamin Disraeli matched his contemporary Heinrich Heine by accepting baptism as the formal price of entry into a Christian society.‡ Disraeli's conversion did not dispose his enemies to think of him as anything but an alien adventurer in fraudulent (and too flamboyant) Christianized costume. He met the anti-Semitism of men such as Thomas Carlyle and Anthony Trollope by the exquisitely ostentatious deployment of the language they took to be their own.§ Disraeli became an ornament of English society and of English literature on what he liked to parade as his own terms: "When I want to read a novel," he said, "I write one." Once baptized and eligible for political life, Benjamin Disraeli adopted the tactics of

---

* Only Alain Minc, in his *Spinoza: un roman juif* (Paris: Gallimard, 1999), has the naughty impulse to suggest otherwise. Minc's novel was the subject of a lawsuit, won by the provincial author of a study of Spinoza that Minc was said to have admired to the point of assimilation.

† Spinoza's London-based friend and admirer Henry Oldenburg, the German-born secretary of the Royal Society, abstained from any such veiled condescension (see Nadler, *Spinoza: A Life*).

‡ Isaac D'Israeli, the book-loving father of Benjamin Disraeli, decided to have his son baptized after a doctrinal quarrel with the elders of Bevis Marks, the oldest synagogue in London. Isaac's commonplace books were Byron's favorite reading. His admiration for D'Israeli probably inspired the poet to write *Hebrew Melodies* and to favor the national liberation of the Jews as he did of the Greeks, though neither of these ancient peoples had had a "nation" for thousands of years, if ever.

§ Louis-Ferdinand Céline maintained, with his customary snarl, that Marcel Proust's *À la recherche du temps perdu* was written in a profuse Hebraic argot that was nothing like authentic French.

flaunting his difference. When prime minister of Great Britain, he teased aristocratic colleagues such as Lord Derby by reminding them that his ancestors had been men of literate resource and social refinement in ancient Israel, while the ancient Britons were prancing about in woad. He also trumped English conceit by going further in pandering to it than any of his predecessors: he put a new jewel in the imperial crown. When he made his annunciation to Queen Victoria that she was henceforth to be empress of India, he at least somewhat mimicked Joseph ben Mattathias when he declared his imminent elevation to Titus Flavius Vespasianus.

Disraeli's premiership was flamboyant and theatrical. His insolence was calculated to be disarming. "A conservative government," he declared, "is an organized hypocrisy." Taking care always to be as amusing as he was outrageous, he was a political actor-manager whose fictions dignified the myth of Jewish superiority with a shamelessness that amused some of the ranks of Tuscany while enraging others. When James McNeill Whistler, at the height of his fame as a fashionable painter, saw Disraeli sitting on a bench in St. James's Park, he had the confidence to approach the prime minister and ask if he might paint his portrait. Disraeli waved a weary hand, saying, "Go away, little man, go away." His fictional self-portraits—another mutation of the Josephan *Vita*—were the only ones he cared to license.

Disraeli's ascent of what he called "the greasy pole" of English politics was achieved with little more than a perfunctory show of renunciation. Unlike Josephus, he was not obliged to grateful servility or literary tact. His youthful role as a dandy, somewhat in the Byronic style,* made isolation into a form of elegance. Deliberately outlandish in dress, Disraeli made a one-man parade of his genius; while he solicited the ballots of the British at large, he had small illusions concerning his acceptance by the ruling class. He depended, at least somewhat, on the idleness of the conservatives who left the brilliant outsider, as Pharaoh had with Joseph, to order things more competently than the

---

* Byron's Venetian gondolier servant and boyguard, Tita, found employment with Disraeli after the poet's death.

natives. Disraeli's coat of many colors set the style for British Jews, though few of them were ever as stylish, or as colorful, again. The only prime minister until Winston Churchill to be graced with an affectionate diminutive, "Dizzy" infuriated the bigots but installed himself in British folklore as no Jew ever contrived to do among the other nations of Europe.*

---

* Eric Roussel's *Pierre Mendès-France* (Paris: Gallimard, 2007) shows that, as France's prime minister, Mendès-France almost achieved similar status, but he lacked the panache—sartorial, literary and rhetorical—that made Disraeli not only a leader but also an entertainer. In the wake of the Dreyfus affair and the anti-Semitic legislation of Vichy, which licensed the deportations of 1943–44, French Jews have had reason to be skeptical of their countrymen's unwavering allegiance to the much-vaunted Rights of Man.

XVIII

JOSEPHUS WAS ONLY THE FIRST of countless Jews for whom the accumulation of pages creates a secret province. By himself, the author can be sovereign. Like Marcel Proust in his cork-lined room, he can mete out retrospective justice or, like Stefan Zweig marooned in Brazil, give vent to incurable, if elegantly composed, nostalgia. In the Passover service, the loss of Jerusalem was formalized in annual longing for a place that, over the centuries, few Jews expected to see. While the lost splendor of their city supplied a myth to match that of Atlantis,* the indelibly alien nature of "the Jews" became a central ingredient of European mythology. They were, for centuries, Christendom's scapegoats of choice. In the 1380s, civil discord inside Paris was resolved with the cry "*Aux juifs,*" and the consequent pillage and massacre of the Jewish quarter, although the contentious issue, in which Jews played no part, was between the citizens and the Crown.†

A post-Christian derivative of theological anti-Semitism has been the stigmatization of Israel. Its right to exist is questioned in accordance with a revision of the same logic that was applied to the insolence of Judaism by Muhammad, Loyola and Luther. The last, in his tract *The Jews and Their Lies*, repeated that the Romans were "God's instruments, punishing the Jews for their delusions regarding their false

---

* Far-fetched versions of the myth of Atlantis and dreams of its retrieval supplied the subject of Pierre Vidal-Naquet's last book.

† See Sumption, *The Hundred Years War,* vol. 3.

Christ and their persecution of the true one." He advocated that they should be deprived of normal civil rights, their property and books burned and they themselves herded into forced labor camps.

Nietzsche remarked that the Germans were "a people who had subordinated themselves to a man like Luther!" Evelyn Juers points out that Thomas Mann's 1937 gloss on Nietzsche's observation was that Hitler was directly in line with Luther and so *"a truly German phenomenon."*[1] Yet some Christian apologists persist with the convenient notion that murderous anti-Semitism was generated only by the Enlightenment. By a perversion of Lutheran logic, the killings and brutality of Kristallnacht in Germany in November 1938 were sanctioned by Joseph Goebbels as righteous "revenge" for the assassination of Ernst vom Rath, the third secretary of the German embassy in Paris.*

The punitive pursuit of heresy marks every monotheism. Islam automatically condemns apostates to death.† Ideologists nurture hatred of schismatics who appear, to rational outsiders, to be scarcely distinct from those who consign them to hell. There were divisions between Jews from the moment Moses turned his back on the refugees he had led out of Egypt in order to trudge up Mount Sinai (it is a long climb to the top), there to seal the covenant with the God who came to be known as Yahweh. Moses descended to find that a good many of the Hebrews were dancing in worship of the golden calf. His first task was to wed them to the singular worship of Yahweh; their uniformity was to be the reflection of His unity.‡ It took forty years in the wilderness to make them into a cohesive force ready, under Joshua's

* He was shot by a seventeen-year-old Jew, Herschel Grynszpan, whose parents had been evicted from their Lubeck house and forced, destitute, across the Polish border. Vom Rath was an anti-Nazi, under observation by the Gestapo, and homosexual. Like Jesus, he became a martyr for a cause he never advocated.

† This rule supplies the "logic" behind the Iranian ayatollahs' fatwa against Salman Rushdie for his "blasphemy" in *The Satanic Verses* (New York: Viking Penguin, 1989), a text almost certainly more often denounced than read.

‡ Even He has been deconstructed by anthropologists, as a conflation of two gods, one of the sky, the other volcanic, whom the Hebrews put together and worshipped as One.

leadership, to take out the Amalekites and assume the lease of the promised land. Its inhabitants' history, and that of their supposed descendants, would be replete with factions, schisms and feuds.

The archetypal theologico-ideological dispute arose between Pauline Christianity and "the Jews" who, in their stiff-necked obstinacy, refused to recognize Jesus of Nazareth as the only son of God. It is a status that Jesus never claimed and that was at odds with Judaism's unbreachable monotheism, which He never questioned. The murderous hostility between early Christian homoousians, who believed that God and Jesus Christ had exactly the same nature, and homoiousians, who maintained that Jesus was of only *similar* stuff to God the Father, matches the controversies that set Essenes against Pharisees and Zealots against their Hellenizing brethren. The stand-off between Sunni and Shia Muslims has claimed many more lives than all the wars between Israel and the Arab states.

For centuries, Jesus was contrasted with "the Jews," quite as if He belonged to a different race. At the same time, He was authenticated because He was descended, as the Messiah was forecast to be, according to Isaiah's prescribed genealogy, from the royal family of David.* The attribution of divine status to Jesus was in line with the practice of Hellenistic monarchs and pretenders since the time of Alexander the Great. The first Roman to flaunt his descent from an immortal was Venus's favorite, Julius Caesar. The latter's jealousy of the great Alexander was among his motives for invading Gaul (money was a more pressing one). Caesar's adopted son, his nephew Octavian, went one better: he agreed to be worshipped, in his lifetime, as the deified Augustus, and even to have temples built in his honor and in that of the goddess Roma, although at first, at his own instruction, he was the object of cult only in the eastern provinces, where Hellenistic kings had established a tradition of self-elevating pretensions to divinity. Subsequent emperors consented to be universally worshipped as a way of

---

* As the Christian festival of Palm Sunday celebrates, Christ's entry into Jerusalem honors a prediction in Zecharaiah (9:9) that the Messiah would ride into the city "on an ass," i.e., on quite a grand form of transport. Most people walked.

deserving their subjects' loyalty (and their tribute). The tradition of assuming their own divine election was resumed, slightly less presumptuously, in the Middle Ages, by the Holy Roman emperors, who were often neither holy nor Roman and had no empire.*

However refined Christian apologetics became, especially after the millennium of 1000 C.E. (when Jesus failed to make His expected return), the righteous disparagement of the Jews has always been validated by their mundane humiliation. The archetypal prophet Elijah the Tishbite set the style for assuming that God was a player in the world's game when he mocked the Philistines' deity Baa-Shamin because he failed to set fire to a pile of wood, which Yahweh then had no difficulty in igniting, even when it was drenched by rain. By the same logic, Christians maintained, the failure of the Jews to prevent the incineration of Jerusalem had to be the proof that Yahweh had deserted them.†

The degradation of the synagogue, literal and metaphorical, remained integral to the practice and rhetoric of Christian Europe. Jesus and His church were custodians of the unique gate through which man could secure access to redemption. Christ's personal history was revised to prove that He had been repudiated, wickedly, by his own people. Accordingly, He and His followers were exempt from the shame of defeat in the Jewish War. Within a short time, they found

---

* As a way of acquiring a faint odor of sanctity, kings and queens of England are institutionalized as heads of the Anglican Church. They also still bear the title of "Defenders of the Faith," bestowed on Henry VIII by the Roman Catholic pope Clement VII, whose authority Henry later repudiated.

† Christians appropriated this notion of divine chastisement to their own case. In *Divided Houses,* the third volume of his history of the Hundred Years' War, Jonathan Sumption reports that when the last great crusading army was wiped out by the Ottoman sultan Bayezid at Nicopolis, Philippe de Mézières, its organizer, concluded that the "*desconfiture lacrimable*" (pathetic disaster) was God's punishment of the chivalry of France for its moral failings. The Vichy government of France took much the same line after the humiliation of 1940 and made "*redressement national*" (national resurrection) the pious excuse for anti-Semitic legislation that exceeded anything that the Nazis had yet enacted. Charles Maurras, the monarchist intellectual who had long advocated the elimination of the Jews and whose Catholicism was too robust for the pope, termed the defeat a "*divine surprise.*" God had looked after His own.

ways to revel in it. Since the earth had proved to be the undeniable realm of the Roman emperor, Jesus Christ was elevated into an otherworldly Lord who had never laid claim to a terrestrial domain: He was a Redeemer of souls, not a practical rebel. The man who had been crucified under the mocking rubric "the King of the Jews" was, in due time, said never to have wanted a Jewish kingdom. If He brought "not peace but a sword," it was to be wielded against his own unbelieving and treacherous kin. Judas became the surrogate, despicable king of the damned Jews. The battle for the theocratic high ground, symbolized by Jerusalem, persisted between Jews and Christians who laid claim to the same God, mystified, in the case of the latter, by the intrusion of the Trinity.

After the sixth century C.E., the rise of Islam (with its many mimetic elements, including a claim to Jerusalem) served to make the struggle triangular. The most keenly observed Judeo-Christian tradition remained that of unforgiving recrimination between contending sects, not least between schismatic popes. Adherents of Christianity kept re-enacting the *stasis* that Josephus had deplored between Jewish factions in the Temple precincts. During the Thirty Years' War, in 1618–38, those who took different views of Christ's message and worship were often more repugnant to each other, dressed as Catholics or Protestants, than even the Jews, with whom Protestants, not least Puritans such as the Pilgrim fathers, were apt to identify. The Treaty of Westphalia, in 1638, dressed the exhaustion of central Europe's contending Christian factions in the mantle of tolerance. The Jews were not relevant to the treaty, but their acceptance, as citizens of a kind, trailed in its wake.

Nineteenth- and early twentieth-century Vienna had some of the cosmopolitan allure of Alexandria in Josephus's time. It gave shelter and a measure of emancipation to a growing number of Jews, many of whom thrived in the artistic and professional liberty of a city that never quite admitted them to parity. The Jews were, in many regards, Vienna's good fortune: they generated both wealth and art. Yet their contributions (and their numbers), even when they enriched or entertained their fellow citizens, fomented rather than allayed the hostility that would lead their audience and beneficiaries to turn against them.

The facility with which so many Jews adapted themselves to Gentile culture gave them, for a while at least, the confidence to speak out more unguardedly than ever before. Among the intelligentsia, they were particularly to be drawn to journalism, of which Josephus was the prototype. The journalist cannot often affect the selflessness of the scientist, but he profits from the putative neutrality of his profession: he describes or pictures what is happening without, in theory, intruding his own personality, even though his prose has almost always to pander to the tastes of the public and (as Karl Kraus stingingly insisted) accommodate the timidities of his editor. Joseph Roth (1894–1939) was perhaps the greatest, because the least cautious, of Jewish journalists to spring from the Germanic world. Never a "success," with a tenured byline, he was an anguished nomad who combined prolific facility with rare accuracy of observation; for example: "Jewish doctors are a kind of atonement for the crucifixion."[2] Roth's novels have a desperate panache unmatched by the works of Jewish writers who have made happy careers in Anglo-Saxon literature.

The personal history of Sigmund Freud reflects specificities and ambiguities he sought to discount or sublimate. His notion of repression, as a feature of all human psychic operations, had a practical correlative in the experience of many Jews in Christian Europe. It could be said that Freud's emphasis on the neurotic consequences of, roughly speaking, *sexual* repression was a Josephan ruse. Donning a scientist's, rather than a historian's, mask, Freud chose, like Spinoza, to indict Christianity *caute*, with argued caution rather than with overt polemic.* The Oedipus complex replaced original sin by cursing all men with the same psychological mark—mental circumcision, as it were. Freud's trick could not be won decisively: like the return of the sexually repressed,

---

* A lover of Greek and Roman antiquities, Freud made the Carthaginian Hannibal his personal totem. The fetishization of the man who almost destroyed Rome stood in for the author whose *The Future of an Illusion* cast doubt on, in particular, Roman Catholicism, whose followers were prominent among Vienna's anti-Semites. One of Freud's papers makes much of an anonymous patient's inadequate memory of Dido's line in the *Aeneid* "*Exoriare aliquis nostris ex ossibus ultor*" ("Let some avenger arise from my bones"). Hannibal and Sigmund were Semitic allies under the skin.

assimilation excited neurotic reactions; anti-Semites who could not accept the loss of their distinction insisted that the divide between Jew and Gentile was elemental.* In neo-Talmudic style, Freud's emphasis— even in the context of his meta-Spinozan naturalism—is on states of mind and their leakage into human activity, rather than on any notion of historical or economic progress.

Freud would never forget how an arrogant Gentile knocked his father's hat into the gutter, and with what obsequiousness he retrieved and replaced it. It is a rare Jew who can absolutely deny the smallest wish to get his own back. Zionism is its geopolitical expression. As J. J. Lawlor has put it, writing about the Platonic myth of Er, "Homesickness has become the proof of the existence of a home." It is also evidence of its loss. Er and errancy have a sweet, if accidental, affinity: both involve interplay between the living and the dead. Walter Benjamin would make a virtue of the Jews' *Irrkunst,* the art of getting lost.

Before their reluctant emancipation by Gentile majorities, the Jews had been forced into ghettos, but there was also a certain acquiescence in the tight domestic consequences: as shtetl life illustrated, Judaism was a communitarian faith.[3] The Viennese psychoanalytic community, under its jealous, if laicized, chief rabbi, the Herr Doktor Freud, mimicked the tradition of the minyan: its social history is of a series of conferences and colloquies, almost always dominated by an authoritarian elder. Josephus reports a similar style of supervision among the Essenes, for whom to be a good Jew required the surveillance of other, better Jews.

In the Christian imagination, the ghetto created a home for covens of bogeymen, a furtive den for necromancy and plots. In anti-Semitic fantasy, the elders of Zion were too cunning to emit any evidence of their plans for world domination. Evidence of their schemes had to

---

* Hitler's preferred philosopher, Alfred Rosenberg, wrote *The Myth of the Twentieth Century,* the flabbiest pseudo-intellectual testament of anti-Semitism; the work of Carl Schmitt was the best-argued. For Schmitt, see *The Concept of the Political,* translated by George D. Schwab (Chicago: University of Chicago Press, 1996; expanded edition 2006, with an introduction by Tracy B. Strong).

be fabricated, as had been the Christological passages in Josephus. Norman Cohn's *Europe's Inner Demons* offers a cool tabulation of how repression of the weak (women as well as Jews) generated fear, among those who crushed them, that they were plotting revenge by the use of arcane powers.[4] The burning of witches and Jews, supposedly a vindication of faith, can be interpreted as an involuntary confession of doubt. Dread of the return of the persecuted disturbed the sleep of the dominant majority.

In a mutation of the same ambivalence, the logic (and vanity) of Jewish guilt persists among, for instance, anti-Zionists who blame the indignation of Islam against the West on the existence of Israel and Israel's existence on the aberrations of Zionism and its lobbyists. The corollary, eagerly embraced by Israel's unsubtle enemies, is that the extinction of the Jewish state, if not of all Jews, will bring world harmony. This modification of pariahdom can be seen as a transposition to geopolitics of various schemes of Christian redemption and rationalizing "science" and historicism. Universal solutions are proposed or "discovered" in order to flush away aberrant, literally disconcerting, exceptions.

From the Enlightenment onward, science seemed to supply an inside track along which clever Jews might transcend "racial" limitations. In physics (and with a white coat), an equation was an equation, a formula a formula, no matter who formulated it. Truth was discovered by genius and confirmed by experiment and by peer review; it had nothing to do with apocalyptic revelation. This impersonalized scheme did nothing to inhibit Nazis from speaking of "Jewish science" when it came to psychoanalysis. Freud had been eager, even before the Great War, to recruit Gentile adherents, Carl Jung in particular, in order to advertise his theory's universal claim.*

---

* The primacy of universalization is now applied to "human rights," just as the ecologists' quasi-deification of Gaia is a metastasis of monotheism. Where Spinoza offered the equivalence *"Deus sive natura,"* the Greens choose nature and make its presumed commandments the creed they claim to be unquestionable. As with the Stoics, the cosmos itself becomes a ubiquitous temple. Man is always trying to rebuild the Tower of Babel with the aid of a common, unaccented creed.

Freud indicted the dominant form of Christianity only en passant, as Josephus's history did the ruthlessness of the presiding emperors. In a modification of Spinozan loftiness, Freudian science dispelled faith without risking specific polemic. The universalization of Charcot's *la chose génitale* dissolved the distinction between Jew and Gentile: all human beings were subject to, if not victims of, a common, undiscriminating nature. As Rudyard Kipling put it, and the psychoanalyst's couch confirmed, the Colonel's lady and Judy O'Grady were sisters under the skin, and the skirt. Yet the trick could not quite be won: similarity is also a form of difference. Freud's entourage was too obviously composed of Jews. However scientific its jargon, psychoanalytic practice had a Jewish accent.* Its theory also manifested involuntary mimesis: the postulate that the human psyche had a tripartite nature became an article of faith that sported a correspondence with the Christian Trinity as well as with Plato.

Without any scheme for historical or economic progress, Freud wanted "science" to be the new, transcendental master of the world. His elevation of science modernized the Josephan *translatio imperii*. This time, the supreme and unifying power would be impersonal. Truth would be determined by dispassionate observers, whose speculations would depend only on scientifically attested evidence. The emergence of the ego from the guilt-making paternal shadow generalizes for all humanity the particular condition of the modern Jew as he seeks to shake free of his specific history. It is only right to say that Freud wished and believed that *his* truth, that of psychoanalysis, would indeed set men free. In practice, however, he imposed his own orthodoxy by the force of a genius that was, in its way, as authoritarian as that of any other prophet.

The allegedly irretrievable otherness of Jews was central to the philosophy of another precocious fin de siècle Viennese Jew. In *Geschlecht*

---

* The promotion of Carl Jung to the status of favorite son, in order to advertise the cross-denominational nature of Freud's "science," generated an Oedipal drama that could only remind the "father" of psychoanalysis of how different small differences could be.

und Charakter (*Sex and Character*), Otto Weininger (1880–1903) attributed virility only to Aryans. He located Jews in an effeminate annex. Weininger's distinctions, like Freud's, were an amalgam of literary insights and metaphysical "science." Without denying his Jewish nature, Weininger crossed the line, if only with one foot. His suicide, soon after he had published his solitary masterpiece, enhanced his Tiresian reputation. Graced with the aura of a last testament, his text had great appeal for anti-Semites, especially since it came, on a Nazi reading, as a confession from the other side. Like Josephus, Weininger has been read as giving comfort to the enemy.*

In philosophy, the famous Vienna Circle of the 1920s and 1930s also had a Josephan aspect: it too attacked the dominant religion by indirection. Its overt animus was against "metaphysics," the system-building "revelations" of other philosophers. Logic, not rhetoric, articulated the syntax of logical positivism; its aggressive neutrality sharpened the guillotine that was meant to sever metaphysicians from respectable academic company. Its English apostle, the precocious A. J. Ayer, denied that the logical positivists had ever been motivated by a desire to assimilate to a universal "religion" of science or for its company to dress itself in the uniformity of men who, with no distinction between Jew and Gentile, worked in the world's supreme laboratory. All the same, the Vienna Circle's cult of science, like Freud's, can be read, from outside, as another attempted great escape from specificity into a godless monotheism to which Yahweh, like the Savior, was irrelevant. Whatever Ayer considered his motives to be,† his attitude

---

* Béla Szabados (*Wittgenstein Reads Weininger*) says that Wittgenstein was indignant to discover that *Sex and Character* was lodged in a part of the Cambridge University Library inaccessible to undergraduates. He was, however, unsurprised when G. E. Moore failed to admire the book, but he maintained that it deserved to be taken seriously, even if it was wise to put a ~ (the logical symbol for negation) in front of Weininger's whole thesis. There were, Wittgenstein implied, interesting ways of being wrong.

† The positivists' relegation of "morals" to matters of personal opinion was, by coincidence, much to the hedonistic taste of both Ayer and his *maître-à-penser* Bertrand Russell. The commandments of revealed religion were relegated to mere

resembles Wittgenstein's ambivalent allegiance to the Vienna Circle, which he attended and then repudiated.

In 1936, as the Nazi threat grew heavier, Wittgenstein wrote to Ludwig Hansel, "I lied to you and several others back then during the Italian internment [at the end of the Great War] when I said that I was descended one-quarter from Jews and three-quarters from Aryans, even though it is just the other way round. This cowardly lie has burdened me for a long time."[5] The confession becomes more touching in the light of the deliberate bravery which Wittgenstein displayed as an artillery observer, in the Austrian army, when under fire during heavy fighting on the Italian front. The element of recycling and reform—inevitable when outsiders become fluent in an adopted tongue—may do something to explain what Wittgenstein acknowledged when he said that Jews were never more than *talented*. It is witless not to read his remark as containing a tincture of irony, not to say false modesty.

Wittgenstein somewhat contradicted himself by proclaiming Otto Weininger to have been a genius, a designation that, in Wittgenstein's own reckoning, exempted him from Jewishness. In his scrupulous biography, Ray Monk takes this opinion to endorse the image of Wittgenstein as a "self-hating" quasi-Nazi who had, as if by psychic osmosis, internalized the Wagnerian notion of the essentially uncreative and parasitic Jew.[6] Béla Szabados's counteroffensive insists that Wittgenstein's attitude was colored by circumstances.[7] The nasty, but more or less bloodless, anti-Semitism of imperial Vienna (typified by its populist mayor Karl Lueger's frivolous claim that it was up to him to define who was a Jew) became lethal only in the policies and practices of Hitler and his followers.* Freud could imagine that his books might one day be burned; he regarded it as an inconceivable anachronism

---

fetishes. Freud put his patients on the couch; modern philosophers have shown an aptitude for joining their pupils there.

* A few Jews, mostly female and intimately linked with Nazi grandees, were granted honorary Aryan status, which allowed them to escape the Shoah. This, it could be said, was an extreme version of the Romanized status granted to Joseph ben Mattathias by the Flavians. The Nazis burned many books by Jews, but Hitler and Goebbels were admirers of the works of Edward Bernays (1891–1995), the German-

that, in our time, an author might be. He died, on September 23, 1939, only just before he could be disillusioned.

Although baptized a Catholic, like the rest of his very rich and ennobled family, Wittgenstein was willing, by 1931, to "confess" that he regarded himself as a "Jewish thinker." In 1949, Szabados points out, he "described his . . . thoughts as '100% Hebraic.'"* What was typically "Hebrew" about Wittgenstein's later philosophy was in line with the Pharisaic tradition: he glossed and commented on issues raised in philosophical discourse but he no more affected to add to the substance of the matter than any Jewish scholiast, however ingenious his reading, would ever claim to have added something substantial to the Torah.† Wittgenstein was never more "Hebraic" than when he said that the problem in philosophy was to "say the new thing in the old language." A Talmudist was, by definition, never original; even the subtlest reading requires a basic text.

Gershom Scholem, who emigrated from Germany to Palestine before the Nazis came to power, claimed that journalistic writing signaled the decline of modern Jewish culture and yet, in an exquisite form, could be a kind of redemption. Even while enthusing about the "messianic" Jewishness of Karl Kraus's style, Scholem contended that Kraus "never had an original thought in his life."‡ He added that his observation "is meant here infinitely more as a compliment than as a criticism": it promised that Kraus, like Wittgenstein, was "a hundred percent Hebraic." Wittgenstein said on several occasions that "if we confuse prototype and object [individual case], we find ourselves dog-

---

born Jewish American pioneer of the mass-selling techniques that lay behind Hitler's notion of the potency of "the Big Lie."

* In retrospect, the famous concluding line of the *Tractatus Logico-Philosophicus,* "Whereof one cannot speak, thereof one should keep silent," could be said to acquire a Josephan ring: Wittgenstein's reticence implies, without overt declaration, what its author really is.

† "Philosophy," Wittgenstein said, "leaves everything as it is."

‡ Edward Timms, *Karl Kraus: Apocalyptic Satirist,* vol. 2, p. 29. Kraus himself had inherited copious private means and, having made a rich marriage, was able to publish his own newspaper without making polite, or circulation-conscious, compromises.

matically conferring on the objective properties which only the prototype possesses."* He reacted with fury when his friend and pupil Norman Malcolm attributed "national characteristics" (fair play being the one at issue) to the British, for whom, he said, it was an impossibility that they should plan to assassinate even a man such as Hitler.

Already translated to a Cambridge professorship, Wittgenstein went in 1938 to Switzerland, soon after the Anschluss, which forcibly united Austria with Hitler's Reich, in order to negotiate with Nazi officials over the fate of his two sisters who were still living in Vienna. He succeeded in buying their immunity, doubtless at a very high price. As a result, they survived while others perished. No transcript exists of the conversation, but it is tempting to speculate in what terms, and in what tone and—to use theatrical terms—in what *character,* Wittgenstein chose to address the well-dressed, civilian plenipotentiaries of Hitler's regime. Whatever his thoughts, his words—like those of Josephus when in the company of the Flavians, *pater et filius*—can hardly have been 100 percent Hebraic. Nor, probably, was his person. Nazi thugs were often in the habit of forcing down the trousers of men they suspected of being Jews who were failing to wear the yellow star. Born a putative Christian, Wittgenstein was most likely uncircumcised.

Karl Popper, a Viennese exile, was a similar case. His father, like Isaac D'Israeli, had a large and cosmopolitan library, in which the young Popper, like any precocious Jew, began the earnest education that took him away from Judaism. By the end of his university studies, Popper had dispensed with religious belief, though not yet with the impatient self-assertion that his enemies associated with his Semitic origins. In wartime New Zealand, Popper elaborated his 1936 essay "The Poverty of Historicism" into a voluminous indictment of the totalitarian tendency in Western philosophy. Published in 1945, *The Open Society and Its Enemies* was an Austrian exile's response—as passionate as it affected

---

* Here, in a nutshell, is the abiding charge against Hannah Arendt: she deduced specific human behavior, especially that of Adolf Eichmann, from an a priori scheme of her own devising. Her (partial) observations of the Eichmann trial were literally prejudiced by her proprietary analysis of "totalitarianism."

to be impersonal—to what Raul Hilberg would call, in his 1961 masterpiece, *The Destruction of the European Jews*. Beginning with Plato and threading through Hegel and Marx, Popper lit a fuse that exploded under the factitious certainties of the closed societies, Nazi and Communist. Both took their warrant from Plato's high-minded false logic. His "guardians," whatever philosophical distinction they affected, were indicted as betrayers of liberty.

Popper, who learned Greek in order to berate Plato with well-read accuracy, seemed to be fueled by a rage with no specific motive. Yet his passion has something of the zeal of the Essenes, who held that the Sanhedrin and the High Priests had defiled the purity of Judaism. He justified his furious devotion to reason by advocating the priority of scientific method. Having shucked Judaism, with an implicit contempt that his husky disciple Bryan Magee has declared overtly, Popper scarcely mentioned religion in his writings. He assumed that postwar society would dispense with unscientific superstitions. In the same tradition, Hannah Arendt never reckoned with the abiding irrationality of dogmatic faith. Her panacea, "universal pluralism," is the complacent prescription of the New York school's haughty principal. The craving for universal "solutions" is, if not malign, more sentimental moralizing than practical politics.

Unlike Leo Strauss, Popper assumed that revealed religion would have no important place in the civilized world after a war that had, in effect, been won by Anglo-American technology (one of the reasons why Martin Heidegger deplored it). Popper assumed that in the future, an Open Society would be secular, democratic and without discrimination. In a spirit germane to the positivists, Freud had wanted nothing so much as to be accepted as a scientist. Wittgenstein insisted that Freud was, on the contrary, in the highest sense, a speculator (D. H. Lawrence remarked on the Jewish genius for "disinterested speculation").

According to Jacques Bouveresse,[8] "For Wittgenstein, a person who thinks that there must be one *correct* explanation and one *correct* reason for the sort of phenomena treated by psychoanalysis is not . . . adopting the dominant scientific attitude but . . . is already on the road to producing a mythology." In this light, the notion that Josephus was always "pro-Roman" and was *essentially* a traitor can be seen as an attempt to make him an anti-icon in the demonology of the Jews. The mutable opportunist resembles Homer's Odysseus, who, when Polyphemus demanded to know his name, replied that he was "*outis*": no one. The wounded Cyclops then cried out, to the fellow Cyclopes who had come to his aid, "No One has wounded me"; whereupon they went away.

In Vienna, the Jew as a nobody (like Josephus in imperial Rome) was transformed—especially when Jews became psychoanalysts and philosophers, even if they devised their own specialities in order to do so—into the Jew as an Odyssean No One, the intellectual without a specific personality who carried out an autopsy on what was left of human illusions. The Vienna Circle's rejection of metaphysics can be seen as an undeclared war on religion. Logical positivism disqualified theology from serious consideration on the formal grounds that its propositions were unscientific. Personal opinions or beliefs did not impinge on philosophy. Objections that began with "I believe" or "I sincerely think" were greeted with "But this is mere autobiography!" The disappearance of the ego was, in theory, a condition of admission to the scientific fraternity.*

Freud's dispassionate pathology had offered a way for Jews to consider their own lives, and to investigate other people's, without sentimentality. After the discovery of what had happened to Europe's Jews under the Nazis, Raul Hilberg composed his account of their mechanized murder by discounting the anguish of the victims. He adopted an unblinking, positivistic method hardly within the scope of an eyewitness such as Joseph ben Mattathias had been of the Roman butchery in Jerusalem. Hilberg's *The Destruction of the European Jews* (1961) resembled *The Jewish War* in that it mounted no explicit polemic. Without the direct menace of a conqueror's commission, Hilberg chose to work as if he were under an embargo imposed by Gentiles. The result was an indictment veiled in alienated and statistical accountancy. More coro-

---

* So-called therapeutic positivism made a bridge between Freud and the Vienna Circle by encouraging metaphysicians to "tell us more" until they cured their own "mental cramps." There is no long record of successful cures.

ner than judge, Hilberg eschewed fine writing; he acknowledged no affinity with the victims whom he enumerated and classified (as Serge and Beate Klarsfeld would in the case of French deportees). With similarly "positivistic" self-effacement, Primo Levi wrote about his experiences as an inmate of Auschwitz in the style of a "factory report." He refrained from overstatement to moderate his anguish, not to ignore it. Affecting to make no moral judgments, both Levi and Hilberg, like Josephus, put on impassive masks for the best expression of their findings.* In his later years, Levi regularly attended his synagogue in Turin, but as a form of remembrance, not because he had come to believe in revealed religion.

Although Arthur Schnitzler's main claim to fame derives from plays such as *The Ring Dance* (*La ronde*), his 1908 novel *The Road into the Open* is one of the shrewdest depictions of the pains and pleasures, illusions and dilemmas of Diaspora Jews. In the early heat of his nostalgic enthusiasm, Theodor Herzl was keen to recruit Schnitzler to Zionism.† He asked his friend to imagine the thrill of writing and having his plays put on in Jerusalem. The reply of the most applauded playwright in Vienna was simply "In what language?" As a medical man, Schnitzler regarded the incurable contradictions of the Jewish condition with unblinking resignation and a certain amusement.‡

---

* Primo Levi nevertheless shows some contempt for an attractive young fellow inmate of Auschwitz, whom he calls only "Henri," who crosses the moral line by making himself sexually available, and attractive, to his jailers. As an old man, "Henri" came out and wrote a book in which, with dignified force, he defended his actions in order to stay alive as beyond any kind of moral assessment. Since he had not betrayed anyone else, he owed no one any account of his tactics. Somewhat like Joseph ben Mattathias, he claimed that he did only what he had to do to beguile his captors, although he did not cite God's will (or absence) in his defense.

† Herzl's notion of a *communal* solution to the existential angst of the Diaspora Jew is typically journalistic; agitprop was his medium. The artist in Schnitzler knew that a true writer had to endure his individuality, just as the doctor in Schnitzler knew that there was no cure for it, no Lourdes for Jews.

‡ Did he smile wryly at the news of his daughter's marriage to an Italian Fascist or did he greet it with the bitterness with which, in Jonathan Miller's 1974 production, Shylock threw Jessica's clothes on the floor on learning that his daughter had "married out"? Miller "outed" himself, to some degree, in the famous and witty line, in *Beyond*

In a personal letter, Freud wrote that Schnitzler had, by the light-ning exercise of his imagination, arrived at conclusions that had taken the inventor of psychoanalysis years of clinical study to reach. One of them, in *Presentiments and Queries,* might have afforded Josephus some comfort when he thought back on that blood-filled pothole in Jotapata: "Martyrdom was only ever a proof of the intensity, never of the cor-rectness, of a belief." Another might not have: "The snob is a person who aspires to apparent self-advancement by means of actual self-abasement. He is the masochist of the social order." His target here may well have been Karl Kraus, whom Schnitzler openly scorns elsewhere:* he described Kraus's pandering to anti-Semitic fashion as "the most repulsive thing I have ever seen." As they did in the Second Temple pre-cinct, attacks of Jews on Jews can still have an unguarded trenchancy.†

Principalities and powers with summary authority over Jews have rarely paid close attention to what Jews choose to say or do to each other. Within the ghetto or the academy, a Jew could make his case against another Jew without the inhibitions that might constrain him in Gentile courts. The venom with which, in the early 1950s, Edward

---

the Fringe, when he claimed that he was no more than Jew*ish*: he didn't, he explained, go the whole hog.

* Schnitzler can be acquitted of criticizing Kraus to get his own back. At the outbreak of the Great War, Schnitzler was alone among Austrian celebrity writers in escaping Kraus's scorn for those who yielded to war fever. Like Kraus, Schnitzler attributed public enthusiasm to "failure of the imagination"—as Josephus had the Jerusalem Jews' appetite for war with Rome. See Timms, vol. 2, p. 300.

† The divided self is not a Jewish monopoly, but the comedy particular to Jews is that they are torn between craving Gentile applause and despising themselves for the desire. Self-hatred can be the dark side of the self-esteem that dares not speak its name. Jews who have already achieved respectability (or imagined immunity from anti-Semitism) cannot be relied on to welcome less comely cousins. Yet Chris-tian fathers, philosophers of history, politicians and ideologists regularly postulate conspiratorial unity among "the Jews." Duplicity has then to be wished on them to account for their loud divisions, which are taken to be camouflage. To preserve their mythical status as a diabolical Other, all Jews, however superficially diverse, are depicted as essentially "the same."

Teller pursued J. R. Oppenheimer over the latter's reluctance to develop the hydrogen bomb is a merciless instance of an intra-Jewish vendetta.*

In the confines of a semiprivate language, Jews have been able to rail at Jews as they could wish to do at their common enemies. Yiddish bristles with scornful and obscene expressions, from *schnorrer* to *schlemiel* by way of *schmuck, schvitz* and *schtup*. Jewish "self-hatred" is as likely to signal introverted anger against the injustice of the outside world as any apprehension of innate inadequacy. Persecution generates compensatory vanities. In the Lodz ghetto during the Shoah, Chaim Rumkowski, whom Hannah Arendt describes as "Eldest of the Jews," nominated himself Chaim the First and issued currency notes bearing his signature and postage stamps engraved with his image. He also rode around his walled fiefdom in a "broken-down horse-drawn carriage." Moshe Merin, in East Upper Silesia, was scarcely less dictatorial. Arendt's own tone, in *Eichmann in Jerusalem,* is more regularly scornful of Jews than of anyone else. "We know the physiognomies of the Jewish leaders during the Nazi period very well" she says and then shows those Jews small mercy. Her use of the word "physiognomies" proclaims the celebrity intellectual's divorce from ghetto-born vulgarity; a fancy term for "faces," "physiognomies" parades the Hellenized makeup she learned from Martin Heidegger (and which would have infuriated the Zealots).

The only European Jewish "leaders" of whom Arendt appears to approve are "a few who committed suicide—like Adam Czerniakow, chairman of the Warsaw Jewish Council, who was not a rabbi but an unbeliever . . . who must still have remembered the rabbinical saying 'Let them kill you, but don't cross the line.'" A stern moralist when it

---

* It was conducted with conspicuous malice by Teller, who sought to benefit from the climate of scarcely surreptitious anti-Semitism displayed by Senator McCarthy and his team, in which Roy Cohn, both a Jew and a crypto-homosexual, was a key player. See *American Prometheus,* by Kai Bird and Martin J. Sherwin (New York: Alfred A. Knopf, 2005). Ray Monk's forthcoming biography of J. Robert Oppenheimer (of which I have seen only a small section in a draft) promises fresh observations on his subject's attitude to and relations with Jews and Jewishness.

came to other people's conduct, Arendt might well have sided with the Zionists, at least in condemning Joseph ben Mattathias for preferring dishonor to death. Never does she suggest that an ordinary German, deputed to murder, should have had recourse to suicide before turning butcher.*

Jews who hope to escape from the ethnico-ethical bunker can be more outspoken in criticizing the habits or morals of Jews than when confronting their Gentile enemies. This posture seems to emancipate the speaker from his or her unwanted origins.† If, in the novels she wrote in the *entre-deux-guerres*, Irène Némirovsky criticized Jews with a relish that is close to inquisitorial, it is, at least in part, because a clever girl could,‡ with impunity (and commercial advantage), pillory the Jewish bourgeoisie the better to appeal to the French. In due time, when the Vichy authorities began the deportations of "stateless Jews," as a result of which Irène herself and her husband were eventually transported to their deaths, the faults of the Jews (especially those of her parents, whom she had satirized remorselessly) were seen by Némirovsky to be venial compared with the self-serving callousness of their supposed betters and onetime colleagues and friends.

Until the arrival of the Germans in 1940, Irène's knowledge of France had been limited to Paris, Biarritz—where her mother went for her annual intake of lovers—and the Riviera. Forced to go into hiding in rural Issy-l'Évêque, she discovered "the marvellously effective mal-

---

* It is remarkable, though rarely remarked, that while several survivors of the camps are known to have committed suicide, often many years after the events they witnessed and the horrors they endured, there is no long list of concentration camp guards or SS officials who found it impossible to live with the memories of their actions. It seems that it is more unendurable to have seen certain kinds of things than to have done them. Innocence, or impotence, can be harder to live with than guilt.

† Noam Chomsky, Jacqueline Rose, the late Harold Pinter and similar moral zealots tend to regard Israel, in particular, in the light of universal virtues that have nothing to do with the contingent circumstances of their advocates. Hence, it is claimed, there is no treachery when a Jew signs up to the humiliation and—with a proud and woeful nod—advocates the destruction of the State of Israel.

‡ Dorothy Parker, an archetypal Algonquin wit, said that she was, in truth, just one more smart Jewish girl who wanted to attract attention.

ice" of peasant life. In an appended passage to her novel *Suite Française*, written at a time when aware at last that she was on her own, she wrote: "Hatred + contempt = March 1942. . . . What is this country doing to me? . . . Let us consider it dispassionately, let us watch it lose its honor and its life blood. . . . Everything that is done in France within a certain social class has only one motive: fear. Pierre Laval and the stench of carrion." Sewing the yellow star onto her daughter Denise's school clothes (two months after her baptized child's First Communion) was Irène's introduction to needlework.

In those months of rural dread, Irène had time to discover that the Vichy myth of *la France profonde* was as fatuous as her trust in Parisian decency: "Everyone lives in his own house, on his own land, distrusts his neighbors, harvests his wheat, counts his money and doesn't give a thought to the rest of the world." Having spent twenty years anatomizing men on the make (and women on the prowl) in the smart world, Irène came abruptly to realize that there were selfish, callous operators pretty well everywhere.

As for Irène's "self-hatred," who can doubt that the mercilessness directed at "her own people" concealed a wider, unspoken scorn? Her underlying topic was the interplay of emotion and callousness, the alternations of vanity and despair, in all the players of the world's game. Imaginative impersonation is the mark of the authentic novelist; fiction is where the truth can be found; documentary is too often where it is confected. Irène could play male or female, be villain or dupe, candid or duplicitous. She moved the black and the white pieces with equal versatility. The insolence of her multiple impostures was a function of an isolation from which neither success nor marriage dispensed her. Those who notice, with glee, that Jew is often hard on Jew fail to read between the lines where it can be divined, by those with eyes to see, with what pitiless accuracy the conceit and cruelty of their enemies might one day be spelled out.

Vasily Grossman's *Life and Fate* (its title a perhaps conscious, scornful echo of Heidegger's *Being and Time*, and arguably a greater Russian novel than *War and Peace*) was one of the earliest post-Holocaust works in which accuracy and imagination combine in an uncompromising account of what Communists and Nazis did to Jews, and to their own people. In it, the narrator's mother, a doctor who has never thought of herself as a Jew, writes to the son whom she will never see again a letter in which she describes the strange sense of freedom she experienced as she marched into the fenced enclosure of the ghetto of Lodz, from which she would emerge only to be taken to her death.

Fruit of the same period, Julien Benda's *Exercice d'un enterré vif (Juin 1940–Août 1944)* is a segment of the *vita* of a Jew living like a ghost in a society where he must remain invisible or risk death. (Ralph Ellison's *Invisible Man,* about the black experience in America, made a bridge, now derelict, between black and Jewish experience as negligible pariahs.) Benda's most famous prewar book, *La Trahison des Clercs* (1927), had denounced fellow-traveling intellectuals. Benda accused them, left and right, of replacing loyalty to facts with ideological pliancy. His own Jewishness was, in his view, irrelevant alike to his criticism and to his way of life. Integrity had no pedigree; veracity, no ideology. Benda's call for the educated to tell the truth, rather than to bend to ideological cant, echoes Titus Flavius Josephus, who claimed to rise above partisanship in his account of *The Jewish War* and of himself.

The Benda of his wartime isolation stands near the end of the road that leads from the fall of Jerusalem to the foundation of the State of Israel. The ultimate Diaspora Jew, he neither denied his origins nor, in his social and intellectual stance, attached importance to them. He treated his enforced eviction from eminence in Parisian literary circles with sour condescension: as if such things mattered! His home was pillaged and his library rifled by the Germans, but—playing the part of a cheerful Timon or a sporting Shylock—he refused to be bitter or dismayed. Like Spinoza, he sublimated pariahdom into a kind of liberation.

Viewing austerity as luxury and solitude as distinction, Benda lacked Hannah Arendt's ambition to be a luminous personage. Arthur Cohen's 1983 novel *An Admirable Woman* is at once a tribute to her intellectual resilience and an involuntary satire on her self-righteousness. One of Arendt's first subjects (and her abiding role model) was the Jewish *salonnière* Rahel Varnhagen, whose ruling ambition, on the cusp of the eighteenth and nineteenth centuries, was to pass as a great lady in Prussian society. She imagined that beauty, wealth and intelligence would enable her to transcend her Jewishness and be an untrammeled citizen of the world. Arendt's attempts to provide a universal political logic, and morality, was of a piece with her heroine's ambition, even as she deplored it. Both women made their mark in the great world but were in the end reconciled, more or less happily, with the irrevocable element of Jewishness in their personalities.

Benda regarded public reputations and desire for the limelight with cool indifference. He declares, without careerist caution, that he cares little for pictorial art or imaginative literature and everything for truth. A zealot without a cause, Benda scorns religious scheme but cleaves to the dispassionate— "white," as it were—propositions of science. It is as if he subscribed to Wittgenstein's gnomic pronouncement, in the *Tractatus Logico-Philosophicus,* "Roughly speaking, all objects are colorless." It can be construed, fancifully, to imply that the essential nature of things is monotone; all color is supplied by human perceptions. Buried alive, Julien Benda becomes a blanched aesthete, cleansed even of the Jewishness he acknowledges only, yet willingly, as a genealogical fact, of small weight except to crackpots or dunces. His severe morality entails a distrust of graven images, and their sensual persuasiveness. Rejection of the bitch goddess Success, and of her mascot the golden calf, disposed him to sublime austerity. He lived perforce and by choice in a blanched, nondenominational, one-man ghetto. His *La France Byzantine,* published promptly after the war, must have been written when he was "buried alive." It denounces the opportunistic cowardice of "clerks" such as André Gide and Paul Valéry* in tailoring their sentiments to accommodate prevailing fashions during W. H. Auden's "low, dishonest decade" of the 1930s.

During the Shoah, doctrinal divisions between Christians had a continuing echo. In wartime France, provincial Protestant communi-

---

* See, for instance Valéry's banal eulogy of Marshal Pétain on the latter's election to the Académie Française, in 1931. Official obfuscation could hardly be more harmlessly or, for a purist such as Benda, more creepily displayed.

ties absorbed and hid large numbers of fugitive Jews, despite the official pogroms sanctioned by the predominantly Roman Catholic *état français*. French Protestants, although indistinguishable, in civil law, from their Catholic fellow citizens, may have been prompted to help Jews by their own long memories of the persecution of the Huguenots by central authority.

By contrast, Romek Marber remembers that Protestants in his native Poland "were in the main of German origin." At the outbreak of war, in 1939, they "considered it prudent to stay indoors. Many emerged, only a few days later, wearing swastika arm bands and highly polished jackboots."[9] On the other hand, relations between Polish Jewish factions, in the worst days of their persecution by the Nazis, are said by Christopher R. Browning to have remained "extraordinarily supportive and harmonious," whether they were "uprooted urban Jews from western Poland" or "beleaguered traditional Jews of south-central Poland. . . . Snide or resentful comments about one another . . . are totally absent from the postwar testimonies."[10]

It is hard to deny that, while Joseph may have offered little or no military advice or help, he was an objective ally of the Romans, if only in the hope of saving Jewish lives. His conduct as Titus's Judaean contact somewhat prefigures that of Rudolf Kasztner's when he negotiated with Adolf Eichmann in Budapest in 1944: Kasztner had the poker player's nerve, the linguistic skills and the cunning charm to confront Eichmann without cringing. His fluent German and willful chutzpah enabled him to make a deal that saved a number of Jews from the transports in which hundreds of thousands of others were consigned to their deaths in Auschwitz and Treblinka. If Kasztner had not made his deal with Eichmann, in which money and jewelry played an alluring part, few, if any, of the almost seventeen hundred Jews he saved would have survived. Among them, however, were Kasztner himself and members of his family. Anyone who has read accounts of his negotiations with the Nazis would have to be a prig or a saint to regard him as a villain. For a while at least, he was a hero. If he had died in Auschwitz, he might have remained one. Budapest was his Jotapata.

After the war, Kasztner became an official spokesman in the Israeli government. In 1953, he was accused in a pamphlet of having given unduly amiable references to a trio of SS officers accused of war crimes. Kasztner was confident of his vindication when the pamphlet's author was sued for libel, but the trial turned, slowly, into an indictment of Kasztner himself. He had, the judge concluded, sold his soul to the devil by failing to warn those whom he could not save of what lay ahead. The verdict of the lower court was overturned, after a lengthy appeal, but Kasztner was a broken man, living in unmitigated loneliness. In 1957, he was shot by Zeev Eckstein and died twelve days later. The killing of Jews by Jews is a tradition without end. In 1995, Prime Minister Yitzhak Rabin—a hero of the wars against the Arabs and "the most secular Jew in Israel"—was murdered by a latter-day Zealot who regarded him as a traitor to Jewish exclusivism, a modern Hellenizer, as it were. The murders of both Kasztner and Rabin, by twentieth-century Sicarii, are instances of how the rage that cannot be visited on unreachable enemies can be displaced sideways onto other Jews.

Hannah Arendt proved that she shared the routine Gentile distaste for nominal slipperiness* by "outing" Theodor Adorno for using his mother's Latin-sounding name rather than the paternal Wiesengrund, which would have proclaimed his Jewish origins.† Arendt pinned a yellow star on the philosopher, who, as it happened, was a scathing critic of her quondam lover Martin Heidegger. Adorno had a habit of asserting himself by the severity of his criticisms; he found time, as Paris was falling in 1940, to make caustic remarks about poor Walter Benjamin's essay on Baudelaire; "Jew" sought to dominate Jew even as the Nazis threatened to murder both of them.

Gentiles have often found it difficult to deny the contributions and even the genius, in the common sense, of some Jews. Not infrequently, even when enlightened, they remain conscious that they are being tolerant, if not condescending. Leibniz's attitude to "the Jew"

---

* Until very recently, applications for membership of country clubs and golf clubs, in Britain and the United States, routinely demanded that the candidate declare "name of father, if changed."

† In fact, both his parents had converted to Christianity.

Spinoza is a paradigm of the arrogant deference Bertrand Russell later showed to "my German genius," as he mistakenly identified the young Austrian student Ludwig Wittgenstein, who had just arrived at Cambridge. Russell's somewhat ironic deference to the author of the *Tractatus Logico-Philosophicus* contrasts with the terse skepticism with which A. J. Ayer—a *demi-juif* issued, like Wittgenstein, from Europe's *haute juiverie*—came to treat Russell's quondam protégé and eventual nemesis, the mature author of *Philosophical Investigations*.[11] If Russell had known that the young Wittgenstein was in truth an Austrian Jew, would he have greeted him as warmly? In his autobiography, Russell sneers at the Semitic origins of the American philosophers who, in the 1920s, welcomed him with guileless effusiveness.

Wittgenstein's reluctance to confess his ancestry, and his homosexuality, cannot be held to explain his early philosophical advocacy of reticence or his later, allegedly conservative, attitude to language, in which common usage was held to carry the essence of what things meant; but his skepticism about "private languages" and his uneasy acceptance of professorial eminence* lie oddly alongside a possessive vanity with regard to his own ideas and status. One of his loudest quarrels was, as might be expected, with a Jewish disciple, Friedrich Waismann, whose emulation of him, in his published work, he read less as homage than as vulgar plagiarism.†

In early-twentieth-century Vienna, Karl Kraus had associated journalistic glibness in particular with feuilletons, the elegantly phrased, long-winded articles that were the speciality of Jewish feature writers and appeared regularly in the *Neue Freie Presse,* the leading Viennese newspaper. For Kraus, such think pieces suffered from "the French disease"; they were apt to dress harsh facts, about death and destruction,

---

* The emblematic open-necked shirt announced that he was a man who disdained formal ties.

† As for himself, Wittgenstein said, "I don't believe I have ever *invented* a single line of thinking. I have always taken over from someone else. . . . What I invent are new similes." But then modesty too has its ironies.

in a form tasty enough for bourgeois breakfasts.* Paul Reitter points out that Gershom Scholem took a similar view: he found structural similarities between journalism and *Musivstil,* the quotation-oriented genre of medieval Jewish writing.[12] Scholem concluded that when Jews become spiritually empty, or "perverted," they turn to, and thrive in, unoriginal journalism† (and, he might have added, if alive today, the trendier kinds of cross-disciplinary scholarship). On the same theme, Kraus insisted that there was a specific accent—he called it *Mauscheln*— that Jews could not eradicate when speaking German and that could be "heard," so he jeered, at the time of the Dreyfus affair, even in their "gesticulating prose."‡ The assimilationist who tries to get away with it can, Kraus implied, always be "outed." Is it unduly fanciful to guess that he was subconsciously pointing the finger at himself?§ Franz Kafka

---

* Edward Timms, in *Karl Kraus: Apocalyptic Satirist* (vol. 1), exemplifies how Kraus's criticism of Jewish journalists could be couched in savage terms: "The blood they [the Jews] have was not siphoned from the body of a Christian, but rather from the human intellect." This was written at a time when Leopold Hilsner, a Jewish shoemaker from Polna, had just been convicted of killing a Christian girl for her blood and was sitting in an Austrian jail. Kraus denounced "this hideous, inane feeling of Jewish solidarity [and] particularist narrowness." In the latter regard and in modern dress, Jacqueline Rose seconds him.

† Jakob Wassermann, in *Von Judentum* (1913), denounced the Jewish "literatus" as a "concentrated cipher for the losses resulting from Jewish integration into modern western societies," claiming that the Jew as an "Oriental," in the mythic sense, can be a creator. The "literatus" (the journalist, in particular) is "*the* person who had been separated from myth," hence the antipode of the creative Jew. (See Timms, *Karl Kraus,* vol. 2, p. 11.) By implication, Josephus stands at the head of the list of the "Occidentalized" transplants on whom Zionists can elect to heap ritual scorn. Self-loathers, it is said, produce only the perishable, and write in newspaper ink.

‡ The poetry of Jews was not spared his barbs: Kraus said of Heine that he had "loosened the corsets of the German language so that every little salesclerk could fondle her breasts." (Timms, *Karl Kraus,* vol. 1, p. 97.)

§ By deriding the style of (Jewish) journalistic reaction to the trials of Dreyfus, rather than concentrating on the innocence of the accused, Kraus himself exemplified what he detested in feuilletonists: the habit of reporting on the color and aura of an event rather than confronting the substantial issue. He was, however, more outspoken in 1922, after Walter Rathenau was assassinated and Kraus's onetime inspira-

denounced the German of acculturated Jews as "the tortured appropriation of foreign property."* Hannah Arendt, on the other hand, wrote of the "reckless magnanimity" with which Jews allowed "host countries" to take credit for their work. As Nachmanides learned from Jaime I of Aragon, a Jew may use all his intelligence to play for a draw, but he should never hope to win.

Karl Kraus crossed the line to become a Catholic and then crossed another (becoming "confessionless") when he abandoned Catholicism for a spiritual one-man's-land in which *Die Fackel,* the periodical he edited and filled with his own work, took no prisoners. Like Joseph ben Mattathias, Kraus thought his countrymen mad, and bad, to go to war. His greatest work, *Die Letzen Tage der Menschheit* (*The Last Days of Mankind*), was an immense collage of the grotesqueries of sentimental, high-flown wartime rhetoric juxtaposed with the bloody horror of actual combat in the Great War. It anticipated, and may have primed, Walter Benjamin's idea of a masterwork that consisted of nothing but a collage—a mosaic, even—of quotations. Endorsing the exorbitant hyperbole of Kraus's style, Benjamin said that the satirist's "non-human characteristics make him . . . a compelling 'messenger of real humanism.' "[13] George Steiner has contrived to find similar qualities in the rabidly anti-Semitic Louis-Ferdinand Céline.

In English-language twentieth-century journalism, the grand manner distinguished the feuilletons and think pieces of commentators such as Walter Lippmann, in New York, and Bernard Levin, in London. In the 1950s, the young Levin derided British parliamentarians with unusual virulence, using the consciously reactionary pseudonym "Taper." His prose often contrived to strike the mordant note to be found in *The Letters of Junius* or in the essays of the first Lord Halifax.

---

tion and recent rival, Maximilian Harden, was almost beaten to death by right-wing thugs. However, Kraus could not resist remarking that Harden had been foolish not to watch out for his safety, despite the frequent threats: "Where a critic can make good use of bravery is [behind] a desk." (Timms, *Karl Kraus,* vol. 1, p. 176.)

* At the end of *The Trial,* Josef K. is finally put to death "like a dog," which sounds like putting down an unwanted stray, but the image recalls Otto Weininger's equation of "dog" and "criminal."

His allusive archaism carried a tincture of self-mockery, but he was liberated by impersonating the grand manner of England's Augustan Age. In 1959, he wrote in the *Spectator* that anti-Semitism was obsolete in England. It was a flight of wishful thinking, and Levin retracted it in the face of undeniable evidence about the Cambridge University "Appointments Board."* In his later career, Levin liked to prove his (syndicated) independence by milling away left and right. In the early 1960s, he described Charles Clore, a London property magnate, as a "Russian Jew." By adopting the vocabulary that had once been the reserve of the prejudiced, he hoped to prove that to call someone a Jew was no longer abusive but simply descriptive. When young, Levin had stepped away from his Semitic shadow, but he resumed it in later years, while attacking racist malice in the Soviet Union. At the last, stricken by Alzheimer's disease, Levin withdrew, with dignity, into the solitary confinement of his disease.

In his long heyday as the leading thinker at the *New York Times*, Walter Lippmann effaced his Jewishness by a show of urbane righteousness. His notion of "the public philosophy" discounted the variety of domestic subcultures and proclaimed the need for common, civilized standards.[14] In 1966, on the eve of retiring from his career as a pundit, he broke ostentatiously with President Lyndon Johnson because, Lippmann declared, the White House had willfully deceived him. Careful to have no trace of a Hebraic accent, he assumed the mantle of an Old Testament prophet, to whom this world's rulers were more than somewhat answerable.

---

* Its "secretaries" kept files on those seeking employment after graduation. Their comments showed systematic and unguarded scorn for anyone who looked Jewish, even if he was "the refined kind." This applied not only to students but also to potential employers who informed the board of possible vacancies.

XIX

IF LEO STRAUSS WAS RIGHT in saying that the language of the Jews was "strictly communal," then the fact that Josephus used the first person singular was an immediate breach of faith. When "meaning in history, meaning of the past, and the writing of history" are linked in the Bible, the book and its reading are implicated in a social web with barbed limits. In the refashioned Judaism that survived the Second Temple, Yosef Yerushalmi says, "collective memory is transmitted more actively through ritual than through chronicle."[1] Tradition is repetitious, by definition, not progressive; it arrests the way of life which it prolongs. Its observers can have nothing to do with the "public happiness" that the Americanized Hannah Arendt advertised as the proper aim of a nondenominational, secularized society. Like so many German scholars who sentimentalized the daily life of ancient Greece, she was pleased to claim that the Greek polis (never Jerusalem) was the emblematic instance of happy times.*

In the Middle Ages, the Jewish tendency to retreat into a timeless spiritual ghetto, with no active attempt to mesh with Gentile life, afforded Christian apologists a chance for fabrication and misrepresentation to which, for various reasons, there was no hot response. Failure

---

* Until very recently, classical scholars rarely went to Greece. Any texts that might have blighted their idealization of "the Greeks" were omitted from the canon, as the history of the Maccabees and other inappropriate books were from rabbinic consideration.

to strike back looked like cowardice and a confession of guilt. Yet it is no more true that passivity and sufferance were *always* the Jewish reflex than that all of them went like sheep to their deaths in the Shoah.*

Leo Strauss, who took competitive issue with Hannah Arendt,† was another modern mutation of Joseph ben Mattathias. He left Germany on the eve of the Nazi takeover, having been the star student of Carl Schmitt, a philosopher who had the ugly consistency never to disengage from his endorsement of National Socialism.‡ Once established in the American academic world, Strauss made duplicity the emblem of integrity. He did not ignore mass democracy, as Arendt did; he deplored it. Modernity was the destroyer of "all authoritative traditions of value" and was as good as "defection from the thinking of classical natural law."²

Strauss was a Pharisee, of a kind, who was also a Hellenist. He wished to revert not to the Torah but to Plato. The vitality of Western civilization came, in his view, from the unfinished, unfinishable playoff between theology and philosophy. Contradiction and dialogue were the fruitful issue of their unceasing rallies. Incompleteness was of the essence of any civilization worth living in. How can there be progress in what is taken to be perfect? "The Western tradition," he said, "does not allow a final solution of the fundamental contradiction. . . . As long as there will be a Western world, there will be theologians who distrust philosophers and . . . philosophers who are annoyed by theologians.

---

* Elie Wiesel was tactless enough to point out that the Jews in the Warsaw ghetto uprising, poorly armed and outnumbered, resisted for longer than the French army after the German breakthrough in the Ardennes in May 1940.

† Nowhere in her work does Arendt reply or even make reference to Strauss. Heidegger says nothing about Wittgenstein, nor Wittgenstein about Heidegger.

‡ With appropriate casuistry, however, irrational antagonisms could become axiomatic. Schmitt's precedent for the Nazi program of ideological homicide was Oliver Cromwell's speech of September 17, 1656, which declared the Spaniard to be "the great enemy of the National Being"; so too "the Jew" of Germany. See Heinrich Meier, *Carl Schmitt and Leo Strauss: The Hidden Dialogue,* p. 20 and following. Leo Strauss denounced Heidegger's lack of "philosophical prudence in mistaking 'the politics of National Socialism for a new stage in the manifestation of Being.'" (Kielmansegg et al., *Hannah Arendt and Leo Strauss,* p. 111.)

While rallying round the flag of the Western tradition, let us beware of the danger that we be charmed or bullied into a conformism which would be the inglorious end of it."[3]

Jürgen Gebhardt synopsizes the Straussian intellectual project as "a restitution of the historical [pre-Christian] form of Western civilisation . . . the city of man set against the modern project of the universal and tyrannical state which aims to eliminate the city as well as Man."[4] It is in this sublime playground that Strauss and Josephus play tag. Uprooted intelligences, men not quite at home, albeit formally enfranchised, they were partial citizens who took it upon themselves to rise above private circumstances to survey what neither presumed to control. Strauss dared to be more prescriptive than Josephus; he lived under Franklin Roosevelt and his successors, not under Vespasian and the Flavians. Strauss and his peers, despite their differences, were products of "the coincidence of Jewish and European origins." Their academic tilts are evidence of their having taken the high road out of the abyss on their way to engaging, in tenured security, with "the Jewish problem."

Walter Benjamin said that "writing history is only possible in the form of exploratory models." He claimed that there was "no longer . . . a law connecting past and present. It is no more possible to explain the course of modern history conclusively by referring to constellations of the past than it is to preclude the incursion of something radically new in [the future]."* Gebhardt glosses this to mean that there can be no

---

* In the same spirit, Hannah Arendt cites René Char: "*Notre héritage n'est précédé d'aucun testament*" (Our heritage is not preceded—i.e., validated—by any testament). The attempt to sever the present from the past by stepping away from their own shadows is common to Europeans of all kinds. The European Union, with its attendant contradictions, can best be understood only in the light of its authors' willful negation of inconvenient distinctions, which, as recent events prove, cannot be eradicated by fiscal homogenization. Isaiah Berlin's sympathetic reading of the philosophy of Johann Gottfried Herder is decorously alert to inescapable incongruities among nations and cultures. It also suggests a sly way of endorsing "national" particularism that only incidentally lends Gentile (and civilian) support to the more pacific forms of Zionism.

"evolutionary notion of progress or theory of linear decline." Benjamin has become emblematic as a tragic figure, at once clairvoyant and blinkered, the diagnostician whose only kill-and-cure prescription for himself was the poison he took, in 1940, in that squat, charmless hotel in Portbou, on the Spanish side of the frontier between France and Spain.

Arthur Koestler, another mutation of Josephus, said later that Benjamin was carrying fifty morphine tablets. He gave half to Koestler, who feared both the Gestapo and the Spanish Fascists, who had sentenced him to death, in Málaga, in the spring of 1937. He had been reprieved thanks to his precocious international fame. Having escaped from Portbou in 1940 (after a period of internment in France), Koestler had the energy and resources to get to England, where he wrote at least two important books, *Scum of the Earth* and *Darkness at Noon,* as well as the first account in English of the extermination of Europe's Jews.*

Koestler taught himself to write precise English, although its composition was always tortuous.† After the foundation of the State of Israel—which he celebrated, in his way, in his 1946 novel *Thieves in the Night*—Koestler advocated an abrupt end to the doubleness that was typical, in some eyes, of the Diaspora. Jews, he said, should now choose between immigration to the Jewish state and wholehearted assimilation with those among whom they lived (he chose to become a patriotic British subject). More razor-edged than practical, the proposal never considered the hyphenate solution, which has allowed all kinds of people—Jews, African-Americans, Hispanics, Irish—to celebrate ancestral allegiances and reconcile their complexity rather than to amputate them.

In the forty-three years between the day when Walter Benjamin went halves with him on those morphine tablets and his own death,

* "Mixed Transport" was published in a special number of Cyril Connolly's magazine *Horizon* in October 1943.

† Peter Green has told me that when Koestler delivered his first book written in English, his publisher (Hutchinson) was dismayed to find that he had mastered every trite trope in his new language. He soon learned better, as he makes clear in *Arrow in the Blue* (New York: Henry Holt, 1984).

Koestler produced not only several durable works but also a few that verged on the cranky.* Unable to forget his days in the condemned cell, he was a dedicated opponent of the death penalty and (along with Victor Gollancz) petitioned for the reprieve of Adolf Eichmann. He also campaigned for the enlightened treatment of prison inmates. *Darkness at Noon* and his contribution to *The God That Failed*—a collection of essays on communism by disillusioned ex-Communists—were said to have led to his being put on a list of those whom the Soviet secret police were eager to murder if given the chance. Koestler was successfully assassinated only posthumously, when David Cesarani lent circulation to the charge (never brought against Koestler during his lifetime) that he had been a rapist. Cesarani's "biography" came out in 1999, almost two decades after Koestler joined the long list of survivors who chose to take their own lives. Suffering from Parkinson's disease and lymphocytic leukemia, he had for several years been an outspoken exponent of the right to die when one chose. He was widely blamed for allowing, or even insisting, that his third wife, Cynthia, die with him. It has been alleged recently that she too was terminally ill, but her suicide note says only that she did not want to live without him.†
Koestler's own exit, as theatrical as Cicero might have wished for, seems linked, if only symbolically, with the suicides of so many of the middle-European Jews who, sooner or later, chose the fate they seemed to have escaped. Although they were not the means of his death, it was as if

* His wish that science could supply a full explanation of human nature and conduct led him to seek a quasi-holistic scheme to account for the irrational, the paranormal and the coincidental.

† According to a profile of Koestler by Peter Kurth (in an article commissioned, but not published, by *Vanity Fair* [1991] and accessible on the Internet):

All their friends were troubled by what Julian Barnes calls "the unmentionable, half-spoken question" of Koestler's responsibility for Cynthia's actions. "Did he bully her into it?" asks Barnes. And "if he didn't bully her into it, why didn't he bully her out of it?"

Because, Kurth claims, the evidence that Cynthia's life had been ebbing with her husband's was all too apparent. Barnes's own widely published dread of death is likely to have colored his reading of the Koestlers' suicides.

Koestler had treasured those twenty-five morphine tablets for when he would need them.

Benjamin killed himself because he was told that, since he could not produce a French exit visa, he was forbidden to remain in Spain and would have to return to France the next morning. He knew that the Gestapo were waiting for him. Fanciful accounts claim that they murdered him in the hotel. The cruel comedy of an impractical man is that he could, in fact, have had the visa, if he had arrived a day sooner or waited a day longer. He could not summon up the energy or the will to cross the Pyrenees illegally, as Heinrich Mann and his wife, Nelly, and nephew Golo had done less than two weeks earlier.* There was no lack of venal *passeurs* who could have led Benjamin over the mountains. His resignation is of a piece with his refusal to concede that he had been wrong to cleave to his Marxist illusions rather than, as Gershom Scholem had been begging him, to accept the particularist solution of emigration to Israel. The belief that there was a cure for Judaism was implicit even in Benjamin's unofficial Marxism.

David Bergelson, a Ukrainian Jewish novelist, offers another variant of the consequences of willful transgression. The fate of Arthur Koestler's Rubashov (the central character in his 1940 novel, *Darkness at Noon*) prefigures that of the writer who was executed, by order of Stalin's politburo, in 1952. Rubashov's long interrogation forces him to realize, as Bergelson eventually would, that he is doomed by the logic of the ideology he volunteered to serve. Like Saturn, the Communist revolution had a habit of eating its own children, with Jews a specialty.

Born in the czarist province of Kiev in 1884, David Bergelson was the youngest of the nine children of wealthy, pious parents, both of whom died by the time he was fourteen. An accomplished amateur violinist, he failed in his efforts to enter university, even—in the last resort—as a dental student. Like Mirel Hurvits, the heroine of his 1913 novel, *The End of Everything*, Bergelson combined intimations of rare

---

* Evelyn Juers recounts, in *House of Exile,* how the obese Franz Werfel and his wife, Alma Mahler-Werfel, wearing "a voluminous white dress," tottered along with them.

destiny with lack of clear focus. He and Mirel shared an appetite for something beyond the shtetl world, in which even the "enlightened" young were liable to be clamped, but neither shows any definite sense of what it should be. Mirel's confinement recalls the chimpanzee who, so Vladimir Nabokov once said, was taught to draw by its keeper: its first picture was of the bars of its cage.

Ambiguity was implicit in the young Bergelson's literary versatility: he wrote first in Hebrew, then in Russian and finally in Yiddish. His decision to remain enclosed within the language of parochial familiarity clashed with an ambition to distinguish himself from, in particular, Sholem Aleichem, whose "volubility" implied folkloric, hence timeless, resignation. Bergelson was split between a desire to remain true to his Yiddish roots and a craving for artistic liberty and success. Unlike Isaac Bashevis Singer (and his brother), he lacked the luck which virility and vanity can sometimes procure. Nazism and Stalinism were the rough beasts that would wrestle for the spoiled world into which the author of *The End of Everything* made his precocious entry.

The novel is said by its editor and translator, Joseph Sherman, to have been a "sweeping departure from the conventions for modern Yiddish literature." Its most evident quality, in its English version, is alienation. Bergelson is at once faithful to his roots and chafed by their entanglements. Like his heroine, he belongs nowhere in particular and has no distinct personality. Neither assimilated nor Zionist, his characters are specimens trapped under the bell jar of *Yiddishkeit*. Bergelson hoped that Yiddish could be the "central component of a secular, modern culture"; yet *Yiddishkeit* itself "perceived the Jewish people as a world nation whose essential characteristic was extra-territoriality."[5]

During its last, callous years, the czarist regime disrupted and dispersed the shtetl society of which *The End of Everything* is the inadvertent obituary. After the murderous post-1918 pogroms, the prospect of Jewish liberation, first in a briefly independent Ukraine and then under the ideological tyranny of the Bolsheviks, was a delusion that led Bergelson eventually to deliver himself to his own executioner. His style is too squeamish to be aggressive or poisonous.

If he pities his Jews, he can neither love them nor leave them. Like Mirel, he tries to pull away, but he and she are stuck on the same flypaper.

After writing *The End of Everything*, Bergelson himself became a lifelong victim of circumstances and, as Marxists would say, of his own contradictions. In the 1920s, he visited America but found it to be an immoral country of "selfish opportunism." He preferred to deliver himself, in 1934, to the Soviet Union and to the literary dictates of "socialist realism." He was richly rewarded, for a while, but the Yiddish culture with which he chose to identify was doomed. During the war he served on Stalin's Jewish Anti-Fascist Committee, liaising with British and American sympathizers, and received a state medal for "Valiant Labor." But after it, when his fellow committeemen accumulated details of the specifically anti-Semitic nature of, in particular, the massacres at Babi Yar, they fell foul of Stalin's insistence that Jews and other Soviet citizens had suffered equally.

The Kremlin's last pro-Jewish act was to endorse the partition of Palestine in November 1947. In early 1948, Stalin determined to eradicate Yiddish culture in the USSR under the rubric of "chauvinistic-Jewish deviation." What had been heroic during the war became treasonous after it. Along with twelve other defendants, Bergelson was accused of the Zionism he had never endorsed and of spying for America by favoring a Jewish homeland in the Crimea. He spent three years in prison and was then sentenced to death after the usual rigged trial. Like Rubashov, he served the regime that betrayed him to the very end, when he confessed to his judges that he was "headed towards attaining the level of a real Soviet man, but did not quite reach it, and of that I am guilty." His fate, like that of Franz Kafka's Josef K., was to die "like a dog," at the hands of Stalin's secret police, of whom one of the most notorious mass executioners was the Jew Lev Zakharovich Mekhlis.*

---

* According to Simon Sebag Montefiore, in *Stalin* (New York: Alfred A. Knopf, 2003), Mekhlis ran a form of institutional Murder Inc., killing preconceived quotas by order of the Kremlin.

Bergelson was a Josephus of a kind—the kind that fails to find hosts as coldly and consistently indulgent as the Flavians.*

The cases of both Walter Benjamin and Bergelson stand in contrast with the nerve and determination of Joseph at Jotapata. Benjamin too furnishes a counter-Josephus, a man incapable of renouncing what was no longer ever going to be available to him, the old country. He lacked the nerve, however, to remake himself, to take the step from being a critic of a civilization that was disintegrating into a future that defied Marxist prediction. Josephus prefigures Benjamin's circuitous thinking: his God plays a regular part, adjacent to human affairs, but in a cyclic, never linear or progressive, sense. He seems to have been alert to the rabbinic renunciation of interest, at and after Yavneh, in general human progress. By concentrating on sacred texts, and their meanings, overt and concealed, the Jews gave up on mundane "history."† The idea of universal laws that was so important to Freud, in his wish to be seen as the discoverer of concealed universal truths, both replaced and, to some degree, mimicked the Yavneh revision of Judaism. Tradition extends itself only by rehearsal and recall.‡

---

* Another, more copious Jewish novelist and journalist, Ilya Ehrenburg (1891–1967), survived Stalin and wrote *The Thaw,* in celebration of the end of the period in which he had served, with a smile, as Russia's unofficial cultural ambassador to the West. He atoned for having gone along with Stalin's refusal to acknowledge the specific sufferings of the Jews in the Holocaust by collaborating with Vasily Grossman on *The Black Book,* which anticipated, in print, the redemptive work of Claude Lanzmann in his film *Shoah.* Ehrenberg evidently had the Josephan charm, and buoyancy, that Bergelson lacked.

† The post-Yavneh deletion of the books of the Maccabees from the "authorized" Bible was due to the "uninspired," mundane nature of their story, which, in its edited form, Maurice Sartre, in *D'Alexandre à Zénobie,* likens to a Hellenistic novel. The romance of rebellion/revolution begins with the embellished success of the Maccabean uprising, which in fact never achieved full independence even from the declining Seleucid Empire, whose rulers allowed the Jews de facto self-government without ceding territorial overlordship. This explains Pompey's presumption of the same authority when he entered Jerusalem in 63 B.C.E.

‡ Franz Kafka's 1919 *Letter to My Father* can be read as a post-Yavneh Jew's letter to his God. Jesus Himself, in the mood of "Father, why hast thou forsaken me?," might have written something along the same lines.

Walter Benjamin's suicide at Portbou, however pitiable, was more resigned than theatrical. It conceded, almost, that he had been "wrong from the start" and that Gershom Scholem, Benjamin's friend who had immigrated to Palestine, had been right. Scholem, who made a lifelong study of the Kabbalah and of the false messiah Shabbetai Zevi, had written, repeatedly, asking Benjamin in effect to renounce modernism and Marxism and repair to the particular virtue of a Jewish life. For more than a decade, the two men had been playing metaphysical chess by correspondence. In that four-square white hotel, Benjamin knocked over his own king. He is commemorated, curtly, in Portbou's blanched *cimetière marin* overlooking the Mediterranean.

Benjamin could not grasp, or fight for, the liberty that would oblige him to concede that he had wasted his ingenuity on detaching him-self from being a Jew in order to be a piece—one that would never quite fit—on the warped board of European culture. There is inciden-tal irony in Benjamin's choosing to die on the threshold of Spain. The Holy Inquisition is still defended on the grounds that its viciousness was sporadic, its officers methodical and its papers invaluable. Histori-ans are grateful to those who keep tidy records.

The comfortable social position of Joseph ben Mattathias's family may have made him complacent; it hardly made him a premeditated traitor. The assistance he rendered the Romans, after his surrender, was offered in order to continue to save his skin; but it was never at the direct expense of other Jews, as has been said of some of the "leaders" of European Jewry. The defiance shown by the inhabitants of the War-saw ghetto in 1943 is beyond praise or reproach. Joseph's Jerusalem was not a similar case. Polish Jews had no hope of being allowed to live, in peace or in any other way. They confronted the killers who had come to murder them all. No great principle was at stake in first-century Judaea, certainly not the physical survival of the Jews. All-out war with the imperial power was not the only course available.

Whatever the moral refinement of the anti-Zionist case, and what-ever the flaws or follies of Israeli policy, critics of the existence of Israel offer no practical recipe for what the remnants of European Jewry should have done in 1945, still less of where else they might have gone or been allowed to go. The British solution was to return survivors of the Shoah to the camps in Germany from which they had been liberated. In *Eichmann in Jerusalem,* Hannah Arendt claims that the surviving Jews would better have sought to reintegrate themselves into the societies from which they had been evicted. However, as Christopher R. Browning shows, a good many Polish Jews who sought to repossess what had once been theirs were either killed or driven away.* In 1945, neither the United States of Harry Truman nor Great Britain under Clement Attlee opened its gates to the remnants of Europe's Jews. As David Cesarani revealed (it was the theme of his 1992 book *Justice Delayed*), the British preferred to admit a Baltic SS division to work in the mines rather than to allow "displaced persons"† to come into the country.

Ever since the triumph of Christianity, the allegation that all Jews are innately devious has justified the severity of those who have conspired to degrade or murder them. The bad conscience of the Christian sees in every new Jew the same old Jew, whose vengeance he dreads. In this light, Josephus typifies the Jew who got away: a traitor in the eyes of his own people and for Gentiles, as for Hannah Arendt, a typically "oily, adroit" customer who makes his deal with the enemy for his own private salvation. Arendt's phrase proved infectious: her close friend Mary McCarthy described the playwright George S. Kaufman and his New York friends as "oily." Prejudice is as much mimetic as "psychological." The poverty of language in almost all anti-Semitic literature is a symptom of the superficiality of the "ideas" which inform it.

The rage of faction against faction inside beleaguered Jerusalem diffused itself throughout the centuries of the Diaspora. The same ferocity was rarely unleashed against Gentiles. Karl Marx, who came from a

---

* In *Remembering Survival.* See also, for firsthand evidence, Anna Bikont's *Le crime et le silence,* passim.

† The phrase was routine code for slave workers and concentration camp survivors, mostly Jews. The Western Allies' use of the anonymous "DPs" echoed Stalin's reluctance to allow the Jews to seem to have suffered more than any other group. The British foreign secretary, Ernest Bevin, mentioned Jews only to say that they were not to be permitted to "push to the front of the queue."

rabbinic family, reserved his most unforgiving animus for "the Jews," whom he arraigned, holus-bolus, as a "huckster race." The Jews took the fall for the bourgeoisie as a whole. Seeking on many occasions to dissociate himself from his origins, Marx made it a habit to refer to his fellow (but sometimes dissentient) socialist Ferdinand Lassalle as a "Yid." Shucking Jewishness onto another, the rabbinically bearded Marx set out to identify himself with an irresistible majority, the Workers of the World.*

The promise to eliminate difference, often through the agency of some new and selfless elite, is an ingredient of all universal gospels. A Communist as sophisticated as Leon Trotsky continued to believe, or at least to maintain, that in the ultimate pseudo-Hegelian synthesis, all humanity would be homogenized—*and* polyvalent—without distinction, as if in a meta-Pauline redemption. In the lifetime of Josephus, the Jew Saul of Tarsus, transfigured into (Saint) Paul, was the prophet of an undifferentiated future bliss in which there would be "neither Jew nor Gentile"; all would be united in Christ Jesus. The young Saul's estrangement from his masters in the Jerusalem Sanhedrin is clear from Paul's letters. By the zeal with which, in his early days, he "persecuted" the small minority of Jews who made a hero, but not yet a Savior, of the recently crucified Jesus, Saul had tried to be holier than the High Priests and so to recommend himself to them. Saul's infiltration of the "Christians" had something in common with that of the czarist police who, in the course of associating with Decembrists and Communists, emulated their revolutionary zeal. The double agent can mimic single-mindedness to such good effect that he becomes half-infatuated with the cause he has been commissioned to sap.

On the Damascus road, Saul / Paul had an electric vision of another way to go: he converted to a line of conduct, and then of belief, diametrically opposed first to the hierarchy and then to "the Jews." A composite of Jew, Roman citizen and provincial, Paul reconciled his confusions—created his "ego-ideal," some might say—by proposing a

* Stalin is reported to have reproached Sergei Eisenstein for his filmed portrayal of Ivan the Terrible because the style of the czar's beard made him look Jewish.

superhuman Jesus, a Savior with a mix of attributes, some lifted from Oriental mystery religions. Detached from his human origins, Jesus was revised into the true incarnation of the Dionysian dying god who figures in any number of Hellenistic cults, not least Asiatic Mithraism, with its ritual of blood-drenched resurrection. The resurrection has become the one miracle that Christianity can never suffer to be subject to Spinozan question. It confirms God as a Christian partisan.

Once Saul of Tarsus had signaled his breach with the Jerusalem authorities by adopting a Greek version of his Jewish name, he was no longer bound by any kind of orthodoxy. As he set out to take the Gospel to the Gentiles, elements of Greek and Zoroastrian cults were assimilated into the Good News. The promised afterlife of the body was exemplified by Jesus's own escape from his "three-day tomb" and his subsequent revelation to the disciples at Emmaus.* Paul's subsequent differences with the Jerusalem "church" can be read as functions of provincial distrust of central authority. In this, Paul prefigured the leaders of the pending Jewish rebellion, men such as Simon son of Gioras and John of Gischala, who detached themselves from subordination to the Second Temple power structure and became candidates for outright hegemony. They then proceeded to murderous competition between themselves, as Lenin and Stalin would, first with the Mensheviks and then with the Old Bolsheviks.

To judge from the crispness of Josephus's counterpunching, in response to critics such as Justus, the main thrust of their charge must have been that he was, from the beginning, a self-interested and treasonous leader. "Anyone who blames me for the accusations I bring against the party chiefs and their gangs of bandits, for my laments over the misfortunes of my country, must excuse my breach of the rules of historical composition. Of all the cities under Roman rule, our own

---

* Celebration of the divinity's triumph over death (and escape from human bondage) was a key element of the worship of Dionysos. The cult of Mithras featured a son of the sun god Ahura Mazda, who died, was resurrected and had twelve disciples. The similarities made Paul's message more plausible and also led to a competition between the two faiths, which lasted until Mithraism withered away with the adoption of Christianity as the official, if never the only, religion of the Roman Empire.

reached the highest summit of prosperity and then fell into the lowest depths of misery."[6]

Jesus of Nazareth is reported, in the Gospels, to have repeated Isaiah's forecast of the fall of Jerusalem, and (so it seems) with relish. Like Saint Paul, Jesus was a provincial with no native fealty to the city that had "stoned the prophets," among whom, by implication, He rode in to be numbered. To Josephus, the misfortunes of all other races might be small by comparison, but the Judaean Jews had only themselves to blame. The possibility of atonement was a key aspect of the covenant; it made adversity tolerable. Religion is less a way of describing the world than of reading meaning, and hope, into it.

Despite everything, Josephus preserved the myth of Jewish election, and hence of redemption. Christianizing Jews would do something similar when they attached their hopes to a resurrected messianic figure who, in Gentile imagery, would evolve into the vengeful and majestic Cristo Rey. The Father had jettisoned the Jews and become the universal God of everyone else. In his retort to Apion, to whom he owed no tactful deference (what did it matter to Flavian censors what was said to a dead Alexandrian academic?), Josephus asserted that the covenant remained unbroken. Jews were used to taking any amount of punishment without flinching. Since they had no graven images, and did not demean themselves by worshipping animals, as Egyptians did, the imagery of their faith was ineradicable and could travel everywhere with them: invisible treasure, sewn into their minds, could never be confiscated. Killing Jews became the only way to obliterate their long memories.

The end of the Jewish War left Jews with no recourse but to expiate their sins and wait for Yahweh to abate his displeasure. The exemplary biblical instance of endurance is in the Book of Job, one of the latest in the canon. There is something of Job's obstinate faith, despite all his adversities, in the figure of Ahasuerus, the shoemaker who, in Christian myth, abused Christ on his way to Calvary and was sentenced to wander alone until He returned. Over time, the pariah was transformed into a man of mysterious, perennial powers, armed with a God-given warrant of survival. The double-edged proverb "the Jew stands at the graveside of his persecutors" both chides and, to a degree, exonerates the anti-Semite (since his activities, however murderous, are always abortive). The persecution and the preservation of the Jews are recurrent elements in Christian pontification. In Pascal's *Pensées,* despite the author's Jansenist animus, Jews are emblematic of human nature itself: "Man must not see nothing at all; nor must he see enough to believe that he possesses it; he must see enough to see that he has lost it; for, to know his loss, he must see and not see; and that is precisely his natural condition." Judas Iscariot, to whom some Jews compare Josephus, and to whom some Christians have compared all Jews, has undergone similar sublimation. He progresses from standing for the archetypal traitor to being a victim of undeserved malice.*

Ignoring the Manichaean dichotomy between Christians and Jews ensconced in the origins of Christianity, Christian apologists make out that anti-Semitism was a function of the Enlightenment rather than of religion. Although inadvertently, Carl Schmitt gave them the lie when he argued that "there is no rational end . . . no programme, however ideal . . . that could justify human beings killing one another over it. . . . If such a physical annihilation of human life does not occur out of the proper assertion of one's own form of existence against a likewise proper negation of this form, that annihilation plainly cannot be justified."[7] Only ideology (of which monotheism is the ur-form) renders killing, for the sake of one's faith, both excusable and "necessary." Christian diabolization of "the Jews" made their slaughter and dispossession a profitable duty. Jean-Paul Sartre's "ideal" anti-Semite decides who, essentially, he is by recognizing himself as a man who hates Jews.

---

* In Robert Graves's *King Jesus* (New York: Creative Age Press, 1946), Judas is the brave zealot who is disappointed by the other disciples' lack of guts, a view somewhat endorsed by the recently discovered manuscript of the so-called Gospel of Judas. The most vindictive elaboration of Judas as "arch-knave," and the impersonation of all Jews, was written by the seventeenth-century German "discalced" (unshod) Augustinian Abraham a Sancta Clara. It took ten years to compose and even today is declared, by *The Catholic Encyclopedia,* to be his masterpiece, "varied with many moral reflections."

The socialism of fools is also the paranoia of the crowd which, in Elias Canetti's view, elides the individual conscience into a mass mentality without memory or remorse.[8]

René Girard argues that the capacity to embody evil—the scapegoat role—is by nature ambiguous. The pariah's social use is as the vessel that evacuates pollution from the community. By objectifying and then removing its sins, the outcast appears to be an instrument of magic redemption. Girard explains how Oedipus, for particular instance, played the part both of the polluted tyrant and, later, of the revered guru. Since, solely by his self-sacrifice, he had the power to dispel the plague that had fallen on Thebes, the guilty one became graced with what seemed to be magical potency. Endowed with supernatural karma, the tyrant and pariah was transformed into the exile at Colonus whom men came to consult as a prophet.

The Jew as demon and miracle worker, and later as medical man, takes on a similar aura of election. According to Vidal-Naquet, Josephus was regarded in pre-Reformation Germany as the author of something close to Holy Writ: he was seen as the "magic healer" who had sustained his community. The archetypal Jew, feared or respected, shunned or solicited, is never just one more ordinary human being. "Jewish self-hatred" can as well be interpreted as the ingestion of Christian attitudes. The prisoner of an alien notation, the Jew stands away from himself and evaluates himself like the stranger that others insist on making him.

Jean-Paul Sartre's 1947 panacea for anti-Semitism (based on small acquaintance with actual Jews or their history) would have the Jew "assume" the character his enemies wish upon him and, by doing so voluntarily, transcend it. He may have been inspired by the story, told by David Pryce-Jones, of the French playwright Pierre Wolff, who, in 1941 Paris, on hearing that Jews had to wear a yellow star, pinned one prominently on his breast, lit a cigar, and hailed a fiacre in order to ride down the Champs Élysées.[9] When a friend murmured that it was not a wise moment to do so, he replied, "My dear fellow, this is no time to hide one's light under a bushel!" *Chapeau,* indeed.

Sartre's clever advice ignores the specificity of Jewish history. The actual fate of Europe's Jews down the centuries renders his prescription condescending and irrelevant. Why "should" Jews be required to conform to what others say they are? On this reasoning, they alone are to be denied the right to existential choice. Aware of Vichy France's complicity in the Holocaust, Sartre became and—unlike most of the rest of the Left—remained a qualified supporter of Israel, never permitting himself the enthusiasm that he displayed for Stalin's Russia or, later, for Mao's China. Sartre's long-serving acolyte Claude Lanzmann's monumental film, *Shoah,* was an unmitigated middle-aged declaration of identity, rage and specificity. An epic of retrieval, as was *The Jewish War,* his nine-hour film passed judgment, if only en passant, on his master's pronounced reticence. Lanzmann's resumption of his Jewishness was social, political and artistic, never religious; to that extent he remained a Sartrean as well as a modernized mutation of Flavius Josephus, unflaggingly persistent in the retrieval and recording of painful memories.* Accurate reminiscence is another way of getting one's own back.

Ahasuerus, the Wandering Jew, impersonated Jewish persistence. As with Judas (and Oedipus), what began as a stigma became a distinction. Because his calvary came to be seen as disproportionate to his offense, the wanderer's pariahdom casts doubt on the justice of the God who ordained it and on the church whose pope claimed to be the "Vicar of Christ." Romek Marber concludes his memories of a Polish childhood during the Shoah by saying:

What had I been witness to? A Catholic Church that had complete control over the Polish Catholic population yet kept silent. Individuals and sometimes small groups of Christians did help, but

---

* To the indignation of, in particular, Simone de Beauvoir, in his old age Sartre fell under the influence of Benny Lévy, a Maoist who later became an Orthodox rabbinic student. Lévy reminded the old atheist of his possible roots in Alsace and wished Sartre into believing himself some kind of a Jew. This was regarded by Simone de Beauvoir as a devilish "*détournement de vieillard.*" After Sartre's death, Lévy himself went to live in Israel and attended a Yeshiva.

they were the exception. Jews escaping from ghettos feared Polish Catholics as much as they feared the Germans. The great corporate body, the Catholic Church, which maintains its universal claim to Christian values, was silent.[10]

Marber's English prose, like Josephus's Greek, is poignant with the stress between the modesty of its expression and the matter he is recalling, after decades of London life, during which he designed dust jackets for Penguin Books. The horror he experienced in his native Poland is so far outside the scope of his mature vocabulary that it issues in a knot of decorum. The stress of writing at all, after so long an interval, and in a language alien to the author's at the time of what happened, fills his autobiography with an air of terse anguish like that to be found in Josephus's *Vita*.

The ancient world heels into the modern with the improbable, and unpopular, return of the Jews to Palestine. However dependent it may have been on the aid and muscle of post-Christian powers, the Jewish state of Israel threatens Christian mythology: it offers the unapologetic Ahasuerus a permanent home. The Zionists' recapture of Jerusalem could never (as at least some of them hoped) be taken to be a merely pragmatic event in world history. As Josephus might have forecast, it carried theological implications. Crusaders had slaughtered all the Jews they could find; the Arabs had put one of their finest mosques where Herod's Temple once stood, and maintained that Muhammad flew from there into the heavens, as Elijah had. Against the odds, the Jews returned and claimed their primacy. The abiding, if seldom admitted, case against Israel is that it threatens the mythological machinery of both Christendom and Islam (and, as the New Left has proved, chimes discordantly with meta-Marxism).

The recapture of Jerusalem in 1967 and the subsequent victory over the combined Arab powers signaled the moment at which the Jews, who had enjoyed the favor of most Europeans, even those on the political left, were transformed, in quite short order, into the oppressors of the Palestinians. General de Gaulle was free to call the Jews "*un peuple d'élite, sûr de lui-même, et dominateur.*" In London, during World

War II, de Gaulle had remarked, wryly, that he had appealed for the French to rally to him, and it was mainly Jews who had responded to his call. He himself had been condemned by the Vichy *état français* as a traitor for deserting his post. At least slightly like Josephus, he preferred to live to fight, and write, another day.

Since, in the end, de Gaulle prevailed and returned to power in France, with the aid of the British and the Americans, Vichy's charge against him lost all merit: he had the last word. Pierre Mendès-France, who had left France with the authority of his commanding officer, was arraigned for desertion by a Vichy government which tried to make him into a second Dreyfus (the Right never accepted that the first one had been innocent). Mendès-France escaped from Vichy custody to join the Free French air force, in which he served as a navigator with rare courage and, according to Romain Gary, some eccentricity. Mendès-France was always conscious that, in many French eyes, he was hardly more than a metic *"curieusement surnommé France,"* as his Fascistic enemies were so often pleased to say.

Raymond Aron, who was among the most assimilated of Frenchmen (and, according to Isaiah Berlin, the most intelligent), reacted with measured scorn to de Gaulle's 1967 remarks, but the general had said what many of his political opponents would soon endorse: the Jews in the new Jerusalem were both domineering and exceptional—they stood out against the "universalism" that was, or should be, the mark of virtuous post-monotheistic ideologies: first Marxism and later "universal human rights," René Cassin's post–World War II recension of Woodrow Wilson's notion of self-determination. The Palestinians were certainly as ill-used as they were ill-advised, by a series of strident demagogues. Yasser Arafat was only the most self-assertive of those whose room for negotiation was hedged by the knowledge that, if they agreed to any reasonable settlement, they would almost certainly be killed.

The increasing isolation of Israel, and the routine of disparagement to which it has been subject in the Western media, coincided with the confidence of the Jewish state that it can be responsible for its own defense. The secularization of what used to be Christendom made it seem that hostility to Israel was either pragmatic (the French sought to endear themselves to the Arabs by cold-shouldering Israel) or moral (which sanctioned the fabrication of Jewish atrocities).* Neither the Quai d'Orsay[11] nor the *bien-pensant* press would be likely to concede that it was affected by the symbolic significance of the Jews taking command once again of the whole of the city that Titus had captured and burned; but Israel's insolence, in claiming exclusive control of Jerusalem, damaged the myth of Christian hegemony on which the vanity of Europe continued to repose. The Israeli victory incidentally refuted the age-old Christian belief that the ejection of the Jews from Jerusalem had proved that God had deserted them.

The authors of the Gospels, from the Jew Mark to the Gentile Luke, read the fall of Jerusalem as if it were the fulfillment of a prophecy by Jesus. The claim, renovated by Richard Bauckham, that the Gospels derive from contemporary documents and testimony, implies that such evidence is itself a verification.[12] He disregards the degree to which a witness's description wishes significance, and interpretation, onto "the facts." What men say they have seen, or choose to recall, is as often founded on what they believe as the other way round. As Géza Vermès has shown, almost everything reported about Jesus of Nazareth, including the place and manner of His Nativity, is colored by partisanship, however honest.[13] The notion that Christian evidence can validate the Gospel stories requires an a priori conviction that they are beyond question. A myth can be fruitful, morally and aesthetically, without its produce—artistic or moral—in any way confirming its truth. Chateaubriand's *Le génie du Christianisme* is a compendium that arrays the splendor of doctrines that it does nothing to prove. Its author did not conduct himself, in his private life, as if in fear of adamantine chains or penal fire.

While Josephus was adopting a largely secular way of looking at

---

* Robert Fisk, for instance, asserted that there had been a "massacre of civilians" in 2002 at Jenin, where Israeli special forces sought to dismantle a terrorist base and suffered casualties almost as great as those of their militant enemy. No evidence of any massacre was ever unearthed. The Internet still records partisan "evidence" that a massacre did take place.

and explaining events, the writers of the Gospels sought to reorient creation. In due time, "the Jews" were depicted as the authors not only of their own misfortunes but of everybody's. Both the Gospels and Josephus's writings hinge on the fall of Jerusalem. The Gospel authors had no more interest in a historically truthful account of events preceding the Crucifixion than pious Jews, in the Diaspora, would show in Gentile history outside the ghetto or the shtetl. The ambition of the evangelists was to portray Jesus of Nazareth—who, for the large majority of Jews in his lifetime, had failed to prove himself the Messiah—as the sole and miraculously resurrected son of God.*

James S. McClaren has declared that it would be "intriguing to consider the type of narrative which Josephus would construct if the [Judaean] revolt had concluded with increased Jewish autonomy."[14] As a rhetorical exercise, such a composition might be entertaining, but the likely answer is, in truth, that Josephus would not have constructed any type of narrative whatever. If the putative Jewish success had come after he had already surrendered at Jotapata, he would almost certainly have been done away with by one side or the other. The retreating Romans would have had no further use for him; the victorious Judaean leaders, such as John of Gischala, would have disposed of him as a traitor. He would have had neither time nor impulse to become a writer whose sole exercise was to retrieve what had been lost to his people and to himself.

It would be no less "intriguing" to consider what type of narrative the evangelists would, or could, have "constructed" if Yahweh had (or could be believed to have) come to the aid of His people and evicted the Romans from Judaea. Would Christianity have been aborted? If the Jews had been historically justified in their dependence on the Holy One, their religion and reputation would have shriveled the appeal of what turned into Christianity. The humiliation of "the Jews" became, and remains, essential to an evangelic reading of the Jewish War. The

---

* Frank Morison's *Who Moved the Stone?*, first published in 1930 and often reprinted, makes divine agency the only possible means of rolling aside the boulder that blocked access to Jesus's tomb and volatilizing his body.

resurrection of Jesus would not have been "disproved" by the success of the Jews, but its consequences could not have been so plausibly interpreted to be of world-historical import. Had the Jewish rebellion succeeded, the myth of Jesus's betrayal by His own people, and its divinely ordained punishment, would have no terrestrial correlative. The abiding Christian need to abuse Judaism and humiliate its "stiff-necked" faithful remains evidence of how great a rival any triumphant form of Jewish community, in an independent Jerusalem, might have been.

It is part of the usual construction of the "Jewish character" (and of "the survivor") that Josephus should be depicted as a man haunted by guilt, as Judas and the Wandering Jew are alleged to have been. His unashamed defense of himself is taken to be proof that he was concealing his shame. He was certainly pained; any kind of exile was experienced, in the ancient world, as an amputation from the body politic. For Greeks, Romans and Hebrews, communal connection gave meaning to life. An exile's punishment, especially if he was an ostracized public figure, lay merely in exclusion. Yet expulsion could lead, if never automatically, to literary innovation and prolificity: *Bacchae,* Euripides's most challenging (because ambiguous) play, was written in exile, as was much of the work of Thucydides and Xenophon.*

Like some prosaic anti-Ovid, the exiled Titus Flavius Josephus spent the last three decades of his life in Rome, regretting the loss of what Pliny the Elder called "by far the most famous city of the East." If he was safe in Rome, he had no future there, only his past. Early in his biography of Isaiah Berlin, Michael Ignatieff reported "His memory is

---

* The fundamental nostalgic book of Western literature is, of course, the *Odyssey.* Israel has, in some ways, been the Jewish Ithaca, the never forgotten homeland to which "the Jew" (James Joyce's Leopold Bloom not least) hopes one day to be headed. Yet as Michael Pieris puts it in an essay in *Ancient Greek Myth in Modern Greek Poetry* (London: Psychology Press, 1996), "there is another version of this Odyssean experience . . . which presupposes the return to and a new exile from Ithaca (*or any other homeland*), due to the hero's inability to accept . . . the realities of his old country. . . . The 'recognition' of the native place is linked to . . . disappointment and despair [and so] leads the hero (whether or not he is called Odysseus) into a second, and this time deliberate, Odyssean adventure [and exile]" (emphasis added).

freakish, so unusually fine-grained as to seem scarcely human, and so effortlessly in command of his past that he gives the impression of having accumulated everything and lost nothing . . . in the labyrinthine archive of his mind. . . . It was a virtuoso display of a great intelligence doing battle with loss." Einstein said of him that he was "a kind of spectator in God's big but mostly not very attractive theater."* If Flavius Josephus was an early candidate in the same class of scribe, the closed tradition of Jewish thought put him under the stress of having to compose his work, at least at first, in parochial terms. The breach between Second Temple ceremonial and what came to be done and said and written in later years opened the pain-filled space in which so many Diaspora Jews stayed true, in one fashion or another, to the old religion. George Steiner designates the "separation of 'word' and 'world' as one of the very few genuine revolutions of spirit in Western history." Josephus by himself, with pen and paper in Rome, is the first man to take a spiritual spin in that direction. He had lost his world; he had only the word.

In the early Middle Ages, even the relatively enlightened Mai-

---

* Berlin never abandoned his Jewishness, but he can scarcely be said to have worn it without reluctance. He became the very model of an Anglicized academic grandee and, during the war, diplomatic civil servant. His black coat and striped trousers, the carnation in his buttonhole and the air of groomed discretion promised that England, his second home, was a theater in which he was delighted to star. He wrote trenchant prose, but without the serrated edge of his fellow Oxonian philosopher A. J. Ayer. Appearing to make a hobby of high intelligence, clever in making no parade of his cleverness, he was British enough to have little time for French intellectuals, of whom he admired only Raymond Aron, an assimilated mandarin of a rather more abrasive, no less meticulous order. Ignatieff says that Berlin was "one of those Jews who, as he remarked of Proust, 'turns his rootlessness into the kind of Archimedean point outside all the world, the better to assess them from.'" It is hardly an epigram for the ages (nor is Proust markedly rootless), but the description is apt for members of the cosmopolitan mandarinate to which Berlin and so many clever Jews have rallied, since the European Diaspora was detonated by the Nazis. Berlin put his wit and brains at the service of the British and managed both to amuse and to instruct them. Attached to the British embassy in Washington, he became Winston Churchill's favorite source of White House gossip. See "Berlin Revisited" in my *The Benefits of Doubt* (Manchester, UK: Carcanet Press, 2003).

monides (who tried to square Judaism with Aristotle) regarded the reading or writing of mundane history as "a waste of time." Harold Bloom says that after the year 500, commemorative lists of martyrs and fast days, in atonement for catastrophes, together with the law, and its Talmudic annexes, "subsumed all the possibilities of history."[15] In that sense, Arnold Toynbee's reference to Judaism as a "fossil religion" had petty pertinence. Freud put a more generous face on it in August 1938, when he wrote to his daughter Anna: "the only possession [the Jews] retained after the destruction of the Temple, their scripture . . . the Holy book and the intellectual effort applied to it . . . kept the people together." These are singular words from the author of *The Future of an Illusion*. Even the avowedly irreligious sage, on his way to exile, seems to say that, for Jews at least, the future lies in the past.

Whatever posture of resigned ruefulness he adopted, Josephus never shed the assumption that God was the literally overall explanation of what happened in history. The God of the Jews was still in control; if He had punished His people, they would have to wait for, and first deserve, His forgiveness. Josephus's view of God as an active, judging agent in the world was alien to the Greeks and the Romans but, in the wake of the destruction of Jerusalem, no longer uniquely Jewish. As the Christians detached themselves from the defeated and despised Jews, they became the antagonists of the people to whom Jesus had addressed Himself. In the second century C.E., the Christian Origen quoted the Greek philosopher Celsus as saying, "See how much help God has been to both them [the Jews] and to you. Instead of being masters of the world, they have been left with no land and no home of any kind." The more recruits Christianity enrolled, the stronger became the urge to parade the growth of the church as proof that God was with them.*

Meanwhile, the High Priest and his entourage, who had practiced the spectacular rituals of the Second Temple, were succeeded by the collegiate style of teaching agreed on by the rabbis who met in discon-

---

* It reached its theological acme in the "proof" for the existence of God "*e consensus gentium*" (from the general agreement of the people)—metaphysics by referendum.

solate conclave at Yavneh after the sack of Jerusalem. As Yosef Yerushalmi puts it, in *Zakhor,* "the rabbis who founded the Judaism that we
know . . . lost all interest in mundane history. They had the written and
the oral law, and they trusted in the Covenant, which assured them the
future." In their eyes, all pragmatic history—Roman, Parthian, even
contemporary work, like Josephus's, on the Jewish past—did not merit
rabbinical scrutiny. Memory was the vessel of Jewish solidarity, but that
was also its prime purpose: "the injunction to remember was felt as a
religious imperative to an entire people."

For fifteen centuries after Josephus, no Jew can be rated a secular
historian until Azariah ben Moses dei Rossi, who was born in Mantua
around 1513. His ancestors were said to have come from Jerusalem with
Titus; if so, it may be that they, like Josephus, belonged to the Roman-
izing class, which no longer dared stay there. Azariah's masterwork,
Me'or Einayim (Light of the Eyes), subjected Talmudic lore to scientific
and linguistic analysis. For instance, he rejected the myth that Titus's
death was caused by a bite from a vengeful gnat dispatched by the
Holy One. Deeply influenced by Renaissance humanism, his books
were deemed heretical and condemned by the Jewish authorities to be
burned. This inquisitorial sentence was later modified to a decree, not
widely obeyed, that Azariah not be read by anyone under twenty-five.
His work exemplified an unresolved problem for modern Jewish historians: if academically respectable to the world at large, their work is
bound to butt against premises that were basic to all Jewish conceptions
of the past: or, as Yerushalmi puts it, "the belief that divine providence
is an actual causal factor in Jewish history, and in the related belief
in the uniqueness of Jewish history itself." Although Yerushalmi stops
short of saying so, from this springs the temptation to find reasons
for the Shoah within Jewry itself. Extreme orthodoxy has been known
to put the blame on assimilation,[16] just as pluralists and assimilation-
ists, such as Hannah Arendt, can point a righteous finger at traditional
"leaders" and the docility of their congregants.

The temptation to find one or another of these "sins" to be endemic
has been eagerly taken up by Gentiles who have always read the inner
uncertainty of Jewry as evidence of corporate guilt. This guilt or "self-

hatred" is not, in most cases, "psychological" but implicit in the logic of Judaism itself (Solomon ibn Verga, a Spanish refugee forcibly baptized in Portugal in 1497, said that it was pointless to pour holy water on Jews since Judaism was "one of the incurable diseases"). What would suit the world's scheme better than to discover that the Jews are guilty of all the things they've been accused of, not least by the Christian churches? By that means, the terrible possibility can be avoided that everything done to "the Jews" in the last millennium was unjustified. In 1942, in Fascist Rome, the German Jesuit Peter Browe wrote of the "manifest failure of the Christian mission to convert the Jews."[17] He sets out reasons for the impasse from both sides, but cannot convince himself that he has said the last word. He then comes to "the reasons from God's side" and dares to guess that "perhaps in the end God Himself did not want Judaism to be obliterated." Yerushalmi wonders whether any sophisticated modern Jewish historian can be imagined attaching an explicit "reasons from God" coda to a work of scholarship. Nor is it conceivable in any work written in the twentieth (or twenty-first) century, other than one seeking some worthy answer to what the cant has been pleased to call "the Jewish question."

In today's civilized world at least, "I am a Jew" sounds like a straightforward declaration. But what exactly is being declared? The practice of Judaism now has a diversity of forms, but Orthodox rabbis do not hesitate to disqualify the deviant or those whom Saint Paul—always more of a Jew than he cared to recognize—accused of "blowing neither hot nor cold." The question remains: is it for individuals to decide whether they are Jews or is there some objective test? The Nazis sought to reconcile a state of law with a murderous ideology by defining a Jew as a person with at least two Jewish grandparents. Circumcision was evidence, but not proof, of a man's Jewishness; lineage was determinant. In earlier centuries, and with varying degrees of coercion or welcome, Jews had been encouraged to purge their inherited taint by converting to Christianity. Under the Nazis, no such salvation was available. The Protestant Victor Klemperer survived to publish his diaries more because he had a "natural" Christian wife than by virtue of his chosen creed, which was dismissed as a camouflage. In Hitler's Germany, ancestry, not faith, determined a man's doom, and a woman's, and a child's.

The legalistic conundrum persists. Jews dispute among themselves, and in public courts, the criteria for admission to full community rights, in particular when it comes to qualifying for "faith" schools. As recent cases in Israel and in Britain have shown, the more Orthodox the judge, the more inflexible his criteria. Even in twenty-first-century England, the Orthodox chief rabbi, in his wisdom, could decide that a mother's conversion to Judaism, however thoroughly supervised, did not automatically certify her son to be a Jew. Yet, in civilized practice, it is not left to a rabbi, however learned, or a judge, however impartial, to determine whether a man is warranted, or obliged, to declare himself a Jew.

"The Jew," as perceived (or defined) by his enemies, is feared or hated as much for his mutability, his capacity to appear in many guises, as he has been, by Christians, for being the reincarnation of Judas. Marx's "huckster race" seemed to have no choice but to practice the mean arts of haggling and usury, whether in the form of the peddler or the plutocrat. Seeking to escape that fate, the assimilated Jew, with his accurate mimicry of whatever society will admit him, is feared and hated, if he is, not least for putting on the style in a way he has hoped will leave him undetected. The Jewish writer, in particular, can become so fluent that his rivals accuse him, if successful, of dominating and perverting the culture in which he parades his excellence.

Josephus, the exile, the traitor, the witness, the reasonable patriot, the pious Jew, the alienated solitary, the sponsored propagandist, melts into and disappears into his textual persona as if it were an alibi. Words supply his coat of many colors. It is, of course, very improbable that he ever returned to Jerusalem—unless, in a flight of fancy, he took ship, perhaps under yet another name, and sailed to Alexandria and then, like Yehuda Halevi a thousand years later, made his way to the city that itself no longer bore the same name it had when he was born. If unlikely to be recognized by whoever still remained whom he had known in his old life, he would be an alien in his own land, even more alone, and more vulnerable, for having come back to where once he belonged.

In truth, no one records when Josephus died or by what means. A modern novelist, if commissioned to supply a plausible or ironic end to his life might fancy that, like those who survived the concentration camps only to kill themselves many years later, he was borne down by the guilt of merely being alive when so many others were dead. The lure of suicide as a form of decisive autonomy, involving a man's own choice of how and when to end things, haunted Seneca, comforted Cicero and dignified Cato.

Josephus's transgression from Jerusalem to Rome would be imitated, mutatis mutandis, by any number of Diaspora Jews. Few gained admission to Gentile society without a measure of guilt or even a deathbed reversion; Benjamin Disraeli is said, perhaps maliciously, to have muttered in Hebrew in his last hours or minutes. By converting to Christianity, Heinrich Heine profited in terms of fame and fortune but was never at ease with the price he had had to pay for social emancipation. Toward the end of his protracted illness (after eight years of agony), someone asked Heine how he imagined God would treat him. "*Il me pardonnera,*" the dying poet said. "*C'est son métier.*" Josephus was not an ironist of the same quality; nor did his God, Yahweh, specialize in letting people off. The author of *The Jewish War* more resembled the unredeemed victim-hero of Albert Camus's *Myth of Sisyphus,* which ended with words of hopeful despair: "*Il faut imaginer Sisyphe heureux.*" As he toiled on in support of what kept rolling back on him, the many instances in his work, and in his memory, of Jews who preferred death to humiliation crowded his consciousness, if not his conscience. Alienation became his way of being at home with himself. Suicide was not his style. Condemning himself to life, he made writing the sentence from which he sought no reprieve.

ACKNOWLEDGMENTS

I could never have written this book without the help, guidance and generosity of scholars and friends. Of these the first was Zuleika Rodgers, of the School of Religions and Theology at Trinity College Dublin, who listed for me a large number of works, without which I should have been fatally unequipped to understand the complexities of the world of Joseph ben Mattathias / Flavius Josephus. Dr. Rodgers has saved me from several inaccuracies and unintentional anachronisms. To call Peter Green, my friend for sixty years, a great scholar of ancient Greece and Rome is to state the obvious. He is also a novelist, an essayist and a translator of wide culture and precise style, and an unflagging enemy of received ideas and ideological elaboration. His advice was first encouraging, then unsparing, and always invaluable. His imprimatur capped three years of work. Paul Cartledge, professor of ancient history at Cambridge, read an obese version of the manuscript and made accurate marks and remarks that saved me from many errors. George Walden was as alert in his comments as I should have expected and as encouraging as I could have hoped. David Goldberg put me right in a number of places; dissented, gently, from some of the things I said; but did not, of course, question my right to say them. I am also indebted to Mark Glanville and Stephen Raphael for their comments. My agent and friend Steve Wasserman has been vigilant and punctual with support, both intelligent and practical. Keith Goldsmith, my editor at Pantheon Books, has been a model of accurate, if not pitiless, patience and persistence. His help in shaping the text may, at times, have been less than graciously received, but he has been a tireless advocate of conciseness and clarity. Bonnie Thompson has proved a dauntless copy editor and has saved me from a number of ineptitudes. Whatever errors or provocations remain are certainly my own. As with all my work, the various versions of this text have been read with unsighing patience, sharp intelligence and pencil in hand by my wife, Beetle, to whom I owe so much more than she will care to read.

NOTES

PROLOGUE

1 Oswyn Murray, *Independent* (London), April 8, 2006.

I

1 *Jewish Antiquities,* XIV: 4.
2 See Mary Beard, *The Roman Triumph* (Cambridge, MA: Belknap, 2007).
3 *Jewish War,* I: 431 and following.
4 Ibid., I: 660 and following.
5 Ibid., II: 16.
6 Ibid., II: 74.

II

1 S. G. F. Brandon in *Jesus and the Zealots.*
2 *Jewish War,* II: 264 and following.
3 In Tessa Rajak, *Josephus.*
4 See chapter 17 of F. W. Walbank's *Polybius, Rome and the Hellenistic World.* Martin Goodman (in *The Ruling Class of Judea*) endorses the notion of the elitist Sadducee style (with its Epicurean savor) being particularly agreeable to the well-off. They had the leisure and means to be more liberally educated and widely read.
5 *Jewish War,* I: 87 and following.
6 Ibid., I: 103.
7 Géza Vermès (with Martin Goodman), *The Essenes According to the Classical Sources* (Sheffield, UK: JSOT Press, 1989).

8   Géza Vermès, in the introduction to the Folio Society edition of *The Dead Sea Scrolls* (London: 2000).
9   *Jewish War,* II: 145.
10 And Steve Mason, in his *Life of Josephus,* politely doubts.

III

1   Acts of the Apostles 24:25. Steve Mason (*Life of Josephus,* p. 176) suggests that bribery may also have been on their agenda.
2   Seneca said that external feelings remind us of simple mortality; such reactions, Paul Veyne says in *Sénèque,* are "slight and skin deep, like dread of the tunnel but excite no violent emotion and no fear. Nothing is to be feared."

IV

1   For *Jewish War,* II: 247 and following.
2   *Jewish War,* II: 467 and following. "Thirteen thousand" is a recurrent number, suggesting that it signifies a great many people rather than any kind of accurate count.

V

1   Arnaldo Momigliano, *Alien Wisdom: The Limits of Hellenization.*
2   *Jewish War,* II: 259 and following.
3   See T. P. Wiseman's 1979 inaugural lecture, "Titus Flavius and the Indivisible Subject," reprinted in H. W. Stubbs, ed., *Pegasus: Classical Essays from the University of Exeter* (Exeter, UK: University of Exeter, 1981).

VI

1   *Jewish War,* II: 587 and following.
2   Ibid., II: 607 and following.

VIII

1   *Jewish War,* III: 407 and following.

IX

1   See Harold Bloom's introduction to Yosef Yerushalmi's *Zakhor,* p. xv.
2   Goodman, *The Ruling Class of Judea,* p. 202.
3   Ibid., p. 180 and following.

Notes

X

1 See Idinopulos, in "Religious and National Factors in Israel's War with Rome."
2 Goodman, *The Ruling Class of Judaea*, p. 198.
3 *Jewish War*, V: 324 and following.

XI

1 See, for example, Rajak, *Josephus*, p. 187.
2 *Jewish War*, V: 548 and following.
3 Ibid., VI: 207.
4 Ibid., VI: 423 and following.
5 In Kenneth Atkinson's contribution to Zuleika Rodgers, ed., *Making History: Josephus and Historical Method*.
6 Ibid.

XII

1 See Idinopulos, "Religious and National Factors in Israel's War with Rome." Johanan ben Zakkai's salute to Vespasian, and his amiable reception, is unmentioned by Josephus, never a man to share credit.
2 Pierre Vidal-Naquet, "Du bon usage de la Trahison," p. 94.
3 Honora Howell Chapman, in "Spectacle in Josephus's Jewish War."
4 Ronald Syme's early, skittish paper on the subject is reprinted in his *Roman Papers*, vol. 5.
5 See Wiseman, in Stubbs, *Pegasus*.
6 *Jewish War*, VI: 230 and following.
7 See Mason's "Figured Speech and Irony in Titus Flavius Josephus," in Edmondson et al., *Flavius Josephus and Flavian Rome*.
8 Hannah M. Cotton and Werner Eck, "Josephus's Roman Audience."
9 Josephus, *Vita*, 429.
10 Cotton and Eck, "Josephus's Roman Audience."
11 Vasily Rudich, *Political Dissidence Under Nero* (London: Routledge, 1993).

XIII

1 In Goodman, "The Fiscus Judaicus and Gentile Attitudes to Judaism in Flavian Rome," in Edmondson et al., *Flavius Josephus and Flavian Rome*.
2 Daniel R. Schwartz, "Herodians and Ioudaioi in Flavian Rome," in Edmondson et al., *Flavius Josephus and Flavian Rome*.
3 Suetonius, *Life of Domitian*, 12.2.
4 Wiseman, "Titus Flavius and the Indivisible Subject," in Stubbs, *Pegasus*, p. 15.

5   Goodman, in "The Fiscus Judaicus and Gentile Attitudes to Judaism in Flavian Rome," cites Cassius Dio (68.1.2) on Nerva's formal rejection of accusations for following a "Jewish life-style."

6   In Gager, *The Origins of Anti-Semitism.*

XIV

1   For the complete meaning of *logos* in Greek, see Richard Seaford, *Money and the Early Greek Mind.*

2   See Brandon, *Jesus and the Zealots,* p. 84ff.

XV

1   Leo Strauss (1899–1973) made an emphatic feature of such discontinuities. Cf., *Faith and Political Philosophy,* his correspondence with Eric Voegelin (Philadelphia: Pennsylvania University Press, 1993).

XVI

1   In *Paschal Homily.* Cited by John G. Gager, *The Origins of Anti-Semitism.*

2   *Jewish Antiquities* 18: 310.

3   In Uriel Rappaport's contribution to Zuleika Rodgers, ed., *Making History.*

XVII

1   See Hillel Halkin, *Yehuda Halevi* (New York: Schocken Books, 2010).

2   Ibid., p. 170.

3   See María Rosa Menocal, *The Ornament of the World* (New York: Little, Brown, 2002).

4   See Leo Strauss, *Persecution and the Art of Writing,* p. 61.

5   See Yosef Yerushalmi, *From Spanish Court to Italian Ghetto.*

6   See Steven Nadler, *Spinoza: A Life.*

XVIII

1   See Evelyn Juers, *House of Exiles,* p. 217.

2   Quoted from Michael Hofmann's 2012 translation of Roth's letters (see Roth, *A Life in Letters*).

3   See, for instance, *There Was Once a World* by Yaffa Eliach (London: Little, Brown, 1998).

4   Norman Cohn, *Europe's Inner Demons.*

5   Ray Monk, *Ludwig Wittgenstein.*

6   Ibid.

7 David G. Stern and Béla Szabados, *Wittgenstein Reads Weininger*. See also Szaba-dos's *Ludwig Wittgenstein on Race, Gender and Cultural Identity: Philosophy as Personal Endeavour* (Lewiston, NY: Edwin Mellen Press, 2010).

8 See Jacques Bouveresse, *La force de la règle* (Paris: Èditions de Minuit, 1987).

9 Romek Marber, *No Return: Journeys in the Holocaust* (Nottingham, UK: Richard Hollis, 2010).

10 Christopher R. Browning, *Remembering Survival*.

11 See A. J. Ayer, *Ludwig Wittgenstein* (London: Penguin, 1986).

12 Paul Reitter, *The Anti-Journalist: Karl Kraus and Jewish Self-Fashioning in Fin-de-Siècle Europe* (Chicago: University of Chicago Press, 2008), p. 34.

13 See Timms, *Karl Kraus*, vol. 2, p. 21 and following.

14 See Walter Lippmann, *Essays in the Public Philosophy* (New York: Little, Brown, 1955).

XIX

1 Foreword to Yerushalmi's *Zakhor*, p. xvii.

2 See Peter Kielmansegg et al., *Hannah Arendt and Leo Strauss*.

3 Leo Strauss quoted in ibid.

4 Ibid.

5 In the introduction to David Bergelson, *The End of Everything*, p. x.

6 *Jewish War*, I: 7.

7 See *Carl Schmitt and Leo Strauss: The Hidden Dialogue* by Heinrich Meier (Chicago: University of Chicago Press, 1995).

8 In Elias Canetti, *Crowds and Power* (New York: Farrar, Straus and Giroux, 1984).

9 In David Pryce-Jones, *Paris in the Third Reich* (London: Collins, 1981), p. 140.

10 Romek Marber, *No Return*.

11 For the pro-Arab history (and delusions) of French foreign policy, see David Pryce-Jones, *Betrayal: France, the Arabs, and the Jews* (New York: Encounter Books, 2006).

12 See Richard Bauckham's *Jesus and the Eyewitnesses*.

13 See Vermès's *Jesus the Jew* and his subsequent works on the same theme.

14 "Delving into the Dark Side: Josephus' Foresight as Hindsight," in Zuleika Rodgers, ed., *Making History: Josephus and Historical Method*, p. 66.

15 In Harold Bloom's 1998 introduction (p. xviii) to Yosef Yerushalmi's *Zakhor*.

16 Cf. www.jewsagainstzionism.com/rabbi-quotes/vayoelmosher.cfm#6million.

17 Quoted in ibid., pp. 90–91.

SELECT BIBLIOGRAPHY

Adler, Laure. *L'insoumise*. Paris: Actes Sud, 2008.

Balsdon, J. P. V. D. *Romans and Aliens*. Chapel Hill: University of North Carolina Press, 1979.

Bauckham, Richard. *Jesus and the Eyewitnesses: The Gospels as Eyewitness Testimony*. Grand Rapids, MI: William B. Eerdmans, 2006.

Benda, Julien. *Exercice d'un enterré vif (Juin 1940–Août 1944)*. Paris: Trois Collines, 1944.

Bergelson, David. *The End of Everything*. Translated and with an introduction by Joseph Sherman. New Haven, CT: Yale University Press, 2010.

Bikont, Anna. *Le crime et le silence: Jedwabne 1941, la mémoire d'un pogrom dans la Pologne d'aujourd'hui*. Paris: Denoël, 2011.

Binet, Laurent. *HHhH*. Translated by Sam Taylor. London: Harvill Secker, 2012.

Birnbaum, Pierre. *Géographie de l'espoir: L'exil, les lumières, la désassimilation*. Paris: Gallimard, 2004.

Boardman, John, Jasper Griffin and Oswyn Murray. *The Oxford History of the Classical World*. Oxford: Oxford University Press, 1983.

Bosworth, A. B. "Vespasian and the Provinces: Some Problems of the Early 70s A.D." *Athenaeum* 51 (1973): 49–78.

Bouretz, Pierre. *Témoins du futur: philosophie et messianisme*. Paris: Gallimard, 2003.

Bowersock, G. W. "Foreign Elites at Rome." In *Flavius Josephus and Flavian Rome*, edited by J. C. Edmondson, Steve Mason and J. B. Rives. Oxford: Oxford University Press, 2005.

———. *Roman Arabia*. Cambridge, MA: Harvard University Press, 1983.

Brandon, S. G. F. *Jesus and the Zealots: A Study of the Political Factor in Primitive Christianity*. New York: Scribner, 1967.

Brown, Peter. *The Body and Society: Men, Women, and Sexual Renunciation in Early Christianity*. New York: Columbia University Press, 1988.

Browning, Christopher R. *Remembering Survival*. New York: Norton, 2010.

Caird, G. B. *Paul's Letters from Prison*. Oxford: Oxford University Press, 1976.

Carroll, James. *Constantine's Sword: The Church and the Jews—A History*. Boston: Houghton Mifflin, 2001.

Select Bibliography

Cartledge, Paul. *Ancient Greece: A Very Short Introduction.* Oxford: Oxford University Press, 2011.

————. *The Spartans: The World of the Warrior-Heroes of Ancient Greece.* London: Pan Books, 2003.

Casson, Lionel. *Travel in the Ancient World.* Baltimore: Johns Hopkins University Press, 1994.

Cavafy, Constantine. *Collected Poems.* Translated by Philip Sherrard and Edmund Keeley. Princeton, NJ: Princeton University Press, 1992.

Chapman, Honora Howell. "Spectacle in Josephus's Jewish War." In *Flavius Josephus and Flavian Rome,* edited by J. C. Edmondson, Steve Mason and J. B. Rives. Oxford: Oxford University Press, 2005.

Cohen, Shaye. *Josephus in Galilee and Rome: His Vita and Development as a Historian.* Leiden: Brill, 1979.

Cohn, Norman. *Europe's Inner Demons: The Demonization of Christians in Medieval Christendom.* St. Albans, UK: Paladin, 1976.

Collins, J. J. *Between Athens and Jerusalem: Jewish Identity in the Hellenistic Diaspora.* New York: Crossroad, 1983.

Coser, Lewis A. *Functions of Social Conflict.* New York: Free Press, 1968.

Cotton, Hannah M., and Werner Eck. "Josephus's Roman Audience: Josephus and the Roman Elites." In *Flavius Josephus and Flavian Rome,* edited by J. C. Edmondson, Steve Mason and J. B. Rives. Oxford: Oxford University Press, 2005.

Davies, Philip R., George J. Brooke and Phillip R. Callaway. *The Complete World of the Dead Sea Scrolls.* New York: Thames & Hudson, 2002.

Davis, John A. *The Jews of San Nicandro.* New Haven, CT: Yale University Press, 2010.

Dawidowicz, Lucy S. *The War Against the Jews, 1933–1945.* New York: Holt, Rinehart and Winston, 1975.

Des Pres, Terrence. *The Survivor: An Anatomy of Life in the Death Camps.* Oxford: Oxford University Press, 1976.

Dodds, Jerrilynn, Maria Rosa Menocal and Abigail Krasner Balbale. *The Arts of Intimacy: Christians, Jews, and Muslims in the Making of Castilian Culture.* New Haven, CT: Yale University Press, 2008.

Edmondson, J. C., Steve Mason and J. B. Rives, eds. *Flavius Josephus and Flavian Rome.* Oxford: Oxford University Press, 2005.

Ferrill, Arther. *Caligula: Emperor of Rome.* London: Thames & Hudson, 1991.

Finkielkraut, Alain. *Une voix vient de l'autre rive.* Paris: Gallimard, 2000.

Finley, Moses. *Politics in the Ancient World.* Cambridge: Cambridge University Press, 1983.

Forrest, W. G. *The Emergence of Greek Democracy, 800–400 BC.* London: Weidenfeld and Nicolson, 1966.

Gager, John G. *The Origins of Anti-Semitism: Attitudes Toward Judaism in Pagan and Christian Antiquity.* Oxford: Oxford University Press, 1985.

Goldstein, Rebecca. *Betraying Spinoza.* New York: Schocken Books, 2007.

Goodman, Martin. "The Fiscus Judaicus and Gentile Attitudes to Judaism in Flavian Rome." In *Flavius Josephus and Flavian Rome,* edited by J. C. Edmondson, Steve Mason and J. B. Rives. Oxford: Oxford University Press, 2005.

———. "Kosher Olive Oil in Antiquity." In *A Tribute to Géza Vermès: Essays on Jewish and Christian Literature and History,* edited by Philip R. Davies and Richard T. White. Sheffield, UK: JSOT Press, 1990.

———. *Rome and Jerusalem: The Clash of Ancient Civilizations.* London: Allen Lane, 2007.

———. *The Ruling Class of Judaea: The Origins of the Jewish Revolt Against Rome, A.D. 66–70.* Cambridge: Cambridge University Press, 1987.

Grafton, Anthony, Glenn W. Most and Salvatore Settis, eds. *The Classical Tradition.* Cambridge, MA: Harvard University Press, 2010.

Green, Peter. *Alexander to Actium: The Historical Evolution of the Hellenistic Age.* London: Thames & Hudson, 1993.

Griffin, Miriam T. *Nero: The End of a Dynasty.* London: Batsford, 1984.

Gruen, Erich S. *The Hellenistic World and the Coming of Rome.* Berkeley: University of California Press, 1984.

Gubar, Susan. *Judas: A Biography.* New York: Norton, 2009.

Hay, Malcolm. *Europe and the Jews.* Boston: Beacon Press, 1960.

Hess, Jonathan M. *Germans, Jews and the Claims of Modernity.* New Haven, CT: Yale University Press, 2002.

Hibbert, Christopher. *Disraeli: The Victorian Dandy Who Became Prime Minister.* London: HarperCollins, 2004.

Hilberg, Raul. *The Destruction of the European Jews* (Chicago: Quadrangle Books, 1961).

Hornblower, Simon, Antony Spawforth and Esther Eidinow. *The Oxford Classical Dictionary.* Oxford: Oxford University Press, 2012.

Idinopulos, Thomas A. "Religious and National Factors in Israel's War with Rome." In *Jewish Civilization in a Hellenistic-Roman Period,* edited by Shemaryahu Talmon. Philadelphia: Trinity Press International 1991.

Jacobs, Louis. *The Jewish Religion: A Companion.* Oxford: Oxford University Press 1995.

Josephus, Flavius. *The Jewish War.* Translated by G. A. Williamson and E. Mary Smallwood. Harmondsworth: Penguin, 1981.

———. *Josephus: The Complete Works.* Translated by William Whiston. Nokomis, FL: Nelson, 1998.

Juers, Evelyn. *House of Exile: War, Love and Literature: From Berlin to Los Angeles.* London: Allen Lane, 2011.

Kalligas, Haris A. *Monemvasia: A Byzantine City State.* London: Routledge, 2010.

Kamm, Antony. *The Israelites: An Introduction.* London: Routledge, 1999.

Kielmansegg, Peter G., Horst Mewes and Elizabeth Glaser-Schmidt, eds. *Hannah Arendt and Leo Strauss: German Émigrés and American Political Thought After World War II.* Cambridge: Cambridge University Press, 1977.

Select Bibliography

Lanzmann, Claude. *Le lièvre de Patagonia*. Paris: Gallimard, 2009.

Lefkowitz, Mary. *History Lesson: A Race Odyssey*. New Haven, CT: Yale University Press, 2008.

——. *Not Out of Africa: How "Afrocentrism" Became an Excuse to Teach Myth as History*. New York: Basic Books, 1997.

Levi, Primo. *I Sommersi e i Salvati*. Turin: Einaudi, 1976.

Loewenstein, Rudolph. *Christians and Jews: A Psychoanalytic Study*. New York: International Universities Press, 1951.

Luttwak, Edward. *The Grand Strategy of the Roman Empire: From the First Century A.D. to the Third*. Baltimore: Johns Hopkins University Press, 1976.

Marrus, Michael. *The Holocaust in History*. Harmondsworth, UK: Penguin, 1987.

Marrus, Michael R., and Robert O. Paxton. *Vichy et les Juifs*. Paris: Calmann-Lévy, 1981.

Mason, Steve. *Josephus and the New Testament*. Peabody, MA: Hendrickson, 2003.

——. *Life of Josephus: Life and Translation*. Leiden: Brill, 2001.

Meier, Heinrich. *Carl Schmitt and Leo Strauss: The Hidden Dialogue*. Chicago: University of Chicago Press, 1995.

Millar, Fergus. "Last Year in Jerusalem: Monuments of the Jewish War in Rome." In *Flavius Josephus and Flavian Rome*, edited by J. C. Edmondson, Steve Mason and J. B. Rives. Oxford: Oxford University Press, 2005.

——. *The Roman Near East: 31 BC–AD 337*. Cambridge, MA: Harvard University Press, 1993.

Million, Pierre, M. Maffesoli, M. Hirschhorn, H. Leroux, C. Mongardini, R. Motta, A. Hahn, P. Schiera, E. Kassab, A. Kelkel, Ph. Raynaud, P. Lecomte and J. P. Sironneau. *Max Weber et le destin des sociétés modernes*. Grenoble: Groupe de recherches sur la philosophie et le langage, 1995.

Momigliano, Arnaldo. *Alien Wisdom: The Limits of Hellenization*. Cambridge: Cambridge University Press, 1975.

——. "The Historians of the Classical World and Their Audiences." *Sesto Contributo alla Storia Degli Studi Classici e del Mondo Antico*. Rome: Storia e Letteratura, 1980.

Monk, Ray. *Ludwig Wittgenstein: The Duty of Genius*. London: Vintage, 1991.

Nadler, Steven. *Spinoza: A Life*. Cambridge: Cambridge University Press, 1999.

Nuland, Sherwin B. *Maimonides*. New York: Schocken / Nextbook, 2005.

Pipes, Richard. *Vixi: Memoirs of a Non-Belonger*. New Haven, CT: Yale University Press, 2003.

Putnam, Hilary. *Jewish Philosophy as a Guide to Life: Rosenzweig, Buber, Levinas, Wittgenstein*. Bloomington: Indiana University Press, 2008.

Rajak, Tessa. "Josephus in the Diaspora." In *Flavius Josephus and Flavian Rome*, edited by J. C. Edmondson, Steve Mason, and J. B. Rives. Oxford: Oxford University Press, 2005.

——. *Josephus: The Historian and His Society*. London: Duckworth, 1983.

Raphael, Frederic. *Some Talk of Alexander*. London: Thames & Hudson, 2006.

Rodgers, Zuleika. "Flavius Josephus." In *Companion to Jewish Biblical Interpretation in the Hellenistic and Early Roman Period,* edited by M. Heinze. Grand Rapids, MI: William B. Eerdmans, 2011.

———. "Justice for Justus: A Re-examination of Justus of Tiberias' Role in Josephus' Autobiography." In *The Limits of Ancient Biography: Genre and Technique,* edited by J. Mossman and B. McGing. Swansea: Classical Press of Wales, 2006.

Rodgers, Zuleika, ed. *Making History: Josephus and Historical Method.* Leiden: Brill, 2006.

Rodinson, Maxime. *Peuple juif ou problème juif.* Paris: François Maspero, 1981.

Rosenbaum, Ron, ed. *Those Who Forget the Past: The Question of Anti-Semitism.* New York: Random House, 2004.

Roth, Joseph. *A Life in Letters.* Translated by Michael Hofmann. London: Granta, 2012.

———. *The Wandering Jews.* New York: Norton, 2000.

Sartre, Maurice. *D'Alexandre à Zénobie: Histoire du Levant antique, IVe siècle avant Jésus-Christ–IIIe siècle après Jésus-Christ.* Paris: Librairie Arthème Fayard, 2001.

Schäfer, Peter. *Judeophobia: Attitudes Toward the Jews in the Ancient World.* Cambridge, MA: Harvard University Press, 1997.

Scheindlin, Raymond P. *The Song of the Distant Dove: Judah Halevi's Pilgrimage.* Oxford: Oxford University Press, 2008.

Schnitzler, Arthur. *The Road into the Open.* Translated by Roger Byers. Berkeley: University of California Press, 1992.

Schwartz, Daniel R. "Herodians and Ioudaioi in Flavian Rome." In *Flavius Josephus and Flavian Rome,* edited by J. C. Edmondson, Steve Mason and J. B. Rives. Oxford: Oxford University Press, 2005.

Seaford, Richard. *Money and the Early Greek Mind: Homer, Philosophy, Tragedy.* Cambridge: Cambridge University Press, 2004.

———. *Reciprocity and Ritual: Homer and Tragedy in the Developing City-State.* Oxford: Clarendon Press, 1994.

Sebag Montefiore, Simon. *Stalin: The Court of the Red Tsar.* London: Weidenfeld and Nicolson, 2003.

Sengoopta, Chandak. *Otto Weininger: Sex, Science and Self in Imperial Vienna.* Chicago: University of Chicago Press, 2000.

Silver, Daniel Jeremy, and Bernard Martin. *A History of Judaism.* New York: Basic Books, 1974.

Stern, David G., and Bela Szabados. *Wittgenstein Reads Weininger.* Cambridge: Cambridge University Press, 2004

St. John Thackeray, Henry. *Josephus: The Man and the Historian.* New York: Jewish Institute of Religion Press, 1929.

Strauss, Leo. *Persecution and the Art of Writing.* Glencoe, IL.: Free Press, 1952.

Sumption, Jonathan. *The Hundred Years War.* Vol. 3, *Divided Houses.* London: Faber, 2009.

Syme, Ronald. *Roman Papers,* vol. 2. Oxford: Clarendon Press, 1979.

Select Bibliography

————. *Roman Papers,* vol. 5. Oxford: Clarendon Press, 1991.

Talmon, Shemaryahu. "The Internal Diversification of Judaism in the Early Second Temple Period." In *Jewish Civilization in the Hellenistic-Roman Period,* edited by Shemaryahu Talmon. Philadelphia: Trinity Press International, 1991.

Tcherikover, Victor. *Hellenistic Civilization and the Jews.* New York: Athenaeum, 1974.

————. *Jewish Apologetic Literature Reconsidered.* Warsaw: Societas Philologae Polonorum, 1956.

Tegel, Susan. *Jew Süss: Life, Legend, Fiction, Film.* London: Continuum, 2011.

Theobald, John. *The Media and the Making of History.* Aldershot, UK: Ashgate, 2004.

Timms, Edward. *Karl Kraus: Apocalyptic Satirist.* Vol. 1: *Culture and Catastrophe in Hapsburg Vienna.* New Haven, CT: Yale University Press, 1989.

————. *Karl Kraus: Apocalyptic Satirist.* Vol. 2: *The Postwar Crisis and the Rise of the Swastika.* New Haven, CT: Yale University Press, 2005.

Turner, E. G. "Tiberius Julius Alexander." *Journal of Roman Studies,* 44 (1954), pp. 54–64.

Vermès, Géza. *The Authentic Gospel of Jesus.* London: Allen Lane, 2003.

————. *Jesus the Jew: A Historian's Reading of the Gospels.* London: Collins, 1973.

Veyne, Paul. *Les Grecs ont-ils cru à leurs mythes?* Paris: Éditions du Seuil, 1983.

————. *Le pain et le cirque.* Paris: Éditions du Seuil, 1976.

————. *Sénèque:* Paris: Laffont, 1993.

Vidal-Naquet, Pierre. "Du bon usage de la trahison." Introduction to Flavius Josèphe, *La guerre des juifs.* Paris: Éditions de Minuit, 1977.

————. *Les juifs, la mémoire et le présent.* Paris: François Maspero, 1981.

Walbank, Frank W. *Polybius.* Berkeley: University of California Press, 1972.

————. *Polybius, Rome and the Hellenistic World: Essays and Reflections.* Cambridge: Cambridge University Press, 2002.

Warmington, B. H. *Nero: Reality and Legend.* London: Chatto & Windus, 1969.

Wilson, Edmund. *Israel and the Dead Sea Scrolls.* New York: Farrar, Straus and Giroux, 1978.

Wiseman, T. P., ed. *Roman Political Life, 90 B.C.–A.D. 69.* Exeter, UK: University of Exeter, 1985.

Wistrich, Robert S., ed. *Austrians and Jews in the Twentieth Century: From Franz Joseph to Waldheim.* New York: St. Martin's, 1992.

Yerushalmi, Yosef. *From Spanish Court to Italian Ghetto: Isaac Cardoso—A Study in Seventeenth-Century Marranism and Jewish Apologetics.* New York: Columbia University Press, 1971.

————. *Zakhor: Jewish History and Jewish Memory.* Seattle: University of Washington Press, 1982.

Yonge, C. D. *The Works of Philo.* Peabody, MA: Hendrickson, 1993.

INDEX

Index

Index

Index

Index

Index